POP CULTURE
INDIA!

Other titles in ABC-CLIO's series

Popular Culture in the Contemporary World

P O P   C U L T U R E
INDIA!

Media, Arts, and Lifestyle

Asha Kasbekar

A B C  C L I O

Santa Barbara, California   Denver, Colorado   Oxford, England

Library of Congress Cataloging-in-Publication Data

Kasbekar, Asha.
    Pop culture India! : media, arts, and lifestyle / Asha Kasbekar.
        p. cm. — (Pop culture in the contemporary world)
    ISBN 1-85109-636-1 (hardcover : alk. paper) — ISBN 1-85109-641-8 (eBook)
1. Popular culture—India. 2. Popular culture—Economic aspects—India. 3. Popular culture—Social aspects—
India. 4. Religion and culture—India.   I. Title.   II. Series : Popular culture in the contemporary world.

DS428.2.K38 2006

306.0954—dc22   2005035247

10 09 08 07 06   10 9 8 7 6 5 4 3 2 1

This book is also available on the World Wide Web as an eBook.
Visit abc-clio.com for details.

Acquisition Editor: Simon Mason
Production Editor: Laura Esterman
Media Editor: Giulia Rossi
Production Coordinator: Ellen Brenna Dougherty
Manufacturing Coordinator: George Smyser
Production Manager: Don Schmidt

ABC-CLIO, Inc.
130 Cremona Drive, P.O. Box 1911
Santa Barbara, California 93116-1911

Text design by Jane Raese

This book is printed on acid-free paper. ∞
Manufactured in the United States of America

Contents

Preface

The purpose of this book is to provide a first step for anyone interested in discovering popular culture in India today. The chapters cover cinema, television, and radio; newspapers and magazines; music, theater, and literature; and sport, providing an explanation of the critical developments in each of these fields. The book also explores the changing lifestyles in India, particularly in the areas of shopping, eating, and other forms of consumerism. Each chapter has its own list of the books, academic papers, and articles in the popular press that I found useful in the compilation of the book.

With the growing number of books on India, it would be useful to explain the need for yet another on the subject. Most books on India tend to specialize in one particular aspect of Indian culture—literature, theater, cinema, the press, and so on. This book strives to provide the reader with an overview of the major aspects of popular culture by providing both a brief history and an explanation of the current situation in each of the areas and portraying a comprehensive picture of present-day India and Indian culture. It also brings into play the role of the Indian underworld, which most academics scrupulously avoid mentioning, despite its extreme importance in the economy of popular culture and consumerism in India.

It has been difficult grappling with the unwieldy diversity of India—its languages, its written scripts, its regional and local cultures—and harnessing it into a cohesive and comprehensive book. I would like to thank Kalindi Philip in Mumbai; without her great help I would never have achieved the task placed before me. I would also like to thank Ravibala Shenoy, reference librarian at the Naperville Public Library in the United States for her help and guidance in compiling this book.

Chronology

1947   India becomes an independent nation on 15 August. The country is partitioned into India and (East and West) Pakistan. Jawaharlal Nehru becomes India's first prime minister. Four million Hindus and Sikhs cross into India from Pakistan and 6 million Muslims from India move to Pakistan. An estimated 200,000 people are killed in the process. The Pakistani army invades Kashmir, and the maharaja of Kashmir hurriedly signs a treaty of accession with India, to make it part of the Indian republic.

1948   Nathuram Godse, a Hindu fanatic belonging to the right-wing Hindu fundamentalist organization Rashtriya Swayam Sevak (RSS), assassinates Mahatma Gandhi. The Indian army occupies Hyderabad and forces the *Nizam* (ruler) of Hyderabad to accede to the Indian Union.

Sombhu Mitra starts his theater group, Bohurupee. S. S. Vasan's spectacular feature film *Chandralekha* becomes an all-India hit, the first-ever film from a Madras studio to do so.

1949   C. N. Annadurai creates the Dravida Munnetra Kazhagam (DMK), a Tamil nationalist, anti-brahmin, anti-North, anti-Hindi party. *Velaikkari* and *Nallathambi*, written by Annadurai, mark the DMK's decision to use cinema as a weapon of political propaganda.

1950   India becomes a sovereign democratic republic. It has a written Constitution and becomes a member of the United Nations. Vijaya Pictures is established and makes its first Telugu film, *Shavukaru*.

1952   India holds its first-ever parliamentary elections. The Congress Party wins, and Jawaharlal Nehru continues as its first democratically elected prime minister.

All India Radio (AIR) ceases to broadcast film songs after a dispute with the film producers. AIR refuses to credit the films from which the songs are taken, because, AIR argues, it is tantamount to free publicity.

1953   The Sangeet Natak Akademi, the first of the three arts institutions funded by the government, is launched to promote music and drama in the country. Prabhat studios cease to operate.

1954   The Lalit Kala and the Sahitya Akademis are launched to promote the fine arts and literature respectively. Bimal Roy's film *Do Bigha Zameen* receives a special mention at Cannes.

1956   The States' Reorganisation Bill is passed and Mysore (later Karnataka), Kerala, and Madhya Pradesh, as well as the Union territories of Delhi, Andaman, and Nicobar, come into existence.

The first Indian newsprint factory at Nepanagar opens. Dr. Bhimrao Ambedkar and 200,000 *dalits* convert to Buddhism. India receives a UNESCO grant to study the possible use of television for education. Philips sells a 500-watt transmitter to India at nominal price.

1960   Bombay state is split on linguistic basis into the states of Maharashtra and Gujerat are created.

The Film Finance Corporation is formed with the aim of providing financial assistance to make serious, experimental, and art-house films. The Film Institute of India is established in Pune in the grounds of the former Prabhat studios.

1962   India is attacked by China over a border dispute, and the Indian army undertakes an ignominious retreat. Nehru loses his international standing as the weaknesses of India are exposed. The Congress Party nevertheless wins the national elections, and Nehru stays on as prime minister. The Bhakra-Nangal Dam, one of the biggest such projects in the world, is completed.

Radio Ceylon captures Indian audiences by broadcasting programs on Hindi film music with Ameen Sayani as host, and sponsored by Ciba's Binaca toothpaste.

1964   Nehru dies and Lal Bahadur Shastri replaces him as prime minister. As a consequence of the Chinese invasion of India, the Communist Party splits into the CPI and the CPI (M). The National Film Archive of India is established in Pune next door to the Film Institute of India.

1965   India fights a second war after Pakistan invades its northwest borders. It is also the year that is supposed to see the installation of Hindi as the sole national language. Violent riots break out in southern India led by non-Hindi speaking populations who decry this imposition. The government decides not to impose Hindi on the South, and English remains the "associate" national language indefinitely.

Daily one-hour television broadcasts begin in Delhi.

1966   Prime Minister Shastri dies in Tashkent while attending peace talks with Pakistan after the war. Indira Gandhi, Nehru's daughter and India's minister for Information and Broadcasting, becomes the new prime minister.

1967   Congress wins the national elections and Indira Gandhi stays on as prime minister. The DMK Party wins in Tamil Nadu, and C. N. Annadurai, a dramatist and screenwriter, becomes chief minister of the state. The violent Naxalite movement, so called because it had its origins in the Naxalbari province in West Bengal, moves to Andhra Pradesh, and the Marxist revolutionaries begin to kill landowners and redistribute their land among poor peasants.

All India Radio bows to the inevitable and sets up a special channel called Vividh Bharati, entirely dedicated to the dissemination of film music. It also begins to accept paid commercials.

1969   Indira Gandhi breaks from the Congress Party to start her own Congress (I). She also embarks on her populist socialistic agenda and nationalizes fourteen of India's private banks. She quells the Naxalite movement with the might of the state.

The success of *Bhuvan Shome* (Mrinal Sen) and *Uski Roti* (Mani Kaul), financed by the Film Finance Corporation (FFC), heralds the beginning of the "new" Indian cinema.

1971   East Pakistan breaks away from West Pakistan and Indira Gandhi helps create the independent nation of Bangladesh. Mrs. Gandhi amends the Indian Constitution to give the legislature (and herself) greater authority while reducing the powers of the judiciary.

India makes 433 feature films and becomes the largest film-producing nation in the world.

1975   In a worsening law-and-order crisis, with Jayaprakash Narayan leading an all-India revolt against the government, Indira Gandhi assumes all powers, suspends the Constitution, and declares a state of Internal Emergency. She imprisons all political and intellectual dissidents. She also declares her own radical twenty-point program, which is made compulsory learning in schools and promises to remove poverty. Press censorship is introduced, and Indira Gandhi's younger son, Sanjay, embarks on a radical sterilization program. It is estimated that around 2.5 million people, mostly poor, are forcibly sterilized.

The one-year SITE project to investigate the possibility of using satellite technology for education with the loan of an American satellite begins. Doordarshan, the government-owned television channel embarks on a project to increase the number of its terrestrial stations. Political goons destroy the only print of the film satirizing Indira Gandhi's dictatorial tendencies, *Kissa Kursi Ka*, by Amrit Nahata.

1977   Indira Gandhi calls national elections and is defeated. Janata Party, a coalition of competing opposition parties, forms the government. It is the first time since Indian independence that the Congress Party is not in power and has not formed the national government. In Tamil Nadu, Tamil screen god M. G. Ramachandran (MGR) becomes the chief minister, having split from the DMK to form his own AIADMK.

1980   The Janata Party splits, and Mrs. Gandhi is returned to power. The FFC merges with Indian Motion Pictures Export Corporation (IMPEC) and becomes the National Film Development Corporation.

1982   The Asian games are held in Delhi and broadcast in color on national television. N. T. Rama Rao starts his Telugu Desam Party (NFDC).

1984   Indira Gandhi is assassinated by her Sikh security guards in retaliation for attacking the holy Golden Temple in Amritsar to flush out Sikh separatists holed up there. An anti-Sikh pogrom is unleashed, and nearly 3,000 innocent Sikhs are killed across the country. Rajiv Gandhi, Indira Gandhi's older son, becomes prime minister. Deadly emissions from the Bhopal plant of Union Carbide (an American company) kill nearly 4,000 people. It is one of the worst disasters in the country's history. Union Carbide disavows any responsibility.

Radio and television licenses are abolished. Funding will henceforth come from the public purse.

1985   Doordarshan begins to accept commercial advertising and launches it first prodevelopment serial, *Hum Log*, modeled on the Latin American *Simplemente Maria*. Television ownership jumps from 2.7 million to 12.5 million.

1986   The district court orders the opening of the Ayodhya Babri Masjid mosque, built in 1528, to Hindu worshippers. According to the Hindus, the mosque stands on the spot of a much earlier Hindu temple to the god Rama.

Shah Bano takes her ex-husband, Mohammad Ahmed Khan, to court for nonpayment of alimony on her divorce. The Supreme Court upholds the Muslim Women (Protection of Rights on Divorce) Bill and orders Khan to pay his divorced wife. The Muslim Personal Law Board accuses the Supreme Court of violating the Muslim Sharia law, and Rajiv Gandhi's government, eager to win the support of the conservative Muslims, passes a new bill taking away all rights from divorced Muslim women.

1987   Rajiv Gandhi sends Indian troops to Sri Lanka to help the Sri Lankan government fight the separatist Liberation Tamil Tigers of Tamil Eelam (LTTE), better known as the Tamil Tigers. Mr. Gandhi's government is plagued by allegations of corruption and scandals—in particular, allegations of kickbacks from arms deals. About 300,000 Muslims attend a rally in New Delhi demanding the return of the Babri Mosque, while militant Hindus gather in Ayodhya to pledge the building of a Rama temple. Doordarshan broadcasts the religious soap *Ramayan*, which attracts a record number of viewers.

1988   Rajiv Gandhi tries to muzzle the press by passing the Defamation Bill, but nationwide demonstrations force him to withdraw it from Parliament.

1989   Militant Hindus lay the foundation stone for a Rama temple, and Gandhi, seeking Hindu support in the elections, allows the ceremony to proceed. However, he is defeated in the general elections by the Janata Dal coalition, supported by the Hindu nationalist right-wing Bharatiya Janata Party (BJP).

Political goons allegedly belonging to the Congress (I) Party kill Safdar Hashmi, a street theater activist in Delhi.

1991   Alleged LTTE terrorists assassinate Rajiv Gandhi in Madras. Congress Party returns to power by a sympathy vote. India's economic situation is in dire straits, and India needs a loan from the World Bank. The new prime minister, P. V. Narasimha Rao, and his finance minister, Manmohan Singh, undertake economic reforms removing industrial licensing requirements that had existed for the forty-four years since independence. Import duties are slashed and the Indian rupee is made convertible.

Doordarshan begins the broadcast of *Parliamentary Question Hour* and for the first time broadcasts from inside the Indian parliament.

STAR TV begins to broadcast from Hong Kong, and its imprint covers all of Asia. Indian viewers begin to tune in with enthusiasm.

1992   Activists belonging to the BJP, the party that had won the state elections in Uttar Pradesh, destroy the Babri Masjid mosque, leading to bloody violence between Hindus and Muslims throughout India.

1993   The government decides to implement the recommendations of the Mandal Commission and reserve 27 percent of higher education and government services for the "backward" castes. Bombs explode in Mumbai at famous sites, including the Air India Radio building and the Stock Exchange, in revenge for the killing of Muslims and the destruction of the Babri Mosque. Dawood Ibrahim, the underworld criminal who had fled to Dubai some years previously, is said to be involved.

Film star Sanjay Dutt, son of film stars Sunil Dutt and Nargis (of *Mother India* fame), is found to be in possession of illegal weapons supplied by the criminal underworld and jailed.

1996   The Congress Party loses the elections, and the BJP forms a government with its coalition allies, but it lasts only thirteen days. It is replaced by a multi-party coalition under H. D. Deve Gowda. Former prime minister P. V. Narasimha Rao is indicted in a corruption scandal.

1997   The liberalization started by the Congress government continues and now includes consumer goods. India joins the Information Technology Agreement of the World Trade Organization, paving the way for a phased reduction in import tariffs on IT products. Bill Gates visits India.

Gulshan Kumar, pioneer of the audiocassette revolution and owner of the T-Series label, is gunned down in broad daylight in Mumbai. Leading music composer Nadeem is accused of contracting out the murder to the criminal underworld; he escapes to London.

1998   India explodes a nuclear device, signaling its capacity to make nuclear weapons. Pakistan does the same within a few days. The two countries are internationally condemned.

The coalition government collapses amid allegations that the DMK, part of the ruling coalition, trained Tamil Tigers in Sri Lanka. The BJP forms the new government, led by A. B. Vajpayee.

Anxious to break the nexus between Hindi cinema and the Dubai-based criminal underworld, the government accords cinema the official status of an industry.

1999   The BJP wins the national elections and forms the new government, with Vajpayee as prime minister. It accelerates the pace of economic reform.

India engages in a war with Pakistan-backed militia, who enter Kargil in Indian-occupied Kashmir. The militia are repelled, but the Indian army suffers heavy losses.

The Prasar Bharati Bill is passed, making Doordarshan and All India Radio autonomous entities under the aegis of the Prasar Bharati.

2000   Economic growth accelerates.

The Indian government agrees to the privatization of FM radio channels.

2001   Pakistan-backed suicide bombers attack the Indian Parliament.

2002   Hindus die in a train fire allegedly caused by Muslim militants in Gujerat. The Hindus retaliate by pursuing a pogrom against the Muslims in Godhra, Gujerat. An estimated 2,000 Muslims are killed. Zaheera Sheikh, a local resident, witnesses a fire caused by Hindu fanatics and becomes a key witness in the "Best Bakery Case," where Hindus massacred her entire family.

Gujerat Chief Minister Narendra Modi, belonging to the ruling BJP, drags his feet in bringing the accused to justice. He is re-elected for a second term as chief minister.

Sachin Tendulkar becomes the first batsman to score 20,000 runs in international cricket.

The government announces guidelines enabling 74 percent foreign direct investment in the non-news and non-current affairs sections of print media.

2003   Mumbai is rocked by bomb blasts in retaliation for the Godhra Hindu-Muslim violence.

The Election Commission makes it mandatory for candidates to declare their criminal past, if any, along with their assets and liabilities, and educational qualifications at the time of filing their nominations.

Jagmohan Dalmiya is elected as president of the Board of Control for Cricket in India.

The United States brands Dawood Ibrahim Kaskar a global terrorist.

2004   The Congress-led coalition returns to power after the general elections. Sonia Gandhi, Italian-born widow of former Prime Minister Rajiv Gandhi and leader of the Congress Party, turns down the prime minister's post, making Dr. Manmohan Singh, former finance minister and architect of the 1991 economic reforms under former prime minster P. V. Narasimha Rao, the first Sikh prime minister of India.

2005   The "Best Bakery" trials get underway, but Zaheera Sheikh retracts her testimony. She accuses the human rights nongovernmental organizations of forcing her to make false allegations. The case continues.

1

Introduction

India has been described as a continent-sized mosaic. With its billion-strong, diverse, multireligious, multilingual, and multicultural population, it is a vast, complex, and confusing country. India is a secular state, but it is home to adherents of all the major religions. Hindus make up around 82 percent of the population, followed by Muslims at around 12 percent; Christians make up 2–3 percent of the population; Sikhs 2 percent; and Buddhists, Jains, and "others" (such as Parsis and Jews) another 2 percent of the population.

It is a plurilingual society with eighteen officially recognized or "scheduled" languages, thirty-three major languages, and a total of 1,652 languages and dialects that belong to four language families (Austric, Dravidian, Indo-Aryan, and Sino-Tibetan) and are written in ten major scripts as well as a host of minor ones. Hindi is the main language, with around 40 percent of the population identified as native Hindi speakers. Its nearest rivals are Bengali, spoken by 8 percent of the population, and Telugu (also 8 percent), followed by Marathi (7.5 percent), and Tamil (6.5 percent). In a north-south divide between the northern Indo-European languages and the southern Dravidian languages (Telugu, Tamil, Kannada, and Malayalam), the speakers of the latter group comprise just 22 percent of the total Indian population. Thus in the mosaic of Indian diversity, no single language has an outright majority, but Hindi dominates.

This mosaic of over a thousand languages has a bearing on the diffusion of all manifestations of new technologies of mass culture—cinema, television, radio, and music. But the picture gets even more complex when literacy rates are taken into consideration. A literate person in India is defined as anyone above the age of seven who can read and write in any language. The figures for 2001 revealed overall literacy rates in India of 65.38 percent (75.85 percent for men and 54.16 percent for women). Literacy rates are highest in Kerala, where the Malayalam language is spoken, with 90.92 percent, while in all of the northern Hindi-speaking states of Uttar Pradesh, Madhya Pradesh, Bihar, Jharkhand, and Chhattisgarh, the literacy rate is below the national average, with Bihar possessing the worst record of just 47.53 percent.

Kolkata at rush hour. (G. Boutin/zefa/Corbis)

The literacy rate, in turn, has a bearing on the circulation of newspapers and magazines: Kerala in the south achieves high readership percentages, although Hindi newspapers have higher absolute figures. The Indian government does not publish any figures for literacy in English, but it is conservatively estimated at between 2 and 3 percent of the population, which translates into between 20 and 30 millions individuals. However, while the native Hindi, Tamil, Bengali, and speakers of other languages are largely rooted within the provinces, English has a pan-Indian presence with strongholds in the cities.

The Position of English

The Constitution of India, written in 1950, decreed that Hindi, written in the Devna-gari script, would be the language of administration throughout the country and that the change from English to Hindi would be completed by 1965. However, there was stiff opposition to the imposition of Hindi as the only official language of India from the non-Hindi-speaking states, particularly the southern states, who saw it as a devious northern plot to ease southern Indians out of government jobs and administrative positions. Thus, a compromise was sought, and English has remained the "associate" language of administration.

Today, English is the de facto linking language among the various linguistic groups as far as national administration, law, science, and technology are concerned. It is the language of power, the language of command, and has a much higher social and economic value than Hindi or any other regional language in contemporary

India. With the growth in information technology and business outsourcing, and India increasingly becoming the "back office" to the world, the value of English has risen even higher.

The Indian use of English while speaking Hindi and Hindi while speaking English has led to the evolution of a new dialect—Hinglish—that is common currency in all the mass media, arts, and advertisements urging the espousal of consumerism. In most Hindi- and regional-language films, plays, and television soap operas, characters lapse into occasional sentences in English to convey their cosmopolitanism; video and disc jockeys on television and radio music channels invariably weave between the two languages. English, on the other hand, has been further indigenized, with many magazines in English using Hindi words to create the illusion of cool, hip, and streetwise journalism; print media in English even publish headlines in romanized Hindi. International writers such as Salman Rushdie and Upamanyu Chatterjee have also incorporated Hinglish into their novels.

Political and Economic Development

Three dates have tremendous significance in the political and economic history of modern India.

The first is that of Indian independence in 1947, when the nation emerged after nearly three centuries of British presence, first as officials of the East India Company and then of the imperial government of Queen Victoria. On the eve of independence on 15 August 1947, colonial India was divided into India and Pakistan. While Pakistan became a Muslim nation, India emerged as a secular socialist republic. Today its secularism is under strain and its socialism has been abandoned, but it remains a vibrant democratic republic with an elected parliament.

India is a federal democracy made up of twenty-eight states (three of them—Chhattisgarh, Jharkhand, and Uttaranchal, all northern states with strong tribal representations—were formed recently from the states of Madhya Pradesh, Bihar, and Uttar Pradesh) and seven union territories. The states vary in size, population, and natural resources.

After independence, the two main parties to emerge in national politics were the left-leaning and secular Congress Party and the right-wing Hindu nationalist Bharatiya Janata Party (BJP), known previously as the Jan Sangh. The Congress, which had led the freedom struggle, won the contest and led the national and state (regional) governments during the decades of the 1950s and 1960s. However, the communists and the Tamil parties (DMK and the AIADMK) have since won state elections and formed governments in the states of West Bengal, Kerala, and Tamil Nadu.

The economy saw GDP growth rates of 4.1 percent in the 1950s, dropping to 3.8 percent in the 1960s and 3.3 percent in the 1970s. These low growth rates, satirized as "the Hindu rate of growth" by economists, hampered the nation's ability to deal with the problems of endemic poverty and rapid population growth (from 381 million in 1951 to 1.02 billion by 2001).

At the time of independence, agriculture comprised over half of the Indian GDP and employed two-thirds of the national population. But immediately after independence India embraced industrialization as a means to achieve rapid economic growth and provide employment opportunities. To assist the process of indigenous industrialization, heavily protectionist policies were pursued by placing limitations on imports through licensing, stiff tariffs, and import substitution. Central planning attempted to regulate the economy with industrial policies that emphasized heavy industries in the "public sector" and the expectation that the private sector would take up the challenge of producing local consumer goods. Industrial licensing told entrepreneurs how much of a particular commodity they could manufacture, and, as some journalists have claimed, encouraged them to do it badly. But while the government took command of the heavy industries, it left agriculture largely in private hands and subsidized the sector through cheap irrigation and fertilizers.

The advantages of pursuing such a policy were that it created a broad and diversified industrial base for the nation, one that included heavy industries and consumer goods as well as mining, electricity, gas, and such. Its disadvantages were that excessive protection from foreign competition and domestic regulation made for inefficiency and high costs, and eroded Indian competitiveness. During the first four decades of Indian independence, Indian exports declined.

The films of the period, particularly those of Mehboob Khan (*Mother India*, 1957) celebrated Nehruvian socialism and the drive for deliverance from poverty via industrialization. Other film directors such as Bimal Roy, Raj Kapoor, and Guru Dutt alternated between hope and disillusionment. There were films about an ideal that had soured, about despair and a moving away from the industrial dream and its corollary of booming cities and urban poverty. The protagonists in both *Pyaasa* (Guru Dutt, 1957) and *Shri 420* (Raj Kapoor, 1955) move away from the city to start a new life somewhere else.

The government-controlled All India Radio (AIR) during this period was engrossed in the process of nation building. It tried to draw in the far-flung, discrete, heterogeneous communities of the multicultural, plurilingual society and to tether them to a Hindi, Sanskritic high culture disseminated from the Center. Thus B. V. Keskar, independent India's minister for information and broadcasting, decided to ban popular film music as cheap; lacking any understanding of, or respect for, high culture; and for being irreverent, confident, and vivacious rather than grave, reverent, and humble. He also banned cricket commentaries from the radio because the sport, although well loved by the Indians, was a colonial pastime and hence an unpleasant reminder of India's less fortunate colonial past.

In 1956, the Indian government reorganized the states along linguistic lines, and the maps of the old administrative "presidencies" and "provinces" under the colonial British rule were redrawn, giving a major boost to the regional languages. The central government retains the power to tax income, production, and foreign trade, and has overall control of foreign policy and defense. The revenue collected is shared out among the twenty-eight states and seven union territories. State governments cannot borrow without the permission of the central government. They can, however, raise revenues through a local sales tax. The film industry provides a useful way for most state governments to raise revenues, and the entertainment tax levied on the sale of cinema tickets can range from 30 to 100 percent.

By the 1970s, after nearly two decades of

central planning and protectionism, it became apparent that the Indian economy was not achieving its goals and the growth rates in the gross domestic product (GDP) had fallen. Furthermore, the high degree of government regulation in all matters had created rampant corruption.

To neutralize the threats to her power, the prime minister, Mrs. Indira Gandhi, espoused even more radical and "progressive" socialist policies and embarked on a wave of nationalizations of private enterprises. In 1969, she nationalized fourteen of India's largest private banks. The following year she introduced a new and more stringent industrial licensing policy. In 1972 she nationalized the coal mines, and she also banned the private wholesale trading of food grains, which led to grain hoarding and a spiraling black market.

Paradoxically, the decade of the 1970s marked a frenzy of creativity in Indian cinema and theater. The birth of the new Indian cinema, pioneered by the art-house films of Mani Kaul, social realism of Mrinal Sen, and other regional filmmakers (particularly from the south) such as Girish Karnad and Adoor Gopalakrishnan, brought an alternative to the hegemonic popular Hindi film industry. There were daring experiments in theater in Mumbai (formerly Bombay), Delhi, and Kolkata (formerly Calcutta), new playwrights and directors such as Vijay Tendulkar, Mohan Rakesh, Satyadev Dubey, Badal Sircar, and many others.

The second crucial date after independence was 1975. Against worsening economic conditions and escalating prices of basic commodities such as grains and cooking oil, in 1975 Indira Gandhi was accused of having indulged in corrupt practices in her 1971 election campaign, and she was barred from holding office for six years. With rising civil unrest, organized by the opposition groups and spearheaded by Jayaprakash Narayan, Mrs. Gandhi retaliated by declaring a state of "internal emergency" that year. She jailed all the opposition leaders, set herself up with dictatorial powers, attacked civil liberties, established a radically populist twenty-point economic program, and embarked on a forced sterilization program of the poor. Two years later, in 1977, under increasing international pressure, Mrs. Gandhi finally announced an election and was trounced by the opposition coalition at the polls.

The Emergency had a direct bearing on the newspapers, whose freedom was severely curtailed. Most proprietors caved in to government demands and began filling their newspapers with progovernment propaganda. Those that did not, such as *Indian Express*, were harassed and their electricity supply was cut, thus preventing them from bringing out a newspaper. The defeat of Mrs. Gandhi in 1977 led to a rapid growth of newspapers, spurred by the political events of the recent past, but also by the development of the new technologies in printing.

Meanwhile, the government media—radio and television—saw themselves as mouthpieces of the government. In cinema, too, there was little sign of protest against Mrs. Gandhi's dictatorial style of government other than the occasional political film protesting the loss of civil liberties during the Emergency. One example of such a "political" film was *Kissa Kursi Ka* (Amrit Nahata 1977). As a privately financed industry, cinema had no desire to invite the wrath of the government and find its films delayed awaiting censorship certification, with debts from high interest rates mounting each day.

The electorate returned Mrs. Gandhi to power in 1980, and she decided to liberalize her socialistic tendencies and allow more freedom in the economy. She also expanded the reach of the government-owned terrestrial (as opposed to satellite) television. She increased the number of satellites in space, introduced broadcasts in color television, and liberalized the importation of television sets. Commercial advertising was allowed, and radio and television licenses were no longer required. The decade of the 1980s was a time of political unrest and secessionist movements—in the Punjab, in Kashmir, and in the northeast. In 1984, two Sikh security guards assassinated Mrs. Gandhi. That year, her son, Rajiv Gandhi, took over as the new prime minister.

Rajiv Gandhi began to liberalize further the economy and reduce domestic regulation, which immediately led to increased productivity. However the growth in GDP to an average of 5.6 percent per annum during the 1980s led to serious macroeconomic imbalances. Fiscal profligacy (through export subsidies, food subsidies, and such) increased government expenditure, while investment slowed down. The Gulf War in 1990 and its effect on the price of oil had a serious impact on India's balance of payments. Furthermore a crisis of confidence in the government's ability to manage the economy led to a drop in foreign exchange reserves to just over US$1 billion, or about ten to twenty days of imports necessary for the Indian economy.

The balance-of-payments crisis in 1990–1991 was a turning point for Indian economic policy as wide-ranging economic reforms were passed, and 1991 marks the third crucial date in the history of modern, independent India. Under pressure from western institutional lenders such as the International Monetary Fund and the World Bank, the Indian economy was opened up to foreign trade. In 1996, a new government formed by the Hindu nationalist coalition accelerated the pace and range of the economic reforms embarked upon in 1991, and the GDP growth rate touched 9 percent per annum during some years of the decade of 1990s. Since then it has stabilized at around 7 percent. Today India continues to be one of the fastest growing economies of the world.

It was also in the decade of the 1990s that India's information technology (IT) industry established itself, and the services sector, particularly telecommunications and IT, have since become the most dynamic areas of the Indian economy. The growth of the services sector of the Indian economy has led to rapid growth not just in the main cities such as Mumbai and Delhi, but also in the southern city of Bangalore, which earlier was nothing more than a lush, green, pleasant retirement town for middle-class Indians. Bangalore today is the hub for the new IT industries. With the establishment of two of the three most important IT companies in the city, Bangalore's population has skyrocketed from 800,000 in 1951 to 6.5 million in 2001. Southern towns such as Salem, Kochi, Mysore, and Hyderabad are now going the way of Bangalore and setting up vital corridors for IT and other services. In the north, another vital new IT corridor has been created around Delhi with the rapid growth of small towns such as Gurgaon and Mohali, as well as the city of Chandigarh, all of which are drawing new middle-class residents. The transformation of these small towns into major cities has had an impact on the culture and lifestyle industries in these areas.

Indian households are keen on appliances such as these televisions, washing machines, and refrigerators, 2001. (Kapoor Baldev/Sygma/Corbis)

Entirely unrelated to the economic liberalization package was the satellite invasion of India in 1991. The satellite revolution in India was the inadvertent consequence of the pioneering efforts of the Hong Kong–based company Hutchinson Whampoa. It sought to create a satellite channel (STAR) in English for the whole of Asia and finance it by advertising luxury goods for the rich consumers created in the 1980s and 1990s by the phenomenal growth of the economies of the "Asian tigers." Whampoa's advertising dollar dreams did not materialize, and they sold a controlling stake to the Australian media baron Rupert Murdoch, who saw an opportunity when the satellite channel found millions of avid viewers among the urban middle-class Indians starved for entertainment. The following year an Indian satellite channel, Zee, was launched. Within a few years there were hundreds of channels uplinking from India in all the main regional languages.

The Indian government's fear of an unbridled Americanization of Indian culture did not materialize. What emerged instead was the growth of regional and local programs, and the real war in Indian television was not waged against America's hegemonic culture industries but between competing regional television cultures within India. The growth of the manufacturing and services sector as a consequence of economic liberalization led to a rise in the number of urban members of the middle class with increasing amounts of disposable incomes. Advertising companies eager to entice the public into a consumerist lifestyle relentlessly drove the spread of a new popular culture through increased advertising budgets for television, radio, newspapers, magazines, music, and sport. The result was changing lifestyles in the big cities and towns in India. Economic liberalization also meant the manufacture and availability of cheap televisions and other consumer electronics, as well as durable consumer and *white goods*, such as refrigerators, freezers, washing machines, dishwashers, and other household appliances, all of which were widely advertised on television. This growing advertising revenue has fueled the growth of popular television, private radio, regional and national newspapers and magazines, the music industry, the sports industry, multiplex cinemas, bars, restaurants, and shopping malls.

In his study on the Indian music industry, *Cassette Culture*, Peter Manuel has demonstrated how the technological revolution, represented by the humble cassette player, sparked an explosion of diversity in Indian popular music and the retrieval of lost musical traditions. Technological innovation in printing has also been at the root of a boom in newspapers and magazines, particularly in the regional languages, and sustained by revenues from advertising. The growth of the middle class and disposable incomes, as well as improved printing technology, has also spurred growth in the book trade and a rise in the number of publishing houses, including Indian subsidiaries of foreign publishing houses.

Only theater has remained relatively unaffected by advertising revenues, although private companies sponsor most theater festivals. In theater, it is the increased numbers in the ranks of the middle classes that has spurred the growth of English, Hindi, and regional-language theaters in all the major towns and cities of India. And it is

the growing divide between the urban middle classes, with their increased disposable incomes and consumerist lifestyles, and the rural poor that has lead to a bifurcation of popular cinema. On the one hand are exclusively urban films largely about cool, hip youngsters pursuing (like their viewers) consumerist lifestyles. On the other hand are classic family melodramas that straddle both the rural and urban viewing populations. The latter feature bombastic rhetoric and operatic emotions about such subjects as twin brothers separated at birth, ailing mothers, and blind fathers.

The Indian Underworld

The criminal underworld in India has for decades been involved in the production and dissemination of popular mass culture. The most important of the criminal gangs has been Dawood Ibrahim Kaskar's D-Company, headquartered in Mumbai, Dubai, and Karachi.

The son of a police constable, Dawood oversees an empire worth Indian rupees (INR) 70 billion (US$1.5 billion) with subsidiaries in Canada, Europe, the Gulf, East and South Africa, and Southeast Asia. His activities range from money laundering, drug trafficking, gambling, and extortion to gunrunning and financing terrorist networks. In 1985 Dawood fled India to escape a police hunt and set up his headquarters in Dubai (with whom India has no extradition treaty). From there he could safely direct his substantial investments in a variety of areas, including popular Hindi films, film videos, and music. His Karachi-based lieutenant "Chhota" ("Little") Shakeel looks after the film and popular culture investments of his business empire

Movie star Sanjay Dutt, 36, is mobbed by fans as he walks out of the high-security Arthur Road Prison in Mumbai on 17 October 1995 after he was granted bail. Dutt was arrested 14 months earlier for purchasing an assault rifle from a member of the city underworld linked to the 1993 Bombay bombings. Dutt is one of 189 suspects on trial in connection with the serial blasts that killed more than 300 people in the city. (Saby Dsouza/AFP/Getty Images)

and stays in constant communication with his henchmen in Mumbai by mobile phone.

The links between the film and the criminal worlds, long talked about but never proven, came to light when the Mumbai police arrested Sanjay Dutt, a leading star of Bollywood cinema, for possession of unauthorized firearms in the wake of a series of bomb blasts in Mumbai allegedly masterminded, according to the Mumbai police and the Indian intelligence, by Dawood and his gang. (Dutt had allegedly acquired the firearms from D-Company.) The blasts were in retaliation for the destruction of Babri Masjid, a Muslim mosque in Ayod-

hya, on the grounds that it had been constructed centuries ago on the holy ground where a Hindu temple dedicated to Lord Rama had once stood. Police investigation revealed that Dawood's enterprises included large-scale music and video piracy worth in 2003 over US$1 billion.

Dawood's and the criminal underworld's investments were largely in the unorganized sectors of the Indian economy such as *hawala*, or the illegal international transfer of funds that bypasses the banks and leaves no paper trail. He was also drawn to the unorganized sector of film financing in India and is supposed to have used Bharat Shah, a diamond jeweler with a thirty-year career in film financing, as a front for his investments. When the U.S. government discovered that much of Al-Qaeda's funding came from *hawala* transactions, they began to try to crack down on such activities. In 2003 they declared Dawood, who allegedly helped Osama bin Laden escape from Afghanistan and American troops, an international terrorist. Dawood escaped from Dubai to Pakistan and is now allegedly either in Karachi or in Southeast Asia.

D-Company's business interests in the popular culture industries encompass film, video, music, television, and cricket. It is active in the area of film finance and is a leading player in film and video, as well as music piracy, which is pushing the music industry toward financial collapse. Assassinations of film and music industry personalities, such as Gulshan Kumar, head of the biggest music cassette company, have also been blamed on the criminal underworld. In the unorganized sector of the cable network, which provides satellite television to individual homes, the criminal network muscles into the network distribution by offering private channels showing nonstop, mostly pirated, film videos, both Indian and Hollywood, as a bonus to loyal customers. In cricket, police investigations have uncovered a close connection between bookmakers and the criminal underworld that culminated in the exposure of widespread match-fixing in the 1990s and exposed the guilt of the late South African cricket captain, Hansie Cronje. In family connections between the underworld and cricket, Dawood's daughter was married to Pakistani cricketer Javed Miandad's son, Junaid, in 2005.

The economic liberalization of 1991 relaxed licensing for foreign imports, including the importation of gold, for which India has an insatiable demand. The rupee was also made convertible. These measures made a huge dent in the core businesses (such as smuggling and *hawala)* of the Indian underworld, forcing the criminals to seek new avenues of business activity. Since 1991, their activities have expanded into extortion, protection rackets, and contract killings, and Chhota Shakeel has regularly threatened (by mobile phone from Pakistan) leading film stars in Mumbai and other successful businessmen across India for protection money.

The Focus of This Volume

With eighteen regional languages and an equal number of oral, visual, and written cultures, any attempt to present an overall view of contemporary Indian popular culture demands strategic choices. It has been my strategy to focus on the most important examples in each sector of the popular culture industry—cinema, broadcast media (television and radio), print media (newspapers and magazines), the performing arts (theater), literature, music, and cricket.

Popular Hindi cinema dominates all the other film industries in India. But the Telugu and Tamil film industries each produce as many films as the Mumbai-based industry, and even though they are watched by just 20 percent of the Indian population, the section on cinema looks at both Hindi and south Indian cinema. Consequently, although Bengali cinema is an important sector of the national film industry, with less than fifty films per year catering to 70 million Bengali speakers, it is but a small sector, particularly when compared with the film industries in Hindi, Tamil, and Telugu.

Indian cricket fans cheer for their team during the third day's play of the first test match between India and Pakistan in Mohali, India, on 10 March 2005. India scored 447 for six wickets at the end of the day's play in reply to Pakistan's first innings' 312 all out. (Ajay Verma/Reuters/Corbis)

With 40 percent of the Indian population speaking Hindi, the broadcast media has focused on television and radio in Hindi. Although Hindi newspapers and magazines have, for the same reason, the largest circulation figures, the English-language newspapers, many of which have multiple editions published from major city centers across the country, have been historically the most influential among the upper classes, the decision makers of the nation. The section on print media therefore focuses largely, though not exclusively, on print media in English.

Historically, Mumbai and Kolkata have been the most important centers for theater, with an impressive body of dramatic literature originating in Marathi and Bengali. Today, theater activity in these two cities is vibrant and abundant. Consequently, the overview of Indian theater traces the development of theater in these two cities. As for literature, Indian literature in English, or "Indo-Anglian" literature, has a pan-Indian readership compared with literature in regional Indian languages. Furthermore, the extraordinary literary achievements of writers from the 20-million strong Indian diaspora, who write mostly about India, have created an international market for Indo-Anglian literature, giving it a national and international importance that far exceeds the impact of regional Indian literatures. Finally, the decision to focus on cricket in the area of sport reflects the fact that it is India's singular sporting passion, and one that straddles its historical past and present. It is also the only sport where India has an international presence and some modicum of global prestige. A legacy of British colonialism, it has now become a thoroughly Indian game and a vehicle for rabid nationalism.

Women and Minorities

In the vast and diverse cultural field that India represents, I have not specifically examined the role of women as a discrete area of study in this broad-based overview. Instead, the achievements of women (such as in literature) have been indicated wherever they have appeared. A specific examination of women's participation in popular culture would be better addressed in more detailed studies of each of the areas of public culture.

India is still largely a patriarchal society and the traditional role of women differs widely between north and south, city and village. Women's roles are still extremely traditional, even in the cities, and marriage and children constitute important aspects of their lives. Urban middle-class women are highly visible, vocal, and have jobs in every sphere of cultural activity. However, while women are an important part of cinema, theater, and music, their contributions in areas such as the broadcast and print media are different from those of men. Innumerable women are editors of newspapers and magazines, although most of these tend to be targeted mostly at a female readership. There are also many women working in the media, in jobs ranging from TV presenters to back-room desk jobs. For example, Ekta Kapoor, daughter of film star Jeetendra, heads Balaji Telefilms, the biggest company to produce television serials.

However, in his book *India's Newspaper Revolution*, Robin Jeffery points out how prevailing social norms, which include a general desire for marriage and children, prevent many women from venturing into challenging jobs as hard-nosed investigative journalists; they opt instead for secure desk jobs in copyediting or the accounts department. In cinema, female stars are generally paid less than their male colleagues, and this is largely because producers have an entrenched belief that women do not have as much "pulling" power to open a new film as male stars do. There have, however, been many exceptions, and female leads such as Madhuri Dixit or Aishwarya Rai (to name the two most recent examples) have often been paid more than their male counterparts. However, it is equally true that most female stars have a shorter screen life than their male counterparts, and by the time the women reach the age of thirty, they are cast aside for younger stars. Furthermore, since most films are romances, producers are always eager to cast young women, and actresses in their thirties have to wait another two decades before they can play matriarchal roles. Many get married and try and find a less demanding career in television.

Dalits

Modern India is divided into large social collectivities such as *dalits*, tribals, "backward" castes, and "forward" castes. Traditional Hindu society was structured around the hierarchical four-fold caste system known as *varna:* at the top were the *Brahmins*, the elite caste of priests, scholars, and the interpreters of the Sanskrit sacred texts; just beneath them were the *Kshatriyas*, the caste of kings and warriors; the third caste was that of the *Vaishyas*, or traders and merchants; below them were the *Sudras*, the caste of artisans and peas-

Madhuri Dixit talks during a press conference in New Delhi 12 July 2002. Sony Entertainment Television, the country's third largest commercial broadcaster, hopes to make marriages happen in the living room of its viewers through a new reality show. Madhuri hosts the show, called "Kahin Naa Kahin Hai" (There Is Someone, Somewhere, Made for You), where boys and girls will meet and get to know each other and their families, and announce whether they wish to get married in front of the cameras. (Reuters/Pawel Kopczynski/Corbis)

ants. The first three castes of Brahmins, Kshatriyas, and Vaishyas today constitute the "forward" castes. However, there is yet another caste known as *untouchables*, so called because they were considered "polluted," and hence any "polluting" physical contact between the forward castes and the untouchables was scrupulously avoided.

Today, the untouchables and other depressed castes and tribal communities comprise the various "backward" castes. The backward castes constitute about 20 percent of the Indian population, and many are still engaged in their traditionally assigned tasks of disposing of garbage and waste matter, as well as taking care of the dead—providing firewood for cremation ceremonies, lighting the cremation pyre, and disposing of any dead animals in the village.

However, the caste system is like a honeycomb, with each stratum in the caste system further fragmented into self-contained regional, even local entities known as *jati*s. Often there is little interaction between *jati*s of different regions. Thus the Brahmins of northern India have little to do with the Brahmins of southern India, and likewise the Vaishyas of eastern India have little to do with the Vaishyas of any other Indian region.

Mahatma Gandhi (1869–1948) dedicated

Mahatma Gandhi, leader of campaigns of nonviolence and civil disobedience, in the Indian independence struggle. (Hulton-Deutsch Collection/Corbis)

a large part of his life to the eradication of "untouchability," which he considered blight on the face of Hinduism. He renamed this fifth group the *Harijan*, or "children of God." The upper-caste Hindus, Gandhi said, must make amends for the atrocities they had perpetrated on the lower castes over the centuries.

The great *Harijan* leader Dr. Bhimrao Ambedkar (1891–1956), generally known as "Babasaheb," who qualified for the bar at Gray's Inn and received his doctorate from the London School of Economics, was a member of the backward castes and a key figure in the drafting of the Indian Constitution written in 1950. Despite Gandhi's efforts at social reform, Ambedkar did not believe that the Hindus would

ever change their attitudes towards the *Harijans*, and he formed the Scheduled Castes Federation in opposition to the Congress. He also urged his caste members to embrace another religion, and in 1956, Ambedkar, along with 200,000 members of the backward castes, embraced Buddhism.

The backward castes are also known as *dalits*. *Dalit* means "broken," "reduced or ground to pieces" in Marathi. The social worker Jyotiba Phule (1897–1890) had first used the word in *dalitodhar*, or upliftment of the oppressed, in his *Satya Shodhak* (Truth Seeking) movement to counter Brahmin suppression of the lower castes. Twenty-five years after Indian independence, in the 1970s, the *dalits* spurred two notable movements: the *Dalit* Panthers and *dalit* literature. The former was a short-lived political movement inspired by the Black Panther movement in the United States, and the latter was a blossoming of writing by *dalits* on the *dalit* experience. Most of the writing is in Marathi verse and prose, and there are just a few translations into English.

The backward castes, along with other oppressed minorities such as tribals and some Muslim communities that have been identified as backward castes, have become powerful political entities in modern Indian democracy. The various communities in contemporary Indian society are now classified as the forward or upper castes, the *dalits* or scheduled castes (SCs), the other backward castes (OBCs), and the tribals or scheduled tribes (STs), all of whom (except the forward castes) benefit from positive discrimination with a percentage of seats reserved for entry to higher educational institutes and job reservations in the public sector. The word "schedule" indicates a government schedule (or list) that names specific castes, tribes, or communities that need to benefit from positive discrimination.

Robin Jeffery, who has scrutinized the Indian print media in detail, discovered that there was hardly any participation by *dalits* in Indian newspapers and magazines. According to Jeffrey, this was not due to any overt discrimination; instead, it appears that a career in journalism is not the premier choice among urban, educated, and middle-class *dalits*, and that many prefer a more prestigious and lucrative career in medicine, engineering, or law to the more volatile one in cinema, television, or the other mass media and arts.

Dalit contribution to Indian popular culture in the areas of media, arts, and lifestyles has not been examined specifically in this survey of popular culture other than to identify it wherever it has occurred within the areas under scrutiny, such as the overarching presence of Baloo Palwankar and his brothers in the field of cricket.

Gay Culture

There is little open homosexuality in Indian society, even in the urban middle class. Homosexuality is against the law, by a decree that dates back to the British colonial times, and the law has not yet been changed. Traditional Hindu society, however, accepted the existence of a "third" sex. (Eunuchs too are part of traditional society and have very specific functions.) The portrayal of homosexuality is extremely rare in cinema, television, and music, although there have been one or two instances of homosexuality as a "comic" theme in cinematic subplots. The existence of one homosexual magazine and themes surrounding homosexuality in stage plays has been noted in the sections on print media and theater, respectively.

2
Music

India is a nation of music lovers, and music is a central feature of most forms of mass entertainment. No film that wishes to reach a mass market would dare to eschew songs. On radio and television, music is a central plank in the programming, with several programs devoted to music, music competitions, and quiz shows. And music remains an integral part of popular and folk theaters across India. No political meeting or celebration—secular or religious—is without musical accompaniment. Every Sunday, loudspeakers blare songs through the streets, the bazaars, and the playing fields. So great is the cacophony, so infernal the din, that the government of Maharashtra has imposed a curfew banning all music in the public domain after 10 PM.

The Indian music industry is one of the world's largest, second only to the market leader, the United States, and India is the largest consumer of music cassettes in the world. Most of the music consumed in India is Indian—film songs, devotional music, and "indigenized" pop. Western music, both popular and classical, has played a very restricted role in India; its sales account for less than 10 percent of the total market. Over the last few years, the Indian music industry has been experiencing a serious crisis precipitated by large-scale piracy and overinvestment in the film industry. The next few years will be crucial in determining whether music companies can rise to the challenges of piracy and free downloading and still remain commercially successful.

History of the Music Industry

The development of the music industry in India can be divided into four main periods:

1. An early start in the 1900s with intense competition between the largely foreign-owned music companies;
2. Almost five decades of near total domination of the market by one company, HMV, and one genre, the Hindi film song;

3. The shattering of the HMV hegemony by the grassroots "cassette revolution" that began in the late 1970s;

4. The satellite revolution that further transformed the Indian music industry.

The Early Years

Commercial records were being marketed in India as early as 1902, just one year after the invention of wax recording (Manuel 1993). Indian performers, including Shashi Mukhi of New Theatres in Calcutta (now Kolkata) and the classical singer Gauhar Jaan, were recorded that year. Initially about twenty recording companies operated in India. Many of them, such as Odeon, Pathé, Nicole, Beka, and Gramophone Company of India (GCI), were foreign-owned with local subsidiaries in the country. Colonial companies marked out their areas of profit in the respective colonies, often producing music under different banners. But the market in the colonies was usually unimportant, since it constituted a very small percentage of their total sales. Nevertheless, the competition for the small, elite Indian market, which included the Indian princes and the newly rich and emerging mercantile classes in the cities of Calcutta and Bombay (now Mumbai), was intense.

In 1908, the British-owned GCI established a pressing factory in Calcutta. GCI could then press recordings for the Indian market locally, while the other foreign-owned companies were obliged to either have the records manufactured in Europe or use the facilities of GCI in Calcutta. By 1910 GCI had released over 4,000 recordings marketed under the HMV (His Master's Voice) label. Not only did GCI own the only record-pressing factory in the country, it had also entered into exclusive distribution arrangements with retailers. By the 1920s GCI had emerged as the market leader, eliminating the competition so ruthlessly that it monopolized the Indian music industry for the next five decades.

However, a few local companies, such as Viel-o-phone and Ramagraph, managed to survive by catering to specific regions. Ramagraph, for instance, specialized in recording the singers of the Marathi stage who starred in the highly successful *sangeet natak*, or musical plays, creating an entire genre of musical recordings—*natya sangeet*. In 1907, the company is said to have recorded 77 Gujerati, 124 Urdu, and 10 Marathi songs from the stage. Bal Gandharva (1888–1967), the musical prodigy and best female impersonator of the Marathi musical stage, recorded about 400 songs for various companies. (Piracy, a major problem plaguing the contemporary Indian music industry, had already reared its head in the 1920s and 1930s, and copies of his songs were recorded by singers who assumed the name of Bal Gandharva.) The early recordings began with a voice announcing the name of the recording company and ending with eulogies such as "Once more" or *Ram Ram Mandali* (Goodbye) instead of applause (Chandvankar 2003). In Calcutta, marching bands and orchestral compositions, the latter performed by the concert bands for stage plays at theaters such as the Classic and the Corinthian, were pressed into records and marketed. Several princely states, too, sponsored recording tours and hired experts from the GCI for advice on suitable music for recordings.

In 1931 GCI was acquired by EMI, and the HMV label became part of the world's biggest record company of the time. By then, GCI had began to issue records in the names of smaller subsidiaries and also offer its pressing services to about 200 smaller companies. That same year the first Indian talkie, *Alam Ara* (A. Irani), was made—a filmed version of the musical production from the Parsi theater stage. The unprecedented success of the film set the trend for the future of the Indian film industry: ever since, most Indian and regional films feature six to eight songs; others may have many more. As film production increased and with it the number of songs and singers available for recording, film songs began to form the most important genre component of HMV records. In turn, film songs began to be guided by the constraints of recording on the 78 rpm format. According to musicologist Bhaskar Chandavarkar:

> The 78 r.p.m. was the only recording format available till other means of recording came to be invented and the film magazine would not allow very lengthy sequences to be filmed without break. These factors made it necessary to have songs of about 3 1/2 minutes neatly cut into 3 stanzas along with the opening "*mukhra*"—the catch words. The three stanzas of the song were again neatly interspersed with musical interludes. These features became so popular that songs which were not recorded for films also emulated them. (Chandavarkar 1985: 249)

In 1961 the arrival of Polydor dented HMV's monopoly, but film songs continued to be the main genre of music marketed by the two companies. HMV maintained its hegemony with 60 percent of the market, while Polydor had to content itself with 40 percent. For the next four decades the mu-

sic industry in India had just one omnipotent recording company (EMI), one omnipresent label (HMV), and one dominant musical genre (the film song). Meanwhile, the music industry suffered a musical sclerosis, with slow growth and even stagnation. But the arrival of the cassette recorder was soon to overturn the hegemony of HMV and the film song, engendering a revolution in popular music.

The Cassette Revolution

In *Cassette Culture*, a study of the musical revolution unleashed by the humble cassette recorder, Peter Manuel uncovers the dramatic restructuring and reorientation of the music industry that resulted from a technological change in the manner in which music was produced and consumed (Manuel 1993). The protectionist policies of the Indian government had for decades banned the importation of electrical goods for personal consumption. However, in the 1970s, migrant workers returning from the Gulf States began to bring home low-cost, Japanese-made radio and cassette players. It was these radio and cassette players, known as "two-in-ones," that gradually changed the face of the music industry in India.

By the early 1980s, Indian prime minister Indira Gandhi had substantially increased the reach of the government-owned terrestrial television and radio, which played a prominent role in the dissemination of Indian film songs as well as Indian classical and regional folk music. Her son, Rajiv Gandhi, who assumed power in 1984 on the death of his mother, saw himself as a modern, "high-tech" prime minister and took the first small steps toward liberalizing the economy by reducing the import duties on electronic goods. He also eased

US$12 million in 1986 to over US$21 million in 1990 (Swamy 1991). By that year, India had become the second largest consumer of cassettes after the United States.

HMV gramophone, ca. 1900. (Bettmann/Corbis)

The cassette recorder, as Manuel points out, had several features that made it entirely suitable for a country like India. It was inexpensive, portable, and could be operated on either electricity or batteries. In contrast, record players or phonographs were big, expensive, and required a consistent electric supply—something that could be guaranteed only in the bigger towns and cities. In fact, fewer than one million phonographs were sold in all of India. Moreover, unlike records manufactured for the phonographs (and before that, for the hand-cranked gramophones), cassettes were cheap and easy to use. Soon the inexpensive, battery-operated two-in-one cassette recorders began to find their way into the Indian hinterland.

the import restrictions on certain items related to the electronics industry, thereby enabling manufacturers to import components for the local manufacture of consumer electronics (Manuel 1993).

The new government policies encouraged foreign (mainly Japanese) firms to seek collaborations with Indian companies. Several emerged—Bush-Akai, Orson-Sony, BPL Sanyo, and Onida-JVC—and began mass-producing players and cassettes. The pent-up demand for consumer electronics, fueled by annual growth rates of 5 percent, and the increasing value of the income brought home from the Gulf by migrant workers, unleashed a dramatic increase in the sale of cassette recorders and cassettes. By the mid-1980s, a decline in the price of raw materials, combined with the local manufacture of tape coating, reduced the purchase price of cassettes. Soon the market was flooded with locally manufactured cassette players, and the consumer electronics industry began to double in size annually. Sales of recorded music rose from US$1.2 million in 1980 to

But cassette technology offered more than just a cheap gadget for listening pleasure. The cassette player was a two-way medium that allowed people not only to play music, but also to record it. It was in this simple music production feature, according to Manuel, the seed of the cassette revolution lay. Furthermore, with the use of two or more cassette players, an individual could even duplicate tapes for distribution. An owner of a cassette player could thus be a consumer, a producer, and a distributor of music, possibilities that were never available to him (or her) when the processes of music production, duplication, and distribution required the high overheads of a record pressing plant.

The consequences of this technological revolution were a profound fragmentation, dispersal, and democratization of the production of music, and an unprecedented diversification in the musical genres available for consumption. No longer were the people at the mercy of the monolithic, monopolistic record producer churning out a single genre of music. Instead, they could manufacture and listen to the kind of music that was closer to their communities and related to their own lives, experiences, and listening pleasures. In place of the single, homogenous musical genre arose a huge heterogeneity of genres of music and music producers that targeted audiences defined by age, class, gender, ethnicity, religion, and even occupation, such as the cassettes of especially bawdy Punjabi songs designed to entertain Punjabi truck drivers as they wound their way along the national highways (Manuel 1993).

New forms of regional music and folksongs aimed at very specific, local audiences began to emerge in local dialects in the different regions of India. Many were linked to the life and harvest cycles of agrarian communities. Scores of new genres and subgenres of music were created, and old, local musical traditions that had lain dying or dormant for decades were revived. One such form was the *ghazal*, a form of Urdu poetry, with origins in Arabic and Persian poetry, set to music. The royal courts in northern India were patrons of this genre of music, and already by the late nineteenth century it had become a very popular form of light entertainment in the towns and cities. Genres such as devotional music, hitherto marginalized by the hegemony of the film song, began to acquire a more audible presence in a rapidly diversifying market. By the beginning of the 1990s and within a decade of the cassette revolution, a completely new musical scene had emerged in India.

HMV was unable to take immediate advantage of its dominant position in the rapidly changing musical scene. Preoccupied with pan-national markets and burdened with a high overhead, the company lacked the flexibility needed to exploit the small, localized regional markets. In contrast, lower income groups, taking advantage of the relatively simple recording capabilities of two or more cassette recording machines, found production—and even mass production—easy and accessible. As a result, the focus of production shifted to these new centers of the music industry. Three hundred new competitors entered the field in the 1990s. Of the 500 music companies operating today, 400 began as small-scale producers. HMV's share of the market dropped from a virtual monopoly in 1960 to less than 15 percent by 2002. In a strong and vibrant market, sales of film music dropped from 90 percent to less than 40 percent of total music sales (Manuel 1993). During the same period, sales in genres such as regional folk music, devotional music, and other nonfilm popular music grew from a negligible percentage to between 40 and 60 percent of the market.

According to Manuel, the cassette revolution *simultaneously* represented a musical development, a specific instance in the international information revolution, a mass-media phenomenon, and a socio-economic development that entailed the demonopolization of the music industry (Manuel 1993).

The Satellite Revolution

In the 1990s a second revolution began with the arrival of satellite television. Al-

From left to right, Jimmy Felix, Vasudha Sharma, Neeti Mohan, and Sangeet Haldipur, members of the musical group Popstars 2, flash a victory sign as they pose in New Delhi 16 September 2003. The musicians were selected out of 15,000 aspirants who wanted to become pop stars, following a nationwide search for the best music talent, organized by Channel V. (Kamal Kishore/Reuters/Corbis)

ready Mrs. Gandhi had embarked on a massive expansion of terrestrial television's reach, and a substantial proportion of the programs offered on national television revolved around music: film songs, folksongs, classical music, musical competition, and music game shows. But with satellite television, Indians were exposed for the first time to music channels such as MTV and, at the same time, to channels dedicated to both Indian and international music.

At first, all the music on MTV was American rock, pop, hip-hop, and similar genres that completely failed to engage the Indian audiences. When MTV stubbornly refused to respond to the desires of its audiences and localize its programming, a new channel, Channel V, emerged that was to provide a platform for Indian music. The result was the birth of a modern, urban, cosmopolitan music known as Indipop, an unabashed fusion (or "confusion" as some purists have disdainfully called it) of Indian music combined with western, African, samba, and other rhythms to create exciting new sounds and a galaxy of singing stars, all delivered by "cool" VJs (video jockeys) in "Hinglish," an amalgam Hindi and English.

The advent of satellite television also coincided with the economic liberalization in 1991, when the government removed several import restrictions and did away with many industrial license requirements. An economic boom followed; growth increased from 5 percent to nearly 7 percent per annum, and with increased industrial production and increased importation of consumer goods, television became an important vehicle for product advertising. Channels such as MTV and particularly Channel V became popular with manufacturers targeting young, urban, cosmopolitan audiences. Even MTV, realizing that it was falling behind Channel V in advertising revenues, changed tack and began to "indigenize" its content. Advertising began to fuel the diffusion of new music, spurring a demand for cassettes and CDs. New Indian companies entered the market. Some already had interests in the print media, such as the Aaj Tak news channel, Times Music (from the Times of India group of newspapers), and Music Today (from the India Today group of magazines). Major international companies such as Sony, Time Warner, and BMG also set up shop in India to satisfy the new and growing demand for film and nonfilm music.

Popular Music in India Today

By the turn of the millennium, with the rising popularity of satellite music channels, increasing access to international music, the emergence of a market for regional music as well as the home-grown Indipop, the arrival of CDs, and the introduction of organized music retailing, the Indian music industry had undergone a complete overhaul. Today India is one of the world's biggest consumers of music.

The music industry in India today is divided along the main genres listed in the following table.

There are five major music companies in India. Of these, T-series controls around 22 percent of the market, Saregama (formerly HMV) 15 percent, Tips 11 percent, and

Film Music	Nonfilm Music
Hindi, 61 percent	Devotional music, 10 percent
Regional, 5 percent	International, 8 percent
	Pop music (Indian), 8 percent
	Other (*ghazals*, Indian classical), 8 percent

(*Source:* FICCI Report 2003.)

Sony and Universal 7 percent each (FICCI 2003).

Film Music

Although the HMV monopoly no longer prevails, Hindi film songs still constitute 61 percent of all music sold by the music companies, while regional films songs (mainly from Tamil and Telugu films) comprise 5 percent of total sales of music in India. Of the Hindi film music consumed, 45 percent of all sales are for songs from new films and about 21 percent for old film songs (FICCI 2003).

Each new film brings to the market a host of new songs. Thanks to sustained economic growth over the last fifteen years and more people with disposable incomes, the consumption of these new issues has increased. New indigenous music companies formed in the wake of the cassette revolution, such as T-series and Tips, entered into a frenzied competition with Sony and Saregama for the music rights to new films, leading to ever-increasing acquisition costs.

The acquisition of music constitutes the single largest expense for the music industry, far greater than the manufacture of cassettes or CDs. For decades, under the venerable umbrella of HMV, film producers were paid only royalties from the sale of a film's music. But in the late 1970s newly formed companies began to offer producers advance payments to lure them away from HMV. Getting major producers to agree to the outright purchase of film music rights was the brainchild of the late Gulshan Kumar. Film producers were delighted with the arrangement, because it meant that they could recover a substantial chunk of their investment, sometimes even before the songs had been recorded.

As more companies adopted this tactic, an aggressive bidding war developed over music rights for films in production with each firm fighting to retain their share of the market. However, the music sales of a film are directly related to the success of the film, so that the greater a film's box office success, the greater the volume of sales for its music. During the boom years, when the film industry was delivering major box office hits, music companies prospered. But generally only one in four Hindi films manages to become a box office hit, and in 2002, the Hindi film industry (Bollywood) suffered its worst losses when 124 films out of a total of 134 crashed at the box office, leaving the music industry in dire financial straits.

To recoup their losses, music companies began to resort to remixes. With the music industry in a slump as a consequence of the slump in the film industry, the return to classic film hits seemed a safe bet for the music companies. But what began as an inexpensive rescue plan to bail out a floundering industry was transformed into a profitable and popular genre of its own. At least four of the top ten albums of the year 2003 were such remixes. They are, according to music critic S. Sahaya Ranjit, "time-tested, extremely hummable with no

dearth of people wanting them for nostalgic value" (Ranjit 2003: 74). According to the Copyright Act of 1957, any music company is free to make a new version of original soundtracks and re-release it in the market two years after its original release. Consequently, these remixes often include fairly recent hits.

Remixes also offer the opportunity to "sex up" an old hit. The lyrics of the old film songs always contained sexual innuendoes, but they were often concealed through a series of stratagems that disavowed any sexual content (Kasbekar 2001). The new remixes highlighted rather than disavowed these sexual innuendoes, leading to frequent confrontations between the government and groups concerned about morality on the one side, and the music (and film) industry and the liberal sectors of society on the other. One recent confrontation was over a music video of a remix of an old film song "*kantaa laga . . .*" The double entendre in the song ("*kaanta laga*" means "I have been pierced by a thorn") passed unnoticed when the original version came out in the 1970s. The remix video, however, is more explicit. It features a woman in blue jeans and a tattoo on her breast performing an erotic dance to accompany the song. The government immediately asked the television channels not to air the video, but because of the publicity, sales of the record and CD skyrocketed. Mobile phone companies vied with each other to offer the melody as a ring tone.

Another genre of music that has grown out of film music is the recompilation. By making new combinations of old and not-so-old Hindi film songs from the archives, the music industry has found a cost-efficient path to profits. The songs sung by

Lata Mangeshkar, the most important Hindi film "playback" singer, are constantly being recompiled. (Since Indian actors can't sing and professional singers can't act or are not beautiful enough to be stars, songs performed by professional singers are recorded and then played back during filming so that actors can mouth the lyrics. The recordings are marketed under the names of the professional singers and carry the name of the film.)

Nonfilm Pop Music

The decentralized music production that characterized the cassette revolution led to both the revival of traditional, long-forgotten forms of music and the creation of new genres that syncretized traditional and contemporary (that is, Western) forms of music.

Bhangra

One of the most dynamic of these fused genres is the contemporary disco *bhangra*, a lively, vigorous folk dance born of the agricultural traditions of the Punjab, a fertile region of the Indian subcontinent. The consolidation of the Punjabi immigrant communities in the United Kingdom and Canada spearheaded the emergence of the disco *bhangra*, an amalgam of Western beats and *bhangra* tunes sung increasingly in a mixture of English and Punjabi.

One of the leading performers of different styles of traditional Punjabi music (*heer* and *bhangra*) is the dignified and respected Gurdas Mann, and of disco *bhangra* is Daler Mehndi, whose tentlike robes and bejewelled turban form an eye-catching spectacle.

Ghazals

One musical form that was revived and reinterpreted during the cassette revolution was the modern *ghazal*. Championed by the Muslim nobility in the nineteenth century in India, the *ghazal*, sung in Urdu or Hindustani, was a light classical mode that consisted of refined poetry and sophisticated musical improvisations expressing unrequited love, mystical devotion, philosophical rumination, ridicule of religious orthodoxy, and celebration of madness and divine intoxication (Russell 1992). When the Moghul empire declined in the eighteenth century, along with the fortunes of the Muslim nobility who patronized the fine arts, the *ghazal* found new appeal among the courtesan class that began to cater to the emerging North Indian Hindu bourgeoisie in *mehfil*s (private concerts).

With the advent of the gramophone records in the early 1900s, recording companies seeking a pan-regional music to record and market hit upon the *ghazal* as a form that could be taken out of the private chambers of the courtesan and publicly marketed to the phonograph-owning upper classes. However, it was not until the arrival of cassette technology and the musical revolution that a mass medium was found for the dissemination of the *ghazal*. In the course of its transformation from a privately performed, light-classical form into a studio-made, publicly marketed form, the modern *ghazal* was born, adapted for a pan-regional North Indian—mainly Hindu—mass audience. Gone were the refined poetry and the sophisticated musical improvisations that were integral parts of the traditional *ghazal*. In their place, a simplified, precomposed musical rendition accompanied a more accessible—though at times sentimental and even mawkish—contemporary versification.

In the course of its transformation from a courtly form to bourgeois one, the *ghazal* also underwent a "Hinduization" in both style and lyrics. Historically, the *ghazal* was linked to the Indo-Muslim culture. With the partition of India and the exodus of most educated Muslims to Pakistan, a Hindu bourgeoisie began to replace the Muslim feudal elite. Knowledge of Urdu had begun to decline, and the courtly Urdu poetry was slowly replaced with simpler Hindi words; at the same time, Muslim singers were replaced by Hindu singers, and a more Hindi diction crept into the singing of the *ghazal*.

The style adopted by the modern *ghazal* singers was one of easy listening—soft, relaxed, soothing, crooning. Although it was dismissed as pedestrian by classical singers, the emerging urban middle classes nevertheless appreciated the new *ghazal*. It was more accessible than the classical music, which required an educated ear, and it was less raucous and raunchy than the film song. Furthermore, the form managed to retain the exotic and romantic associations of the courtesan world and Urdu poetry, and convey them to a more contemporary, less aristocratic, and less sophisticated audience (Manuel 1993).

As a musical form, the *ghazal* has the distinction of not only predating the Hindi film song but also of being one entirely independent of Hindi cinema. Hindi films absorbed innumerable contemporary and traditional Indian and foreign influences into their songs. They also incorporated the traditional *ghazal* and created a subgenre, the "film *ghazal*," to accompany the courtesan scenes in the films. Nevertheless, despite being devoured by the film music industry, the *ghazal* as a distinct musical form managed to remain independent of the Hindi film song.

Indian singers such as Anup Jalota, Pankaj Udhas, and Jagjit Singh are the prominent singers of this genre. Pakistani *ghazal* singers, such as Abida Parveen, have also found fame and success in India, while *qawwali* singers, such as the Sabri brothers and the late Nusrat Fateh Ali Khan, have been recognized as international star performers of the genre. Hariharan, famous for his album *Colonial Cousins* with Leslie Lewis, is also an accomplished *ghazal* singer.

Indian singer Jagjit Singh (left) hugs Pakistani singer Ghulam Ali as they prepare to address a joint press conference on the eve of their music concert in Bangalore, India 4 March 2005. The concert is organized to promote friendship between the two South Asian neighbors. (Dibyangshu Sarkar/AFP/Getty Images)

Adnan Sami, India-based Pakistani singer, gestures during an interview in New Delhi. Sami has been roped in by Channel V to hunt for the best music talents in the country, 2004. (Kamal Kishore/Reuters/Corbis)

Indipop

In a bid to target the Indian audiences and offer greater variety, the global music channels began to feature Indian artists in all kinds of popular nonfilm music. The music that has emerged from this trend is an eclectic mix of genres called Indipop, a hybrid of Indian and western musical traditions. With its easy East-West fusion, Indipop is open to all kinds of musical interpretations and has created a series of new subgenres, including Sufi pop (songs of Islamic mysticism in a jazzed up version by artists such as Kailash Kher, whose voice is said to resemble that of the late singing sensation Nusrat Fateh Ali Khan) and Indian hip-hop (performed by artists such as Aneida, Xenia, and Adnan Sami). It has also given birth to pop singers such as Remo Fernandes and Asha Bhonsle, the latter a sixty-seven-year-old playback singer of over 12,000 songs, most of them from Indian films, who made a late transition to this music to become the new pop icon in the late 1990s. It has also given rise to rock groups such as Parikrama and Zero, and fusion that blends jazz, Carnatic classical, and samba rhythms as in the music of Trilok Gurtu.

In addition to artists performing in these fusion genres, a clutch of Indian artists record western pop music, most often cover versions of chart toppers. There are a few exceptions, however, such as Remo Fernandes, who sings original songs in English. These groups are given a platform by music channels such as MTV and Channel V, and some have even inspired fan clubs in places such as Israel and Malaysia. Although they have captured 8 percent of the Indian market within less than a decade, Indian musicians performing western music generally do not seem to enjoy much success in international markets.

Indian devotees play music during the Jagannath Rath Yatra festival in New Delhi 1 July 2003. During the festival, images of Jagannath, his brother Balabhadra, and his sister Subhadra mounted on ceremonial chariots are taken out in a procession. Lord Jagannath is the incarnation of Lord Vishnu, the preserver, one of the trinity of the Hindu pantheon. (Prakash Singh/AFP/Getty Images)

Devotional Music

The devotional music section in the industry constitutes about 8 percent of the market and is considered a reliable niche and an "evergreen" seller by the industry. *Bhakti*, or devotion, constitutes an important part of Hindu religious practice, and the most natural expression of *bhakti* is singing. While Hindu religious music comprises a major part of this segment, Muslim, Sikh, Christian, and other religious music, too, forms a part of this market.

In Hindu music, songs about gods, myths, folklore, legends, and festivals are all part of the repertoire. The broad sweep of devotional music includes chants and readings of scriptures such as the *Vishnusahasranam* (the thousand names of the god Vishnu), *Shivamahimnah stotra* (verses in praise of the god Shiva), *Bhagavad Gita*, *Ramayana*, *Ramcharitmanas*, and holy mantras, such as *Om Namah Shivaya*. These recordings are often used in daily, weekly, or occasional sessions of prayer, contemplation, and private worship. No religious subject is too small or too obscure to merit its own cassette.

Devotional songs—*bhajan* and *abhanga*—composed by saints, such as Surdas, Mirabai, and Tukaram, and other spiritual guides celebrated over the centuries, have a steady, year-round market and are used both at home and at large religious gatherings. Celebratory songs and devotional music for specific religious festivals, such as *Ganesh Chaturti*, *Navratri*, *Dussera*,

Diwali, and *Durga Puja*, are seasonal favorites. On festival days these songs are often played in temples and other areas of religious celebration and relayed over loudspeakers for the local population (regardless of whether they want to listen to it). In addition, since Indian films exploit every form of song in their repertoire of musical offerings, there are also the film *bhajan*s available for these occasions.

Fusion also pervades celebrations linked to religious festivities. For example, *dandiya* and *garbo* are traditional forms of communal dances performed each night during the nine consecutive nights of *Navratri* celebrations. Today there are modern versions of the same traditional music performed with synthesizers and other electronic equipment, creating new musical genres that have emerged in order to make traditions more relevant to modern-day India. The more contemporary accompaniments to the traditional rhythms make them more appealing to the younger generations, who see the celebrations primarily as an occasion for socializing with the opposite sex.

In Muslim religious music, readings from the Koran and *qawwalis*, mystical Sufi songs of ecstatic worship, constitute the two major categories, while in Sikh religious music, *kirtan* (sung religious commentaries) and *shabad*, or readings from the holy texts of Sikhism, are most commonly marketed.

As a genre, devotional music requires simplicity of style and content. Sincerity of emotion and religious feeling take precedence over musical virtuosity. All great classical singers, both Hindu and Muslim, conclude their public performances with a *bhajan* or some kind of devotional song. This is in keeping with the classical tradi-

tions of the performing arts, where salutations to the divine are offered both at the beginning and end of a performance. The devotional renditions of the great classical singers also form part of the devotional music repertoire.

There are best-selling recordings of *bhajans* by Bhimsen Joshi, Kumar Gandharva, the late Omkarnath Thakur, and the late M. S. Subbalakshmi. The most famous of light classical *bhajan* recordings are those of D. V. Paluskar, who died at the age of 35 in 1955. Well-known contemporary performers of devotional music include Hari Om Sharan, Pankaj Udhas, Anup Jalota, and Anuradha Paudhwal.

The leading producer of religious music is T-Series, which controls about 77 percent of this niche market. It releases between 150 and 200 devotional titles every year—nearly three a week. Although none of the other companies can compare with the T-series assembly line, Tips and Saregama control about 4 percent of the market and release thirty to forty titles year. Venus commands around 5 percent of the market, even though it releases only ten titles a year, thanks to its extensive distribution network (FICCI 2003). Smaller companies such as Plus Music and Baba Audio, which are not players in the high-stakes film-music genre, depend entirely on devotional releases such as *bhajans*, prayers, recitations from the epics, and other religious texts for economic survival.

For music companies, devotional music constitutes a sound business strategy. It is a low-cost genre and, unlike film music, it requires no expensive rights or glamorous marketing. The market for devotional music is not as unpredictable as that of film music or subject to erratic changes in fashion; thus it has the added advantage of a much longer "shelf life" than film music. The overseas market for devotional music among the Indian expatriate and immigrant communities is also very steady. Best of all, thanks to India's rich heritage of religious literature, there is an inexhaustible corpus of material. Singer Anuradha Paudhwal, who moved from film to devotional music and has over a thousand *bhajans* to her credit, observed that "there is so much material that even if I were to sing for 100 years, it wouldn't get over" (Chopra and Joshi 1997: 76–77).

International Music

With increased exposure to western popular music via the music channels of MTV and Channel V, international music, which includes pop, rock, rap, reggae, hip-hop, and jazz, has increased its market share from 2 percent to about 8 percent in the last few years.

Issues

The rapid growth of the music industry in India has been accompanied by a parallel growth in problems that have plagued the industry for the last few decades. The single most pressing problem of the cassette revolution has been the uncontrolled spread of piracy.

The Growth of Piracy

"Everybody is listening to our music," laments V. J. Lazarus of Universal Music, "but nobody is buying it" (Goyal 2003: 38). The music industry in India currently stands at INR 10.4 billion (US$230 million), of which only INR 6.2 billion (US$137 million) constitute legitimate sales. In terms of units, total sales in 2003 stood at 230 million cassettes and 11 million CDs, of which the legitimate market accounted for 138 million cassettes and 7 million CDs (FICCI 2003). However, the "unorganized" nature of the sector defies measurement, and in the absence of any reliable data, most reports on the size of the music market are just estimates.

Most of the piracy takes place in Hindi film music, the most popular genre in the market. According to the London-based International Federation of the Phonographic Industry (IFPI), the volume of piracy in the Indian music markets ranks third highest and the value of pirated products ranks sixth highest in the world.

The same factors that fueled the cassette revolution—low cost and ease of duplication—were instrumental in facilitating the emergence of the vast pirate sector in the music industry. But over the decades, piracy has ruined many fledgling music companies. In 1980, pirated tapes accounted for an estimated 10 percent of sales, but by 1986 the share increased to nearly 95 percent of the music market. Thanks to a series of measures begun in the 1990s that lowered the retail price of legitimate cassettes and CDs and abolished certain taxes, the Federation of Indian Chambers of Commerce and Industry (FICCI) estimates that piracy now accounts for around 40 percent of all music sales in India (FICCI 2003).

Until 2001, music piracy consisted solely of the unauthorized copying and selling of music on cassettes. However, with the emergence of CDs as well as new technologies that allow free downloading, digital piracy has also become an alarming phenomenon. The market for CDs still comprises a very small segment of the music market because of its cost compared with cassettes, but it stands to suffer even greater threats from the piracy networks.

Writer Peter Manuel identifies various forms of piracy in the music industry, including bootlegging (the marketing of unauthorized recordings of a live performance, a feat impossible before the advent of cassette recording) and the dubbing of selected songs on request for individual customers. Various cassette retailers, electronic repair shops, and dubbing kiosks, all of which specialize in piracy, conduct these operations as a side business. Typically, an individual provides the dubber with a list of songs, such as the hit numbers from a variety of contemporary films. The dubber duplicates the requested songs from his own archives onto a cassette for a fee. Such is the success of these operations that in cities like Chennai (formerly Madras), kiosks release weekly tapes of compiled hits from various labels (Manuel 1993).

The most prolific form of piracy in India is the unauthorized mass duplication and sale of legitimate commercial recordings. Although this sector is theoretically "unorganized," Manuel argues that it is actually quite well organized into small-scale dubbers, on the one hand, who primarily copy regional music catering to specialized, local audiences, and on the other hand, large-scale corporation-like enterprises that command vast resources and pan-Indian distribution networks. These latter enterprises copy film songs for nationwide markets. Most of these pirated cassettes are sold openly in the market, sometimes alongside retail outlets selling legitimate cassettes and CDs. The distribution networks include street vendors who, in cities like Mumbai, have even established their own trade associations. Manuel points to the Maharashtra Cassette Dealers Sena (Army) affiliated with the right-wing Hindu nationalist party Shiv Sena, which offers protection from police prosecution in exchange for membership dues for the organization (Manuel 1993).

Yet another form of piracy involves the production of cover versions. Cover versions are recordings of (usually old) songs performed by new singers, but using the same tunes and lyrics as the originals. Legally, cover versions are permitted, subject to the fulfilment of certain formalities, such as permission from the original producers and payment of fees to them. But often the producers of cover versions ignore such formalities. Furthermore, by copying the same labels or inserts as the original versions, consumers are duped into thinking they are buying low-priced originals, only to discover that the songs are being performed by different, often less familiar, singers.

The primary advantage of the pirated tape is price. Since music pirates enjoy all the advantages of the music industry without having to pay taxes or overhead costs such as recording fees and royalties or the costs of production, promotion, and advertising, their retail price is very low. Nor do they risk their resources experimenting with new artists or new kinds of music; instead, they can stand back and cherry-pick the successes. And by acquiring recording materials such as blank cassettes from unlicensed producers or smugglers they manage to keep even the costs of recording to a minimum.

In the past, the Indian government's onerous taxation and unreasonable demands of the recording companies (that they export 75 percent of their stock, for example) meant even greater advantages for the music pirates. And by overpricing their products, the legitimate recording companies drove consumers into the arms of the pirates. In an attempt to curb piracy, the government has now abolished excise duties and reduced sales tax, and music companies have recently reduced the price of cassettes and CDs.

Music piracy began to grow rapidly when it became apparent that the monopolistic recording companies such as HMV were unable to abandon their sluggish commercial practices and meet the sudden explosion of demand for music (particularly film music) that accompanied the cassette revolution. HMV never kept account of its own music catalogs during the seven decades of almost complete domination of the market and was unable to supply reissues of old film songs. Pirates, who took advantage of improved technology, quickly met the pent-up demand for old songs. The legitimate companies were also slow in arranging for adequate distribution throughout the country, particularly in smaller cities, towns, and the rural areas, so nimble pirates stepped in and met the demand.

Indian consumers are not averse to purchasing pirated products. Most are not even aware that their purchases are pirated. While cassettes with hand-written, photocopied, or cheaply printed labels betray their pirated provenance, those bearing well-printed but bogus labels of bona fide or bogus companies are hard to discern and require intimate knowledge of the market on the part of the consumer. According to an Indian government report on piracy in 1999, nearly half the consumers of pirated products interviewed were unaware that they were buying pirated copies of the original. Those who were aware were unperturbed by the inferior sound

quality and poor durability, because the money they saved by buying pirated cassettes was substantial, at least in the short term (Government of India 1999). Besides, consumers were used to substandard products churned out by the inferior technology of the legitimate music industry, and the cassette players too were initially of poor quality. Today, with improved technology, both the originals and pirated copies of the originals are of a very high sound quality as are also the cassette and CD players. (Because of their higher costs, CDs constitute just 3–5 percent of the music market.)

Sometimes innocent companies are accused of piracy because of crimes perpetrated in their names. T-series, for example, often accused of piracy, has also been a victim of piracy. Pirates pasted T-series logos and labels on pirated versions of HMV and other companies' recordings (Manuel 2003).

Legitimate producers could not initially resort to the law to restrain the music pirates. The only extant copyright act dated from the colonial period when cassette players did not exist and piracy was not an issue. To overhaul the copyright law in the face of the sudden boom in cassette piracy required time, and there were long delays in the passing of amendments to the act. Besides, the government regarded music and other creative industries as frivolous sectors of the Indian economy, and parliamentarians, with more pressing concerns, were in no great hurry to change the status quo.

Lax policing and lenient judicial sentencing have encouraged the pirates to proliferate. Seen as a victimless crime, the police are reluctant to devote their meager resources towards eliminating a crime that they consider less of a threat to law and order than many others, such as murder, kidnapping, and burglary. Most police investigations and criminal prosecutions have taken place only at the insistence of the producers or the Indian Phonographic Industry (IPI). The music industry has declared the police resources devoted to apprehending music pirates by the government as totally inadequate. The annual budget for rooting out piracy currently stands at INR 50 million (US$1.11 million). In the 1980s, the IFPI gave the IPI INR 43 million (US$950,000) to fight piracy. But policing digital piracy is extremely difficult, since anyone with an Internet connection and MP3 software can download music with ease.

Justice in the courts is slow, and legal cases can take a very long time. Even in the rare instance that a case comes to court, judges tend to be lenient, since the person in the dock is often a first time offender. The pirates have come up with a system that ensures minimal punishment: a new person is produced as the culprit each time a company is taken to court. In 1997, there were 5,500 cases of piracy registered, of which only 200 cases were addressed in court. Out of these there were only thirty-five convictions, and in most cases the penalty was a fine of about INR 500 (US$10). Small fines, short sentences, lengthy and expensive litigation, and low recoveries often result in companies having little hope for relief, and piracy has now been accepted as an unavoidable business hazard (FICCI 2003).

For artists, piracy ensures widespread distribution and sales of their music. Often artists are employed on flat-fee contracts and receive no royalties, but even those who are entitled to royalties find that the widespread distribution of their music leads to more public performances and handsome income from such live events. However, poorly recorded pirated versions can also do injustice to artists by presenting their talents in an unflattering light.

It has also been noted that legitimate companies have sometimes depended on private arrangements with pirates to help them meet demand when they are unable to do so themselves. For instance, when a "sleeper" film unexpectedly becomes a hit, the producers cannot meet the sudden demand for its music without help from the pirates. So a private agreement is reached, whereby the legitimate company unofficially subcontracts the production to a pirate company. Such a deal was allegedly struck by the producers of the film *Maine Pyar Kiya* (S. Barjataya, 1989): officially, 3 million copies were sold, but actual sales numbered nearly 10 million. Sometimes legitimate producers of cassettes sell pirated versions of their own music to save on taxes, default on royalties, and obscure the smuggled or unauthorized sources of their raw materials. Such allegations were directed against T-series when the company was still in its infancy (Manuel 1993).

Fortunately, the level of piracy appears to have dropped, at least according to a survey by the IFPI. Their report indicated that piracy in India had fallen from a high of 95 percent in 1985 to about 30 percent in 1995 (FICCI 2003). Nevertheless, local cassette producers and sellers are not optimistic. They report that piracy is on the increase. It is possible that, while the actual numbers of pirated cassettes on sale in India has risen because of the growth in the overall market, the percentage of pirated cassettes and CDs is on the decline.

Members of the electronic and music industries have strong incentives to conceal or misrepresent aspects of their operations. Tape-producing companies may also seek to under-report production to save on excise duties and sales tax. Such common practices seriously misrepresent the size of the industry, so it is assumed that the actual sales of prerecorded cassettes are several times larger than that which is officially declared.

Links with Organized Crime

It appears that there may be a link between piracy and organized crime, and that profits from the music industry are used in other operations, including terrorism. It is alleged that the murder of an important personality in the world of music is linked to the Dubai-based Bombay Mafia.

In 1997, Gulshan Kumar, founder-owner of T-series, one of biggest music companies in India, specializing in devotional music, was shot dead in the streets of Mumbai. Investigations revealed that the killer was Abu Salem, one of Dawood Ibrahim's henchmen, and that it was allegedly a contract killing at the behest of Nadeem Saifee, one half of the Bollywood film music-composing duo Nadeem-Shravan. Saifee, who was said to have close contacts with the Dubai-based criminal underworld, took refuge in London. He later sought political asylum to avoid extradition to India. While some have mentioned professional rivalry between Saifee and Kumar, others say that music companies were losing money because of Kumar's piracy and that Kumar was treading into Indian Mafia territory. The police have been looking at a possible convergence of interests. The case remains open.

Conclusion

Today more Indians listen to music than ever before, and more music is available to them. But as one critic has noted: "Music is booming, but the music industry is going bust" (Goyal 2003: 38). Reeling from the combined effects of film flops in 2002, the high costs of acquiring music rights, piracy, and digital downloading, the music industry's worth has fallen by half, from INR 12 billion (US$350 million) in 2000 to INR 6 billion in 2003. In response, music companies are slowly moving away from new film music and opting for remixes. They are also looking to expand other genres, such as lounge, Sufi pop, and hip-hip, bringing greater diversity to popular Indian music. With music companies slowly initiating more stringent measures against large-scale piracy, better retaining and pricing of products, and the corporatization of the Indian film industry, the Federation of Indian Chambers of Commerce and Industry predicts the currently flat sales figures will grow by 60 percent by 2007 and that despite a somber mood in the music industry, the future looks bright (FICCI 2003).

A to Z Index

Asha Bhonsle (1933–), together with her sister, Lata Mangeshkar, dominated the Hindi film-music industry for three decades, recording over 20,000 songs in fourteen languages. She is the most popular, cool, hip, and trendy senior singer in the young world of Indian rock, fusion, and remixes. The matriarch has also done *ghazals* and pop, and as early as the 1980s had teamed up with western singers such as Boy George (*Bow Down Mister*).

Alisha Chinai (1972–) is the pioneer and undisputed Queen of Indipop—that's the verdict of the music industry. Her first major hit album was *Jadoo* (Magic). Further platinum albums included *Aah Alisha*, *Baby Doll*, *Madonna*, and *Kamasutra*, but it was *Made in India* that established Indipop as a discrete genre and Chinai its prime proponent. *Om—The Inner Voice* was followed by *Dil ki Rani* (Queen of Hearts). She gained notoriety for accusing composer Anu Malik of molesting her and also accused Magnasound of cheating her of her royalties. The music company countersued for defamation. Chinai occasionally sings playback songs for Hindi films.

Remo Fernandes (1953–), the grand old man of Indian pop music, was one of the first Indian singers to attempt to fuse rock with Indian music. He gained recognition in the early 1980s when one of his concerts was televized on Doordarshan. Although he only sang in English he soon became a household name and was invited to compose music for films (Shyam Benegal's *Trikaal*, 1985, and Pankaj Parashar's *Jalwa*, 1986).

Trilok Gurtu (1951–), son of the late Indian classical vocalist Shobha Gurtu, is a world-class musician who has played with jazz bands in Europe and the United States. His debut album, *Usfret* in 1988 established him as a serious vocalist and musician. He was the first musician to blend the Indian, jazz, rock, and African musical traditions. In 2004, he composed the background score for Sidhartha Srinivasan's film *Amavas*.

Hariharan (1955–) trained in Carnatic (south Indian classical style) music and then moved into the north Indian *ghazal* genre. He became one of the pioneers of Indian fusion music when in 1996 he and Mumbai-based Leslie Lewis released the first fusion album, *Colonial Cousins*. Hariharan has also sung for Hindi and Mani Ratnam's Tamil films.

Anup Jalota (1953–) is the son of *bhajan* exponent Purshottam Das Jalota. He specializes in *bhajans* but is equally popular for his renditions of *ghazal*, *geet* (chanson), and film songs.

Kailash Kher (1985–) is the hottest new singer to break into Bollywood playback circles. His voice resonates like the late *qawwali* singer Nusrat Fateh Ali Khan. He is now celebrated for his rendition of Khan's *Allah Ke Bande*, in homage to the late genius, and *Rang de ne* for the film *Dev*. He also sang for *Swades* (A. Gowatrikar, 2004) and *The Rising* (Ketan Mehta, 2005).

Lata Mangeshkar (1929–) is the queen of Indian film songs and has recorded over 25,000 songs in fourteen languages. In the late 1980s, she is said to have recorded two songs a day. She specialized in singing in a high-pitched voice (in the key of C sharp), a feat that had to be repeated by all new playback singers. Her film hits are a central part of the music industry's repackaging of nostalgic songs from old Hindi films, and most remixes feature at least one of her songs.

Gurdas Mann (1957–), a Punjabi folk singer, got his break in music with an exuberant number, *Dil da Mamala*, that he wrote and performed for a Punjabi play, *Sasi Punnu*. The song was aired on Jullandhar TV and became an overnight sensation. It was commercially recorded by HMV (now Saregama) in 1982. Since then he has produced over twenty-seven albums and written over 200 songs, mainly in Punjabi, and has single-handedly revived Punjabi folk music. His most famous album is the *Apna Punjab* track.

Daler Mehndi (1967–), the king of disco *bhangra*, began singing in the local *gurdwara* (place of Sikh worship), then worked as a taxi driver before bagging a contract for *Bolo Ta Ra Ra*, which made recording history. It was followed by other successes such as *Ho Jayegi Balle Balle* and *Tunak Tunak Tun*. In 2003, he was accused of human trafficking but was cleared of all charges, although his estranged brother remains implicated in the scandal.

Shubha Mudgal (1959–), disciple of the celebrated maestro Pandit Kumar Gandharva, is a versatile performer straddling several genres, from the classical to Sufi to devotional and Indian pop. She is also a composer for ballets and films.

D. V. Paluskar (1921–1955) achieved legendary status as a classical singer despite a life cut short by poverty and ill health. Trained in classical Hindustani music by his famous classical singer father, V. D. Paluskar, he cut several classical records with Columbia and HMV but will always be remembered as one of the greatest singers of *bhajans* (devotional songs). The most famous of these are collected under the title *Payoji Maine Ram Ratan Dhan*, which contains some of the best-loved *bhajans*,

including Mahatma Gandhi's favorite, *Raghupati Raghava Raja Ram*.

Parikrama, one of India's top rock bands, is a Delhi-based pop group that started in 1991 and has survived the competition. Their latest single, "But . . . It Rained," was downloaded from their website by over 100,000 music lovers.

Abida Parveen (1954–) is one of the celebrated Pakistani singers of *ghazal* and Sufi songs (*Sufiana kalaam*). After the death of Nusrat Fateh Ali Khan, she is considered the best singer of Sufi mystical lyrics. An album released by Times Music in 2003 entitled *Abida, Mere Dil Se* made her an international star.

Anuradha Paudhwal (1954–) began her career as a playback singer for films in the 1970s. Her rapid rise in the industry suffered a setback with her open criticism of the singing sisters Lata Mangeshkar and Asha Bhonsle, and producers dropped her from film projects. She turned to Gulshan Kumar for a recording contract—he was then just breaking into the world of film music with his company T-Series—and she later concentrated on devotional songs.

A. R. Rahman (1966–) began his career by composing jingles for television commercials and has risen to become one of the most talented and prolific composers of Indian film and nonfilm music. His big break came with the films of Mani Rathnam. Since the 1990s, he has composed for innumerable Hindi films and collaborated with the American pop star Michael Jackson and the British composer Andrew Lloyd Webber, the latter for his stage musical *Bombay Dreams*. He was also the composer for Gurinder Chadha's film *Bride and Prejudice* (2004) and for the Oscar-nominated Chinese film *Warriors of Heaven and Earth* (Zhang Yimou 2004).

Adnan Sami (1973–) is one of the hottest stars of the Indian pop music world. Educated at Rugby, an English public school, he moved to India from Pakistan and collaborated with the great Indian film singer Asha Bhonsle before achieving even greater fame and popularity with the album *Tera Chehra* and his single *Lift Kara De*. His music videos invariably feature top film stars such as Amitabh Bachchan and more recently Rani Mukherji. His newest release is *Abstract*, a series of compositions on electric piano.

Jagjit Singh (1941–) is a renowned *ghazal* singer. Initially he sang with his wife, Chitra, and the two were one of the earliest husband-wife teams in the early 1970s. Their most famous album, *The Unforgettable*, was released in 1976 and set a new high in record sales. However, grief at the sudden death of their son led Chitra to abandon all public engagements. Jagjit Singh continued as a solo singer, and his collaborative album *Sajda*, with Lata Mangeshkar, marked another milestone in his career.

Pankaj Udhas's (1951–) speciality is the *ghazal*, and he was one of the early exponents of the musical form when it re-emerged in its current form as part of the cassette revolution of the 1980s. His first album of ghazals, *Aahat*, was released in 1980. His most successful *ghazal* album to date has been *Aafreen*, which achieved triple platinum status in 1986, the year of its release. That same year he began his career as a singer of playback for the Hindi film screen's unmusical screen stars.

Xenia (1980–) became one of the newest Indipop sensations with the success of her first album *Meri Ada*. She is also the first pop artist from the disputed region of Kashmir. Her major influences come from such diverse musical sources as Diana Ross, Asha Bhonsle, and Abida Parveen.

Zero is a Mumbai-based rock band that in 2000 began playing in pubs and discotheques before finally winning the Great Indian Rock competition in 2004. Their early albums, *Albummed* and *Hook*, were self-financed, but they now have recording contracts with major music companies.

Bibliography and References

Appadurai, Arjun, Frank Korom, and Margaret Mills, eds. *Gender, Genre, and Power in South Asian Expressive Traditions*. Philadelphia: University of Pennsylvania Press, 1991.

Baruah, Teena. "Border Crossing." *The Sunday Express*, 6 June 2004.

Chakravarti, Sudeep. "Daler Mehndi: The Sardar of Swing," *India Today*, 29 June 1998.

Chandavarkar, Bhaskar. "Indian Film Song." In *70 Years of Indian Cinema*, edited by T. M. Ramachandran. Bombay: Cinema India-International, 1985.

———. "Tradition of Music in Indian Cinema." *Cinema in India*, April–June 1987.

———. "Now It's the Bombay Film Song." *Cinema in India*, July–September 1987.

———. "The Power of the Popular Film Song." *Cinema in India*, April–June 1990.

Chandra, Anupama, with Kavitha Shetty. "Audio Cassette Industry: Hitting the Right Notes." *India Today*, 30 November 1993.

Chandvankar, Suresh. "History of Music." *Screen*, 6 June 2003.

Chopra, Anil. "Magnetic Tape: To Import or Not to Import." *Playback*, December 1986.

Chopra, Anupama. "Devotional Songs: Singing a Divine Tune." *India Today*, 29 December 1997.

Dagli, Kinjal. "Music: Out of the Garage." *The Week*, 20 June 2004.

Deshpande, Haima. "Killed for a Song." *The Sunday Express*, 27 June 2004.

Eremita, Bosco de Sousa. "Remo Fernandes: Rocking and Rolling at Fifty." *The Week*, 18 May 2003.

Federation of Indian Chambers of Commerce and Industry (FICCI). "The Indian Music Industry: Fast Forward" and "The Indian Radio Industry: In Play Mode." In *The Indian Entertainment Sector: In the Spotlight*. Mumbai: KPMG, 2003.

Government of India, Department of Education. *Study on Copyright Piracy in India*, New Delhi, 1999.

Goyal, Malini. "Music Industry: Missing Notes." *India Today*, 5 May 2003.

Gupta, Sulakshana. "Thorn Bird: Kanta Lagaa's Shefali Jariwala Is Back to Shaking Her Booty." *Indian Express*, 16 June 2004.

Joshi, G. N. "A Concise History of the Phonograph Industry in India." *Popular Music* 7 (2), May 1988.

Joshi, Namrata. "Music Channels: Music Mongering." *India Today*, 15 June 1998.

———. "Music Video: Trying to Be Picture Perfect." *India Today*, 3 August 1998.

Joshi, Namrata, and Anupama Chopra. "Super Cassettes Industries: All in the Family." *India Today*, 13 October 1997.

Kasbekar, Asha. "Hidden Pleasures: Negotiating the Myth of the Female Ideal in Popular Hindi Films." In *The History, Politics and Consumption of Public Culture in India*, edited by Rachel Dwyer and Christopher Pinney. New Delhi: Oxford University Press, 2001.

Katyar, Arun. "Indian Pop Stars: Going for a Song." *India Today*, 15 April 1993.

———. "Film Lyrics: Obscene Overtures." *India Today*, 15 January 1994.

Kinnear, Michael. "Odeon in India." *International Talking Machine Review*, Spring 1990.

Kohli, Sangeeta. "Bawdy Tones." *The Week*, 15 June 2003.

Koppikar, Smruti, Anupama Chopra, and Anita Anand. "Gulshan Kumar Murder: Suspect No. 1." *India Today*, 29 September 1997.

Krishnakumar, K. "Yesterday Once More: Indian Rock Bands Find Their Voice as People Warm Up to the Sound." *The Week*, 11 June 2004.

Manuel, Peter. *Cassette Culture: Popular Music and Technology in North India*. Chicago: University of Chicago Press, 1993.

———. "A Historical Survey of the Urdu Ghazal-song in India." *Asian Music* 20 (1), Fall–Winter 1988.

Ranade, Ashok. *On Music and Musicians of Hindoostan*. New Delhi: Promilla, 1984.

Ranjit, S. Sahaya. "Medley: Remixes Are the Best Bet." *India Today*, 9 June 2003.

Raval, Sheela. "Asha Bhosle: Reinventing a Diva." *India Today*, 27 October 1997.

Reddi, Usha. "Media and Culture in Indian Society: Conflict or Cooperation?" *Media, Culture and Society* 11 (4), 1989.

Russell, Ralph. *The Pursuit of Urdu Literature: A Select History*. Calcutta: Seagull Books, 1992.

Shukla, Archana, and Reshmi R. Dasgupta. "Bhangra's a Tara-ra-rage on the Circuit" and "Punjabi Music Has a Pan-India Audience, Draws Advertisers." *The Economic Times*, 9 September 2003.

Skillman, T. "The Bombay Hindi Film Song." In *Yearbook for Traditional Music 1986*. New York: International Council for Traditional Music, 1986.

Wajihuddin, Mohammed. "Magic Numbers." *The Sunday Express*, 30 May 2004.

3

Theater

In the preface to his book on political theater in India, Rustom Barucha decries the general tendency to view Indian theater as a single, unified entity. "It needs to be stressed," he writes, "that there is no such thing as *an* Indian theater. It may have existed centuries ago when it was synonymous with Sanskrit classical drama, but today we can speak only of the Bengali theater, or the Marathi theater, or the Tamil theater, and so on. There are as many theaters as there are languages in India" (Barucha 1983: xi).

With sixteen major languages and hundreds of dialects in India, there are indeed hundreds of theaters in India. Also, since most of the languages and dialects are not entirely understood outside their particular province or region, there has been little or no communication among the various theaters. Moreover, translations of regional plays into other regional languages have been few and remain so even today. And, as Barucha argues, apart from differences in language, the various regional theaters also reflect divergences of culture comprising the bewildering variety of customs, traditions, and folklore that are inextricably linked to particular regions. Consequently, the theaters in India are often specifically related to the cultural inheritance of particular communities. A play set in Bengal, for instance, may not be fully understood by an urban audience in Tamil Nadu, while the contemporary resonances of a Marathi play may elude an audience in Rajasthan. The various Indian theaters have thus developed as discrete regional and independent entities. "It should be remembered," observes Barucha, "that there are difficulties in understanding Indian theaters within India itself" (Barucha 1983: xii).

Despite the bewildering variety of dramatic activity, almost all contemporary theater in India has in some way been informed by certain crucial developments. The first two are the classical Sanskrit theater, which flourished between the first and eighth centuries AD, and the *Natyashastra*, a scholarly treatise attributed to Bharata (circa second century AD) on the aesthetics of the Sanskrit stage. Modern Indian theater is also influenced by the traditional popular and folk theaters of the regions, such as the *jatra*, *tamasha*, and *nautanki*, which flourished after the decline of the classical theater. These folk and traditional theaters continue to thrive despite intense competition from film, television, and the modern stage. The legacies of the colonial British stage of the eighteenth and nineteenth centuries, the Parsi theater of the late nineteenth and early twentieth centuries, and the Indian People's Theater Association during the World War II years have also informed the development of the modern Indian stage.

The arrival of the British colonials in the nineteenth century led to the creation of an exclusively British theater for the consumption of the colonial residents of Kolkata. The curiosity of the Indians was aroused both by the novelty of the plays (Shakespeare, for example) and the exotic theatrical conventions (proscenium stage, curtains, sets, props) of western stage productions. In the 1850s, universities were established in the cities of Bombay, Calcutta, and Madras, and the teaching of drama and literature brought both Shakespeare and Sanskrit literature into the reach of the growing number of Indian students (Gokhale 2003). The dramatic conventions of the British performances in colonial India soon seeped into vernacular Indian productions.

Borrowing elements from the British stage and from the prevailing local popular theaters (such as the *nautanki* and *tamasha*), the Parsi theater was born in the mid-nineteenth century—a splendid amalgam of Indo-European-Islamic influences designed to entertain the growing urban population. The Parsi theater's extravagant spectacles in some of the local languages later inspired the growth of local theaters in Hindi and other regional languages, such as the Marathi theaters in Bombay and Poona (now known as Pune)

and the Company Nataks in southern India. In the 1940s, the rise of the Communist Party gave birth to the Indian People's Theater Association (IPTA), created as the cultural wing of the Communist Party. IPTA helped bring into existence the modern, vibrant theater in Calcutta and other cities.

Today the most dynamic and vibrant theaters are those that animate the stages of the cosmopolitan cities of Mumbai and Kolkata. Both cities host a vast variety of theaters and performances from all parts of the country. Both professional and amateur groups perform in at least three different languages in each city: in Mumbai, the Marathi-language theater dominates the cultural scene, followed by theater in Hindi (the national language), Gujerati (the language of the neighboring state of Gujerat), and English. Less frequent but nevertheless enthusiastically received are plays performed in Tamil for the Tamil-speaking population of the city. In Kolkata, the Bengali theater holds the prime position, with theatrical activity in Hindi and English. Both the cities also benefit from the frequent visits of touring theater groups from other towns and cities of India.

Sanskrit Theater

The origins of classical Sanskrit theater are still obscure. The surviving plays (and fragments of plays) are the main sources of information about this early theater, as well as Bharata's crucial treatise (circa second century AD) on the performing arts, the *Natyashastra*, which provides information on how these plays may have been performed. Normally performances were private or semiprivate and took place in theaters built within the precincts of palaces

Kathakali is dance-drama wherein the actors don intricate makeup, headgear, and ample skirts. This form of dance-drama is enacted in the courtyards of temples of Kerala, the southernmost state of India. No words are spoken, but the story is told by movements of hands and expression in the eyes. It is widely regarded as a connoisseur's dance. *Dussasana Vadham* (killing of Dussasana) is perhaps the most popular play in Kathakali repertoire. This story is from a Hindu epic, Mahabharata, wherein the Kauravas, led by their wily uncle Shakuni, challenge their cousins the Pandavas to a game of chess. The Pandavas lose all, including themselves and their wife, Draupadi. Duryodhana (the eldest of the Kauravas) asks Dussasana to drag Draupadi to the royal court by her hair and disrobe her. Lord Krishna comes to her rescue and protects her honor. A seething Draupadi curses the Kauravas, saving the worst for Dussasana. (Baldev/Corbis)

or the homes of the rich. The actors expressed emotions, or *bhava*, which created a variety of feelings or sentiments among the spectators. This "essence" of feeling experienced by the spectator was called *rasa*, and Bharata enumerates eight such *rasa*s or feelings: erotic, humorous, heroic, compassionate, furious, apprehensive, marvelous, and horrific.

Sanskrit drama was performed without scenery and with a minimum of properties: the highly developed gesture language of dance made up for the absence of both. Every part of the body was used to help tell a story, and the well-trained audience recognized from conventional movements of hands, limbs, and features that the king was riding in his chariot, or that the heroine was caressing her pet fawn. The splendid attire of the actors was also regulated by convention, so that heroes, heroines, gods, demons, and villains were immediately recognizable (Basham 1994).

Dancing (*nrtya*) was closely connected with acting (*natya*); the words themselves are forms of the same root word, and both dancing and acting were aspects of a single art, *abhinaya*, the portrayal of emotions that would produce eight corresponding sentiments (*rasa*) in the hearts of the spectators. The drama employed chiefly word and gesture, and the dance chiefly music and gesture. The poses and gestures were classified in detail: thirteen poses of the head, thirty-six of the eyes, nine of the neck, thirty-seven of the hand, and ten of the body are mentioned. With so many combinations available, the dancer could tell a whole story that was easily comprehensible to the observer who knew the conventions. The most distinctive feature of the dance was the hand gesture (*mudra*). By a beautiful and complicated code, the hand alone was capable of portraying not just a wide range of emotions, but also gods, animals, men, natural scenery, and actions (Basham 1994).

The performance generally began with an invocation to one or more of the gods, and a prologue in which the chief actor and stage manager (*sutradhar*) humorously discussed with the chief actress the occasion of the performance and the nature of the play to be performed. The main dialogue of the play was in prose, freely interspersed with verses. The verses were declaimed or intoned, but contrary to the practice in popular theater, they were not sung. The main play was generally preceded by a prelude (*praveshaka*) in which one or two characters set the scene and described what had gone before (Basham 1994).

The theatrical conventions allowed no tragedy. They also forbade the portrayal of violence, although these and other rules were sometimes ignored, as in the plays of Bhasa (second century AD). Tragic and pathetic scenes were common, but endings were almost invariably happy. But if the ancient Indian theater lovers rejected tragedy, they delighted in melodrama and pathos. Sanskrit drama contained many melodramatic scenes: noble heroes led to execution for crimes they did not commit declaimed their innocence to their sorrowing wives and children, only to be saved from the stake at the last moment; wives were unjustly expelled from their homes by their husbands; long-lost children were reunited with their parents in the final act (Basham 1994). The plots of Sanskrit drama seem to be reincarnated in those of the popular Hindi films, which also have a propensity for romance, family relationships, and melodrama.

Traditional Theaters

The terminal decline of the classical Sanskrit stage in the eighth century AD, which started with the political disintegration of the powerful Hindu and Buddhist states in northern India, was hastened by the conquest of the subcontinent by hordes of Muslim invaders who entered through the northwest.

The political fragmentation of northern India and the Deccan, and the rise of small, regional kingdoms resulted in interest concentrating more immediately upon local concerns and resources, and the whole of northern and central India became preoccupied with local rather than countrywide matters (Thapar 1966). These new states based on local cultures and histories crystallized local and regional loyalties. At the same time, the Sanskrit theater declined with the loss of an imperial patron. In the absence of a new and elite form of drama to replace it, it was the turn of the popular and "folk" theaters to gain ascendancy. Old legends, tales from the *Puranas* (religious literature of the first millennium*)*, mythological lore, philosophy, and stories of Sanskrit plays were popularized by bands of players scattered around the land.

These forms of theater were flexible, varied, and heterogeneous. (Early performances were usually of a religious nature, although later more secular forms of theatrical entertainment began to develop.) Certain common features, however, linked the multifarious forms of popular entertainment and celebration. Performances of popular or folk theaters were part of the local, religious, and agricultural calendar. Unlike performances in the private and elite nature of the Sanskrit theater, the popular or folk performances took place in public spaces, either after harvest or between the planting seasons. Most performances took place at night, after the day's toil. Players usually belonged to a particular castes of performers (for example, the Kolhati and Dombaris in Maharashtra were caste of tumblers and jugglers), although later, toward the beginning of the nineteenth century, actors in *maanch* of Madhya Pradesh and *nautanki* of Uttar Pradesh came from the artisan classes and included goldsmiths, tailors, carpenters, gardeners, and coppersmiths. As in the Sanskrit theater, most performances, whether secular or religious, began with an invocation of the gods (usually Lord Ganesh), either on stage or off. The performances invariably combined song and dance. Most performances comprised merely musicians and the players, and there were no sets or props. The performances were loud and unsophisticated, lacking the rigid fastidiousness of the Sanskrit theater and its elaborate science of *abhinaya*, or the portrayal of emotions and *mudra*, or gestures (Gargi 1966).

The surviving forms of popular theater can be loosely categorized as religious or secular although the boundary has never been clear. An irreverent and bawdy element has always been present in religious popular theater, such as the *Ram Lila*, introduced through the comic figures and the dancing; at the same time, secular theater, such as the *tamasha*, *nautanki*, and *jatra*, includes some serious moments of religious reverence and instruction.

Ram Lila *and* Ras Lila

The *Ram Lila* is a cycle of plays based on the life of Ram as recounted in Tulsidas's *Ramacharitamanas*. It is said that during his lifetime, Tulsidas (who died in 1624) often listened to the chanting of Valmiki's *Ramayana* in Sanskrit, held during the Hindu festival of Navratri. Inspired by it, he wrote a long poem in Hindi about Ram's life. The Brahmin priests of the northern Hindu holy city of Varanasi (formerly Benares) were shocked to see the worship of Ram conducted in the tongue of the common man and boycotted Tulsidas. But this only helped to make his epic poem even more popular. Two years after Tulsidas's death, Megh Bhagat, a devoted follower and dealer in bows and arrows, enacted the *Ram Lila* on the basis of Tulsidas's *Ramacharitamanas* during a five-day festival of pilgrimage. The tradition of *Ram Lila* spread to other parts of the region, and slowly the five-day celebrations grew into a festival that can today last as long as an entire month, reaching its climax when Ram destroys the villain Ravana. The all-night performances of the *Ram Lila* are characterized by plenty of singing, dancing, bombastic rhetoric, sword fights, comic interludes, and pageants (Gargi 1966).

While the *Ram Lila* is a spectacular pageant spread over several nights in different acting locales with multiple sets, the *Ras*

Effigies of (from left to right) Meghnath, Ravana, and Kumbh Karan are ready for the celebration of Dussehra, the triumph of good over evil, where the giant-sized effigies created are then burned. As legend has it, the Lord Rama killed Ravana after Ravana abducted Rama's consort, Sita. (Baldev/Corbis)

Lila retains its devotional focus and is characterized by poetry and song. It takes place in temple courtyards. Three inspired saints, Narayan Bhatt, Ghumand Dev, and Hitharivanshare, are said to have originated the genre (Gargi 1966). It has the fervent intensity of a religious congregation. It binds the audience in a bond of devotion and is an acceptable release for repressed emotions and tensions. Audiences join in the chants. Cymbals, chanting, drums, and slogans add to the fury of the maddened ecstasy. The form was used as an effective political weapon by the Hindu fundamentalists during the partition of India into Pakistan and India (Gargi 1966).

Chavittu Natakam

The *Chavittu Natakam* is an unusual example of Christian religious theater. Chinna Thampi Annavi, a Tamil Christian missionary, founded it in the seventeenth century with the aim of spreading Christianity. For its style, the theater drew on an eclectic amalgam of martial arts (such as *Kalaripayattu*), temple arts (such as *Koothu* and *Kodiyattam*), and European opera and Shakespearean plays as performed in India. For its material, it drew on stories from the Bible, Renaissance Europe and the Holy Wars, and most frequently, the life of King Charlemagne. In this form of theater, the story of Charlemagne (known as *Karalman Charitham*) acquires the grand proportions normally the preserve of the Hindu epics, and requires at least fifteen nights for its performance. Elaborate costumes and songs are its key features. Traditionally fisherman enacted these performances, and until recently, the Roman

Catholic Church sponsored them. However, the shortage of sponsors has led to the gradual demise of this form of theater. Currently there are just four performances a year in the southern state of Kerala (Abraham 2004).

Jatra

The *jatra* of Bengal provides an interesting example of a traditional theater whose origins lay in religious entertainment but became increasing secular over the course of its history. According to Hindu mythology, the child Krishna left behind his foster parents and milkmaids in the woods of Vrindavan and traveled to Mathura to punish his evil uncle, King Kamsa. His journey, or *jatra*, to Mathura was revived and popularized by Chaitanya (1485–1533), who, along with devotees of Krishna, went singing and dancing on pilgrimages to Mathura. The heartrending separation from his loved ones as Krishna leaves for Mathura began to be celebrated in the *palas* (plays) and became the favorite theme of singers and players, and *jatra* soon came to be associated with the dramatic form that grew out of these enactments and singing.

Over the centuries, *jatra* underwent changes in its themes, acting style, and music. In the latter half of the nineteenth century, the *palas* had degenerated into erotic singing and dancing. But throughout its development, *jatra*, like all traditional theaters, maintained its loose, flexible form of narrative, where an evening's performance included several episodes from different religious sources. An evening's performance might begin with the traditional invocation to the gods, followed by an episode from Krishna's life. This would be followed by an episode of the life of Shiva. (There are two major strands of Hindu thought, Shaivism and Vaishnavism, associated with the gods Shiva and Vishnu respectively. Shiva's life concerns mystical power and meditation while Vishnu's life usually features the life of Krishna, one of the incarnations of Vishnu, and focuses on love.)

An example of a *jatra* story concerning Shiva follows. A demon worships Shiva by sitting in yogic meditation. Shiva is pleased and grants a boon. The demon asks to be unconquerable by any man. The boon granted, the demon goes on to conquer and destroy the world. Many gods try to defeat the demon but he is unconquerable. Finally the goddess Durga appears and kills him, with the fight ending in a tableau. Durga with her ten hands, her gory tongue sticking out, sits triumphant astride her tiger (Gargi 1966).

One characteristic particular to the *jatra* is that the play always starts with a climax. It could be the entry of a demon with a dripping head. The historical *Samrat Zahandarshah* opens with the firing of a gun; *Bargo Elo Deshe*, on the Maratha invasion of Bengal, begins with invaders looting the people; and *Neel Kothi*, on the indigo planters, begins with laborers being whipped by the plantation owners. The shock tactics silence the audiences. It may help to alert bored audiences awaiting the start of the show, get the attention of people wandering around the arena, and quiet conversation (Gargi 1966).

The *jatra* was mobilized by the Indian People's Theater Association (IPTA) during World War II to win support for the Communist Party's association with the Allies after Germany invaded Russia. The celebrated actor-director Utpal Dutt invariably used the *jatra* form for his people's theater in Kolkata, as did Sombhu Mitra's Bohurupee Company.

Between the 1930s and 1960s, with the growth of film and a powerful realistic acting tradition in the professional theaters, *jatra* suffered a setback. The form also fell into disrepute because of excessive use of murder, horror, and eroticism. The middle-class leaders of the Bengali intellectual revolution condemned the vulgarity of the comic scenes. But the *jatra* never died in the rural areas. Even in the city of Kolkata, it still crops up at night in various squares and alleys. There is hardly a Bengali who in his or her childhood has not sat for hours watching the colorful *jatra*. Today a *jatra pala* can last for four hours and is filled with action-packed dialogue. Its six to eight songs compete in popularity with those from films (Gargi 1966).

In Kolkata there are currently twenty-one *jatra* troupes, ten permanent professional and eleven *thekawali* (with actors engaged temporarily on contract). Each offers about three plays a year. The leading *jatra* troupes visit the states of Assam, Orissa, and Bihar, and distant towns of Bengal, and are invited for festivals, fairs, marriages, and housewarming ceremonies. They even perform as far away as Varanasi and Delhi, which have large Bengali populations. Political color is especially apparent in the *jatra*. Plays on the partition of India, Hindu-Muslim unity, and patriotism are a big draw. Mukand Das, a freedom fighter and *jatra* composer-singer who died a few years ago, was jailed many times for his anti-British *palas* during the struggle for Indian independence (Gargi 1966).

Tamasha

Some traditional theaters, such as the *tamasha* and *nautanki*, had completely secular origins.

The austere Moghul emperor Aurangzeb spent the last eighteen years of his life (1689–1707) quelling rebellions led by the chiefs of southern India and the western Ghats. The sturdiest resistance to the emperor was from Shivaji, who led the expert guerrilla warriors, the Marathas in the Deccan. The imperial army, camped in the valleys and hills away from home, hungered for entertainment. Singing girls and dancers were imported from northern India to amuse the bored soldiers. The Dombari and Kolhati, acrobats and tumblers of the local communities, learned the northern dance style readily and joined the entertainers. The local poets composed songs in Marathi. The traditional Gondhalis, who sang and danced in praise of the goddess Parvati, created their own bastardized version of the northern *Kathak* dances, copied from the company that had accompanied the Moghul soldiers, and a new form of entertainment was born. It took the name of *tamasha*, a Persian word that traveled to Maharashtra and the Deccan through the Moghul armies and means "fun, play, entertainment" (Gargi 1966).

The performance begins with a round of loud drumming, intended to alert the audience that the performance has begun. The drumming is followed by an invocation of the god Ganesh. The musicians stand with their backs toward the audience and move upstage and down singing the invocation. (Vijay Tendulkar employed a similar invocation in his modern Marathi play *Ghashiram Kotwal.*) This ceremony, called *avahan* (invocation of the gods), is also popularly known as *gana*, an abbreviation of Ganesh. Sometimes Shiva and Parvati are also praised in the song because they are the parents of Ganesh. No woman is present on the stage while the *gana* is sung. The buffoon (called Songadya) is allowed to join the invocatory song, but at this moment he is serious and dignified.

The next preliminary is the appearance of Gaulan, a milkmaid in Krishna's legend, played by a *tamasha* woman. She enters with rhythmic steps and does an erotic dance, hiding her face with the end length of her sari, though her head is uncovered. She tantalizes the principal singer and the instrumentalists, who move in quick steps round and round the stage. They talk with the Songadya, the buffoon, who impersonates Krishna. His friend Paindia, a deformed, club-footed, quarrelsome cretin, accompanies Krishna. The incident, taken from Krishna's life, has sexual innuendoes and confirms the nonreligious note of the *tamasha*. The familiar pattern of dialogue is as follows:

DRUMMER: Oh, friend, where are we going now?

KRISHNA (*walking fast in a circle*): To Mathura.

DRUMMER: What work have you there?

KRISHNA: Not in Mathura, I have some business on the way.

DRUMMER: I see! You are going to sell milk and meet the maids.

KRISHNA: What a wise fool you are! My hands are empty. How could I sell milk?

DRUMMER: Why are you hurrying, friend? You are walking fast. What's the job?

KRISHNA: My job is . . . don't you know? My job . . . to tease the milkmaids and drink their milk.

MANJEERA PLAYER: From the pots they carry on their heads or from . . . ?

KRISHNA: I pull at their saris and waylay them. Only then will they yield . . . milk.

TUNTUNA PLAYER: Arrr! There she is!

ALL: Where?

TUNTUNA PLAYER (*walks like a woman*): Here she comes jingling her bells and swaying her hips. Listen to the music of her footsteps!

(*The* tamasha *woman enters casting glances from behind her sari.*)

PAINDIA (*holding the* Gaulan): Pay the toll to Krishna. Your milk!

(*She takes down the imaginary pitcher from her head, tilts it, pours milk into Krishna's cupped hands, and sings.*)

(Gargi 1966: 78–79)

The main play or *vag* follows the above preliminaries, and its themes can vary. They deal with military chiefs and kings, a merchant and his mistress, a warrior meeting a young maiden in a foreign land, two brothers quarreling over a piece of land, a henpecked husband with two wives. Mythological and historical romances abound. Like all folk plays, the *vag* concludes with the moral that truth will shine and falsehood will perish. The hilarious jokes, erotic songs or *lavanis*, provocative dances, and powerful singing and drumming constitute the main body of the play (Gargi 1966).

The erotic is the dominant sentiment in a *lavani:*

We came to enjoy your body,
Your breasts,
And we decided to win the two round fortresses.
Don't tantalize us;
We shall enjoy your body forthwith.
(Gargi 1966: 97)

In the eighteenth and nineteenth centuries *lavanis* were specially composed and well rehearsed, while the dialogue was left to the inventive faculty of the actors. They were simply given the main points of the story and they improvised the dialogue on the spot, adding to the text and injecting freshness at every performance. The singers then completed the dialogue by singing a *lavani* and carrying forward the story. Today, however, the modern *vag* is written like a play, with dialogue and songs, and the actors no longer improvise their lines.

The Maratha court patronage ended with the British occupation of India. In the nineteenth century landlords and their dissolute sons, with no awareness of art or music, became the patrons of *tamasha*. In their courtyards *tamasha* became vulgar. Today there are 800 full-fledged *tamasha* troupes employing 40,000 people (actors, dancers, instrumentalists, and their families). Three thousand women actresses on tour perform in the village squares (Gargi 1966).

Contemporary playwrights have exploited the *tamasha* form in their works. Vasant Sabnis wrote *Viccha Majhi Puri Kara* (1968) in the *tamasha* form. The actor-playwright P. L. Deshpande used the *tamasha* form in *Sarvodya*, a political satire. Vasant Bapat also has many successful modern *tamasha* to his credit.

The *tamasha* has been a strong propaganda weapon. Active in the leftist movement for over twenty-five years, Anna Bhau Sathe, from the Mang community, wrote political satires using the *tamasha*. His colleague, Amar Sheikh, thrilled huge gatherings of workers with his *lavani* singing. Government cultural troupes have also used the *tamasha* for promoting the Five-Year Plan and new projects to rural audiences (Gargi 1966).

Nautanki

The secular form of *nautanki* theater originated in northern India and represents an exciting blend of the Hindu-Muslim folk cultures. The austere Muslims who came as conquerors in the eleventh and twelfth centuries slowly adopted the ways of local Hindus, and the Hindus slowly accepted Muslim influence in their arts. During the long Moghul rule (1526–1712), the arts reflected a synthesis of the two cultures. Even religious tales digested in the traditional all-male *nautanki* performances have a secular coloring. In as sacred a play as *Raja Harishchandra*, when the noble queen Taramati begs money for the cremation of her dead son, she dances, kicking her heels and swinging her hips. In a religious tale Sita sings of her tragic plight while casting "come-hither" glances (Gargi 1966).

Except for the opening prayer song, *mangalacharana*, which is invariably in high-flown Hindi to emphasize its religious nature, the songs and the alliterative dialogue are a mixture of Hindi and Urdu. The writers also mixed in Braj, Rajasthani, Hindi, and local dialects; consequently *nautanki* plays are not generally highly regarded as literary works, despite their dramatic quality. Nevertheless, they are tremendously popular with rural audiences. Most villagers are acquainted with the plays, and because of their musical appeal and the directness of the language, *nautanki* literature sells better than the best sellers in Hindi or Urdu. In fact, people buy this folk literature by weight. Wholesale dealers generally weigh cheaply printed plays on a scale and hand them over to retail shopkeepers, who then circulate them among the aficionados (Narayana 1987). The courtly language of the plays required the composer to choose elaborate music drawn from classical tradition, although in the actual performance the singers made the melodies, or *ragas*, more folk than classical.

Munshiji, or "the accountant," is invariably the clown. He wears a coat buttoned backward with a patched, multicolored shirt and trousers and carries a split bamboo in his hand. He is a stereotypical character belonging to the nineteenth-century palaces of *nawab*s and landlords, always appearing at an unfortunate moment to remind people of their outstanding bills. No stranger to the seamy side of life, Munshiji moves among cuckolds, disguised lovers, mistresses, and gallant warriors, breaking the serious mood by his financial logic. In *nautanki* performances he appears as an all-knowing man whose incongruous remarks make people laugh. Whenever the play begins to drag, he is brought on to liven up the proceedings.

Because of its commercial nature and its secular character, *nautanki* has become increasingly lewd. After the Suppression of Immoral Traffic Act was passed in 1959, many prostitutes and *nautch* (dancing) girls, forced to leave their professions, opted to join *nautanki* troupes. When the Kanpur city corporation banned the *nautanki* performances within its municipal limits, the troupes began to perform on the outskirts of the city, and townsmen flocked to the performances. But it is the old-style *nautanki* troupes with their all-male casts that preserve the traditional vigor, singing style, and operatic charm of the form (Gargi 1966).

The Colonial British Theater

Although the classical Sanskrit and the popular theaters have had a lasting impact on contemporary Indian theater, the colonial British theater activity had an even greater impact on it. Far from home and eager for some kind of familiar entertainment, the British had begun to build theaters for the expatriates in Calcutta soon after they arrived.

The Calcutta Theater was built in 1779, and with it began an unbroken period of expanding theatrical activity in the English community that lasted more than 100 years. The climate for theatrical activity was congenial. There was peace in this part of the country, the rule of law had been established and was enforced, and trade was booming. Money was there for the taking—at least for the officials of the British East India Company, whose numbers steadily grew but whose social life was rather limited. Except for Christmas and such infrequent social occasions as the governor-general's "at home" and ball, there was little by way of social festivities for the Englishman and his *memsahib*. Under these circumstances, the English theater in Calcutta, nourished by a steady inflow of histrionic talent from England, became a center of English social life (Raha 1978). A number of additional theaters were built in the early nineteenth century: Chandernager Theater (1808), Chowringhee Theater (1813), Dum Dum Theater (1815), and Sans Souci Theater (1839) (Raha 1978).

The plays—Shakespeare and a medley of comedies, farces, and serious plays that had proven popular in London and on the provincial stages of England—were performed exclusively in English. There were productions of *Hamlet*, *Macbeth*, *She Stoops to Conquer*, *School for Scandal*, and *Earl of Warwick*, alongside productions of less worthy plays—*Honeymoon*, *The Weather Cock*, *The Sixty-Third Letter*, and

Nariman Point culminates in the National Center for Performing Arts with the Parsi-sponsored Tata Theater (1981), designed by the American architect Philip Johnson, and the Jehangir Nicholson Museum of Modern Art. Bombay, 1997. (Lindsay Hebberd/Corbis)

many others, long since forgotten. There never seemed to be a shortage of acting or managerial talent, and an almost unbroken chain of gifted actors and actresses performed in Calcutta's English theaters. Tickets were highly priced (Raha 1978).

Initially, both the audience and the performers were exclusively white. The Calcutta Theater engaged only Englishmen, even as ushers and doorkeepers. The colonial theater's only contact with Indian theater was an English production in 1839 of Kalidasa's *Abhijnanashakuntala*, which had been translated by Sir William Jones in 1789, at the Sans Souci Theater (Bandyopadhyay 1986). In August 1848, however, a "Native Gentleman," one Baishnav Charan Auddy, was taken into the cast and assigned the role of Othello in a production

at Sans Souci. In the words of a letter in *The Calcutta Star*, the announced "debut of a real unpainted nigger *Othello*" had set "the whole world of Calcutta agog" (Raha 1978: 197).

The concept of going to see a play in a theater was initially novel to the elite Indian spectator. Traditionally, performances had taken place in the homes of wealthy landowners and aristocrats. However, the three cities of Calcutta, Bombay, and Madras had become important trading centers, and a new class of moneylender-traders was beginning to form the nucleus of a commercial aristocracy whose tastes began to acquire an urban orientation. The founding of universities in Bombay, Calcutta, and Madras in 1857 produced a new corpus of Indian students who were familiar with both western and Sanskrit literature.

Drama critic Shanta Gokhale points out that the land-owning aristocratic or caste-empowered members of the old feudal order gradually gave way to the cultural leadership of urban, university-educated young men from the upper castes who had been exposed to ideas from the West. Amateur drama groups were formed at universities and other places. Ideas were borrowed from the touring British theater companies, with their sets and painted scenery (Gokhale 2000). In 1842, Jagannath Shankar Seth built a theater in Bombay that was available for hire to the British and Indians alike. Soon more theaters were built in the three main cities. The elite class of English-educated Indians flocked to see plays of the kind watched by the British colonials in these new theaters.

The western plays were in English, a language understood only by the elite. What pleased the majority of the Indian urban theatergoers, however, was an amalgam of the European and Indian theatrical traditions—a theater that would offer Indian subject matter in Indian languages but also incorporate the exotic conventions of the proscenium stage, with its painted backdrops and ornate curtains separating the audience, seated in neat rows, from the stage. The first theater to offer just that kind of fare was the Parsi theater.

The Parsi Theater

The growing urban population, with its corollary of a growing middle class and a growing working class in the nineteenth century India, saw two streams of theater: the popular, traditional forms such as

tamasha in Mumbai and *jatra* in Kolkata, which found their way from the villages to the cities, and the Parsi and European theaters for the middle classes. Until the advent of sound films in 1931, the Parsi theater was the most widely available form of theatrical entertainment for urban Indian audiences. An entrepreneurial community, the Parsis (or Zoroastrians, originally from Persia) established many theatrical companies in Bombay, and their theater came to be known as the Parsi theater. It was the first example of a fully commercial theater with a professional repertory.

Around 1850, amateur theater groups were beginning to emerge in Mumbai, and a few enterprising Parsi business managers organized some of the theatrical clubs into professional touring companies. The Parsi theater absorbed some of the conventions of the colonial English theater, witnessed on the stages in Kolkata and Mumbai, and blended them with conventions of the indigenous popular and "folk" theaters. In style, the new theater was a happy marriage of the colonial English theater and the robustly musical popular Indian theater. The names of the theaters bear witness to the British influence: New Alfred Company, Empress Victoria Theatrical Company, and Original Theatrical Company, although the plays that were performed were Indian. When the Parsi theater companies began to travel around the country in 1874, local entrepreneurs formed copycat companies offering similar fare and gave their companies similar British or Anglo-Indian names such as the Albert Natak Company in Chennai (Madras), the Ripon Indian Club (in Peshawar), the Oriental Opera and Dramatic Company (in Lahore) (Hansen 2001).

Initially, the plays were in Gujerati (the language spoken by Parsis), but with the huge commercial success of these ventures, the troupes soon began performing in Urdu and other regional languages, and later even in English. Traveling companies performed in Calcutta, Madras, Lahore, and even in London. Their productions featured a heterogeneous cast of players and catered to a heterogeneous crowd.

The plays produced by the Parsi theater largely comprised heroic legends from the Persian *Shahnamah* (for example, *Shirin Farhad*), Indo-Islamic fairy romances (for example, *Indar Sabha* and *Alam Ara*), stories from classical Sanskrit drama (most notably *Shakuntala*) and the Hindu epics, and adapted Shakespearean comedies and tragedies staged in the proscenium theaters first built by British and later by Indian entrepreneurs in Bombay. The Parsi theater had a stable of writers (known as *munshis*) on their payroll, and their output was on an industrial scale. Two scribes, Mohammed Mian "Raunaq" Banarasi and Hussein Mian "Zarifa," are said to have together authored more than fifty plays. Many plays by the Parsi theater writers were published and sold by the *seer* (an Indian measure) in the markets downtown (Narayana 1987).

The scripts were designed to cater to popular feelings with deliberate contrivances to provide for a variety of tastes. The makeshift arrangement of the auditorium without the modern facility of sound amplification imposed certain limitations. The lines had to be delivered in a loud manner. In the task of making themselves heard, the performers utilized rhymed sentences, which helped the dialogues to be heard in the last row.

Makeup on these stages was confined to indigenous material, and mica powder was often utilized as a tantalizer. But the absence of powerful modern electrical lights meant that the makeup, too, had to be loud, and that the gestures had to be highly stylized and loud to form one complete pattern with the painted curtains and cut scenes (Narayana 1987).

Sensationalism prevailed in most productions. *Vira Abhimanyu* of the New Alfred Company used to end with a bang, with the following stage directions: "Exit all, change scene. The father of Jayadratha is performing penance. The head of Jayadratha falls in his lap. The father gets up and his head breaks into a hundred pieces." *Buddhadeva* of Vyakula Bharata Company has this scene: "Scene change. Storm. Lightning and thunder. Stars dislodged from the sky. Huge demons seen. Some are spouting fire and some smoke. The sky is riddled with arrows in the background" (Narayana 1987: 41).

As their popularity grew, the productions began to devote themselves to more and more spectacular scenery, ornate curtains and drapes, and special effects in the lighting that highlighted the elaborate settings and enhanced the visual and emotional intensity. Songs and dances were plentiful, as were comic interludes.

The theater nevertheless adhered to the Indian convention of male actors playing female roles. Indeed, the New Alfred Theatrical Company banned female actors for nearly forty years. Women who did attempt to gain a foothold on stage faced physical danger. Kathryn Hansen, who has written extensively on the Parsi theater, points to the case of Latifa Begum, an accomplished courtesan and actress who was abducted after her first performance (Hansen 2001).

According to Hansen, the success of the Parsi theater companies could be attributed to several factors: new marketing techniques, such as newspaper advertisements and printed handbills; exotic names that evoked the British monarchy (Empress Victoria Theatrical Company, New Alfred Company); the novelty of the proscenium stage with its elaborate painted scenery and special effects; the allure of operatic singing and declamatory acting techniques; and a sudden desire among the urban populace to see one another and to be seen at the theater. The polyglot, pan-regional and culturally heterogeneous Parsi theater was an appropriate expression of the burgeoning urbanization, industrialization, and capitalism (Hansen 2001).

Eventually the Parsi theater succumbed to competition from the "all-talking, all-dancing" films that began to emerge from the film factories set up in Mumbai. However, the influence of the Parsi theater on popular Hindi films was apparent. *Alam Ara*, the first Indian talkie, made in 1931, was a recreation of a Parsi theater production, as were *Shirin Farhad* (1931) and *Indar Sabha* (1931).

The influence of the Parsi theater on other urban theaters was immense. Through a process of selection and adaptation to contact with local forms, the Parsi theater influenced a number of regional styles of musical theaters, such the Marathi *sangeet natak* genre in Maharashtra, the company *natak* in Karnataka and Tamil Nadu, the *nautanki* in northern India, and the Bengali theaters in Calcutta. It also exerted an important influence on new urban drama in the subcontinent. Through its productions and its traveling companies, it was the first cultural phenomenon to connect the four major cities with one another and with the hinterland, a feat not repeated until the recent developments in Indian television.

One of the theaters it was to influence greatly was the Marathi theater, which is today the most vibrant of modern Indian theaters.

Marathi Theater

A central feature in the development of the Marathi stage has been the *sangeet natak*, a unique form of operatic theater. Before its emergence on the Marathi stage, *tamasha* and other folk performances entertained the rural masses while more sober forms of dramatic expression—such as *keertan* and *harikatha*—entertained the higher castes. Missing from upper-caste entertainment, however, were secular performances that drew on the emotions and music without being vulgar or bawdy as the lower caste entertainment was.

Sangeet Natak

In 1843, the *rajah* of Sangli (in southern Maharashtra) asked Vishnudas Bhave, who worked in his palace, to put together some sort of secular performance that would both entertain and edify the female members of the royal household and other courtiers. Bhave set about his task with earnestness and vigor and presented *Sita Swayamwar*. The musical "play" was constructed around a well-known and well-loved episode from the Ramayana where Sita chooses Ram as her husband. The performance was declared a resounding success, and Bhave was entrusted with producing more such entertainment for the royal household. Unfortunately the *rajah* did not live long enough to enjoy the new productions, and a change in the royal arrangements forced Bhave to set out with his band of players and seek his fortunes elsewhere. His travels in the region including visits to Bombay, and his plays enjoyed great success for nearly a decade.

While Bhave is honored for the first attempt at bringing forth a modern Marathi theater, the true father of the *sangeet natak* is Balwant Pandurang Kirloskar (1843–1885). A professional actor who had watched many of the Parsi theater productions that were crowding the stages of Bombay, he decided to present more refined, less spectacular, and more classical productions in Marathi. The result was *Sangeet Shakuntal*, first staged in Poona (now Pune) in 1880. The play, with 7 acts and 209 songs (Gokhale 2000), incorporated none of the crude attempts to dazzle the audience with gimmicks that had become so commonplace on the urban stages. Despite the inordinate number of songs, there was also an actual script with written dialogues that actors had to learn. Although female impersonators continued to play female roles, it was nevertheless the first public performance of a Marathi play in a proscenium theater and the first step toward modern theater in Marathi.

The success of *Sangeet Shakuntal* and Kirloskar's second play, *Sangeet Saubhadra* (based on a story from the epics), led to more playwrights writing musical dramas. Soon the Marathi theater seemed to have created a unique theatrical genre—the *sangeet natak*.

Subsequent writers who embraced the genre introduced their own contributions. Govind Ballal Deval (1855–1916) broke new ground in 1899. A student and "rehearsal master" of Kirloskar, Deval abandoned the standard stories from the Hindu epics and introduced social themes. In *Sangeet Sharada*, a lonely seventy-five-year-old widower seeks to marry Sharada, a fourteen-year-old girl—a practice quite common under the patriarchal Hindu family system. The young girl's excited hopes for her future, and her horror when she realizes what destiny has in store for her, made a powerful impact, coming at a time when British attempts at social reform were becoming particularly contentious.

To mark the centenary of Bhave's *Sita Swayamwar*, a huge festival of Marathi theater was held in 1944 at Mumbai's Chowpatty beach. Forty-one groups participated, and the performance held in the open air lasted all night. It is estimated that around 8,000 spectators made their way to the venue each night. Plays from the repertory of the *sangeet natak* were revived, with Deval's *Sangeet Sharada* and Kirloskar's *Sangeet Saubhadra* drawing the largest number of spectators (Gokhale 2000).

The beginning of the twentieth century is often described as the golden age of the *sangeet natak*. A confluence of talent, including the playwrights Krishnaji Prabhakar Khadilkar (1872–1948) and Ram Ganesh Gadkari (1885–1919), composer Govindrao Tembe (1881–1955), and the celebrated female impersonator Bal Gandharva (1888–1967), took the productions to an unprecedented level of excitement, pleasure, and professionalism.

Khadilkar's most famous play was *Keechakavadh* (the Slaying of Keechak), a story from the Mahabharata. It contained powerful undertones of political symbolism, which was not surprising as Khadilkar was editor of the firebrand Marathi broadsheet *Kesari*. In the episode where Draupadi, wife of the five Pandava brothers, is made to serve Keechaka as a servant after the brothers lose their kingdom and possessions to their cousins in a game of dice,

Khadilkar clearly sets out two opposing sides. Keechak and his attempts to ravish Draupadi was a veiled reference to the Viceroy of India, Lord Curzon (1859–1925), and Draupadi as the victim of his priapic lust symbolized the Indian people. Not surprisingly, the play was banned in 1910.

Another celebrated play from Khadilkar was *Manapaman* (1911), a comment on class and caste that has entered the annals of Marathi theater as a classic—not for its negligible social comment but for its musical virtuosity. Central to the success of *Manapaman* was Bal Gandharva (1888–1967), the first Marathi stage star and the most elegant female impersonator ever. Describing Gandharva's centrality to the genre, drama critic Shanta Gokhale writes:

> If Bal Gandharva was the jewel in the crown of Marathi theater, then his setting had to be designed to offset every facet of his personality and performance: his movements, his expressions, his music, his clothes. There was satin, velvet and gold aplenty in his furnishings. Arches were constructed to frame him, steps for him to climb down in the full majesty of a trailing sari. Richly covered seats and bolsters, period furniture and carpets embroidered in real gold thread abounded. The colours were striking and the textures smooth and heavy. As a last touch of opulence, the air was scented with perfume. To see Bal Gandharva in such a setting, bathed in the mild but abundant moonlight glow of "daylight" electric lights, made the audience wonder whether they were not actually witnessing a scene set in the abode of the gods. (Gokhale 2000: 67)

Among those who consciously moved away from the Hindu epics and Sanskrit plays was Ram Ganesh Gadkari (1885–1919), whose musical drama *Ekach Pyala*, written in 1917, still draws full houses whenever it is performed. The play was "modern" in its attempts to present a contemporary theme yet still adhered to most of the conventions of the *sangeet natak* genre. The plot concerns the pressures of urban life and competition, which destroy the career and eventually the family of a brilliant young lawyer. The stresses of modern urban life, work, and competition cause Sudhakar to take to drink. Then his alcoholism causes his career to slip away, and his wife labors to stave off starvation. Unable to give up his drinking and unable to cope with reality, Sudhakar kills his wife and child before killing himself. The impact on the high-minded middle-class Marathi audiences was sensational, and Gadkari's early death added to the play's intensity and impact.

Within a decade of the flowering of the *sangeet natak* genre and the Marathi stage came the "all-singing, all-dancing" Indian movies of the 1930s. Actors, technicians, and musicians from both the Marathi and the Parsi theaters rushed to join the celluloid revolution, where they were better paid than in the theater. The Marathi theater was left struggling to survive.

The impact of cinema on theater was more far reaching than first imagined. The commercial success of the talkies caused more and more playhouses in Bombay and Poona to be converted into cinemas. This left the theater with fewer and fewer venues for staging plays. As long as films were silent, the Marathi theater had felt safe. But with the arrival of the talkies in the 1930s and Marathi films, Marathi theater lost its monopoly over entertainment in the language. These films lasted just three hours, and the musical dramas that ran from eight at night until three in the morning suddenly seemed too long. And in the cinema, real women, not female impersonators, played female roles. As more and more Marathi-speaking people, mesmerized by the new medium, began to frequent the cinema, the audiences who patronized the theater shrank. Gradually plays became shorter, with fewer songs, and Marathi theater began to accept the presence of women on stage. However, despite these concessions to changing times, the *sangeet natak* as a genre had already seen its heyday.

Modern Marathi Theater

With the advent of cinema, Marathi theater, too, felt the need to modernize. Modernity on the Marathi stage was understood as the staging of a three-act play on contemporary reality with a credible plot, realistic characters, natural dialogue and acting, women playing women, and most significantly, no songs. The first Marathi dramatist and stage designer determined to bring "modernity" was Bhargavram Vitthal Warerkar (1883–1964) or "Mama" Warerkar, as he was known to his public. The pioneering work of Warerkar owed much of its inspiration to Ibsen. He began writing at the age of twenty-one, but his first important play, *Sonyache Kalas*, was written in 1931, when he was nearly forty. It was based on his own novel about the confrontation between factory workers and their industrialist adversaries. Warerkar earlier wrote *Turungachya Darat* (1922), a play about the scourge of the caste system. As a backdrop for the play, he used cricket, a colonial sport adopted by the Indians, and the subject of caste discrimination in the selection of team players for the very popular Quadrangular matches in Bombay.

Warerkar's contribution to Marathi theater—and to the theater in general—was immense. He was the first to hire craftsmen and create a box set, and to relieve the stage of ornate velvet curtains. It is said that his realistic sets brought a thunder of applause from the audiences (Gokhale 2000). As member of Parliament he introduced the first national theater festival in Delhi in 1954. His dedication to theater was complete. According to one story, when he went to see a play directed by the celebrated Ebrahim Alkazi (1924–) in New Delhi, he was surprised and impressed to see that the play began precisely on time, even though the auditorium was far from full and the expected dignitaries had not yet arrived. When a decision to choose a director for the newly formed National School of Drama in New Delhi was to be made, Warerkar's unambiguous vote was for Alkazi, who became became its director in 1961.

Another dramatist of the 1930s was Prahlad Keshav Atre (1898–1969)—a writer, pamphleteer, orator, satirist, and journalist who produced a sizeable body of literature. Atre, who acknowledges the influence of Gadkari, Molière, and Noel Coward, is best known on the Marathi stage for his acerbic wit and biting satire. His first great commercial success was *Sashatang Namaskar* in 1933, the very first original comedy in Marathi (Gokhale 2000). Several of the twenty-five plays he wrote were huge commercial successes, and Atre remains an inspiration to aspiring satirists.

The next great flowering of Marathi theater occurred in the 1960s when a rich variety of writers, actors, directors, and theater groups suddenly emerged—along with young poets, novelists, and short story writers in Marathi. The new dramatists sought inspiration from sources as varied as Shakespeare and Sanskrit drama, as well as Shaw, Ibsen, and other European and American playwrights. Many translations and adaptations (not always acknowledged) from world literature were also performed on the Marathi stage.

Much of the impetus for this blossoming of talent came from drama competitions and theater festivals organized by state and philanthropic institutions. Organizations formed to promote Marathi theater that saw the emergence of professional drama companies. In the early 1960s, the Maharashtra state government embarked on the construction of dedicated theaters in Bombay, Pune, and Goa, the latter having been recently liberated from Portuguese rule. It also instituted annual one-act drama competitions in Marathi for amateurs. At around the same time, the Bharatiya Vidya Bhavan, a charitable trust dedicated to promoting Hindu culture, also began to organize one-act drama competitions. Though earlier dramatists were content with adaptations, translations, or revivals of plays, a new confidence emerged and original plays began to be written. These competitions became a venue for the showcasing of new talent and encouraged new playwrights to risk bold and daring themes and narrative forms. Another reason for the reflowering of Marathi drama during the sixties was the demise of Marathi cinema. Unable to compete with the Hindi films from Bollywood (also headquartered, like Marathi cinema, in Bombay), Marathi films were gradually pushed to the margins, where Marathi filmmakers barely survived by making films for rural audiences on rural themes about young women and lascivious village chieftains. The Marathi theater audiences, being urban sophisticates, had little patience with this kind of piffle and returned to the theater.

A range of genres emerged in the theater of the 1960s. There were ground-breaking psychological dramas, such as Vasant Kanetkar's (1922–) *Vedyache Ghar Unhat* first performed in 1957 and *Raigadhala Jewhan Jaag Yete* first performed in 1962. The latter is a psychological analysis of the father-son relationship between the great seventeeth-century Maratha king Shivaji and his son Sambhaji, where the historical hero of Maharashtra was shown as a complex human being. It was a bold venture, since Shivaji, who died in 1680, had always been the subject of adulation; to portray him as a flawed human being to a reverent Marathi audience required skill and courage.

Comedy was the forte of P. L. Deshpande (1919–2000), whose sharp observations poked fun at the self-righteous do-gooders of the nation, as in *Tujhe Ahe Tujhya Pashi* in 1957. Even more popular was *Batayachi Chawl* (1960), a one-man show on lower-middle-class life in a housing tenement.

In 1967 the playwright Purushottam Darvhekar revived the *sangeet natak* genre with *Katyar Kaljat Ghusali*. But instead of adapting a conventional story from mythology or Sanskrit drama, he ushered in a new era in the genre by constructing a plot where music formed a natural part of expression through confrontation (and romance) between two schools of music. The play celebrated its thousandth performance in late 1976 and still draws an audience whenever it is staged.

The 1960s was also a time when Vasant Sabnis (1923–2002) updated the *tamasha* genre with *Viccha Majhi Puri Kara* in 1965, which made a star of the lead actor

Dada Kondke, who went on to dominate the Marathi screen for decades. Bal Kolhatkar reigned supreme as a playwright with *Dooritanche Timir Jaavo*, a classic family melodrama filled with conservative Hindu sentiments first performed in 1957. Another success of Kolhatkar was *Vahato Mee Durvanchi Judi* (1959). At the "absurdist" end of the drama spectrum was C. T. Khanolkar (1930–1976), whose complex *Ek Shoonya Bajirao* (1966) was inspired by Luigi Pirandello's *Six Characters in Search of an Author*.

Vijay Tendulkar

However, the biggest discovery of the 1950s–1960s was Vijay Tendulkar (1925–), one of the greatest playwrights of the Marathi stage. Tendulkar's plays arrived with a completely new vocabulary, and his impact on Marathi drama can be compared to that of Harold Pinter on the English stage. His early plays, such as *Shrimant*, first performed in 1955, and *Manus Navacha Bait*, first performed in 1956, poured scorn on the hypocrisy and materialism of the middle classes. He also exposed the underbelly of the sanctimonious bourgeoisie by placing an unmarried pregnant daughter at the heart of the narrative as the parents try desperately to find her a husband to save face.

The three most famous of Tendulkar's plays came in the 1970s, which was a decade of rich creativity and experimentation, both in theater and in cinema. In popular cinema, there were the new violent action films starring Amitabh Bachchan, while the art house film circuit showcased the experiments in narrative form in the works of Mani Kaul, Kumar Shahani, and G. Aravindan, among others. Marathi theater, too, saw a serious attempt to create a new kind of serious and intellectual drama by some playwrights.

Tendulkar's *Gidhhade*, written in 1961 but not performed in Marathi until 1970 (Gokhale 2000), showed the middle classes as a congregation of vultures, ready to prey on others. His *Sakharam Binder*, first performed in 1972, exploded on the stage like a bomb. Its protagonist was the eponymous Sakharam, who debunks all the sacred traditions of the self-righteous Hindu middle class to the point of sacrilege. In both plays, in addition to the savage characterizations, Tendulkar's dexterous use of language and dramatic tensions were entirely new and thrilling, and the reaction was volatile. Some loved him. Others thought him depraved (Gokhale 2000).

It was *Ghashiram Kotwal*, with its completely new form and dramatic idiom, that secured Tendulkar his position in the history of Indian drama. The play tells its story entirely in verse and dance movements. The plot debunks the myth of the nineteenth-century ruling Peshwas, heroes to the Maharashtrians for having held off the advances of the colonizing British. In the play, however, they emerge as wily, lascivious, and depraved. The foolish Ghashiram is elevated to the position of *kotwal*, or chieftain, so that the gray-eyed Nana Phadnavis, the Peshwa (ruler), can seduce his daughter.

Violent protests broke out at its first performances in 1972. The theater community ruptured, and long-standing associations splintered. When the director, Jabbar Patel, and his production company were invited to Germany, many erudite Marathi scholars and writers protested, arguing that the visit would besmirch the reputation of the country. Finally, a compromise was sought. It was agreed that they could perform the play overseas as long as they presented a disclaimer saying that the play distorted historical facts (Gokhale 2000).

Talent abounded in the 1970s. Other important dramatists of the period included the award-winning Ratnakar Matkari, whose body of work includes radio plays, children's plays, experimental plays, and mainstream plays. He is most famous for *Lokkatha '78*, a play that laid bare the stark brutalities of everyday life for *dalits* (untouchable castes) in rural India. The script evolved from improvisations of actors based on a real life incident, where a low caste girl was raped and killed by leading members of the community.

Meanwhile, the mainstream continued to thrill audiences with grandiose melodrama and equally virtuoso acting, as in Vasant Kanetkar's *Natsamrat*, first performed in 1970, about a Marathi Shakespearean actor whose life begins to mirror the tragedy of King Lear. The role of *natsamrat*, or thespian, soon became the most sought after role for an actor of merit on the modern Marathi stage and remains so even today.

After Tendulkar

The next generation of playwrights included Achut Vaze, Satish Alekar, and Mahesh Elkunchwar. Vaze has been mostly connected with experiments in the "theater of the absurd." His *Chal Re Bhoplya Tunuk Tunuk* (1974) was inspired by Samuel Beckett's *Waiting for Godot*, as its characters try to find a meaning in life. The *bhopla* (pumpkin) in the title symbolized the big zero or nothingness. Although Becket's plays do not come under the category of absurd, that was how Becket had been categorized in India, and Vaze's work, peppered with incoherent expressions of angst, disjointed sentences, repetitions,

and nonsequitors, and concerned with crises of identity and deep alienation, was not met with much empathy from the Mumbai audiences. As critic Shanta Gokhale points out, some spectators genuinely wondered if they had been victims of an elaborate hoax (Gokhale 2000).

Satish Alekar, on the other hand, is rooted in the Pune Brahmin culture, and his work concerns their obsession with narrow, middle-class values. He first achieved fame at a workshop organized by Satyadev Dubey in 1973. His seven full-length plays, all written in the 1970s, explore small town politics—*Doosra Samna* (1989), for example—and changing middle-class values—*Shanivar-Ravivar* (1980), *Mahanirvan.* The latter, first performed in 1974, is about the burden a father places on his son, even after the father's death, with his insistence on customs and rituals. *Begum Barve* (1979) is one of Alekar's best plays, and many have described it as one of the finest plays in Marathi theater. It concerns a female impersonator, Barve, ironically referred to as *begum* (queen) from the heyday of the *sangeet natak* genre, who has fallen on hard times and now sells incense sticks for a living. The play deals with dream and reality, escape and brutality. Alekar's latest play *Pidhijat* (2003) explores the political and bureaucratic cultures of contemporary India.

Mahesh Elkunchwar is the best-known contemporary playwright after Tendulkar, and his work about the stark brutalities of everyday life has been widely translated into other Indian languages. He is best known for plays such as *Party* (1975), about pretentious art people at a party whose shallow lives are counterposed by a true citizen who works with tribal communities or *adivasis*. The *Wada Chirabandi*

(1987) trilogy is a fin de siècle type of drama, almost Chekovian in its evocation of the passage of an era explored through the death of a patriarch. An ancestral home and socioeconomic changes are central to the plots of the trilogy. In 2002 Elkunchwar wrote his first play in English, *Sonata*, which explores feminine/feminist themes.

Another playwright influenced by Vaze is Shafaat Khan (1952–). His plays include *Bhoomitecha Farce* (1988) about the god Ganesh and his mouse as metaphors for hierarchy and rigid geometrical divisions. Khan has also made forays into the world of cinema. In 2005, his play *Shobhayatra*, a sardonic comment on contemporary India and its newly found consumer culture, was made into a film by director Vijay Ghatge. Tushar Bhadre (1959–) and Premanand Gajvi (1947–) both write on social change. The latter's *Gandhi Ani Ambedkar* (1997) explores the mental attitudes and relationship between the two national leaders Mahatma Gandhi and Babasaheb Ambedkar. Makarand Sathe's (1957–) *Thombya*, first performed in 1996, is a fragmented construction about slippages between thought and action, belief and nonbelief, an object and its image, the real and the unreal. No connections are offered and no answers provided. Also in the mid-1990s Chetan Datar's (1964–) *Zulva* is about a ritual whereby a man takes a woman who has been dedicated to the gods, and *Savalya* (1989) concerns three granddaughters and their grandmother who once had an affair with their father, causing the mother to kill herself and the father to leave home. The girls long to escape the dismal shadows of their lives. Prashant Dalvi's (1961–) *Char Chaughi* (1991) is a story about four women, a mother and her three independent-minded daughters, all born out of

wedlock (Gokhale 2000). Sushma Deshpande performs one-woman shows based on the lives of real women whom she interviews and studies in depth. The first and most successful was her play and performance in 1989, as the wife of social worker Jyotiba Phule. The second was on the lives of *tamasha* female performers.

Currently, the biggest challenge for Marathi theater is the growth of Marathi television due to the proliferation of cable and satellite networks, which have poached talent from the stage for television productions. As a consequence, today, an actor first establishes himself on television and then does the occasional play on stage. Stage actors without a television profile remain less interesting to the Marathi public. Similarly, writers seek fortune and exposure on television. The result is that theater today is relatively less important to the Marathi people than it has been in the recent past.

Bengali Theater

In the late nineteenth century, the *jatra* remained unchallenged as the medium of popular entertainment and instruction in the rural areas of the Bengal. Even in Calcutta and the major towns of eastern India, until the turn of the century, *jatra* never lacked for patrons or an audience.

But, by the turn of the century, Calcutta had become an industrial and financial hub with a thriving port and a large multilingual population. The growth of trade and industry led to the unparalleled affluence of trading families and the rapid expansion of the middle class. With the spread of British education during the nineteenth century and contact with English dramatic literature and English theatrical forms in the playhouses of Calcutta, the educated elite started to look down upon the *jatra* as a degenerate form of entertainment fit only for the lower orders. And, as Rustom Barucha writes in his book on political theater in Bengal, by that time, the devotional fervor of *vaishnavism* (which had been at the root of this dramatic form) had spent itself as a reforming social force, and the *jatra* had gradually become a "rag-bag" of monotonous song sequences, crude vulgarities, and rusted religious motifs (Barucha 1983).

The Early Playwrights

In 1795 a Russian violinist, Herasim Lebedeff, came to Calcutta, studied Bengali, built a playhouse, and staged a Bengali play. Even though nothing much happened for decades thereafter, 1795 marks the birth of modern Bengali theater. During the mid-1830s, a few affluent city dwellers began to stage plays in their palatial homes. The trend caught on, and by the 1860s the staging of plays in private homes for invited audiences had become a regular pastime (Raha 1978).

These first stirrings of a modern Bengali theater became visible thanks to the literary efforts of three playwrights: Ramnarayan Tarakaratna (1822–1886), Michael Madhusudan Dutt (1824–1873), and Dinabandhu Mitra (1830–1873). Tarakaratna wrote and staged several original social dramas. His first, *Kulin-kula-sarvasva* (1854), was a condemnation of the elite castes. The play's run was promptly stopped by the *kulin*s, an elite Brahmin caste group who organized a protest. In 1865, he attacked the prevailing custom of polygamy in his second play, *Nabanatak*. Tarakaratna also translated several San-

A Bengali mask for a theater ritual. It represents Parvati, wife of Shiva, the Hindu god of theatre and performers. (Charles & Josette Lenars/Corbis)

skrit plays into Bengali. It was while watching just such a translation that Dutt rushed off to write a "better" play. The result was *Sharmistha* in 1859.

Niladarpan, written by Mitra in 1860, is considered one of the greatest plays in Bengali theater and made Mitra famous overnight. It dealt with the extreme hardships faced by the indigo planters in India. Around the mid-nineteenth century, the colonial British entrepreneurs were forcing subsistence farmers to cultivate indigo as a cash crop so that the expatriate traders could sell it in India and overseas for very high margins. When the farmers refused, they were forced by a variety of means to comply. The play recounts the miseries of these farmers. Mitra, who worked for the postal department and had traveled widely in the villages, was very familiar with the peasants' predicament, which he exposed in the play. The political impact of *Niladarpan* has been compared to that of *Uncle Tom's Cabin*, written just eight years earlier, in the United States.

Commercial Theater

Although a group of playwrights was already creating a body of dramatic literature, theater as a commercial enterprise—that is, available to the general public by sale of tickets—did not arise until December 1872. One of the driving forces behind the newly emerging commercial theater was Girishchandra Ghosh (1844–1911). Ghosh took over one of the theaters in Calcutta and focused his energies on publicizing his productions and selling tickets to the entire population, not just the elite, of Calcutta. Such was the success of the commercial theater he inaugurated that he began to run out of plays to perform. Furthermore, Ghosh's talents as an actor were unbounded (he has even been compared to David Garrick) and the urban audiences seem to have developed an insatiable desire for new plays starring Ghosh. Out of the need to keep the commercial theater going, Ghosh began to churn out plays and soon developed into a prolific playwright as well.

The success of Ghosh's theater soon drew the attention of financiers, who saw the new development as a profitable enterprise. They established a number of new theaters such as Star, Minerva, Kohinoor, Aurora, and others. The plays produced were religious and mythological stories (many of them written by Ghosh), and operas, as well as farces and comedies that ridiculed the moral failings of the rich and the pretentiousness of city-bred men and English-educated women (Raha 1978). The average run of the plays was twenty to twenty-five performances. With three or four playhouses and three performances a night (from 8 PM to 3 AM), new plays were in constant demand.

But Ghosh was not the sole luminary of the new professional theater. Another star performer was Ardhendu Mustafi (1850–1909), who, along with Ghosh, would dominate Bengali theater for the next four decades. There were few productions that did not feature either Ghosh or Mustafi, or both. A third figure to join their august company was Amritlal Basu (1823–1929), an excellent comic actor. Actresses, rather than female impersonators, began to play the female characters on stage, although initially the women recruited were from the flesh trade. One of the most interesting actresses of the epoch was Binodini Dasi (1862–1941), who joined the stage at the age of twelve and retired at twenty-four, after a glorious run of twelve years. Her autobiography, *Amar Katha*, and an incomplete memoir, *Amar Abhinetri Jiban*, are invaluable contributions towards the understanding of the conditions of Bengali theater of the time (Raha 1978).

One major event in the history of theater was the Dramatic Performances Control Act, passed in 1876 by the British colonial government. Its aim was to suppress any expression of political dissent and any display of nationalism on stage. The trigger for the act was an incident involving a visit of the Prince of Wales to Calcutta that same year. Invited to a leading lawyer's residence, the prince was introduced to the womenfolk of the household. This exposure of the women to an outsider, worse still to a foreigner, was considered a breach of the Hindu code of conduct. A farce called *Gajananda and the Prince* was promptly produced that lampooned the Anglophile lawyer. The viceroy promptly intervened and passed an ordinance prohibiting performances that were "scandalous, defamatory, seditious, obscene or otherwise prejudicial to the public interest" (Raha 1978: 30). The act was repealed in 1954, seven years after independence.

Until the 1930s, the commercial theater was a chaotic world of stupendous profits, equally impressive losses, litigation, intrigue, and scandals. But already by the beginning of the twentieth century, the initial spurt of enthusiasm and creativity had left the theater. Bengali drama critic Kironmoy Raha explains: "The theatre had not really changed whereas the theatergoer had. Education had spread and a new generation had come up. Even as they flocked to the theater for momentary sensations the people were becoming tired of old faces and familiar plays . . . One saw the gaudy, ornate dresses of kings and princes, the unrestrained exhibition of patriotism and cheap idealism, the ceaseless ranting passing for heroic emotions, the excesses of ululating expressions of grief and desperation in cracked voices amidst a flood of tears shed by the audience and noisy waves of tasteless ribaldry; all this and the conventional set pattern of characterisation" (Raha 1978: 78–79).

More importantly, the talkies had arrived, and the new films in Bengali had begun to enthral their spectators. Several Bengali studios were set up in Kolkata. Of these the most important was undoubtedly New Theatre, whose films had begun to enchant not just Bengalis but all Indians;

some went on to win awards at international film festivals. New Theatre even began to remake their successful films in Hindi, thereby reaching a more extensive audience. Faced with such competition, the theatrical companies began to lose money.

One personality dominated the final days of the golden age of Bengali theater: Sisir Bahaduri (1889–1959). Famed as the ultimate actor with tremendous stage presence, his virtuoso performances in the historical and mythological plays confirmed to the critics and writers of the times that they were in the presence of genius. In his career, he played about eighty different roles. But his talents did not just lie in acting; he was also an innovative director. He effected changes in sets and décor, and transformed the manner in which plays were lit. His efforts gave the Bengali theater a new lease on life.

Then, in the years of World War II, the Indian People's Theatre Association (IPTA) suddenly burst upon the stage. Its life was relatively short, but it had a tremendous impact on the development of theater within India.

Indian People's Theatre Association

IPTA was established in 1943 by the Communist Party of India (CPI) to spread its ideological message. One of the urgent needs of the CPI was to justify the stand it had taken vis-à-vis World War II. The Congress Party, which had been spearheading the fight for Indian freedom from British colonial rule, had denounced Britain for dragging India into what it saw as an essentially imperialist war. How could the British fight for freedom, they asked, when it was denying India its own freedom? At first the CPI concurred. But later, outraged by Nazi Germany's attack on the Soviet Union, it supported the Allies by arguing that the war was a war against fascism. The Indian communists thus pitted themselves against the Indian nationalists, and a propaganda war was necessary to explain their change of stance.

IPTA was created out of the cultural squads that were part of the CPI. The model that IPTA adopted for the presentation of its plays was that of the folk and popular theaters, such as the *jatra*, *tamasha*, *kathakala*, *burrakatha*, and the *jarigan*, that flourished in the rural areas of India. IPTA's most crucial contribution to the Indian political theater movement was its production of Bijon Bhattacharya's *Nabanna*, directed jointly by the playwright and Sombhu Mitra, first produced in October 1944. Radical in form and content, terrifyingly honest in its depiction of suffering, and daringly innovative in its use of language and stagecraft, *Nabanna* was a landmark in the Bengali theater; in many ways its ambition and courage have never been surpassed. The subject of the play was nothing less devastating than the deaths of five million peasants during the Bengal famine of 1943–1944 (Barucha 1983). The play's reception was beyond expectation. It invariably attracted larger crowds than any playhouse could accommodate. One performance was said to have had 7,000 spectators (Raha 1978).

IPTA was responsible for changing the very structure and concept of theater in various parts of India. By performing for the masses rather than for limited audiences, it mobilized theater and made it more accessible to those sections of society that had previously ignored it, or had been prevented from seeing it. Although many of the productions were hectic and hastily improvised, they succeeded in conveying the exigencies of the historical moment to their mass audiences (Barucha 1983). The imminence of India's independence was so intoxicating to the masses that IPTA had no difficulty in rousing their patriotic fervor. Theater was no longer mere entertainment with some social and political significance; it had become the very forum of the people.

However, once independence was achieved in 1947, IPTA not only lost its appeal, but fell victim to the ideological infighting between rival groups within the Communist Party that led to its splintering into CPI, CPI (Marxist), and even CPI (M-L) (Marxist-Leninist).

Modern Bengali Theater

The biggest contribution of IPTA was the creation of a huge corpus of trained, energetic, and dedicated actors and writers, such as the poet Kaifi Azmi (1925–2003) and the actor Balraj Sahni (1913–1973), who would make an enormous contribution to the emerging theaters and cinemas in India. Two figures who emerged from IPTA to dominate the Bengali theater for the next three decades were Sombhu Mitra and Utpal Dutt.

Sombhu Mitra and the plays of Tagore Actor-director Sombhu Mitra (1916–1997) has been deemed one of the most influential figures of modern Indian theater. After *Nabanna* (staged in 1944), Mitra's association with IPTA was controversial and brief. In 1948, he formed his own company, Bohurupee, and staged many poetic dramas, notably Rabindranath Tagore's masterworks, such as *Raktakarabi* and *Raja*. The staging of the former in 1954 has been proclaimed a landmark in Bengali theater.

Mitra's greatest allegiance as an artist had been to the works of Tagore, and he devoted a substantial part of his career and life to unraveling the mysteries and consonances of Tagore's dramas. In fact, until Mitra's historic productions, the plays of Tagore, who won the Nobel Prize for literature in 1913, were deemed too "symbolic" or too "mystical" to be performed on stage. Many critics saw Mitra's orientation as an artist as too ethereal, too poetic, and ultimately too deeply personal (Barucha 1983). Considered one of the greatest actors since Sisir Bahaduri, Mitra was also an important figure in the cinema of the 1940s and 1950s.

Utpal Dutt and the Theater of Revolution

Another figure to emerge from the shadows of IPTA was Utpal Dutt (1929–1993). Blessed with a demonic energy, Dutt first worked with Geoffrey Kendall's group that toured India performing Shakespeare. He briefly joined the Bengal unit of IPTA, performing agit-prop plays on street corners and at political rallies. Dutt later embraced the popular *jatra* form for his own plays. One of his plays was *Chargesheet*, written overnight in 1950 following the arrest of the Communist Party workers. An unabashed ham actor, his theater of revolution (in which he often played the enemy of the people) was often constructed around his own larger-than-life figure—a figure that was at times a villain and at times a buffoon (Barucha 1983).

His political plays—*Angar* in 1959 (about the death of coal miners), *Kallol* in 1965 (a battleship Potemkin–inspired production on the Indian naval mutiny of 1946), and *Tiner Talwar* (on the early years of the Bengali theater)—were con-demned by some as too theatrical and spectacular to be revolutionary. But the very same theatrics and extravaganza endeared him to his huge audiences. In the 1970s, his subject matter was not confined to Indian episodes—*Barricade* was about the rise of fascism in Germany, *Manusher Adhikarey* was about the trial in Alabama of African American youths on a trumped up charge of raping two white girls, *Lenin Kothai* was about the Kerensky regime and the Bolsheviks, and *Ajeya Vietnam* about the brave fight of the Vietnamese against the Americans (Barucha 1983).

Dutt also acted in several Bengali and Hindi films. But as he often explained in newspaper interviews, he made his seasonal trips to Bombay, where he hammed his way through a clutch of the Bollywood films, in order to finance his work in the theater.

Badal Sircar and the Poor Theater

The influences on Badal Sircar (1924–), unlike those on Mitra and Dutt, emanated from western theaters—from Joan Littlewood, when he spent two years in London, to Antony Serchio (and the Polish theater director, Jerzy Growtowski) of La Mama Theater and Richard Schechner from the Performance Group, both in New York. Sircar's first play, *Ebong Indrajit*, has been hailed as one of the finest in modern Indian theater. First published in Bohurupee's journal in 1965, it was immediately lauded for its originality of form and relevance of context, and it remains one of the most widely translated plays within India. *Ebong Indrajit* is about a perceptive middle-class youth in Bengal who is unable to fulfil his dreams, yet, at the same time, unable to accept the bourgeois triviality of society around him.

Sircar created his work as strictly non-commercial theater. Not only did Sircar believe that it was possible to work outside the commercial theater tradition, he felt that it was necessary to do so. Instead of advocating revolution with bombastic rhetoric, his theater urges spectators to feel compassion for the underprivileged who have been denied the basic necessities of life. Over the years, Sircar gradually minimized the use of sets, costumes, background music, tape recorders, and projections. The body of the actor and its relation to the space on stage were Sircar's most immediate concerns as a director.

Sircar wrote several plays and directed many more. His most important work after *Ebong Indrajit* is the trilogy comprising *Baki Itihas*, *Tringsanga Satabdi*, and *Sesh Nei*. Of these, *Baki Itihas* is a particularly fascinating play in its juxtaposition of domestic comedy and a bleak vision of history.

The contemporary theater personalities of the Bengali stage are Manoj Mitra, Mohit Chattopadhyay, Debasis Majumdar, and the much younger Bratya Basu. Mitra made known his immense talent with his first play, *Chakbhanga Madhu* (1972), written for his company, Sundaram, about social conflict and moral dilemmas. His most famous plays include *Narak Guljar* (1976), *Raj Darshan* (1982), *Sajanao Bagan* (1977), *Naisha Bhoj* (1986), *Alakanandar Putra-kanya* (1989), and *Sobhajatra* (1991). Mohit Chattopadhyay belongs to Sudrak Theater Company, and his most famous play is *Rajrakta* (1971). Debasis Majumdar's first play, *Amitaakshar* (1978), was a huge success. This was followed by *Isabasya* (1986) and *Swapna Santati* (1990) (Raha 1995).

Bratya Basu—playwright, director, and actor—belongs to Ganakrishti Theater Company in Kolkata. With eleven plays to his credit, he has become one of the leading playwrights of the Bengali theater. His first play, *Asaleen* (1995), is considered the first post-modern Bengali play. In 2004, he wrote *Winkle Twinkle* (an allusion to Washington Irving's classic story "Rip van Winkle"), satirizing the Communist government that had ruled West Bengal for twenty-six years. The play established Basu's reputation as the political conscience of Bengali theater. It concerns a Communist who disappears from police custody during the Emergency in 1976, only to re-emerge in 2002 and discover a very different Communist government. His son has embraced a different political ideology, and the self-seeking and ambitious Communist Party members have marginalized his erstwhile comrades. The Communist Party, the butt of Basu's ridicule, volubly criticized the play in the party mouthpiece newspaper *Ganashakti* (Ganguly 2003). In 2005 Basu wrote the powerful play, *Satorie July*, which dealt with the aftermath of the violent Hindu-Muslim confrontation in Gujerat and criticized religious fundamentalism.

Hindi and English Theaters in India

Unlike the Marathi and Bengali theaters ensconced in the Mumbai-Pune and Kolkata (and surrounding regions), respectively, the Hindi and English languages have no special headquarters. Hindi plays are staged in Delhi, Mumbai, and Kolkata, and English-language plays staged in Mumbai, Delhi, Bangalore, and Kolkata.

The blossoming of the Hindi stage came in the decades of the 1960s and 1970s, marked by the productions of two Hindi plays: litterateur Dharamvir Bharti's *Andha Yug* and Mohan Rakesh's (1925–1972) *Ashadh Ka Ek Din*. Published in 1954 and 1958, respectively, neither play was performed until the 1960s. *Andha Yug*, which deals with the senseless fratricide that is the theme of the epic *Mahabharata*, was first staged by Satyadev Dubey in Mumbai in 1962 and later by theater director Ebrahim Alkazi with the National School of Drama in New Delhi in 1966. Shyamanand Jalan in Kolkata first staged *Ashadh Ka Ek Din*, on the life of the Sanskrit poet-playwright Kalidasa, in 1960. The play was later staged by Alkazi in 1962 in New Delhi and by Dubey in 1964 in Mumbai and established Rakesh's reputation as the first modern Hindi playwright in India. Rakesh went on to write *Lehron Ka Rajhans* (1968) and the bestselling *Adhe Adhure* (1969), the latter about the crises of identity and masculinity that face modern man.

Many of the plays written in the creative surge that seemed to have enveloped the nation during the 1970s were rapidly translated and staged in these three main cities, creating a pan-Indian body of dramatic literature. Thus, plays originally written in Marathi by Vijay Tendulkar, Satish Alekar, Mahesh Elkunchwar, and G. P. Deshpande; plays written in Kannada by Girish Karnad (*Tughlaq, Hayavadana*) and Adya Rangachary (*Suno Janmejay*); plays written in Bengali by Badal Sircar, Mohit Chattopadhyay, and Debasis Majumdar, as well as many others, were performed in translations all over the country.

While directors such as Dubey, Jalan, and Usha Ganguly were at the forefront of Hindi theater in Mumbai and Kolkata, in Delhi the impetus for theatrical activity came from the National School of Drama, established in 1959. The school staged an array of productions, from intimate student productions to the grand historical spectacles of *Tughlaq* and *Andha Yuga*—productions that often included the entire student body. The school also invited several directors from overseas. The most famous of these was the East German director, Fritz Bennewitz from Weimar, who made the German playwright Bertolt Brecht a firm favorite with Indian audiences—not just in Delhi but also in Mumbai and Kolkata.

In the 1970s, street theater in Hindi was made famous by director Habib Tanvir (1924–), who trained at the Royal Academy for Dramatic Arts in London and later with IPTA. His productions of *Charandas Chor, Agra Bazaar, Mitti Ki Gadi* (based on the Sanskrit play *Mrcchakatika* by Sudraka) were performed by his company, Naya Theater, and his Chattisgarh players from Madhya Pradesh. Other directors of street theater, such as Safdar Hashmi (1954–1989) and his Jana Natya Manch, staged short plays in the street. Hashmi had rejected the traditional forms of popular theater for being too embedded in feudal and obscurantist structures. Instead, he found his own forms of direct address to his street audiences. His play *Machine*, performed in 1978, lasts just thirteen minutes and is about conditions faced by workers in a chemical factory. It played to audiences of over 160,000 in Delhi before being taken up by enthusiasts all over India. *Aurat*, his most popular production, has had over 2,000 performances in eighteen years and has been translated in almost every Indian language (Yarrow 2001). Hashmi was murdered by political opponents in 1989.

Theater in English

Plays staged in English are gradually becoming another body of pan-Indian theater. One of the most important Indian playwrights who wrote in English was Asif Currimbhoy (1928–1994). All his plays were set against the changing social and political events of India of the 1960s and 1970s. His first play, *The Doldrummers* (1960), about the loss of faith among the urban poor of Mumbai, was promptly banned by the government of Maharashtra for "sexual promiscuity"; *The Dumb Dancer* (1962), a play within a play, explored the Kathakali form of dance drama; *The Captives* (1963), about Hindu-Muslim trust—or the lack of it—during the Chinese invasion of India; *Goa* (1964), an account of India's occupation of the Portuguese enclave; *Inquilab* (1971), about the appeal of the extreme and violent left-wing Naxalite movement for Bengali youth; *Sonar Bangla* (1972), about the liberation of Bangladesh; and *Om Mane Padme Hum* (1981), about the escape of the Dalai Lama from Tibet (Lal 1995).

Unfortunately, despite Currimbhoy's prodigious talent and his ability, as critic Shanta Gokhale has pointed out, to use all kinds of devices—songs, slide shows, mime, monologues, choruses—to dramatic effect, he never found favor with Indian audiences, and most of his plays were first performed to acclaim in the United States rather than in India (Gokhale 2000).

Indian audiences have been kinder to the Bangalore-based actor-director-playwright Mahesh Dattani (1958–), the bright new talent who writes in English. His first play, *Where There's a Will*, about family relationships and overbearing fathers, was first performed in 1988. In *Dance Like a Man*, written the following year, the protagonist faces intense opposition from his father when he decides to become a *bharat natyam* dancer and marries another dancer. In 1990, Alyque Padamsee, the stalwart director based in Mumbai who specializes in productions in English, directed Dattani's *Tara*. In this play, the female protagonist becomes a victim of the Indian preference for sons rather than daughters. Tara is a conjoined twin, with three legs between Tara and her twin brother. The parents decides to let the boy have the second leg and let Tara remain handicapped, even when the doctor advises against this decision on medical grounds.

The subject of homosexuality is raised in *Bravely Fought the Queen* and *On a Muggy Night in Mumbai* (1991). In the former, one of the three women portrayed as victims in the play is married to a homosexual; the latter traces the lives of four affluent homosexual men. *Final Solutions* (1993) (based on Hindu-Muslim violence and distrust) is Dattani's only overtly political play, and he returns to the familiar themes of family relationships and homosexuality in his radio play *Do the Needful* (1997) for the BBC. His most recent play is *Thirty Days in September*, written in 2001. He has since progressed into film direction with *Morning Raga* (2003), about a tragedy that draws together three characters through the theme of music. His plays reflect the hopes and anxieties of the new urban India.

Despite Dattani's success, most English-language theater depends on sponsorship, and according to playwright Rookie Dadachandji, sponsors are not willing to back indigenous scripts. Instead, "they want money-back guarantee plays like musicals, comedies or classics" (Chowdhury 1998: 79). In an effort to make English theater more popular, literary circles have begun play readings. Crossword, a Mumbai-based bookstore, has also begun staging informal, dramatized play readings, attracting the literati and ordinary people alike.

Unlike the Marathi and Bengali theaters that have professional or semiprofessional companies, actors, and a permanent theater to perform in, many Hindi and English troupes depend on institutions like Prithvi Theaters for a venue. Stage and film star Prithviraj Kapoor first set up Prithvi Theaters in 1944. In 1978, actress Jennifer Kendall (from a British family of actors and married to film star Shashi Kapoor, the youngest son of Prithviraj Kapoor) revived the theater. Prithvi Theaters, located in Juhu, Mumbai, and managed by Sanjana Kapoor (Shashi and Jennifer Kapoor's daughter), has been an important venue for theater festivals since 1984. Plays in all Indian languages are performed there, and over the years it has also become an international venue for performances.

Issues

Dearth of Good Plays

One of the complaints from those involved in theater is the dearth of good plays available for actors and directors. The issue surrounding stage plays is a complicated one. That there was a flourishing Sanskrit dramatic literature until the eighth century AD is apparent from the variety of surviving plays and fragments of plays. But with the decline of the Sanskrit theater and the emergence of the popular theaters, the writing of plays went into decline. The performers of popular and folk theaters were

men of the soil and usually illiterate, and writing a script or learning written lines did not constitute part of the theatrical activity. The performances were geared toward dance and song. Dialogue was often minimal, and whatever dialogue did exist was usually improvised. In fact, the contribution made by the upper castes, when they lent their talents to the popular theater, was mostly in the composition of lyrics, such as in the *tamasha lavanis*.

In the 1950s, state government agencies decided to use local forms of theater as vehicles for their various social and health-care messages. However, when the directors of the programs wrote out the scripts, they were astounded to discover that none of the traditional actors could read. Instead, the actors asked to be told the kernel of the plot and the general gist of the message, delivering the scenarios in their own manner and in their own words (Abrams 1974). In Marathi drama, Bhave's *Sita Swayamwar*, performed in 1843, had no written dialogue; it was an evening's performance made up entirely of songs and mime. In 1880, Khadilkar was the first to actually write dialogue and make his actors learn it in his play *Sangeet Shakuntal*.

When theater was revived in the eighteenth and nineteenth centuries, at first the new playwrights chose the same subjects as traditional theaters: episodes from the epics (the *Ramayana* and the *Mahabharata*), stories from Sanskrit drama (for example, *Abhijnanashakuntala*), and historical legends. (Early Indian cinema, too, was comprised almost entirely of mythological films.) The early plays of Marathi drama were invariably based on stories from Hindu mythology or Sanskrit drama. Bengali drama, too, tended toward mythological themes. Playwright Ramnarayan

Tarakaratna translated many Sanskrit plays into Bengali for production on stage, and Michael Madhusudan Dutt's first play was based on a mythological tale. However, along with the mythological themes, Bengali drama also built up a rich and varied corpus of social dramas. Even the Parsi theater preferred fairy tales, legends, and historical dramas. Although there were tentative efforts toward modernism, it was only in the 1960s, with the arrival of playwrights such as Vijay Tendulkar, Badal Sircar, Mohan Rakesh, Girish Karnad, and Adya Rangachary, that a culture of modern writing for the stage emerged.

The absence of a history of realistic drama was deeply felt by all modern Indian playwrights, who now had to leapfrog from feudal themes to the contemporary concerns of urban Indians eager for entertainment. That the new playwrights needed direction became apparent in 1971, during a conference on theater organized by the Sangeet Natak Akademi and held at the National School of Drama. The general discussion was about dramatic form, and several established and aspiring playwrights complained that the three-act structure of western plays was too confining and even artificial to Indian sensibilities. Several claimed to prefer drawing inspiration from authentic Indian tradition rather than resorting to alien sources emanating from the West. The consequence of that seminar was the sudden emergence of Indian plays using certain conventions of the traditional theaters.

The idea of using traditional forms of theater was not new. The Parsi theater companies adapted popular theater techniques and conventions for their productions in proscenium theaters. Rabindranath Tagore, the Nobel laureate, mocked the garish décor of the commercial Bengali theater and used traditional forms of entertainment and instruction in his plays—*keertans*, songs by Baul singers, and *jatra* conventions (as in his plays *Sanyasi*, *Phalguni*, and *Muktadhara*). Utpal Dutt, who trained with IPTA, was a prolific plunderer of the *jatra* form for his political theaters. Habib Tanvir directed the Sanskrit play *Mrcchakatika* (*Mitti Ki Gadi*) without curtains or props or sets in 1959. He even brought six tribal players for his production of *Nai Nautanki*. Dina Gandhi and Shanta Gandhi championed the *bhavai* form of traditional theater of Gujerat. The latter wrote *Jasma Odan*, now part of the National School of Drama repertory. Shivram Karanth wrote operas based on the *yakshgana* of Karnataka, while G. D. Madgulkar and P. L. Deshpande revived the *tamasha* traditions for an elite audience. Girish Karnad wrote *Hayavadana* in the form of the *yakshgana*. However while having the freedom to deploy traditional Indian forms was an option available to modern playwrights, the inability to create new dramatic forms has hampered modern Indian drama.

Another reason for the paucity of dramatic literature has been, as Barucha has pointed out, the reluctance to translate plays from one Indian language to another (Barucha 1983). One reason for the absence of a cohesive body of dramatic literature accessible to all Indians regardless of their linguistic differences is the shortage of writers well versed in two completely different Indian languages. Most Indians tend to speak two Indian languages (their mother tongue and sometimes Hindi) and English. To find a writer able to translate from one Indian language into Hindi is not unusual, but to find a writer who can go from one regional language to another regional language is more difficult. *Enact*, published until the 1960s, was one of the very few publications that translated plays into English, from where they could be then retranslated into an Indian language.

Plagiarism

One of the consequences of the dearth of good Indian plays has been plagiarism. The concept of intellectual property and plagiarism when viewed from a traditional perspective is complicated. For centuries, the Indian stage has been used to appropriating stories from the Hindu myths, epics, and Sanskrit drama. In many regions these stories comprised the only subjects for any form of performance, and an original play was a novel concept. Also, it has been common practice to translate an original play, often emanating from the United States or Europe (and in some cases from Eastern Europe), into the regional language and perform it without crediting either the playwright or the translator. Perhaps this custom had to do with concerns about royalties—the foreign liabilities would be equivalent to several times the cost of an entire production and hence unaffordable.

The "borrowing" of plots and at times entire plays by playwrights remains a problem in Indian theater. (It also exists in Indian cinema, where films are remade by adding songs and dances to the original story.) Gokhale points out that the practice of borrowing from foreign sources on the Marathi stage is widespread, from plays merely "inspired" by the original through degrees of adaptation to straight translations (Gokhale 2000). Even celebrities of the Marathi stage cannot escape censure. Tendulkar, Matkari, and Kanetkar have all

adapted plots or general themes from western originals. Thus Tendulkar's highly successful *Ashi Pakhare Yeti* (1970) was based on the play *Rainmaker*, a fact acknowledged in the preface to the play; *Shrimant* was inspired by Luigi Pirandello's *The Pleasure of Honesty. Shantata! Court Chalu Ahe* (1967) owed its inspiration to several sources—the film *We're No Angels*, the German novel *Dangerous Game*, and J. B. Priestley's *Time Plays* (Gokhale 2000: 172). Matkari's *Jodidar* was based on *Man, Woman and Child*, while the film *The Apartment* inspired his play *Birhad Vajla*. Kanetkar's *Be-iman* (performed in 1973) took its central idea of friendship and duty from Jean Anouilh's *Becket*. Gokhale points out that a staging of the translation of the original play took place at the same time as the staging of *Be-iman*, allowing viewers to compare directly the two versions.

Competition for Audiences and Performance Space

Another problem that faces Indian theater is competition for viewers from television. Initially, the impact of state-owned television was not great, largely because most Indians did not possess a television set, and in any case, the programs were not very exciting. In the 1980s, Prime Minister Indira Gandhi decided to mobilize the propagandist advantages that the medium of television offered and rapidly expanded the reach of the national network. Color television was introduced and the taxes on television sets were lowered. As more and more people began to own television sets, the impact on cinema and theater was immense. In the 1990s, satellite television began to offer viewers hundreds of channels for low monthly subscriptions. Since then, theaters and cinemas have had to struggle to entice people away from their television sets.

Not only does theater have to compete for viewers, it has also to compete with other forms of entertainment for performing space. As the Indian film industries began to consolidate their positions in the 1950s and 1960s, more and more theaters were converted into cinema halls. In Mumbai, most of the theaters, including the prestigious Opera House, were rewired for the talkies.

And not only does the theater have to compete with cinemas for performing space, it has to also contend with marriage parties for venues. Hindu marriages are social rather than religious events and take place not in temples, but in secular settings—clubs, *maidans* (playing fields), and open-air spaces. College and school halls are also pressed into service for evening receptions. Rentals are high, and theater groups with limited funds find it very hard to find viable venues. When low-cost venues are found, such as the small auditorium at the Chhabildas School in Mumbai's Dadar district, the result is impressive. The Chhabildas phenomenon offered young and innovative theater companies a chance to experiment and showcase their talent to theatergoers. There has also been some help through dedicated theaters built by the state governments, but a few theaters in a city like Mumbai, with a population of nearly 15 million, is far from sufficient. Organizations like the National Centre for the Performing Arts (NCPA) and the Prithvi Theater, both in Mumbai, do offer some resources, and the relentless search for space goes on. In the meantime, scarcity of performing space continues to stifle the growth of theater in India.

Conclusion

Despite the struggle of theater companies to survive in an increasingly competitive field, several indicators bode well for the future of theater in the big cities and towns. Numerous competitions organized by state governments, the National School of Drama, and other organizations, like Nandikar and Ganakrishti in Kolkata, the Sri Ram Centre in Delhi, and the Prithvi Theater and the National Center for the Performing Arts in Mumbai, have encouraged innovation in all aspects of drama—writing, stage design, lighting, costumes, and acting. The proliferation of television has also allowed actors, writers, and designers to earn a living and work in the theater without having to seek employment in banks or government offices. Actors such as Naseeruddin Shah, who trained at the National School of Drama, act in popular films, Hollywood films, and on Indian and British television while maintaining a perennial presence on the Indian stage.

The National School of Drama and other training organizations have, over the years, trained hundreds of students from the various regions and provinces of India, most of whom have returned to their provinces to mobilize the theater as a meaningful form of entertainment. Many have acquired national stature while working in their respective regions, such as Rattan Thiyam in Manipur, B. Jayashree and Prasanna Kumar in Karnataka, Neelam Man Singh Chaudhary in Chandigarh, and Bhanu Bharti in Jaipur. Although theater may not overtake cinema and television as the prime entertainer in India, it remains a varied, broad-based, innovative, and politically alert form of contemporary popular culture.

A to Z Index

Abhijnanashakuntala: The Story of Shakuntala (Sanskrit drama): On a hunting trip, King Dushyanta encounters Shakuntala, a young maiden who lives in a forest refuge. They fall in love and he marries her, giving her a ring as a token of his affection. The ring, however, is cursed: should she lose it, Dushyanta will lose all memory of her. Duty calls, and the king returns to the capital city and his palace. One day Shakuntala loses the ring in the nearby river. Finding herself pregnant with the king's child, she travels to the palace, only to find that he has no memory of her. In the meantime, a fisherman who recovers the ring, which had been swallowed by a fish, recognizes the royal signet and takes it to the palace. With the ring recovered, the king recovers his memory, and Shakuntala is welcomed into his palace.

Ebrahim Alkazi (1924–) trained at the Royal Academy of Dramatic Art in London and worked for many years in Mumbai with Theater Unit before becoming the first director of the National School of Drama (NSD) in New Delhi in 1961. One of India's foremost directors, his attention to detail in costume, lighting, makeup, sets, diction, and performance was unrelenting. His most famous productions were the grand historical productions of *Andha Yug* and *Tughlaq.*

Mahesh Dattani (1958–) represents the new generation of stage personalities. An actor-director and playwright who writes only in English, the Bangalore-based Dattani drew national attention with his *Dance Like a Man* (1989), about the problems of being a male classical *bharat natyam* dancer. Dattani has also raised the taboo subject of male homosexuality in his plays. He has since progressed into film direction with *Morning Raga* (2003), about a tragedy that draws together three characters through the theme of music; his plays reflect the hopes and anxieties of the new urban India.

Satyadev Dubey (1936–), one of the foremost directors of the Hindi stage in India, made his name in 1962 with Dharamvir Bharti's *Andha Yug*, based on the *Mahabharata* epic. Over the last four decades he has directed hundreds of plays and discovered scores of new plays and playwrights. Dubey has unwaveringly supported young talent and novice writers, inspiring them to better and more exciting work. He runs theater workshops and training sessions; he has also written and directed films, including a filmed version of Tendulkar's *Shantata, Court Chalu Ahe!*, for which he won a Sahitya Akademi award.

Utpal Dutt (1929–1993) was a stage and screen actor. Dutt was renowned for his grand, exuberant political theater mostly delivered in *jatra* style. He became a national figure with his frequent appearances in Hindi films, where he played retired soldiers or bluff comic stereotypes with aplomb.

Indrasabha (*Nautanki* and Parsi theater): An important nineteenth-century musical drama was *Indrasabha* ("The Court of the God Indra") by Agha Hassan Amanat (1816–1859), the Urdu poet of Lucknow. Amanat used traditional melodies, folk tunes, and seasonal dances, adding to these his dramatic lyric talent. The operatic play went into many editions during his lifetime. Every professional theatrical company during the second half of the nineteenth century staged *Indrasabha*. Various *nautanki* troupes modified the original to include their local myths, characters, situations, and melodies. *Indrasabha* stands between literary drama and folk play. Its popularity invigorated *nautanki* writers, who sought to emulate its whimsical and otherworldly atmosphere of fairies, devils, gods, princes, wizards, and dancers.

The events take place at the court of Indra, king of the gods, who sits in state flanked by beautiful fairies. The Emerald Fairy (Sabz Pari) falls in love with an earthly prince (Gulfam), and with the assistance of the Black Demon (Kala Dev) she smuggles Gulfam into Indra's heaven. Displeased at this infraction, Indra casts Gulfam into a well and clips the wings of Sabz Pari, who plunges to earth. Undaunted, she disguises herself as a female mendicant (*jogin*) and, singing irresistible songs of separation, gains readmission to the heavens, whereupon she wins the king's favor and eventually earns her lover's release.

Shyamanand Jalan (1932–) is an actor, director, and founder (with Pratibha Agrawal) of the pioneering Hindi-language theater group Anamika, established in 1955. In fifty years the group produced over seventy-two productions in Hindi, along with one-act plays, children's theater, and ballets. During the 1970s, he averaged three productions a year. Jalan discovered Hindi drama's modernist genius Mohan Rakesh in 1960. He also brought Badal Sircar to the rest of India by producing the Bengali plays *Ebong Indrajit* and *Pagla Ghoda* in Hindi.

Chandrasekhar Kambhar (1937–) is a Kannada playwright, poet, folklorist, and film director. Kambhar is most famous for his *Jokumaraswamy*, written in 1972 in the style of the traditional *Yakshgana* theater. He turned to filmmaking in the late 1970s, and his handling in 1978 of *Kaadu Kudure*, based on the Spanish playwright Federico Garcia Lorca's *The House of Bernada Alba*, established his reputation in film direction.

B. V. Karanth (1929–) is a renowned stage and film director who joined Gubbi Veeranna's Gubbi Company in 1944. He established his reputation as a serious film director with *Chomanna Dudi* (1975). A graduate of the National School of Drama, he was its director from 1978 to 1981. He now runs the Karnataka state repertory theater, Rangayana.

Girish Karnad (1938–) is a film and stage actor, director, and Kannada playwright. Karnad wrote his first play, *Yayati*, while still a student at Oxford University. Part of the new Indian film movement, Karnad also explored new avenues in screen and playwriting: his play *Tughlaq* is written like a Greek tragedy, and *Hayavadana* is written in the *yakshgana* style. Karnad also was one of the pioneers of the new Indian film movement with Samskara (1971) and Kaadu (1973). He served as director of the Film and Television Institute of India from 1974 to 1975.

Shyam Manohar (1941–) is a playwright and novelist. Manohar bridges the gap between the mainstream and experimental theaters. His first play, *Yakrit* (Liver), was conceived of when he tried to give up smoking and decided to write about how time hangs heavily on an individual in that situation. His other plays include *Hriday* (Heart), *Yelkot*, which deals with questions of sex and desire, and *Darshan.*

Sombhu Mitra (1916–1997) was a great Bengali actor and director. Mitra set up his own theater company, Bohurupee, in 1948 after a stint with IPTA. His production of Rabindranath Tagore's *Raktakarabi* is a landmark in the development of modern Indian theater. Mitra also directed several films in Hindi and Bengali, the most celebrated being *Jagte Raho* (1956), starring Raj Kapoor.

Alyque Padamsee (1931–) is a media personality—an advertising guru and the father of English theater in India. He works mainly in English, bringing to the Mumbai theaters all the latest stage hits from London's West End and New York's Broadway (*Evita, Cabaret, A Streetcar Named Desire*). He has also pioneered some Indian playwrights in English translations.

Mohan Rakesh (1925–1972) broke onto the Hindi stage in 1958 with *Ashadh Ka Ek Din*, about the personal dilemmas faced by the classical Sanskrit playwright Kalidas. Like its predecessor, his next play, *Lehron Ka Rajhans*, was set in historical times but grappled with modern problems—in this case, about Buddha and the issue of renunciation. *Adhe Adhure* was the first to be set in modern-day India. It concerned masculine anxieties and feminine despair and alienation.

Pune-based architect **Makarand Sathe** (1957–) began his writing career with short stories and poems before turning to plays. He is greatly influenced by Eugene

Ionesco. Of the Indian playwrights, he claims his greatest influences to be those of Satish Alekar and P. L. Deshpande. His full length plays include *Charshe Koti Visarbhole* (1987), about time and money; *Aees Paees Soyinay Baees* (1995), about a girl who refuses to be bullied into marriage by her aunt and other family members; and *Surya Pahilela Manus*, where he uses the personage of Socrates to elucidate modern politics.

Naseeruddin Shah (1950–) is a graduate of the National School of Drama as well as the Film and Television Institute of India. Shah is one of India's finest actors, whether on stage, in experimental films, or in mainstream cinema. He made his film debut with the films of Shyam Benegal and won international attention with his performance in Mira Nair's *Monsoon Wedding*. Shah keeps up a perennial presence in Hindi and English plays when between films.

Vijay Tendulkar (1925–) is one of the foremost contemporary Indian playwrights. Tendulkar's plays form part of the canon of modern Indian drama. His *Sakharam Binder* (1971), about a debauched Brahmin, and *Ghashiram Kotwal* (1972), about debauched Peshwas, created a scandal among the Maharashtrian elite. Tendulkar has also written screenplays for directors of the new Indian cinema.

Bibliography and References

Abraham, Vinu. "Chavittu Natakam: Stamp of Devotion." *The Week*, 27 June 2004.

Abrams, Tevia. *Tamasha, People's Theater of Maharashtra State.* Unpublished Ph.D. diss.,

East Lansing, Michigan State University, 1974.

Bandyopadhyay, Asit Kumar. *History of Modern Bengali Literature*. Calcutta: Modern Book Agency Private Limited, 1986.

Bandyopadhyay, Samik. "Theatre: From Metropolis to Wasteland." In *Independent India: The First Fifty Years*, ed. Hiranmay Karlekar. Delhi: Oxford University Press, 1998.

Barucha, Rustom. *The Politics of Cultural Practice: Thinking through Theatre in an Age of Globalization*. London: Athlone Press, 2000.

———. *Theatre and the World: Performance and the Politics of Culture*. London: Routledge, 1993.

———. *Rehearsals of Revolution: The Political Theater of Bengal*. Honolulu: University of Hawaii Press, 1983.

Basham, A. L. *The Wonder that Was India*. New Delhi: Rupa, 1994.

Benegal, Som. *A Panorama of Theatre in India*. New Delhi: Indian Council for Cultural Relations, 1967.

Bhattacharya, Malini. "The Indian People's Theatre Association: A Preliminary Sketch of the Movement and the Organization 1942–47." *Sangeet Natak* 94, Oct.–Dec. New Delhi: Sangeet Natak Akademi, 1989.

———. "The IPTA in Bengal." *Journal of Arts and Ideas*, January 1983.

Chaitanya, Krishna. "The Aesthetics of *Kathakali*." *Sangeet Natak* 80, April–June 1986.

Chowdhury, Nandita. "Acts of Courage." *India Today*, 16 February 1998.

David, Stephen. "Rangayana: Under the Sword." *India Today*, 29 February 1996.

Desai, Sudha R. *Bhavai*. Ahmedabad: New Order Books, 1972.

Devi, Mahasweta. *Truth Tales*. London: Women's Press, 1987.

———. *Five Plays*. Calcutta: Seagull, 1997.

Dutt, Utpal. *Towards a Revolutionary Theatre*. Calcutta: M. C. Sirkar, 1982.

Ganguly, Tapash. "Setting the Stage: *Winkle Twinkle* Marks the Return of Political Satire to Bengali Theatre." *The Week*, 13 April 2003.

Gargi, Balwant. *Folk Theater of India*. Seattle: University of Washington Press, 1966.

———. *Theater in India*. New York: Theater Arts Books, 1965.

Gehlot, Deepa. "Theatre Hits the Highway." *The Times of India*, Bombay, 5 June 2004.

Ghosh, Manmohan. *Natyasastra*. Calcutta: Asiatic Society of Bengal, 1958.

Ghosh, Nemai. *Dramatic Moments: Theatre in Calcutta since the 60s*. Calcutta: Seagull, 2000.

Gokhale, Shanta. *Playwright at the Centre: Marathi Drama from 1843 to the Present*. Calcutta: Seagull, 2000.

———. "The Dramatists." In *An Illustrated History of Indian Literature in English*, edited by Arvind Krishna Mehrotra. New Delhi: Permanent Black, 2003.

Government of India. *India 2004: A Reference Annual*. Publications Division, Ministry of Information and Broadcasting, New Delhi, 2004.

Guha Thakurta, P. *The Bengali Drama*. London: Kegan Paul, Trench, Trubner, 1930.

Hansen, Kathryn. *Grounds for Play: The Nautanki Theatre of North India*. Berkeley: University of California Press, 1992.

———. "The Indar Sabha Phenomenon: Public Theatre and Consumption in Greater India (1853–1956)." In *The History, Politics and Consumption of Public Culture in India*, edited by Rachel Dwyer and Christopher Pinney. New Delhi: Oxford University Press, 2001.

Hashmi, Safdat. *The Right to Perform: The Selected Writings of Safdar Hashmi*. New Delhi: Sahmat, 1989.

Jain, Nemi Chandra. "Contemporary Productions of Bhasa Plays." *Sangeet Natak* 87, January–March, 1988.

Jayasankar, Menaka. "Dramatis Personae: The New Generation." *The Indian Express*, 16 May 2004.

Kalidas, S. "A Space for Stage." *India Today*, 3 April 2000.

Kapoor, Shashi, with Deepa Gehlot. *The Prithviwallahs*. New Delhi: Roli, 2004.

Karanth, K. S. *Yaksagana*. New Delhi: Indira Gandhi Centre for the Arts/Abhinav, 1997.

Karnad, Girish. *Hayavadana*. Bombay: OUP, 1972.

———. "Tughlaq." In *Three Modern Indian Plays*. New Delhi: OUP, 1989.

———. *Naga-Mandala*. New Delhi: OUP, 1990.

———. *The Fire and the Rain*. New Delhi: OUP, 1998.

Lal, Ananda. "Theatre in English: Some Postcolonial Hopes." In *Rasa: The Indian Performing Arts in the Last Twenty-five Years*, edited by Ananda Lal. Calcutta: Anamika Kala Sangam, 1995.

———, ed. *Rasa: The Indian Performing Arts in the Last Twenty-five Years*. Calcutta: Anamika Kala Sangam, 1995.

Mathur, J. C. *Drama in Rural India*. London: Asia Publishing House, 1964.

Mehta, Dina. *Brides Are Not for Burning*. Calcutta: Rupa, 1994.

Menon, Ramesh. "Street Plays: Drumming for Literacy." *India Today*, 30 September 1993.

Misra, Rama Darasa. *Modern Hindi Fiction*. Delhi: Bansal, 1983.

Mitra, Amal. "The English Stage in Calcutta, Circa 1750." *Sangeet Natak* 88, April–June 1988.

Mukeni, Sumitra. "Encounters with Cultures: Contemporary Indian Theatre and Inter-culturalism." *Seagull Theatre Quarterly* 4, 1994.

Mukhopadhyaya, D. *Lesser Known Forms of Performing Arts in India*. New Delhi: Minimax, 1976.

Nadkarni, Dyneshwar. *Balgandharva and the Marathi Theatre*. Bombay: Roopak Books, 1988.

Narayana, Birendra. *Hindi Drama and Stage*. Delhi: Konark Publishers, 1987.

Pillai, G. Sankara, ed. *The Theatre of the Earth Is Never Dead*. Trichur: School of Drama, University of Calicut, 1986.

Radhakrishnan, M. G. "Ningal Are Communistakki? Comarades See Red." *India Today*, 31 August 1995.

Raha, Kironmoy. *Bengali Theatre*. New Delhi: National Book Trust, 1978.

———. "Bengali Theatre." In *Rasa: The Indian Performing Arts in the Last Twenty-five Years*, edited by Ananda Lal. Calcutta: Anamika Kala Sangam, 1995.

Rangachary, Adya. *The Indian Theatre*. New Delhi: National Book Trust, 1971.

Richmond, Fancy P., Darius L. Swann, and Philip B. Zarilli. *Indian Theatre: Traditions of Performance*. Honolulu: University of Hawaii Press, 1990.

Popular Book Depot. *The Marathi Theatre: 1843 to 1960*. Bombay: Popular Book Depot, 1961.

Sircar, Badal. *Third Theatre*. Calcutta: Naba Granth Kutir, 1973.

———. *Evan Indrajit*. Calcutta: Oxford University Press, 1977.

———. *Three Plays: Bhoma, Procession, Stale News*. Calcutta: Seagull, 1984.

Srampichal, Jacob. *Voice to the Voiceless*. New Delhi: Manohar Publishers & Distributors, 1994.

Tanvir, Habib. *Charandas Chor*. Trans. Anjum Katyal. Calcutta: Seagull, 1996.

Tapas, Vijay. "Marathi Theatre." In *Rasa: The Indian Performing Arts in the Last Twenty-Five Years*, edited by Ananda Lal. Calcutta: Anamika Kala Sangam, 1995.

Tendulkar, Vijay. "Silence, the Court Is in Session." In *Three Modern Indian Plays*. New Delhi: Oxford University Press, 1989.

Thapar, Romila. *A History of India*. Middlesex Penguin, 1970.

Thiyam, Ratan. "The Audience Is inside Me." *Seagull Theatre Quarterly* 14/15, 1997.

Thomas, Prince Mathews. "Theatre: A Happy Denouement." *The Week*, 4 April 2004.

Varadpande, M. L. *Loka Ranga: Panorama of Indian Folk Theatre*. New Delhi: Abhinav Publications, 1992.

———. *Mahabharata in Performance*. New Delhi: Clarion, 1990.

Vatsyayan, Kapila. *Traditional Indian Theatre: Multiple Streams*. New Delhi: National Book Trust, 1980.

Warder, A. K. "Classical Literature." In *A Cultural History of India*, edited by A. L. Basham. Oxford: Clarendon Press, 1975.

Yajnik, R. J. *Indian Theatre*. New York: E. P. Dutton, 1934.

Yarrow, Ralph. *Indian Theatre: Theatre of Origin, Theatre of Freedom*. Richmond Surrey: Curzon Press, 2001.

4

Indian Literature in English

India is a multicultural, multilingual country. Its diversity is reflected in its 1,652 mother tongues belonging to four language families (Austric, Dravidian, Indo-Aryan, and Sino-Tibetan) and written in ten major scripts as well as a host of minor ones (Pattanayak 1998). Out of all of these languages and dialects, the Indian government has recognized eighteen languages as "scheduled" or official. Hindi is the national language of the country, but English, initially to be retained for just fifteen years after independence, has now been granted the status of "associate" official national language.

The position of English in this Babel is a privileged one. Historically, it was the language of the colonizer, the language of higher education, of science and technology, of law and commerce. It was also the language of the elite, of getting on and getting ahead (Mehrotra 2003). Today, it is the language through which the elite of India can communicate with one another and with the rest of the world. Unlike the other Indian languages, English does not emanate from any Indian region or province, nor is it concentrated in any one particular area of India. Instead, English is an elite pan-Indian language, with English speakers concentrated in the bigger cities and towns across the entire country.

In its annual reference book published by the Ministry of Information and Broadcasting, the government of India does not offer any statistics on the number of people literate in English. Overall literacy rates in any Indian language stand at 65 percent, and estimates place literacy rates in English at between 2 and 3 percent of the population. For that reason, Indian literature in English cannot be construed as part of a popular or mass culture. However, even the low percentage of literacy in English represents between 20 and 30 million people who can speak and read English. And these numbers are not concentrated in any corner of India but are dispersed across the nation. Thus, within the context of a burgeoning middle class and an avid consumer culture, Indian literature in English has become an important commodity to be sold, purchased, and consumed.

India is the world's third largest market for books. Overall India publishes approximately 70,000 books in eighteen languages each year, mak-

English-language bookstore on a flooded street. Calcutta, 1990. (Bruce Burkhardt/Corbis)

ing it the seventh largest producer of books in the world. It also is the third largest producer of books in English, just after the United States and the United Kingdom.

The Development of Indian Literature in English

The Early Years

Many historians designate the year 1800 as the starting point for the history of Indian literature in English, although the first book written and published by an Indian in English was *The Travels of Dean Mahomet* (1794). Dean Mahomet, who had followed his master, a British officer in the army of the East India Company, back to Ireland and settled there, wrote the travelogue in epistolary form (Mehrotra 2003). By 1800 the British had emerged the unchallenged

rulers of India. With the supremacy of the British came the spread of the English language, the most lasting legacy of British colonization of India. The early books in English were grammars, dictionaries, teaching aids and phrase books, and translations of literary works, digests, and compendiums written by the early Orientalists in Britain to facilitate colonization and explain the new acquisition—both to the East India Company's servants in India and to an avid literary and scientific community back home in England (Mehrotra 2003).

In 1825 came the famous and oft-quoted "Minute on Education of 1835" written by Thomas Babington Macaulay, where he declared that "we must at present do our best to form a class who may be interpreters between us and millions whom we govern; a class of persons, Indian in blood and colour, but English in taste, in opinions, in morals, and in intellect." However, the class that Macaulay aspired to create had, in fact, long been in the formation, largely comprising the new urban elite of Calcutta (now Kolkata). Many of them were land-owning immigrants who were drawn to the city by the promise of office jobs in the expanding British administration, the key to which was the knowledge of English (Mehrotra 2003).

The founding of universities in Calcutta, Bombay, and Madras in the nineteenth century also had a direct impact on these middle classes and on the legacy of Indian literature in English. At first English education was available in India only through private and missionary establishments. The Hindu College (which later became the Presidency College) was set up at the request of, and with funding from, a group of elite but orthodox Hindus in 1817, well before the colonial agenda for an English education had been fully formalized. It was only when the British realized that the spread of western education would establish and perpetuate their own power that they began to encourage the establishment of institutes of higher education throughout the country. English soon became the language of governance in India, and quickly replaced Persian as the language of the law courts, of official business, and of higher education.

The introduction of English found favor with many Indians. It was already the dominant language of the world. English was, according to the great social reformer Ram Mohan Roy (circa 1772–1833), not only the language of power and command but also of documentation, histories, narrative, theological disputation, and personal reflection. The introduction to English literature at the new Indian universities also led Indians to discover a new world of prose and the realist novel. Furthermore, English novels were cheaply and abundantly available to the Indian readers. The books they devoured were the works of Benjamin Disraeli, Bulwer Lytton, Marie Corelli, Wilkie Collins, Charles Dickens, and G. W. M. Reynolds, and it was to these figures of the Victorian era that Indians turned when they first crafted their first fictions (Mehrotra 2003).

Another consequence of the growth in university education was that the Indians began to master the colonizer's language and by the 1820s had begun to adopt it as their chosen medium of expression. These pioneering works of poetry, fiction, drama, travel, and belles-lettres are little read today, but when they were published they were audacious acts of mimicry and self-assertion by the mere fact of being in English. Many of the new Indian writers took stories from the *Annals and Antiquities of Rajasthan* (1829), written by Col. James Tod and published in 1829, for their poems, ballads, and romances (Mehrotra 2003).

The influence of English literature was not contained within the English-speaking elite. Colonial education also brought about a transformation in regional-language literatures. It brought the attention of regional-language writers to the potential of prose, and the new works created in the regional-language literature displayed a remarkable hybridization and variety brought about by the collision of the two cultures. The new books in regional Indian languages began to be written along the lines of English novels and romances. By the early decades of the nineteenth century, a tumultuous intellectual and cultural awakening was under way in Bengal, the place where the British and Indian cultures first encountered each other. It then spread to other parts of the country, especially in the decades following 1857, the year of the Indian rebellion against the British colonial powers. The second half of the nineteenth century marked the birth of a new Indian novel and literature characterized by the narration of ordinary lives in everyday language. Regional readers embraced the new literature with enthusiasm.

The earliest Indian texts in English may well have been two tracts of imaginary history written by Kylas Chunder Dutt and Shoshee Chunder Dutt in 1835 and 1845, respectively. These were "A Journal of Forty-Eight Hours of the Year 1945," published in the *Calcutta Literary Gazette*, and *The Republic of Orissa: A Page from the Annals of the 20th Century.* Both texts, published as journals, imagined a future insurrection against British rule by Indian patriots: in the first, after initial successes, the Indians are routed; in the second, the insurrection is led not by an English educated urban youth but by a tribal from the province of Orissa. Victory does not elude him as it does his predecessor, and the story ends with the British Empire in terminal decline (Mukherjee 2003).

In the early school of Indo-English poetry, poets did not dare to experiment with the European metrical forms. Instead, their ballads and sonnets were usually imitations of the English style that even looked at their subjects from a Western point of view. An important figure in Indian poetry in English was Henry Derozio (1809–1831), a Eurasian of Portuguese origin who wrote verse in the style of Lord Byron. At Hindu College, where he taught, Derozio gathered around him a band of young progressives

called the "Young Bengal" and inspired them not just to write in English but also to scrutinize and question every aspect of Indian tradition.

One of those whom he inspired was Michael Madhusudan Dutt (1824–1873), a student of Derozio at Hindu College and an anglophile who converted to Christianity and preferred to write exclusively in English in his early years. His first attempt was a long narrative poem, *Captive Ladie*, published in 1849. He also wrote an essay on *The Anglo-Saxon and the Hindu* (1854), replete with classical references to Herodotus, Virgil, Homer, Petrarch, Byron, and several others (Mehrotra 2003). However, his plays in English—*Razia, Empress of Inde* (1858), and *Sermista* (1859)—were translations from the Bengali. In 1869, Dutt translated into English Dinabandhu Mitra's now classic play *Niladarpan* (1860), about the inhuman exploitation of workers on indigo plantations. Thereafter Dutt began writing exclusively in Bengali. He wrote a version of the *Ramayana* by using epic devices borrowed from Milton.

The Indian novel had its birth with Bankimchandra Chattopadhyaya's (1838–1894) *Rajmohan's Wife*, about middle-class life in Calcutta. In 1864, it was serialized in a short-lived journal called the *Indian Field.* It was Chattopadhyaya's only attempt at writing fiction in English. He subsequently wrote fourteen powerful novels in Bengali. Lal Behari Day (1824–1894) wrote about village life in *Govinda Samanta, or the History of a Bengali Raiyat.* The novel chronicles the fortunes of the Samanta family as it moves from a rural idyll to famine, debt, the loss of land, migration, and death. It was later revised and enlarged and published in 1908 as *Bengal Peasant Life* (Mukherjee 2003).

The only woman writer writing in English during the nineteenth century was Krupabai Satthianadhan (1862–1894), an Indian Christian who published two books—the first an autobiographical account about her education and marriage, the second about the struggles of a female misfit with a thirst for reading and knowledge. In her novels, outcastes and tribal men and women were presented as individualized characters, probably for the first time, and the idea of a nation was linked to cultural, rather than religious, identity (Mukherjee 2003).

Although some of the books written in the nineteenth century were published in the metropolitan centers of book production, such as London, Calcutta, Bombay, and Madras, a good proportion were published by small presses with limited distribution located in small towns across India. These early novels lacked the abject servility that would characterize the later novels. Resistance to colonial rule appeared as a frequent theme, either major or minor, although most of these attempts at resistance are unsuccessful. Unfortunately, most of the books have perished.

One curious fact about these books is, according to the writer Meenakshi Mukherjee, the eagerness reflected in the titles (*Glimpses of . . .*, *Peeps into . . .*, and so forth) to unveil some of the mystery about a homogenous place called India. Unlike the writers in regional languages who were confident about their readership within their specific region, the writers in English suffered from an uncertainty about their audience. It could have been the British reader or the colonial administrator in India, and for their benefit it was necessary to make life in India more accessible through literature. Thus in Bankimchandra Chattopadhyaya's *Rajmohan's Wife*, leafy vegetables become "salad," although India had no concept of eating uncooked greens. Lal Behari Day in *Govinda Samanta* announces that there are no "taverns" for the Bengali peasants to spend their evenings in, and that they lack the concept of courtship among the young (Mukherjee 2003: 92–93).

However, by the end of the nineteenth century, a new phenomenon is apparent: novel after novel in English seem to be paying direct or veiled tribute to British rule. Although many writers evoke the greatness of India's Hindu past, obsequiousness toward the British rulers is demonstrated at regular intervals. By the beginning of the twentieth century, even though the stirrings of nationalism had become conspicuous among the creative writers in the Indian languages, in Indo-Anglian writings the obsequiousness continued.

Familiarity with the English language and western culture were markers of power, and some novelists in English began to display their acquaintance with the classics of western literature more obviously than the others. Interestingly, they never mentioned lowbrow writers (although there was no doubt that they were voraciously devoured by the Indian public) like G. W. M. Reynolds, Wilkie Collins, Marie Corelli, and Benjamin Disraeli, whose influence on the Indian-language novels is well known. Instead, the Indian writers in English took care to align themselves with only the best in a variety of ingenious ways. Epigraphs from Byron, Scott, Cowper, Shakespeare, and Coleridge were common, and quotations and references were generously woven into the narrative, whether the context called for them or not (Mukherjee 2003).

In fact, such a premium was placed on an author's facility with the English language that sometimes it became the chief selling point of his novel. The publishers of *The Prince of Destiny*, for instance, claimed that since readers in Britain could not believe that its author Sarath Kumar Ghosh was anything but an Englishman in masquerade, they deemed it expedient to publish the author's portrait in the British edition in Indian dress in order to convince British readers that he was truly Indian (Mukherjee 2003).

According to Mukherjee, "Echoes of canonical English novels are often perceptible in these texts. For example, Henry Fielding's famous 'bill of fare' metaphor at the beginning of his novel *Tom Jones* is replicated on the first page of Day's *Govinda Samanta* . . . The convention of closure found in the Victorian novel, where all the characters are neatly served with their just desserts and the loose ends tied up, is also faithfully repeated in novel after Indian novel" (Mukherjee 2003: 98–99). However, such mimicry often coexisted with fierce cultural pride and an assertion of the antiquity and superiority of Indian civilization in relation to that of Europe. Ambivalence about western civilization— on the one hand seen as liberating and on the other as a threat to Hindu identity— prevailed, and many novels featured a *guru* or spiritual guide who pointed to a transcendental, ancient Hindu wisdom.

Novelists of the 1930s and 1940s

The early 1930s were a period of optimism about the prospect of Indian independence, and the novels of the 1930s and 1940s played an important role in embodying and imagining the anticolonial nationalism spearheaded by Mahatma Gandhi that was gathering pace within India. Three major Indian writers in English emerged in the course of these two decades: Mulk Raj Anand, Raja Rao, and R. K. Narayan. Anand and Rao were cosmopolitan creatures who had spent their formative years in the West, and their writing displayed the same cultural schizophrenia that has since become the hallmark of many contemporary Indian writers, whereas Narayan's talents were nurtured at home in India.

In 1935, the Progressive Writers Association (PWA), a movement of Indian writers led by Sajjad Zahir, was formed in London. It was inspired by the meeting in Paris of the International Association of Writers for the Defence of Culture against Fascism led by Maxim Gorky, André Gide, André Malraux, and others the same year. Radical Indian students and intellectuals began to meet regularly at the Nanking Restaurant in Denmark Street in London to discuss and formulate the organization's original manifesto. The PWA believed that "the new literature of India must deal with basic problems of existence today—the problems of hunger and poverty, social backwardness and political subjugation, so that it may help us to understand these problems and through such understanding help us to act" (Russell 1992: 205).

Most of the members of the organization returned home after finishing their studies in London, Oxford, Cambridge, Paris, and elsewhere, and soon Marxist ideology began to inform the work of the Indian writers, both in English and in the regional languages. As the first major cultural initiative involving the independent Left and the Communist Party of India, the PWA made a formidable impact, introducing a politically aware realism into the predominantly feudal and reformist traditions of the literatures of India (Rajadhyaksha and Willemen 1999).

Mulk Raj Anand   Among the many writers who frequented the PWA meetings was Mulk Raj Anand (1905–2004), seen as the "father" of the Indian novel in English. Anand combined the competing ideologies of nationalism and cosmopolitanism, modernism and Marxism, and nonmodern Gandhism and Nehruvian socialism. A student at the University of London, he was gradually drawn into the Bloomsbury circle. He simultaneously developed an interest in Indian philosophy and aesthetics. His writing career began in England with short essays on books in T. S. Eliot's magazine, *Criterion*. But his reputation as a writer was established upon his return to India with the publication of his first three novels. His first, *Untouchable* (1935), demonstrates his decisive shift from Bloomsbury to Sabarmati (Gandhi's abode). It narrates one day in the life of a sweeper, and its theme of oppression is continued in his two subsequent novels, *Coolie* (1936) and *Two Leaves and a Bud* (1937).

In all his books, Anand explored the oppressive lives of the Indian peasant, the caste system, "untouchability," and rural poverty or the degradations of urban existence. His later novels include the famous trilogy *The Village* (1939), *Across Black Waters* (1940), and *The Sword and the Sickle* (1942), whose central character, Lal Singh, a Punjabi peasant, ends up fighting in World War I.

In the 1950s Anand embarked on a seven-volume autobiography after Shakespeare's "Seven Ages of Man." However, he only managed to complete *Seven Summers* (1951), *Morning Face* (1968), *Confessions of a Lover* (1976), and *The Bubble* (1984)

before his death in 2004. Anand was also a pioneer in transcribing the exuberant Punjabi and Hindustani dialects of northern India into his English writings, a trend that was to be popularized half a century later by Salman Rushdie. Anand also founded *Marg*, the first fine arts and literature magazine in English in India.

Raja Rao   Another major figure of the times was Raja Rao (1908–), who left for France to study western philosophy and mysticism in 1927 and thereafter divided his time among India, Europe, and the United States. Rao's preoccupation was with form and cultural translation, with the problem of translating Indian modes of feeling and expression into English (Gandhi 2003).

His first novel, *Kanthapura* (1938), describes the daily life in an Indian village during a revolt against an overbearing plantation owner. The story uncovers the gradual arrival of Gandhism to a small caste-ridden village called Kanthapura on the Malabar Coast. Rao's commitment to Gandhian nonviolence is clearly revealed in his description of the peasants' conversion to the principle of civil disobedience. The story is narrated as a series of reminiscences of an old woman, and its tone is informed by her preliminary invocation to the goddess Kenchemma, who functions as the presiding deity over the events. Like a *harikatha*, a form of traditional theater in southern India, it has Gandhi as the "epic" hero. Rao combines the dynamic force of women (whom Gandhi urged the national movement to embrace) and the socialist principle of equal distribution of wealth within the self-sufficient village.

The Serpent and the Rope (1960) is a semi-autobiographical account of a marriage between intellectuals that is destroyed by philosophical discord. It explores the philosophy of Vedanta through an Indian male protagonist in the West (Rao) and the breakdown of his various relationships with western and Indian women. His metaphysical novel *The Cat and Shakespeare* (1965) is a tale of individual destiny. *Comrade Kirillov*, written much later (1976), also explores Rao's dual interests in Gandhi and Marxism through an examination of the political complexities of Indian liberalism. All four works are profoundly serious, reflecting Rao's abiding concern with the potential clashes between pragmatism and ideals. He has also published two collections of short stories, *The Cow of the Barricades and Other Stories* (1947) and *The Policeman and the Rose* (1978).

R. K. Narayan   R. K. Narayan (1906–2001), author of thirty-four novels, was one of the few Indian writers to have honed his skills entirely in India. He did not even travel overseas until late in his life. His first book was *Swami and Friends* (1935), set in Malgudi, a fictional colonial district town—complete with a post office, bank, middle-class suburb, small roadside shops, low-caste slums, a missionary school, and government bungalows—where his characters had to find their place (Mishra 2003). *The Bachelor of Arts* (1937), his second book, was about a young graduate, whereas *The Dark Room* (1938) takes up the condition of women. In this book, the protagonist, Savitri, runs away from home when her husband begins associating with a modern woman, but in the end she returns to her suffering at her husband's place.

After independence, he published *Mr Sampath* (1949), *The Man-Eater of Mal-*

gudi (1980), *The Talkative Man* (1985), and *The World of Nagaraj* (1990). He first came to the attention of the West when Graham Greene hailed his work in the United Kingdom. His novel *The Financial Expert* (1952) was the first of his novels to be published in the United States. His best book is judged to be *The Guide* (1958), which was made into a film by the Hindi film industry in Bombay. It is about a professional guide who invents history for bored tourists, seduces a married woman, steals, and then becomes a holy man whose devotees look to him to provide water during a drought. It won the Sahitya Akademi Award, the highest literary recognition awarded by the Indian academy for letters, in 1960.

Most of Narayan's stories center on a modest hero surrounded by eccentrics. Narayan's books portray a world of inchoate longing and vague dissatisfaction. They are peopled by characters who revolt against the dreary life as clerks in business and administrative offices but ultimately abandon the dreams that would have helped them escape and settle down to drab, unromantic surroundings. His characters display a love for restless drifting and travel to the edge of their world, only to surrender to the inevitable and accept it by reconciling themselves to it. He describes the bewilderment, anxiety, and disappointment of a generation of Indians expelled from the past into a new and unfamiliar world. A Brahminical formality circumscribes the relationships within families, the father being especially aloof, often cold; romantic love when it occurs is either beset by loss of control (*The Bachelor of Arts*, *Mr Sampath*, *The Guide*, *The Talkative Man*) or by anxiety and fear (*Waiting for the Mahatma*), so that love's failure comes as a relief, as in *The Painter of Signs* (Mishra 2003).

For decades Narayan had difficulty finding a publisher for his books, and it was only after various recommendations from Graham Greene that Narayan's works were finally published.

Other Writers   Other important writers of the period include Ahmed Ali (1910–1994), who brings a Muslim perspective to his books, as in his short story "Our Lane." A founding member of PWA, Ali's only pre-partition novel, *Twilight in Delhi* (1940), is about the Nihal family, the claustrophobia of a particular class of Muslim families, and the erosion of a whole culture and way of being. He emigrated to Pakistan after partition. His only other novel was *Ocean of Night* (1964), a tragic romance.

Another important writer in English was Aubrey Menen (1912–1989), who brought into the open the complex contradictions of a homosexual existence in a sexually repressive society. His cultural hybridity (his mother was Irish) and his sexual dissonance were the subjects of his books. His first novel, *The Prevalence of Witches* (1947), brings to the forefront his mixed parentage, and he exposes the hypocrisies and delusions of British society in India. His play *Rama Retold* (1954) was the first play to be banned in independent India (Gandhi 2003).

1950s–1970s

During the first two decades after India attained independence in 1947, many writers felt that it was unpatriotic to write in English, the language of the newly departed colonizer. These were unpromising times to embark on a literary career in English. The spirit of nationalism was still strong but the initial enthusiasm of independence had given way to the despair of partition (of India into India and Pakistan), alienation, and dissatisfaction. The ruling triumvirate of Mulk Raj Anand, Raja Rao, and R. K. Narayan continued to write. But it was not until 1960, when Narayan's *The Guide* (1958), a novel in English, won the Sahitya Akademi Award, that the orthodox Indian literary establishment welcomed Indian writing in English in its midst.

The 1950s and the 1960s era was not a period of great innovation for Indian writing in English, but they did witness the emergence of many women writers who explored the conflict between tradition and modernity directly in relation to the condition of women. In these novels emancipation is often figured as a personal release into what seems a very literary realm of transcendence. Of the several that emerged during this period, the three most significant were Kamala Markandaya, Nayantara Sahgal, and Anita Desai.

Kamala Markandaya   Kamala Markandaya (1924–2004), was the pseudonym of Indian-born novelist Kamala Purnaiya Taylor, who wrote ten novels that present a stunning array of characters against a backdrop of neo-colonialism and a conflict between East and West. All her writings explored the tensions between western and Indian values, and between rural and urban life.

Born in Mysore, Markandaya studied history at Madras University and made her name with her first novel, *Nectar in the Sieve* (1954), which narrated the intense suffering of Rukhmini, an Indian peasant woman. It became a best seller in the United States. Following American writer Pearl Buck's chronicles of famine and suffering in China, Markandaya's novel describes the stoic endurance of Rukhmini, who, married at the age of twelve, uncomplainingly suffers extraordinary tragedies. In her second novel, *A Handful of Rice* (1966), she explores the lives of the urban poor, and her third, *The Golden Honeycomb* (1977), looks at the lives of Indian princes. In *The Nowhere Man* (1972) she deals with racial prejudice against Indian immigrants in Britain. It was followed by *Two Virgins* (1973). Her last novel was *Pleasure City* (1982), where the East-West confrontation is replaced by the competing demands of modernity and tradition. In this novel, a multinational company wishes to build a holiday resort by the sea, and the new development changes the lives of the quiet fishing village that has for centuries eked out a subsistence living from the sea (Narayan and Mee 2003; Naik and Narayan 2001).

Nayantara Sahgal   Nayantara Sahgal (1927–) is the daughter of Vijaylakshmi Pandit, sister of Jawaharlal Nehru, India's first prime minister. Her novels portray the life of the western-educated Indian elite— their hypocrisies, their lack of values, and how they have taken on the mantle of political power—seen from the vantage point of her privileged and powerful Nehru household. All nine of her novels are set against a background of major political events and often read like an extended lesson in Indian and world history. For instance, *A Time to Be Happy* (1958) is informed by the events leading to Indian independence; *Storm in Chandigarh* (1969), the partition of Punjab into Punjab and Haryana; *Rich Like Us* (1985) is set during the Emergency imposed by her cousin, Mrs. Indira Gandhi. The latter won the Sinclair Prize for fiction

as well as the Indian Sahitya Akademi Award.

Her next novel, *Plans for Departure* (1985), examines the complex Indo-British relationship through the story of a Danish woman who comes to India and leaves on the eve of World War I to marry an Englishman. Several decades later her son marries an Indian political activist. Her next novel, *Mistaken Identity* (1988), is set in the 1920s. The playboy son of a maharaja finds himself accused of sedition by the British colonial government and sent to prison for three years. The result is a hilarious encounter with militant union leaders and pacifist Gandhians, both trying to win him over to their separate causes (Naik and Narayan 2001).

Sahgal's recent *Lesser Breeds* (2003) is once again set during the freedom movement. Conceived in two halves, the first half is about a lecturer in English literature who fires up his students with enthusiasm for the freedom struggle only to find that three of them are beaten to death by the colonial police. In the second half, the lecturer's daughter goes to the United States for further education and is looked after by the sister of a liberal American journalist who had covered the freedom movement in India.

Anita Desai   Anita Desai (1937–) is one of the internationally best-known Indian women writers, and her themes are usually about dysfunctional relationships among individuals from the upper middle classes. Her early books all explore the fraught existence of women from this class— whether it is the daughter and young wife in *Cry, the Peacock* (1963); the middle-aged wife and mother in *Where Shall We Go This Summer?* (1975); the grandmother in

Fire on the Mountain (1977); or the sister in *Clear Light of Day* (1980).

In a change of style, Desai switched to male protagonists in her later books—*In Custody* (1984), about a journalist seeking out an Urdu poet for an interview at a time when Urdu poetry is dying in India, and *Baumgartner's Bombay* (1988), about the lonely life of a Jewish émigré who flees Nazi Germany and seeks refuge in India, only to witness Hindu-Muslim religious hatred. Desai moved to the United States in the early 1990s. Her novel *Journey to Ithaca* (1995) is a completely cliché-ridden, Eurocentric vision of India as a place of squalor and filth, god-men and fraudsters, heat and dust, thus occupying territory originally claimed by Ruth Prawar Jhabvala. (Jhabvala [1927–], a Polish writer married to an Indian, wrote about India, but essentially from a white woman's point of view. She is also a screenplay writer for many of the James Ivory–Ismail Merchant films. She moved to the United States in 1975.) Desai's *Fasting, Feasting* (1999) returns to the subject of dysfunctional Indian families, except this novel straddles India and the United States. In her recent novel *The Zigzag Way* (2004), she bids farewell to the Indian milieu to embrace an Irish American professor's search for roots via the history of Irish miners in Mexico.

Other Writers   India is the basis of the nonfiction books of Nirad Chaudhuri (1897–1999), who saw India as an essentially anti-intellectual country. His diatribes against his countrymen and women and most minorities were very provocative. His most famous book was *The Autobiography of an Unknown Indian* (1951), about growing into adulthood in the early decades of the century. He began writing in the year of independence when he was fifty, and his first trip to England is narrated in *Passage to England* (1959). His next book was *The Continent of Circe* (1965), where he expounds his theory that the climate of India made its colonizers into brutes regardless of whether they were Aryan or British. He saw Indians as a warlike race and fond of bloodshed, a shocking revelation to his countrymen, who saw themselves as most peace loving. In the early years of his writing career, he failed to find an Indian publisher, and *The Intellectual in India* (1967) was one of his first books to be published in India.

Khushwant Singh (1915–) wrote about the trauma of partition in his most famous book (considered by many as the best on the subject), *Train to Pakistan* (1956, published in the United States as *Mano Majra*). The partition of the country into India and Pakistan is represented as an event that the simple villagers of the Punjab who have lived together peacefully regardless of religious differences just cannot fathom. Finally, a generous and impulsive Sikh peasant, Jugga, saves the situation at the cost of his own life.

Singh has also written a well received two-volume *History of the Sikhs* (1963 and 1966) and was editor of the popular Indian magazine *The Illustrated Weekly of India* (1969–1978). In his general writings, he was an iconoclast who urged Indians to be less prudish and write more openly about sex. His recent essays in *The End of India* (2003) reveal his transformation from bawdy raconteur into melancholic doomsayer, but he recovers his bawdy touch with *Paradise and Other Stories* (2005). That novel was preceded by *Burial at Sea* (2004), a slim novella on Jawaharlal Nehru's supposed sexual relationship with a Hindu nun, Shraddha Mata. Although the names have been changed, Singh's lurid and sensationalist thesis states that Shraddha Mata was in fact an Indian Mata Hari, planted by the Hindu nationalists to subvert Nehru's secularist vision of India.

Another writer of the times was Ruskin Bond (1934–). An Anglo-Indian, Bond's first novel, *The Room on the Roof* (1956), won the John Llewllyn Rhys Memorial Prize. It presents a lonely Eurasian boy's quest for friendship and his whole-hearted enjoyment of the noisy life of the Indian bazaar, from which narrow-minded guardians have kept him away. Bond is best known for his short stories and as a children's writer. He writes in simple and unpretentious English and demonstrates great control over the language. Like R. K. Narayan, Bond specializes in writing about life in the small towns of India. In 2005, Bond published *A Face in the Dark*, a collection of ghost stories for both children and adults.

What was striking about the novelists of these two decades was that they demonstrated complete command of the dominant forms of the English novel; they showed that Indian novelists ought to be taken as seriously as western novel writers. In doing so they paved the way for the next generation of writers of the 1980s and 1990s.

1980s Onward

The appearance of Salman Rushdie's magnum opus, *Midnight's Children*, in 1981 ushered in a new era of Indian writing in English.

Rushdie, born in 1947 a few months before India achieved independence, was educated in Bombay and England. His second book, *Midnight's Children* (1981), was a runaway success and won the Booker Prize that year. (In 1993, it won the "Booker of Bookers"—the best of the twenty-six books that had won the Booker Prize from the time it was instituted in 1969.) The novel's protagonist, Saleem Sinai, is born at the same moment as India achieves independence—at midnight on 15 August 1947—and over the next twenty-five years the history of his life is closely linked to the history of the nation. Funny, irreverent, magical, and powerful, the book recounts the birth and coming of age of a man and a nation simultaneously. Rushdie's novel covers the most important events of the period—the war with Pakistan, the creation of Bangladesh in 1971, and the Emergency imposed by Mrs. Indira Gandhi in 1975. Just like the Hindu epics that featured a master narrator who dictated his narrative to an amanuensis, in *Midnight's Children* Rushdie rewrites India's history in epic narrative style using a narrator. Rushdie paints a vast canvas, and despite the novel's rambling style and digressions, he weaves together several different strands—political fantasy, comedy, surrealism, or its contemporary counterpart *magic realism*—and then ties up the narrative with vivacious word play, puns, and scores of stylistic experiments.

His next book, *Shame* (1983), looks at political events in Pakistan, in particular the execution of the democratically elected prime minister, Zulfikar Ali Bhutto, by the military dictator Zia ul Haq. His *The Satanic Verses* (1984) takes creative liberties in the retelling of certain parts of the Koran and was banned in India and many other Muslim countries. It earned Rushdie a *fatwa*, or death sentence, from the Ayatollah Khomeini, forcing him to go into hiding. During his seclusion, he wrote *Haroun*

Salman Rushdie, England, 2000.
(Rune Hellestad/Corbis)

and the Sea of Stories (1991), stories for adults and children, and also put together a collection of essays, *Imaginary Home-lands* (1991*)*. His later books are *The Moor's Last Sigh* (1996), *The Ground Beneath Her Feet* (1999), and *Fury* (2001). His most recent novel is *Shalimar The Clown* (2005), a story about love, betrayal, and revenge.

According to many historians of Indian literature in English, Rushdie's imaginative use of language, with wit, puns, satire, and magic realism (or surrealism) on a vast canvas of characters and events recalls the work of G. V. Desani (1909–2000), born in Nairobi, Kenya, and of Indian origin. Broadcaster for the BBC as well as poet and playwright, Desani's most important contribution was *All About H. Hatterr*

(1948), where Indian English jostles against the rules of grammar and diction, Shakespeare combines with Indian legal-ese, and cockney with *babuisms.*

Desani's novel concerns the growing up story of a mad-hatterish hero, H. Hatterr, son of a European merchant seaman and a lady from Penang. Set in British India, the story tells Hatterr's attempts to find a higher truth amid the hypocritical religious affectations of Indian culture on the one hand and the social hypocrisies of British culture on the other. Desani heralds the fiction of latter-day writers such as Salman Rushdie in *Midnight's Children* (1981) and also I. Allan Sealy's *The Trotter-Nama: A Chronicle* (1987). In fact, his linguistic experimentation and irreverence were even more revolutionary than those found in contemporary Indian fiction.

In Rushdie's books, the teeming metropolis of Bombay (now Mumbai), a city of immigrants, and Rushdie's own status as an immigrant, first in the United Kingdom and later the United States, are brought together. Rootlessness is a common theme. The use of the colloquial English dialects of Bombay and the film industry made him the first to put to use in his books both the high culture of India and its popular culture. But most important, Rushdie showed the rest of the Indian writers how to be post-colonial—how to appropriate the English language and bend it in any direction to sensational effect. He gave the Indian writers in English the confidence to exploit the rich diversity of India and Indian culture for their own ends.

The success of *Midnight's Children* gave new writers the confidence to address the issues such as "imagining the nation." Prior to Rushdie's example, the writer in English tried to demonstrate how "Indian" he or she could be while writing in an "alien" language. Rushdie's success paved the way for Indian writers to be published by major publishing houses, and new, untried Indian writers have begun to sign lucrative contracts. The change in circumstances for Indian writing can be gauged by comparison with the early careers of Anand and Narayan. Anand's first novel, *Untouchable*, was ignored by nineteen British publishers in 1935, and R. K. Narayan managed to secure a publisher only due to the intervention of British writer Graham Greene (Naik and Narayan 2001).

Rushdie's fame also identified an international audience for Indian writers in English as well as an English-reading public in India. Consequently, there have been commercial developments in English-language publishing within India that have enabled a new crop of Indian writers to come forward. Penguin India was set up in 1985, and Rupa Paperbacks and IndiaInk have emerged to provide a marketing network able to deliver affordable English-language fiction to the expanding urban middle class.

In the wake of Rushdie's success came a torrent of new talent writing in English. Shama Futehally (1952–) wrote *Tara Lane* (1993), about a Muslim industrialist class. Her most recent book, *Reaching Bombay Central* (2002), is about a train journey undertaken by a Muslim woman and her encounter with different people.

Amit Chaudhari (1962–) wrote *A Strange and Sublime Address* (1991), *Afternoon Raag* (1993), *Freedom Song* (1998), and *A New World* (2000). His books are imbued with a lyrical sense of loss and disorientation at the diversity of India, the very diversity that Rushdie revels in. Heterogeneity is also the theme of Kiran Nagarkar's (1949–)

Ravan and Eddie (1995) and *Seven Sixes Are Forty-Three*. The author translated the latter from his Marathi version published in 1974.

Rohington Mistry (1952–), who lives in Canada and has twice been short-listed for the Booker Prize, often describes his Parsi background in his novels. His first novel, *Such a Long Journey* (1991), uses as background the real-life mysterious "Nagarvala" case of a bank fraud perpetrated by a Parsi, a fraud that even had implications for the political career of Mrs. Indira Gandhi. His second novel, *A Fine Balance* (1996), a tale of two tailors set against the horrors of the Emergency in 1975, was also short listed for the Booker Prize but panned by the feminist writer, critic, and media personality Germaine Greer. He returned to his roots in *Family Matters* (2002), a story about a dying man and his two daughters set against the Mumbai riots and Hindu extremists. Oprah Winfrey chose the book for her Book Club.

I. Allan Sealy (1951–) wrote *The Trotter-Nama: A Chronicle* (1988), a sprawling saga of a family of Anglo-Indians, a community whose presence troubles the imagining of the nation in terms of a homogeneous cultural authenticity. Sealy's later works include *Hero* (1990), a parody of a south Indian film star who moves from cinema to politics; *The Everest Hotel: A Calendar* (1998), about the plight of some soul-searching Anglo-Indians trapped in a world to which they no longer belong. His recent book *The Brain-Fever Bird* (2003) is a post-Soviet novel about an unemployed scientist from the now redundant Soviet biological weapons program who works as a chauffeur at the Indian consulate. He flies to India to sell his knowledge but is waylaid en route by a puppet artist.

Many writers feel that there are countless Indian forms that can be revived and intelligently reworked so that Indian modernism need not be a wholesale imitation of Western forms. Rather than simply placing contemporary material in traditional forms, which would tend to define India in terms of the glories of an unchanging past, novelists of this period have been much more willing to rewrite the genres of Indian literary tradition. Nor has Indian tradition simply been understood as a repertoire of classical literary forms but as popular culture as well. Hindi film has had an important influence on recent fiction, providing a set of symbols, new kinds of narrative technique, and a new subject matter, as in Ruchir Joshi's *The Last Jet-Engine Laugh*, 2001, and Sealy's subsequent novel *Hero*. Shashi Tharoor (1956–) wrote *The Great Indian Novel* (1989) and followed it with *Show Business* (1994), a spoof on the Hindi film industry. He has since moved to a biography with *Nehru: The Invention of India* (2003).

Two novelists who address the issue of translating Indian history into the novel are Mukul Kesavan and Vikram Chandra. In *Looking through Glass* (1995), Kesavan (1957–) looks at the Muslim community, which has often been erased from nationalist history, and offers a different perspective on the closing years of the struggle for independence. The protagonist falls out of a train and finds himself in 1942, amid the Quit India agitation, and a Muslim family offers him refuge. In the novel, not only has he traveled across time but also across cultures.

If these novelists share an interest in retrieving suppressed histories, they also bring to the fore the act of narration. In these historical novels, the nation is written in terms of its "unruly excessiveness."

According to critic Jon Mee, the Sanskrit aesthetic principle *atyukti*, or excessive saying, is practiced to demonstrate it. Digressions, repetitions, and fantastic events push the traditional form of the novel to its limits and often at the center of the textual carnival is the body itself (Mee 2003).

Unlike the magic realist mode of Rushdie and his followers, Vikram Seth's *A Suitable Boy* (1993), which took ten years to write, is a 1,300-page romance set in the classic realist mode and placed in post-independent India of the 1950s as it progresses toward a secular, commercial society in the image of conventional western models of development. He reveals an Indian bourgeoisie emerging from religious superstition and social snobbery and shows progress as secularism that requires the casting away of concerns about traditional identities and pursuing a liberal economic mode (Mee 2003). Seth moved away from the subject of India and Indians to focus on music and Europe in his next novel, *An Equal Music* (1999). His most recent novel, *Two Lives* (2005), is about the lives of the author's uncle and his German-Jewish wife buffeted by World War II and its aftermath.

The new young writers include Pankaj Mishra (1969–), author of the travelogue *Butter Chicken in Ludhiana: Travels in Small Town India* (1995), and more recently the ambitious *An End to Suffering: The Buddha in the World* (2004), which tries to explain Buddhism in the world and Mishra's own quest for meaning. The book covers a wide sweep from Vedanta to the Enlightenment to Osama bin Laden via Nietzsche, Marx, Schopenhauer, and Borges, to mention just a few fellow travelers.

Suketu Mehta's (1963–) nonfiction *Maximum City: Bombay Lost and Found*

(2004), about the New York–based writer's personal rediscovery of Mumbai via the Indian underworld, extra-judicial police killings, the Hindi film industry, the Hindu fundamentalists, transvestites, and bar girls, has won widespread praise.

Women Writers The contemporary women writers of India do not replicate the epic scale of the books by males where Indian history is rewritten and the nation reimagined. Instead, while the men explore history, the women writers explore the domestic space in their novels. One of the leading contemporary female writers is Shashi Deshpande (1938–), who began as a writer of short stories. Her novels—*The Dark Holds No Terrors* (1980), *Roots and Shadow* (1983), *The Long Silence* (1988), *The Binding Vine* (1992), and *Small Remedies* (2000)—present the situation of women trapped in an urban, middle-class life. Critics concur that it was with *The Long Silence*, which won the Sahitya Akademi Award, that Deshpande emerged as a mature writer. In the book, an upper-middle-class woman with two teenage children finds that her husband has engaged in fraud and that they must move to a cheaper and less salubrious locality. Deshpande uncovers the shallow middle-class values of convenient arranged marriages, the upwardly mobile husband, and children in "good" schools. Her recent novel, *Moving On* (2004), returns to the theme of the Indian family and the trapped woman.

Gita Hariharan (1954–), novelist, short story writer, and children's writer, experiments with narration, but not in the epic mode like her male counterparts. *The Thousand Faces of Nights* (1992) and *The Ghosts of Vasu Master* (1994) are concerned with rewriting folk tales and chil-

dren's stories wherein problem children are won over by story telling. Her recent novel, *In Times of Siege* (2003), is about a university professor of history who inadvertently invites the wrath of the Hindu fundamentalists with his treatise on the twelfth-century poet Basava's radical opposition to the caste system.

A new woman writer on the Indian diaspora is Jhumpa Lahiri, born in 1967 to Bengali parents in the United Kingdom and educated in the United States, whose first collection of short stories, *Interpreter of Maladies* (1999), won her the Pulitzer Prize. In her first novel, *The Namesake* (2003), she explores the world of the Bengali expatriates.

The most famous of the women writers is Arundhati Roy (1960–), a social activist whose first and, so far, only novel, *The God*

Arundhati Roy won the Booker Prize for her book *The God of Small Things.* New Delhi, 1999. (Robert van der Hilst/Corbis)

of Small Things (1997), won the Booker Prize. Again the use of narration, of the space of women, and the bigger picture of politics driven by patriarchs forms the deep tragedy that lies at the center of the book. The domestic and personal lie in an uneasy relationship with the wider national and political context.

Pulp Fiction

Shobhaa De (1948–), better known as the "Maharani of Muck" (as well as the "Princess of Porn," the "Rani of Raunch," and the "Sultana of Sleaze") is loved by her readers and hated by the critics. None of this distracts from the fact that she is India's best-selling English-language author. Even in a traditional and conservative society like India, sex sells. De, a one-time model and editor of gossip magazines, found a gap in the market and decided to put her talents to writing about it from a female point of view. She has completed over a dozen titles. The object of her scrutiny has invariably been the lives of rich and bored urban cosmopolitan women.

De sharpened her writing skills in the 1970s as editor of *Stardust*, founded by Nari Hira, owner of Magna Publications, who has often been compared to Rupert Murdoch because of his penchant for yellow journalism. *Stardust*, which offers an unrelenting fare of salacious gossip and innuendo, shocked and captivated Indian readers, who had never read anything on such a thrilling scale before. Adding to his stable of lightweight magazines, Hira followed up *Stardust* with *Society*, once again edited by De. (All of Hira's magazines start with the *S* sound: Stardust, Society, Showbiz, Savvy, Citadel, and so forth.)

De's first foray into novels (which she took to writing after allegedly falling out with Hira over stock options) was *Socialite Nights* (1988), an autobiographical novel with the more complex bits neatly airbrushed out of her narrative. This was followed by *Starry Nights* (1991), her all-time best seller about a Bollywood starlet who sleeps her way to the top of the pyramid. (Following her mentor's example, all of De's book titles also begin with the letter *S*.) The book sold 35,000 copies. That may seem a small number to anyone outside India, but it was enough to keep Penguin Books in business. Penguin had opened in India in 1985, but had initially struggled to stay afloat. The average sales for successful books are between 7,500 to 10,000 copies. The spectacular selling power of De's novels helped Penguin to stay in business. Her subsequent books—*Sisters* (1992), *Strange Obsession* (1992), *Sultry Days* (1994), and *Snapshots* (1995)— brought her run of soft-porn chick-lit to a temporary halt. She then moved to writing more of the same for television soaps (*Swabhimaan*).

There has always been a large market for popular English fiction in India, from Mills and Boon romances to "airport" novels. But such fiction was always imported or reprinted in cheaper Indian editions. Never before was it written by Indians in India (Dwyer 2000). For being the first to introduce the "sex and shopping" genre into India, De's place in Indian popular literature is assured.

De has also accepted credit for introducing "Hinglish" or Hindi slang into novels written in English, although the trend was originally started by the late Devyani Chaubal, a sensational, subversive, irreverent, fiery, and much feared film journalist who signed her gossip columns as "Devi." De borrowed Devi's techniques in *Stardust*, and during their reign as gossip queens they were the Hedda Hopper and Louella Parsons of India. Rushdie incorporates this form of Hinglish into his novels, as do other Indian writers in English. Upamanyu Chatterjee's *English, August* (1988) opens with the words: "Amazing mix . . . *Hazaar* f***ed. Urdu and American . . . I'm sure nowhere else could language be mixed and spoken with such ease" (quoted in Mee 2003: 320).

De is also important because she is a "brand" in her own right and has heralded the incipient consumerist culture of India. Her novels are all set in a world of consumerist fantasies, where sex and shopping are locked in a lusty embrace. *Starry Nights* was a groundbreakingly lascivious book about Bollywood films, which borrowed freely and unabashedly from a variety of sources and included a sex act in an aircraft washroom taken straight from the soft-porn French film *Emmanuelle* (1973). *Sisters* was set in an industrialist family, while *Sultry Days* and *Strange Obsession* explore the world of advertising and modeling respectively, the latter via lesbianism and kinky sex.

De claims her women as winners. They may well be, but they do so through sex and manipulation. They are conspicuous consumers in the modern capitalist societies in the burgeoning cities of contemporary India. Most Indian feminists hotly contest her alleged feminist credentials, and Kali for Women, a publishing company set up in 1984 by two feminists to publish fiction by women, has never shown any desire to publish her books.

De, as skilled as Madonna in constantly reinventing herself, according to feature writer Miranda Kennedy, is currently trying to establish her reputation as a thinker and serious columnist. This is a pity, because she is best when she is irreverent and subversive (Kennedy 2004).

Amar Chitra Katha and the Revolution in Indian Comic Books

Amar Chitra Katha is the most celebrated form of comic books in India. It was started by Anant Pai for International Book House in 1967, and the genesis of the Indian comic book genre, until then a monopoly of British and American publishing houses, is an interesting one. According to Frances Pritchett, who conducted an indepth study of the genre, Pai was horrified to see that during a quiz show on Indian television in Delhi the juvenile contestants knew all the answers to the questions on Greek mythology but none on Hindu mythology—and this in a city where each year for ten long days they enact scenes from the *Ramayana* (Pritchett 1995).

He returned to Mumbai determined to remedy this failing. Earlier, the company had tried unsuccessfully to translate Classics Illustrated Comics into Hindi. This time, instead of rendering English comics into Indian languages the company decided to produce Indian comics in English. At first success eluded them, but eventually the series made (and continues to make) publishing history.

The subject matter at first was Hindu mythology, particularly the epics—the *Ramayana* and the *Mahabharata*. The very first volume was on the life of the Hindu god Krishna. But, uncertain about its reception in the mass market, they printed only 10,000 copies. It went on to sell over a half-million copies. After that, Amar Chitra Katha went on to produce over 500 titles covering a vast range of subjects, each overseen by a central editorial committee comprising Pai and his assistants, and each in a standard format of thirty-two pages.

There are currently ninety titles on Hindu mythology in the Amar Chitra Katha series. There are also comics on Indian folktales and legends (fifty-six titles), teachers and saints (twenty-seven), Buddhist tales (twenty-four), tales from ancient Indian history (fourteen), makers of modern India (thirteen), great women of India (thirteen), and an assortment of stories from Sanskrit classics, histories, and biographies of kings, scientists, doctors, and others. By 1993, its total sales were over 78 million copies (Pritchett 1995).

Most of these retellings from the epics are an amalgam of different sources and different tellings of the same myths. Sex, violence, and any form of strife or controversy are deliberately avoided, and great pains are taken to avoid issues of superstition. The ignominies of caste and "untouchability" are often roundly condemned in the texts. The series soon became the ultimate source of information for a lot of readers, both children and adults. Pai recounts an incident in which two senior officials decided to settle their dispute over a minor historical fact by consulting the comic book on the subject (Pritchett 1995).

The most important objective of the series was to educate Indian children about their classical and religious heritage. Written in English, although there were translations into some (though not all) of the Indian languages, the series was aimed primarily at middle-class children as a vehicle of both entertainment and education. Children who have been educated in En-glish generally have attended urban Christian missionary or westernized schools where a western ethos prevails. Children educated in the vernacular languages are generally less westernized and more aware of their own regional cultures.

Consequently it was felt that large numbers of the urban, English-speaking, school-going Hindu population remained unacquainted with their own culture. The Amar Chitra Katha responded primarily to the perceived need to educate these urban children on the glories of their own Hindu traditions. The series also educated whole generations of expatriate Indian children on Indian mythology, folklore, history, and other aspects of Indian culture, taking on the role, in many ways, of the grandmother and becoming for these children the primary source of stories about India (Pritchett 1995).

The series dominated the Indian comic book scene and soon became a victim of its own success. It has been found guilty by academics of a variety of sins. It has been accused of being excessively nationalistic, contriving to show India as a homogeneous entity and ignoring the inner political and social tensions during its fight for freedom against the British. It has also been accused of sins of omissions in its library of modern hagiographies with regard to particular religious minorities, such as the Muslims, women, and the lower castes.

Compiled at a time when nation-building and national integration were seen as important goals for a young country that had already suffered partition into India and Pakistan, it is not surprising that the series strove to provide a harmonious and homogeneous portrait of the nation and its peoples with all dissension and internal tension cut out of the narratives.

There is no doubt that each new issue of the Amar Chitra Katha is created within a field of tensions—commercial versus educational values, accuracy versus the need to appease particular interest groups, a commitment to Indian history versus a commitment to national integration. The end products have been the fascinating result of an extraordinarily complex series of choices. And despite the criticisms, Amar Chitra Katha remains a unique feature of the histories of Indian publishing and Indian popular culture.

Seeing a bright future for comics in India, Marvel Comics launched an indigenized version of *Spiderman* in August 2004. In a joint venture between Marvel Enterprises, the owners of the Spiderman brand, and Gotham Entertainment Group, the Indian publishing licensee of Marvel Comics, the radioactive arachnid Peter Brubaker becomes Pavitr Prabhakar and his love, Mary Jane, becomes Meera Jain (Padmanabhan 2004).

Issues

Writing in English

At the heart of Indian literature in English lies a conundrum: Is English really an Indian language? The language introduced by a colonizing power has remained entrenched in India for over two centuries. It is, in India's political history, a language of power and command. But because of India's cultural and linguistic diversity, it has also become the language through which India communicates with its diverse populations. Consequently, it has become yet another of India's languages—but one with a privileged position. Today it remains an elite language, the language of business,

the language associated with modernity. English is also the language with which India communicates with the rest of the world. The problem that arises within India is the inequality of access to English, which brings with it the problems of communication among classes.

Raja Rao's preface to his first novel, *Kanthapura* (1938), explains the difficulty of bridging the cultural and historical gap between the English language and the Indian tale: "One has to describe in a language not one's own the spirit that is one's own" (Gandhi 2003: 180). The problem, he suggests, can be resolved by an indigenization of English—by infusing it with the breathless and unpunctuated "tempo of Indian life." Furthermore, faced with the indisputably western origins of the novel form, the Indian writer in English is required to undertake the rather more difficult task of generic appropriation by relocating his narrative within the epic traditions of the *Ramayana* and *Mahabharata*. This project inevitably requires a departure from the necessarily secular content and structure of the European novel to admit, instead, the random magic or "legendary history" of some "god or godlike hero." This objective is secured through a formal "magic realist" blend of the fantastic and the mundane, just as the postcolonial writers such as Rushdie and the others have since done. Thus there is a simultaneous need for indigenization as well as a globalization (Gandhi 2003: 182).

The initial espousal of English in the nineteenth century by reformers and modernizers such as Ram Mohan Roy led to the introduction of English as the medium of instruction in schools and universities. Many with an English education urged other Indians to write in English. However, as the independence movement gathered strength, and nationalism took hold of the educated classes, the question of language became a vexatious one. Some, such as the great Bengali poet and Nobel Prize winner for literature in 1917 Rabindranath Tagore (1861–1941), had reservations about Indians writing in English. But other leaders of the independence movement were very robust in their defense of the English language. Gandhi, with his legendary pragmatism, saw it as an instrument of communication. He opposed what it stood for—colonialism and cultural degradation—not the language itself. Gandhi wrote many of his books in English, as did Nehru, and both leaders were beneficiaries of a western education. C. Rajagopalchari resolved the dilemma by astutely claiming English as "Saraswati's [a Hindu goddess's] gift to India" (Gandhi 2003: 173).

Gandhi and Nehru, both leaders of the struggle for Indian independence, wrote extensively in English. Nehru's long spells in prison resulted in a prolific output of history writing—such as *Glimpses of World History* (1934) and the *Discovery of India* (1946). Writers also sought inspiration from Gandhi's journals, such as *Young India* (1919–1932) and *Harijan* (1933–1948). It was in the pages of the former that Mulk Raj Anand read Gandhi's account of the untouchable Uka, which informed his subsequent book *Untouchable*. Raja Rao claimed familiarity with Gandhi's autobiography *The Story of My Experiments with Truth* (vol. 1, 1927; vol. 2, 1929).

Thus it was through texts such as Gandhi's *My Experiments*, Nehru's *Autobiography* (1936), General Mohan Singh's *Leaves from My Diary* (1946), and Vijaylakshmi Pandit's *So I Became a Minister* (1935)—not to mention the profusion of

prison letter-writing in this period—that practitioners of the novel form acquired a quite specific understanding of the contiguity between personal and political prose, between narratives of subjectivity and those of nationalism. Moreover, many of the writers of the 1930s and 1940s wrote both in English and their regional languages: Bhabani Bhattacharya wrote in Bengali and English, Raja Rao in Kannada and English, Ahmed Ali in Urdu and English, and Mulk Raj Anand in Punjabi, Urdu, and English.

After independence, the Indian Constitution made Hindi the national language, but English was to be allowed to continue as the language for all official purposes of the Union for a period of fifteen years, that is, until 1965. Many had felt the absence of a national language that could draw together a nation. But in the political climate of the time, English symbolized everything that was wrong with the country and Hindi and the mother tongues everything that was right. English was to be the language of the colonial past, Hindi and the mother tongues the languages of the future. But Nehru wanted no legislation on languages. He felt allowing English to continue would in fact revitalize Indian languages.

Besides, the south was opposed to Hindi, and soon the nation was divided into anti-English and pro-English lobbies. "We are Indians not Hindians!" read one of the banners at an anti-Hindi demonstration in the south. Eventually English was retained in the south, and after 1960 English was accepted as an Indian language. The same year the Sahitya Akademi offered for the first time its prize to an English-language novel.

Although after independence Nehru fought to retain English in India for national communication, the Indian fiction writer in English felt that the end was nigh. Many felt that writing in English was a sign of "Anglo-mania," and many of the novels of the 1950s and 1960s seem to be highly skeptical of the dominant forms of Indian culture and society, choosing to find a more "authentic" idea of India in traditional village life. Maybe, suggests critic Jon Mee, there was a denial by the elite writers about their situation of writing in English in a land of uneducated millions. Indeed, few writers of the period show any affection for the elite, metropolitan personal lives that most of them led (Mee 2003).

Animosity toward English was largely the animosity felt towards the social class that English had come to be identified with: a narrow, well-entrenched, metropolitan-based ruling elite that has dominated Indian life for more than fifty years. But those who write, in any case, belong to a privileged group. For some critics the very playfulness of language used in the post-Rushdie novels confirms the privileges of a class of Indians who have no anxieties attached to their uses of English and who are secure enough in their own elitism to experiment with a language that they have spoken since birth. There is no doubt that the provenance of writers of English is a narrow class band comprising academics, editors, and other inhabitants of the book trade. English is thus a "supra-language" that is "cultural-written-formal" rather than "social-oral-conversational" within the national linguistic context (Mehrotra 2003: 18), and it is this middle-class world that provides the most obvious context for the new Indian writing in English. Over the decades the nation has moved from the village centrism of the Gandhian era to the city centrism of the post-Nehru period.

Today, the reason for writing in English in India is also a commercial one. English literature by Indians has come of age both in India and overseas. Both new and old writers have been landing contracts worth multiple millions of dollars. (Vikram Seth is said to have signed a US$1.8 million contract for *A Suitable Boy*.) Some critics believe that India's writers in English retreat into a metropolitan or cosmopolitan elitism that produces a literature intended only for the English-speaking privileged classes within India and the international public outside. Others feel that Indian writing in English is writing for export as an exoticized spectacle of "otherness" for a western readership.

The Publishing Industry

India has around 11,000 publishers and produces a total of 70,000 titles annually in eighteen different languages (Mehta 2004). The industry is valued at around US$1 billion a year. Before independence India was an export market for British publishing houses. Since then, most Indian publishers have concentrated on textbooks for schools and universities in Hindi, English, and the eighteen regional languages. In 1961, the Indian government set up the National Council of Educational Research and Training (NCERT) to develop model textbooks for adoption and publication by all Indian states. By the late 1960s the various Indian states had set up their own state textbook boards. Even today, the Indian government is the largest publishing house in India, and the combined efforts of NCERT, the State Text Book Boards, the National Book Trust, and the Publication Division of the Government of India have, until now, constituted the largest share of the publishing industry. Some of the subject areas were farmed out to private publishing houses that survived on such government contracts for textbooks. Publishing houses began to specialize in specific areas of study. Thus, Popular Prakashan cornered the market in textbooks in English on medicine and social studies, whereas Jaico Books poured its energies into books on engineering and management.

However, since the boom in Indian literature in English, particularly after the success of Salman Rushdie's *Midnight's Children*, the publishing industry has grown dramatically (10–12 percent annually), and the number of private publishers has risen. Furthermore, thanks to improved technology and rapid developments in Indian printing, publishing houses from overseas have also awakened to the potential of the Indian market and have set up Indian imprints. One of the first publishing houses to set up in India was Penguin Books (followed later by its children's section, Puffin), which established Penguin India in 1985. Initially, it brought out about 6 titles annually; today it publishes over 200. Other major publishers in English include Rupa Co. (an Indian imprint of HarperCollins), Picador, IndiaInk, Permanent Black, Yeti, Roli Books, and Sage. There are also publishing houses devoted to women's literature and women's studies, such as Katha, Kali for Women, and Women Unlimited.

In global terms, however, the Indian publishing industry represents just 0.5 percent of global publishing. The challenge of the Indian market is to deliver good quality printing at low costs. Unlike the United States and the United Kingdom, where a minimum print run is around 5,000, in India it is just 2,000 (Mehta 2004). Penguin India has a 10,000 Club for writers who have achieved sales of 10,000 copies and more. There are however just 103 members of the club, and most of them are veterans such as R. K. Narayan, Khushwant Singh, Rabindranath Tagore, Ruskin Bond, and Shobhaa De. Around 25–30 percent of books published achieve sales of 7,500–10,000, and of these, one in two might sell 25,000 copies over two years.

The problems that plague the still nascent publishing industry are myriad. First of all, India does not have a culture of literary agents. Writers regularly accuse publishers of a lack of professionalism and complain that they provide them with little or no support. For instance, there are sometimes book launches without books on hand. Another problem is that of little or poor editing by publishing houses. Furthermore, most publishers have no publicity divisions, and even the organization of book reviews is completely uncoordinated. Additionally, most bookshops are small, independent, and family owned. Crossword is the only significant retail book chain, with sixteen outlets; Oxford University Press has five. Finally, there are few literary magazines that can provide space for short stories and opportunities for a writer to be known.

Conclusion

Despite the issues surrounding the complex position English holds in India and with Indian publishers, the Indian publishing industry expects a bright future, thanks to the variety of talent that has blossomed since Rushdie's international success. Indian writers are today supremely confident of their skills and are aware of their global potential. Besides, the Indian diaspora has undoubtedly provided an exciting new dimension to Indian literature in English. With better access to books, improved libraries, better book marketing, and a young population (half of India's population is under the age of twenty-five), the future of Indian literature in English is promising.

A to Z Index

Mulk Raj Anand (1905–2004) is known as the father of Indian literature in English. A Gandhian-Marxist and versatile writer, his best-known work is *Untouchable.* He is also famous for his trilogy *The Village*, *Across Black Waters*, and *The Sword and the Sickle*, which critiques the prevailing social injustices in India.

Upamanyu Chatterjee (1959–) is part of the Indian administrative service, and his novels reflect the preserve of the elite administrative class. *English, August* (1988) is a humorous account of the life of the civil servant in the districts. Director Mahesh Dattani has made it into a film. Chatterjee wrote a sequel, *The Mammaries of the Welfare State*, in 2000.

Nirad Chaudhuri (1897–1999) was a controversial writer of nonfiction. His most famous book was *The Autobiography of an Unknown Indian* (1951), about growing into adulthood in the early decades of the century.

Shobhaa De (1948–) has been a model, newspaper columnist, and editor of film gossip and society magazines. She is also the queen of Indian pulp fiction in English. She scandalized the Indian intelligentsia with her brand of "sex and shopping" books.

Anita Desai (1937–) has written fourteen novels to date. She moved to the United States in the early 1990s, and her recent novel, *The Zigzag Way* (2004), moves away from the subject of India to trace the Irish roots in Mexico of an American professor.

G. V. Desani (1909–2000) was born in Nairobi, Kenya, of Indian origin. His most important literary contribution was *All About H. Hatterr* (1948), where he creatively experiments with language by mixing up the rules of grammar and diction. His humor, wit, wordplay, and irreverent boisterousness have been considered the inspiration to Salman Rushdie and the post-Rushdie writers.

Shashi Deshpande (1938–) is a writer rooted in the Indian tradition, and she writes mainly about urban women, their claustrophobic family relationships, and the crises and tragedies that they survive. Her most famous novel is *The Long Silence* (1988), for which she won the Sahitya Akademi award. To date she written nine novels, short stories (published in six collections), and children's fiction.

Gita Hariharan (1954–) is a novelist, short story writer, and children's writer. Her latest novel, *In Times of Siege* (2003), is about a university professor of history who inadvertently invites the wrath of the Hindu fundamentalists with his treatise on the twelfth-century poet Basava's radical opposition to the caste system.

Jhumpa Lahiri (1967–), born in London to Bengali parents and educated in the United States, is a writer on the Indian diaspora. Her first book, *Interpreter of Maladies* (1999), is a collection of short stories that won the Pulitzer Prize. Her recent book, *The Namesake* (2003), is a novel on the Bengali diaspora in the United States.

Kamala Markandaya (1924–2004) was one of the early women writers who made a valuable contribution to the canon of Indo-Anglican literature. She wrote about villagers, poverty, and female suffering. Her most famous book, *Nectar in the Sieve*, is about the stoic suffering of Rukhmini, who endures with dignity all the tragedies that befall her.

Rohington Mistry (1952–) evokes his Parsi background for his first novel, *Such a Long Journey*, by investigating the mysterious Nagarvala case about bank fraud that had implications for Mrs. Indira Gandhi. He returns to his roots in *Family Matters* (2002), a novel about a dying man and his two daughters set against the Mumbai riots and the Hindu extremists.

R. K. Narayan (1906–2001), the author of thirty-four novels, was one of the few Indian writers to hone his skills entirely in India. His name is synonymous with Malgudi, a fictional colonial district town, which he created in his first book, *Swami and Friends* (1935). He was the brother of India's greatest cartoonist, R. K. Laxman.

Progressive Writers Association (PWA) was a Marxist group of radical Indian writers formed in 1935 in London. The PWA believed that the new literature of India should actively deal with the problems of hunger and poverty, social backwardness, and political subjugation.

Raja Rao (1908–) studied in France and has since lived in Europe and the United States. His novels explore philosophy and Indian mysticism. *The Serpent and the Rope* (1960), his most celebrated novel, is a semi-autobiographical account of a marriage between intellectuals that is destroyed by philosophical discord.

Arundhati Roy (1960–) is a social activist who won the Booker Prize with her first and only novel, *The God of Small Things*, set in Kerala. She was the second Indian after Rushdie to do so. Some critics found the book exhaustingly "overwritten."

Salman Rushdie (1947–) paved the way for a new chapter in Indian literature in English. Almost all his books have won awards. His most famous book is *Midnight's Children* (1981). His style of writing is reminiscent of a riotous carnival: exuberant, surreal, and witty, heralding magic realism.

Nayantara Sahgal (1927–) is the daughter of Vijaylakshmi Pandit, sister of Jawaharlal Nehru, India's first prime minister. Her novels portray the life of the western-educated Indian elite. Her most famous novel, *Rich Like Us* (1985), is set during the Emergency imposed by her cousin, Mrs. Indira Gandhi. It won the Sahitya Akademi Award.

I. Allan Sealy (1951–) wrote his first novel, *The Trotter-Nama: A Chronicle*, a sprawling history of his Anglo-Indian family in the style of the great royal Indian chronicles. His *The Everest Hotel: A Calendar* (1998) was short-listed for the Booker Prize. His recent book *The Brain-Fever Bird* (2003) is set in post–Soviet Union Russia.

Vikram Seth (1952–) is best known for his 1,300-page saga *A Suitable Boy* (1993), which took him ten years to write. Set in post-independence 1950s India, it is about marriage-making and fragile Hindu-Muslim relations. In his next novel *An Equal Music* (1999) he moved away from the subject of India and Indians to set a romance among Europeans in London and Vienna. He has also written a collection of poems, *The Golden Gate* (1986).

Khushwant Singh (1915–) is a sensationalistic journalist, editor, and libidinous writer, with over 100 books to his credit. His best-known works are *Train to Pakistan* (1956) and two scholarly tomes on the *History of the Sikhs* (1963–1966).

Bibliography and References

Dash, Sandhyarani. *Form and Vision in the Novels of Anita Desai*. New Delhi: Prestige, 1996.

Dhar, T. N. *History-Fiction Interface in Indian English Novel: Mulk Raj Anand, Nayantara Sahgal, Salman Rushdie, Shahsi Tharoor, O. V. Vijayan*. New Delhi: Prestige, 1999.

Dhawan, R. K., ed. *The Novels of Mulk Raj Anand*. New York: Prestige, 1992.

———, ed. *Nirad Chaudhuri: The Extraordinary Scholar*. New Delhi: Prestige, 2000.

Dingwaney, Anuradha. "Salman Rushdie." In *An Illustrated History of Indian Literature in English*, edited by Arvind Krishna Mehrotra. Delhi: Permanent Black, 2003.

Dodhiya, Jaydipsinh, ed. *Shobha De: Critical Studies*. New Delhi: Prestige, 2000.

———, ed. *The Fiction of Rohington Mistry: Critical Studies*. New Delhi: Prestige, 1999.

Dwyer, Rachel. "Pulp Fiction? The Books of Shobha De." In *All You Want Is Money, All You Need Is Love: Sexuality and Romance in Modern India*. London: Cassell, 2000.

———. "Shooting Stars: The Indian Film Magazine, *Stardust*." In *Pleasure and the Nation: The History, Politics and Consumption of Public Culture in India*, edited by Rachel Dwyer and Christopher Pinney. New Delhi: Oxford University Press, 2001.

Gandhi, Leela. "Novelists of the 1930s and 1940s." In *An Illustrated History of Indian Literature in English*, edited by Arvind Krishna Mehrotra. Delhi: Permanent Black, 2003.

George, K. M. *A Many Branched Tree: Perspectives of Indian Literary Tradition*. Delhi: Ajanta Books International, 1991.

Government of India. *India 2004: A Reference Annual*. Publications Division, Ministry of Information and Broadcasting, New Delhi, 2004.

Harikrishnan, Charmy. "Dina N. Malhotra: Paperback Patriarch." *India Today*, 20 December 2004.

Iyengar, Srinivasa K. R., and Prema Nandakumar. *Indian Writing in English*. New Delhi: Sterling, 1985.

Kaushik, Neha. "Indian Publishing Industry on a Global Trail." *The Hindu Business Line*, 23 August 2003.

Kennedy, Miranda. "The Maharani of Muck." *The Nation*, 27 May 2004.

Khair, Tabish. *Babu Fictions: Alienation in Contemporary Indian English Novels*. New Delhi: Oxford University Press, 2000.

King, Bruce, ed. *New National and Post-Colonial Literatures: An Introduction*. New Delhi: Oxford University Press, 1996.

Krishna Rao, A. V., and Madhavi Menon. *Kamala Markandaya: A Critical Study of Her Novels 1954–1982*. New Delhi: B. R. Publishing, 1997.

Malik, Ashok. "Offshore Publishing: Budgeting Words." *India Today*, 13 March 2000.

Mee, Jon. "After Midnight: The Novel in the 1980s and 1990s." In *An Illustrated History of Indian Literature in English*, edited by Arvind Krishna Mehrotra. Delhi: Permanent Black, 2003.

Mehrotra, Arvind Krishna, ed. *An Illustrated History of Indian Literature in English*. Delhi: Permanent Black, 2003.

Mehta, Sonny. "Cinema and Literature: Exploiting India's Soft Power." *India Today*, 29 March 2004.

Mishra, Pankaj. "R. K. Narayan." In *An Illustrated History of Indian Literature in English*, edited by Arvind Krishna Mehrotra. Delhi: Permanent Black, 2003.

Mukherjee, Meenakshi. "Beginnings of the Novel." In *An Illustrated History of Indian Literature in English*, edited by Arvind Krishna Mehrotra. Delhi: Permanent Black, 2003.

———. *The Perishable Empire: Essays on Indian Writing in English*, New Delhi: 2000.

Naik, M. K. *A History of Indian English Literature*. New Delhi: Sahitya Akademi, 1982.

Naik, M. K., and Shyamala A. Narayan. *Indian English Literature 1980–2000: A Critical Survey*. Delhi: Pencraft, 2001.

Narayan, Shyamala, and John Mee. "Novelists of the 1950s and 1960s." In *An Illustrated History of Indian Literature in English*, edited by Arvind Krishna Mehrotra. Delhi: Permanent Black, 2003.

Natarajan, Nalini, ed. *Handbook of Twentieth Century Literatures of India*. Westport, Conn.: Greenwood Press, 1996.

Nelson, Emmannuel S. *Writers of the Indian Diaspora: A Bio-Bibliographical Critical Sourcebook*. Westport, Conn.: Greenwood Press, 1993.

Padmanabhan, Anil. "Comics: Scaling East." *India Today*, 5 July 2004.

Pattanayak, D. P. "The Languages: A Multicultural Plurilingual Country." In *Independent India: The First Fifty Years*, edited by Hiranmay Karlekar. New Delhi: Indian Council for Cultural Relations, 1998.

Pritchett, Frances W. "The World of *Amar Chitra Katha*." In *Media and the Transformation of Religion in South Asia*, edited by Lawrence A. Babb and Susan S. Wadley. University of Pennsylvania Press, 1995.

Rajadhyaksha, Ashish, and Paul Willemen. *Encyclopedia of Indian Cinema*. London: British Film Institute, 1999.

Russell, Ralph. *The Pursuit of Urdu Literature: A Select History*. Calcutta: Seagull, 1992.

Sadiq, Muhammad. *Twentieth Century Urdu Literature*. Karachi: Royal Book Company, 1983.

Sampemane, Sumati K. "Rising Popularity." *Business India*, 17 February–2 March 2003.

Satchidanandan, K. "Literature: Signing in Different Scripts." In *Independent India: The First Fifty Years*, edited by Hiranmay Karlekar. New Delhi: Indian Council for Cultural Relations, 1998.

Sebastian, Mrinalini. *The Novels of Shashi Despande in Postcolonial Arguments*. New Delhi: Prestige, 2000.

Singh, Prabhat K., ed. *The Creative Contours of Ruskin Bond: An Anthology of Critical Writings*. New Delhi: Pencraft, 1995.

Varughese, Suma. "An Unsuitable Writer." *Society*, March 1993.

Walsh, William. *Indian Literature in English*. London: Longman, 1990.

Who's Who of Indian Writers: 1999. 2 Vols. New Delhi: Sahitya Akademi, 2000.

Williams, H. M. *Indo-Anglian Literature, 1800–1970*. Madras: Orient Longman, 1976.

5

Print Media in India—
Newspapers and Magazines

One of the greatest legacies of the British colonial rule in India was that of a free and robust press. Although Indian-owned newspapers and magazines appeared a long time after the first British-owned newspapers and journals had begun publication in India, they made up for the slow start by proliferating rapidly in accordance with the political needs of the last decades of colonialism. The growth rate of the print media has multiplied in geometric progression since independence, the effects of the "newspaper revolution" becoming apparent during the 1980s.

Until the 1980s, English-language newspapers dominated the Indian print media scene, but since then the balance has shifted in favor of the Indian-language press, particularly the Hindi-language press, which caters to over 40 percent of the Indian population. Today there are newspapers in all the languages of India and in all the ten Indian scripts (Devnagari, Bengali, Gujerati, Gurmukhi, Kannada, Malayalam, Oriya, Perso-Arabic, Tamil, and Telugu) as well as English, thus reaching nearly every corner of the nation.

The growth of the Indian-language press has resulted in a beehive structure with no single pan-Indian newspaper or monopolistic publisher. Instead, regional-language newspapers, fueled by ballooning advertising revenues, themselves a product of increasing levels of prosperity and expanding consumerism since 1991, compete ferociously in catering to discrete and localized linguistic groups. All of this has resulted in a huge diversity of newspapers and magazines that seems to inure the medium to threats from a rapidly expanding television and radio network.

History of the Indian Press

The Early Years

The earliest newspapers in India were printed in English by British expatriates living in Calcutta (now Kolkata). On 29 January 1780, James Au-

Indians waiting at a bus stop read details of the terrorist attacks in Washington, D.C., and New York in newspapers in the eastern Indian city of Calcutta on 12 September 2001.
(Jayanta Shaw/Reuters/Corbis)

gustus Hicky brought out the first newspaper in India, a four-page weekly called *The Bengal Gazette* (also known as the *Calcutta General Advertiser*). Hicky's tabloid had faced all the pressures that would preoccupy a newspaper today—advertising, competition, and censorship. Advertising, very prominently displayed, along with subscription revenues, kept Hicky's paper solvent, particularly when in November of that same year a rival weekly, the *India Gazette*, began publication. For a couple years the two tabloids competed intensely. In order to garner a larger readership, the *Bengal Gazette* indulged in frivolous tittle-tattle, gossip, and scandal. One of the tar-

gets of the witty and scurrilous tabloid was Warren Hastings (1732–1818), the governor general of Bengal, whom Hicky relentlessly lampooned in his cartoons. But Hicky soon learned the dangers of earning the enmity of the most important Englishman in India. He was imprisoned for defamation, but he managed to bring out his paper. However, by March 1782, his printing machines were seized by the police at the behest of Hastings, and the newspaper was forced to close down.

Within two decades of Hicky's initial venture, scores of weeklies and monthlies appeared in Calcutta, and the city became not just the birthplace of Indian journalism but also the very center of it. But for nearly forty years the press in India, which by now had extended to the cities of Bombay (now Mumbai) and Madras (now Chennai), was entirely in the hands of the British residents in India: it was owned by the British, edited by British residents, and designed for the exclusive consumption of the expatriate British and European community, which was, in large measure, affiliated to the East India Company. Most newspapers carried an undistinguished fare of social news interspersed with gossipy accounts of alleged amorous liaisons, letters from local readers, and reprints of articles from British newspapers. There were also government notices, fashion notes, and advertisements.

Many of the English journals that had begun to proliferate also took up the cause of their particular political leanings with regard to British politics. Thus the *Calcutta Journal*, owned by some merchants in Calcutta, voiced Whig (Liberal Party) opinions, while *John Bull in the East* set itself up as the Tory (Conservative Party) voice in India. There were no censorship laws. If an editor was seen to overstep the mark in the reporting of social scandal, the dispute was either resolved in a gentlemanly way or he was assaulted and challenged to a duel by the aggrieved party. If the transgression was serious enough to annoy the company administration, then the editor was sued for libel and jailed or deported back to the British Isles.

The social world of the British in the mid-eighteenth century was cocooned from that of the Indians, and news pertaining to or of interest to Indians had no place in these early publications. It was not until the 1820s that newspapers owned by Indians made a tentative appearance. In 1816,

the first British-owned Indian-language journal, the Bengali monthly *Digdarshan*, appeared, with news in both Bengali and English. It soon switched to a weekly publication schedule and changed its name to *Samachar Darpan*. Its news stories focused on events in India and problems relating to Indian society. However, the newspaper steered clear of any political controversies, thus winning the approval (and postal concessions) of the British authorities (Padhy and Sahu 1997).

It was an article written by Christian missionaries denigrating the great Hindu philosophy of Vedanta and published in *Samachar Darpan* that set the stage for a burst of publishing activity from the Indians. An outraged Ram Mohan Roy (circa 1772–1833), the great Indian social and religious reformer, responded to the article in a forceful letter, only to find that his missive was completely ignored by the editor. Spurred by indignation and eager to counterbalance the Christian missionary propaganda, Roy started his own *Brahminical Magazine*. In 1821, Roy founded the short-lived *Sambad Kaumudi* as well as a Persian-language weekly called *Mirat-ul-Akhbar*. Together with Dwarkanath Tagore and Prasanna Kumar Tagore, Roy started yet another weekly, the *Banga Dutt*, which appeared in four languages: Hindi, Bengali, Persian, and English.

All of Roy's newspapers were progressive publications urging social and religious reform. He himself was a champion of civil rights and is said to have held a public dinner in celebration of the French revolution of 1830. Roy's enthusiasm for the written word as the medium to promote his causes was infectious and engendered a sudden blossoming of journalism in Indian languages. Thus Roy is often referred to as the "father" of Indian-language journalism.

Between 1831 and 1833, nineteen new Indian journals were added to the thirty-three English-language and sixteen Bengali newspapers and journals already in publication (Parthasarthy 1989). Most of the growth of the Indian-language press took place in the cities of Calcutta and Bombay. The Indian-language newspapers were generally more concerned about the failures of the colonial government and the misdeeds of its servants than tales of European scandal and gossip. Many were antigovernment, but not anti-British. In fact, they all revelled in India's association with the British parliamentary institutions.

After 1857

Attitudes changed after the Indian Rebellion (also referred to as the "Indian Mutiny" or the "First Indian War of Independence") of 1857. Its aftermath was a period of national awakening, and there was a dramatic parting of ways between the British-owned English-language press and the Indian-owned English and vernacular press. The British-owned press launched vicious tirades against the Indians, using virulent and racist language in writing about the "treacherous natives." They bayed for blood and closed ranks against the Indians. Tory and Whig rivalries were buried, and the British expatriates urged the colonial government to be even more ferocious in the repression of the rebellious natives. The Indian press, for its part, turned nationalist, a nationalism that was to reach its peak a few decades later under the leadership of Mahatma Gandhi in the struggle for Indian independence.

The Hindi and other vernacular newspapers made an immense contribution to the political awakening of the Indian masses and the struggle for freedom. The Hindi-language weekly *Oodunt Mardant* was started in 1826 and printed in Calcutta, but the British authorities refused to grant it postal concessions, causing it to close within a year. The editor, Jooghul Kishore Sookool, tried again with *Samyadani Martand*, but that too failed. Between 1830 and 1850 scores of newspapers emerged and submerged with regularity. It was not until the 1860s that Indian-owned newspapers and journals began to remain solvent and even proliferate. Most of these were published in regional Indian languages and cheaply made, with small print-runs for local circulation—although by that time the expanding rail network and an efficient postal system had made it possible for weekly journals to command a more extensive readership.

What fueled the growth of the Indian newspapers was the unheralded arrival in the mid-nineteenth century of a new middle class in the cities of Calcutta, Bombay, and Madras. It was a class that had imbibed ideas from reading western literature and coming into contact with western education—an education that advocated concepts of democracy, liberalism, and nationalism. In fact, from 1870 onward an "education explosion" took place, with Indians setting up private colleges and demanding new universities. Although this new, articulate middle class was still a microscopic minority, it "now possessed a language, ideas, and attitudes in common; it had a common mind and speech, as no other class in India had had before, and it could take an all-India view" (Spear 1970: 169).

At first, much of the emerging Indian-language press had, like Roy's newspapers, focused on social reform, arguing eloquently for the abolition of evil social practices such as *sati* or the immolation of widows on their husband's funeral pyres, child marriage, and the caste practice of "untouchability." But after the Indian Rebellion of 1857 and the poisonous attacks of the British-owned English-language press in India, the Indian-owned press took up the cudgels and demanded greater respect and increased political and administrative powers for Indians. The *Amrita Bazaar Patrika* was founded in 1868 to defend the cause of the peasants fighting the owners of the indigo plantations. *The Hindu*, one of the leading newspapers of contemporary India and the oldest Indian-owned English-language newspaper, was started as a weekly in 1878 in Madras. By 1889 it had become a daily newspaper and was beginning to counter the vicious criticism from the British-owned papers at the appointment of an eminent Tamilian as judge at the Madras High Court. In 1881, Sardar Dayal Singh Majithia, an ardent admirer of Ram Mohan Roy, started the English-language *Tribune* in Lahore "to advance the cause of the mute masses" (Parthasarthy 1989: 279). That newspaper was to become the most eloquent bearer of public opinion in the northwest of India.

While the British colonial regime pampered the British-owned pro-*raj* press and was willing to tolerate the Indian-owned English-language press, they saw the Hindi and other regional-language presses as clearly dangerous to their rule. They believed that educated Indians who read the English newspapers were likely to appreciate the benefits of British rule but that the masses were prone to the undesirable influences of the provocative and seditious writings in the regional-language presses.

But with the wide array of Indian languages and scripts, it was impossible for the government to have a comprehensive understanding of what was being said in all of them. To keep track of the vernacular press, the government of India demanded that each provincial government compile a fortnightly or monthly report on the "native newspapers," with highlights from each of the local-language presses. The practice continued until the 1930s, and the compilations became a major source of information for historians and provided the only surviving record of many newspapers of the period (Jeffery 2000).

When Lord Lytton (1831–1891) assumed his post as viceroy of India in 1875, officials clamored for strong action against the vernacular press, which they accused of publishing vituperative falsehoods against British officialdom. Most of the attacks on the government at the time were on subjects such as racial discrimination, unjust treatment of Indians in punishment of crimes, unfairness in job opportunities, the tyranny of the colonial government, and the overbearing conduct of the British and European residents in India. It was also alleged that the vernacular press was publishing seditious material, in some cases even going so far as to encourage Indian soldiers to rebel against their commanding officers as they had done during the mutiny in 1857.

Increasingly unnerved by the angry fulminations of the vernacular press, Lord Lytton passed the draconian Vernacular Press Act in 1878. Targeted specifically at the malcontents nestling in the provinces, it imposed severe restrictions on the Indian-language press but exempted the English-language press from its strictures. It demanded that the printer or publisher

Lord Lytton was an English politician, diplomat, and poet. He was viceroy of India from 1875 to 1880. (Corbis)

of a newspaper in an Indian language furnish a bond undertaking not to publish abusive and inflammatory articles, while tacitly condoning the largely English-owned English-language press and its racist ranting. It empowered the British colonial government to search the premises of any Indian-language press and confiscate material. Similarly, the government could demand a security from the printer or publisher and force them to forfeit the money paid, if they suspected any anti-government propaganda.

To escape the constraints placed upon the vernacular press, the recently founded *Amrita Bazaar Patrika* changed overnight into an English-language newspaper. The

most important aspect of the Vernacular Press Act was that while the government could undertake all these actions without having to seek the permission of the law courts, the printer or publisher could not seek judicial redress for the arbitrary actions of the government. However, the act had little actual effect, and with the election of a Liberal government in Britain and the arrival of a new viceroy in India, it was repealed in 1881.

It would be wrong to assume that there was unqualified unity among the Indian-owned newspapers. There was a clear hierarchy among the newspapers, and the attitude of the Indian-owned English-language newspapers towards the vernacular press was not dissimilar to that of fastidious Brahmins disdainful of the hoi polloi. Unlike the erudite opinions and intellectual ponderings penned in the Indian-owned English-language newspapers, crude personal abuse of British officials was commonplace in the small regional presses. In 1889 the Punjabi *Halishaher Patrika* described the province's lieutenant-governor, Sir George Campbell, as "the baboon Campbell with a hairy body . . . His eyes flash forth in anger and his tail is all in flames" (Parathasarthy 1989: 219). Writing on the subject of the Indian-language press in 1897, G. Subramnia Aiyer, editor of *The Hindu*, loftily observed:

The vernacular press, as it is called, is in the hands of an inferior set of men. It must be confessed that these men, not possessing sufficient education, often commit errors. It must be noticed that the vernacular languages are not quite suited to the discussion of public questions . . . Those gentlemen who conduct the vernacular press are often at a loss to find suitable words to express themselves and, as is often the case with people that want to express their feelings, they resort to exaggeration or hyperbole without meaning the slightest offence by the language they make use of. (Parathasarthy 1989: 217–218)

The Freedom Struggle

In the decades of the 1880s and 1890s, the movement for greater self-administration was beginning to gather momentum. The Indian National Congress, established in 1885, demanded a greater say for Indians in the administrative affairs of India. One of the leaders of the movement was the fiery Bal Gangadhar Tilak (1857–1920), who had understood the political importance of mass communication. In 1881, he had started two newspapers—the Marathi-language *Kesari* and the English-language *Mahratta*. The former was a provocative publication intended for the Marathi-speaking people, and within a year it was the best-selling newspaper of the region. His English-language publication, however, adopted a more magisterial and dignified tone.

By the turn of the century, some Indians had begun to believe that violence could be the more effective means to achieve independence from Britain, and the country began to witness bombings. Tilak was accused of fomenting violence by the Anglo-Indian press and in 1908 was sentenced to six years of imprisonment. Also in 1908, the government passed the Newspapers Bill in tandem with the Explosives Substances Bill. The move was intended to stop newspapers from inciting the populace to murder. It gave the government the right to confiscate the printing press of any newspaper that was perceived to encourage violence, to imprison, and even to transport the alleged offenders. Under the

provisions of the bill, seven printing presses were confiscated in just one year while scores of publishers were arrested and imprisoned.

In 1870 there were 280 newspapers in the whole of India, but by 1910 there were 280 publications in the United Provinces alone (Jeffery 2000). The acerbic press had made it harder and harder for the colonial government to implement policies unpalatable to the Indians. Besides, the telegraph carried news fast from one part of the country to another and was impossible to control. Yet the government persisted. Two years later the Press Act of 1910 was passed, which revived most of the strictures of the Vernacular Press Act of 1878, except that because there were several Indian-owned English-language publications at this time, it was equally applicable to the English-language press.

During World War I, Indians (including Tilak) supported the British, but British policy toward Indian aspirations for greater autonomy and administrative powers remained largely ignored. Attempts to control the Indian-language press continued apace. Between 1917 and 1919, 963 newspapers that had existed before the Press Act of 1910 were proceeded against in legal actions, and 173 new printing presses and 129 newspapers were killed off commercially by demands for security; over 500 publications were banned under the act, and the government collected over a half million rupees in fines (Parathasarthy 1989). The Press Act was repealed in 1922.

It was when Mahatma Gandhi returned to India from South Africa in 1915 that the Indian freedom movement gained a new dynamism and direction. In 1913, the theosophist Annie Besant (1847–1933), who had already started *New India*, launched the Home Rule movement in 1916 to fight for Indian self-government. Gandhi's policies of *ahimsa* (nonviolence), *swadeshi* (the boycott of imported goods), and noncooperation with the British colonial government drew millions of men and women from ordinary walks of life to participate in the struggle for independence.

Gandhi started two newspapers, *Young India* (in English) and *Navjivan* (in Gujerati), and wrote in a very simple, accessible style. Since he did not believe in either copyright or the protection of intellectual property, he gave permission to all newspapers to freely reproduce his articles. Gandhi's message was thus widely disseminated in different languages throughout the country, inspiring journalists and writers to redouble their efforts to attain the goal of freedom. He later started the *Harijan*, *Harijan Sevak*, and *Harijan Bandhu* to give voice to voiceless multitudes from the untouchable castes. Gandhi was charged with sedition in 1922 for his writings and sentenced to six years of rigorous imprisonment.

For the wealthy Indians, it became an act of patriotism to launch a newspaper, and Indian-language newspapers mushroomed all over the country, enthusiastically supporting the struggle for freedom. Many of the newspapers founded in this period were fervently nationalistic and would play an important role in the press in modern India: *Aj*, the Hindi-language nationalist daily was set up in 1920 by Shiv Prasad Gupta; the *Swarajya*, which was founded in Madras in 1922 by T. Prakasam, espoused the teachings of Mahatma Gandhi but failed to survive; the English-language *Hindustan Times* was started in 1923 and bought by the G. D. Birla family in 1927; the *Free Press*

Journal was created in 1930 to keep afloat the Free Press News Agency that dispatched nationalist news to its subscribers and had begun to feel the effects of the government's heavy-handed closures and confiscations.

Often ill equipped and poorly resourced, the editors saw the newspaper as a weapon in their fight against colonialism. Many of the editors suffered privation, imprisonment, and even deportation at the hands of the British. The *Amrita Bazaar Patrika* suffered serious financial losses for having espoused the cause of the Indian National Congress and Mahatma Gandhi, and its editor was imprisoned for defamation. The *National Herald*, founded in 1938 by Jawaharlal Nehru, and the *Hindustan Times* were relentlessly persecuted by the government. By 1942 the government had suppressed ninety-two journals (Parthasarthy 1989).

A robust, adversarial press had an enormous impact on Indian politics, because the educated classes were avid newspaper readers and, like their counterparts elsewhere in the world, tended to believe what they saw in print. Unrelenting criticism of government policy, jeers at officials, and allegations of abuses were corrosive and seriously undermined the prestige of the colonial government. To counter these attacks, the colonial government embarked on a system of rewards and punishments for individual proprietors and journalists.

The most effective of these was the buying of advertisements in newspapers, because even a small increase in revenue made a big difference to newspapers struggling to remain solvent. In the 1920s, official advertising to a select group of Indian journals increased substantially. According to Robin Jeffery, who has written extensively on the Indian press, "The combination of commercial and official pressure inhibited larger newspapers from confronting the government too aggressively. The management of *The Hindu* at one point refused to carry banned nationalist material and explained to Mahatma Gandhi that they had made too large an investment in their presses to risk confiscation and ruin" (Jeffery 2000: 186).

At the end of World War II, Gandhi launched the Quit India movement. Newsprint was scarce, and the colonial government controlled allocation of its limited supply. The nationalist press, particularly those newspapers that endorsed Gandhi's rallying cry of "Quit India," found it difficult to obtain the allocations necessary to bring out a daily newspaper. The Indian and Eastern Newspaper Society (INES) was formed in 1945 to lobby the colonial government for a fairer distribution of newsprint to all newspapers, regardless of their political leanings.

After Independence

Once the nationalist goal was achieved and India won independence from the British in 1947, the Indian newspapers had to find ways to make their publications financially viable. During the freedom struggle, just launching a newspaper and providing a forum for the dissemination of nationalist opinions was an act of patriotism. But now the businessmen had to recoup their investment. Many have pointed out that this was the period when the editor lost his preeminent position to business managers and accountants.

Most British proprietors of the English-language papers either closed or sold out to the Indians before returning home. The *Times of India*, contemporary India's biggest selling English-language newspaper, which belonged to Bennett, Coleman & Company, was sold to Ramakrishna Dalmia in 1946, who in turn sold it to his son-in-law to pay government fines incurred by his fraudulent financial activities in other commercial sectors. The *Statesman*, a British-owned newspaper, continued in India as long as it could but eventually was sold to Indian ownership in the 1960s.

The new government of an independent India did not introduce any new legislation specifically designated to guarantee freedom for the Indian press. Instead, it was covered under Article 19 (1) of the new Indian Constitution, which protected the "freedom of speech and expression." This general provision would govern the Indian press henceforth.

However, no government is ever content to live with a completely free press. With India reeling from the devastating effects of the violent partition of the country in the west (West Pakistan) and east (East Pakistan, later Bangladesh), and communist insurgencies elsewhere within the country, the same nationalist leaders who had condemned the British press censorship now sought to rein in the power of the press by passing amendments to the Constitution. After independence in 1947, publication of material likely to cause public unrest, incite people to crime, or harm relations with a foreign power was banned.

The Official Secrets Act passed during the British *raj* in 1888, which forbade the unauthorized publication of government papers, also remained on the statute books. Similarly, the Press and Registration of Books (PRB) Act of 1867, which required all printers and publishers to register their newspapers with the local authorities and carry their names and addresses on the publications, remained, with some minor amendments.

In 1952, the Indian government established a Press Commission to look at the state of the Indian press, its printing presses, the freedoms it enjoyed, and the working conditions of journalists. One of the commission's recommendations was the creation of a Press Council to oversee ethics and to hear complaints from the reading public.

One of the early measures of the Press Commission was the well-meant "price-page schedule." The quasi-socialist thinking that informed the policies in the early days of independent India made the government suspicious of large companies. To prevent rich newspapers, fattened with advertisements, from engaging in a price war and wiping out medium and small newspapers with less advertising revenues, it decreed that the minimum price per newspaper page should be fixed. The decree was immediately challenged in court by the Marathi-language daily *Sakal*, which emerged victorious, and the government had to back down (Jeffery 2000).

In a move to assist journalists, the government also appointed three wage boards over the three subsequent decades to ensure that newspapers adequately recompensed their journalists and workers. It also tried to provide subsidized housing in Delhi for those who were members of the parliamentary lobby. In Bombay, where the cost of housing is high, it offered land at subsidized rates to build a *patrakar* colony—a journalists' enclave of affordable housing.

The Office of the Registrar of Newspapers for India (RNI) was created in 1956. It was required to monitor the press and verify circulation figures, which tended to be exaggerated by most newspapers. But because of its slow-moving, inadequately resourced bureaucratic machinery, the audited circulation figures of the Audit Bureau of Circulation (ABC), established in 1948, were more acceptable to the advertising agencies (Bhatt 1997). According to the RNI, there were 330 daily newspapers and 3,203 periodicals in 1952. By 1960, their number had grown to 531 daily newspapers and 7,495 periodicals, with combined circulations of over 4 million for newspapers and over 13.5 million for periodicals.

Another of the functions of the RNI was the allocation of newsprint. From the 1960s until recently, the Indian government controlled the importation of newsprint. India did not produce sufficient newsprint, and the shortage of foreign exchange in the first few decades after independence did not permit uncontrolled importation of goods. To meet the demand India resorted to indigenous production, which was entirely in keeping with the government's quasi-socialistic policy of "self sufficiency" and "import substitution." Production of newsprint in India began in 1956, and by 1997 there were twenty-two newsprint mills, state-owned as well as private. Import substitution's first casualties were the forests of Madhya Pradesh, which were, in the absence of any coherent program for replanting or replacement, completely wiped out (Bhatt 1997). The restrictions were removed in 1997 and importation of newsprint liberalized.

Registration with the RNI not only guaranteed a regular supply of scarce newsprint from the government at controlled prices, it offered further perquisites, such as access to concessional postage. It could also qualify a young, start-up newspaper for additional benefits, such as land at concessional rates for the construction of newspaper offices, offered by some state governments (Bhatt 1997).

The Directorate of Audio-Visual Publicity (DAVP), under the auspices of the RNI, carried out government advertising for all public sector recruitment and notifications. Around 25–30 percent of the DAVP's budget was targeted at the print media, and it placed advertisements in almost all newspapers, paying rates worked out by a special government formula that ended up being lower than those paid by private sector advertisers. Nevertheless, it was a boon to many of the smaller newspapers, particularly the regional papers that found it difficult to attract advertising from the city-based advertising firms and agencies. Not only were these advertisements an important source of income, but they also helped increase their circulation, since educated young men and women eagerly perused the columns for employment opportunities. For some bigger newspapers, however, the government rates were so low that they preferred to do without them.

All these worthy measures and instances of assistance made many critics very cynical about the government's largesse. J. N. Sahni, the veteran nationalist-newspaper editor, made a caustic comment on the attitude of Indian editors. "Under the British," he wrote, "the fear of iron chains or a series of coercive measures threatened press freedom. These also served as a challenge which journalists had to meet. After Independence, silver chains made cowards of many a star writer rather than penal restrictions" (Parthasarthy 1989: 331).

Mrs. Gandhi and the Emergency

In 1975, Prime Minister Indira Gandhi declared an Internal Emergency to stem the growing law and order problem. Opposition leaders, political activists, intellectuals, and nearly 250 journalists were jailed. Newspaper editors were required to adhere to a set of written guidelines issued by the government concerning what they could and could not publish. Three ordinances—banning "objectionable" material and abolishing the Press Council and the freedom to report proceedings of the houses of parliament—were also passed.

These bullying tactics were not the only methods that Mrs. Gandhi's government used to harness the press. It also resorted to covert bribery. It tripled the amount of government advertising (Jeffery 2000), dramatically improved the advertising rates, and used these "improvements" to reward compliant newspapers. The allocation of newsprint was yet another means by which the Indian government could ensure a docile press.

Most publishing houses submitted to the exigencies of the Emergency government. Seeing the number of compliant newspaper editors, L. K. Advani, an opponent of Mrs. Gandhi and later Minister of Information and Broadcasting in 1977–1979, is said to have remarked that "journalists were told to bend but chose to crawl" (Jeffery 2000: 190). But not all of them made that choice. The biggest and most famous of these objectors was the Indian Express Group of Newspapers under the ownership of Ramnath Goenka. For defying Mrs. Gandhi's orders the *Indian Express* often found that its electricity had been cut, which prevented it from bringing out a newspaper the next morning. Other rebellious newspapers, such as those from the southern state of Tamil Nadu where Mrs. Gandhi had simply removed the elected state government from power, were simi-

Indian Prime Minister Indira Gandhi reads the *National Herald* newspaper at home, 1978. (Kapoor Baldev/Sygma/Corbis)

larly harassed. Most newspapers and magazines saw a decline in sales. The sole exception was the *Punjab Kesari*, which adopted a magazine-style format and put cultural news, art news, and travel features on the front page, relegating the pared-down political news to the center pages. It saw a doubling of its sales (Jeffery 2000).

Mrs. Gandhi also merged the four Indian news agencies into one, Samachar. These were the English-language Press Trust of India (PTI), which in 1947 inherited the premises and equipment of the Reuters subsidiary, the United Press of India (UPI). The first Press Commission, concerned about ensuring healthy competition, urged the creation of a second news agency, and the English-language United News of India (UNI) came into being in 1961. Hindustan Samachar, set up as a regional-language news agency in 1948, was

suspected of having links with the Rashtriya Swayamsevak Sangh (RSS), an extreme Hindu nationalist group that supported the Hindu nationalist Jana Sangh Party, political opponents of the secular Congress Party. Samachar Bharati, the second Hindi-language news agency, was created in 1967 as an alternative to the Hindustan Samachar.

The "Newspaper Revolution"

After Mrs Gandhi called and lost the general elections in 1977, the new government lifted all reporting restrictions and restored the status quo ante. It also set up the Second Press Commission to investigate the abuses of the newspaper industry during the Emergency. Mrs. Gandhi was re-elected to power in 1980 and ironically, under her new tenure, the decade saw a spectacular growth in the number of newspapers and magazines. It was also the first time that the circulation of an Indian-language newspaper, *Dainik Bhaskar*, overtook that of any English-language newspapers. The post-Emergency era began to witness an unprecedented "newspaper revolution."

Until the declaration of Emergency by Mrs. Gandhi in 1975, Indian newspapers were described as dull and cliché-ridden. The Nobel Prize–winning writer V. S. Naipaul complained in *A Wounded Civilisation* that their vision was limited and that there was an absence of inquiry—the absence of what may be called human interest. The liveliness of the Indian press was confined to the editorial pages. Elsewhere the papers were filled with communiqués, handouts, and reports of speeches and functions.

With the end of the Emergency and the defeat of Mrs Gandhi at the elections in 1977, the Indian press suddenly came to life. A number of political magazines such as *India Today* (in Hindi—the English-language version was started in 1975), *Sunday*, *The Week*, and *Outlook* emerged across the country, in English, Hindi, and other major languages. In them, the excesses of the Emergency and the abuses of authority were exposed on a weekly or fortnightly basis. The investigations and exposés by Arun Shourie, journalist, editor, and later government minister, set off an enthusiasm for investigative reporting. Sensational violence, crime, and dirty politics became the main diet of even the staid newspapers. A new generation of journalists emerged—young, self-assured, forceful, and disdainful of politicians—bringing with them a fresh and exuberant style.

Several factors account for this exponential growth in newspapers.

First, the experience of government repression had created an increased interest in political matters and news, which could support more and more newspapers.

Second, with an average population increase of 23 percent each decade, the actual numbers of Indians had nearly doubled from around 450 million at the time of independence to nearly 800 million by the 1980s. The increase in population signaled an increase in readers, whose demands could be met with more newspapers and greater circulations.

Third, the increase in population was accompanied by an increase in literacy rates, which had risen from 19 percent in 1951 to nearly 44 percent by 1981 (*India 2004*). With more literate people in India, circulation figures for newspapers rose higher and higher each year. Much of this new literacy was in the regional scripts. India has eighteen official languages and ten different scripts, and in 1980, for the very first time in the history of India, the circulation figures for newspapers in Hindi overtook those for newspapers in English.

Fourth, economic growth also meant that more Indians had a greater proportion of disposable income, which could be spent, in part, on newspapers and magazines (Jeffery 2000). The easing of government controls and creeping economic liberalization had already begun with Rajiv Gandhi, who took over as prime minister in the aftermath of his mother's assassination in 1984. India's economic growth rate was inching up to 5 percent from the previous 3 percent "Hindu rate of growth" that had been its standard performance. With even greater economic liberalization in 1991, economic growth rates reached 7 percent, increasing the wealth and purchasing power of a large number of people. The economic growth fueled greater levels of consumption for the emerging middle classes in the towns and cities across India, which in turn fueled an advertising boom that drove the growth of newspapers and particularly magazines.

Fifth, road transport and infrastructure also played a role in the distribution of the print media. From the early years of the twentieth century until soon after independence, railway and postal deliveries were the principal means of transportation for newspapers and magazines. With the growth of road transport, the distribution contractors arranged for local vans and bicycles to deliver farther into the hinterland not accessed by the railway (Bhatt 1997).

In addition, writer Robin Jeffery points to other crucial features that led to the increase in both the number of vernacular newspapers and periodicals and in the circulation figures for these newspapers during the 1980s. These include advances in technology, such as offset printing and computer typesetting, that liberated the cumbersome Indian scripts that are so much more difficult to compose on the old systems of printing. Telephone modems also liberated the vernacular newspapers from the handicaps of distance, allowing for the successful establishment of more and more regional-language newspapers away from the big metropolises (Jeffery 2000).

Simpler language was also used in the regional-language newspapers, making them accessible to all. Hindi newspapers, in particular, moved away from the high-flown Sanskritized vocabulary favored by the government-run All India Radio to an easy, uncomplicated style of writing. Magazines

such as *Stardust* even espoused the cause of "Hinglish" (a mixture of Hindi and English), making the reading of English simpler and more fun, particularly for those whose command of English was tenuous. Since the 1980s, all magazines, including political journals, write easy-to-digest Hinglish, bringing to the practice a certain ethnic-urban chic.

The new regional newspapers focused on local news, local events, births, marriages, and deaths, all of which was important information in the local communities. In doing so, they offered something that the big English-language newspapers, national radio, and the nascent government-owned television could not, and still do not, provide. Jeffery cites the example of a local farmer for whom the death of a much-loved stud bull merited an obituary notice in the local newspaper, while the Marathi-language *Sakal* published the daily price of fresh vegetables in the Pune market for the convenience of the housewives (Jeffery 2000).

The combination of all these factors led to an extraordinary boom in newspapers. By 1996 the number of daily newspapers had grown to 4,558 and that of periodicals to 37,830, with circulations of 45.2 million and 44 million respectively (Bhatt 1997).

While all newspapers—national, regional, provincial, and even tribal, in all languages—doubled, tripled, or even quadrupled their circulation figures, the biggest growth was in Indian-language newspapers. Hindi-language newspapers alone constituted over 40 percent of the entire print media in India. This growth of the Indian press provided a dizzying diversity of choice for the regional readers.

The central Indian city of Hyderabad provides a useful microcosm of the newspaper world in India. Hyderabad, capital of the state of Andhra Pradesh, has a trilingual population: Telugu, Urdu, and English. The leading English dailies are *The Hindu* and the *Indian Express*. Hyderabad also has its own city-based English-language papers, *Deccan Chronicle* and *Newstime* (from the Eenadu group). The city also has an evening English daily, *Skyline*, and a Hindi-language daily, the *Milap*.

In addition, the city has Urdu-language dailies, such as *Siasff*, *Munsiff*, *Rehnuma-e-Deccan*, and *Angarey*. Smaller Urdu papers include *Aina-e-Hyderabad*, *Bhagyanagar Observer*, *Bhagyanagar Times*, *Haq Baat*, *Khateeb*, *Kamamder Maheshar*, *Naveed-e-Deccan*, *Rehnuma-e-Hind*, *Saz-e-Deccan*, *Shan-e-Hind*, *Siasi Mahz*, *Takeed*, *Tulway Sahir*, *Voice of Hyderabad*, and *Watan Ki Pukar*.

Furthermore the city has Telugu-language newspapers such as *Eenadu*, *Andhra Jyoti*, *Udayam*, *Andhra Prabha* and *Andhra Bhoomi*. These newspapers also cover the district towns or have district-specific editions. In addition to these, the nearby town of Eluru has three of its own Telugu-language newspapers: *State Times*, *Gopi Krishna*, and *Eluru Times*; Nalgonda has *Praja Por* and *Praja Portam*; Warangal has *Warangal Vani*; and Guntur has the *Guntur Express* (Bhatt 1997).

Magazine Revolution

The newspaper revolution also saw the emergence of scores of magazines in English, Hindi, and all the regional languages. The first Indian magazines began to appear in the early 1900s and were initially in Bengali and exclusively devoted to literature. In 1901, Ramananda Chattopadhyay began *Prabasi*, an illustrated Bengali literary monthly that pioneered the popular mix of book excerpts, poetry, and one-act plays alongside reviews and essays. It also serialized fiction, including Rabindranath Tagore's *Gora* (1907–1909). Later, with the advent of cinema, magazines devoted entirely to this new form of entertainment began to appear as well. The first periodical exclusively devoted to cinema was the Gujerati-language *Mouj Majah*, launched in Mumbai in 1924. The earliest film magazine in English was *Filmindia*, published from 1935 to 1961. The magazine targeted an elite readership and was the handiwork of a single individual, Baburao Patel. The prewar years saw a gradual decline in the studio system and the rise of the independent film producer and with it, the star system. Magazines were used to promote the star persona, and soon there was proliferation of glossy film magazines that focused on the stars and their lifestyles. At the same time there were some serious film trade magazines such as *Screen*, started by the Indian Express group of newspapers in 1951. Another film trade magazine was *Tradeguide*, started in 1954.

The growth of magazines continued over the decades, with several famous literary figures lending their names to literary periodicals. After independence, several publishing houses, such as the Times of India group of newspapers, offered magazines devoted to cinema (*Filmfare*), women (*Femina*), or general interest (*The Illustrated Weekly of India*). The gradual increase in magazines reached its apogee in the 1980s.

Most of the new magazines of the 1980s were the consequence of greater advertising budgets from manufacturers of consumer goods. In addition to the growth of political magazines mentioned above, the 1980s saw the sudden rise in society, lifestyle, home decoration, and women's magazines. *Society, Debonair, Gentleman, Inside Outside, Interiors, Savvy,* and *Women's Era* began to compete with the older publications such as *Eve's Weekly, The Illustrated Weekly of India,* and *Femina*. In the face of such intense competition, both *Eve's Weekly* and the *Illustrated Weekly of India* eventually ceased publication. In the regional languages, the most important women's magazines were *Manorama Weekly* (Malayalam), *Grihashobha* (in several regional languages), and *Ghar Shringaar* (Punjabi). They covered a range of subjects of interest to many women: cooking, home care, fashion, films, and gossip.

In the 1980s film magazines began to comprise a very important sector of the magazine trade. The magazine with the biggest circulation was *Filmfare,* followed by its closest rivals, *Cine Blitz* and *Screen*. The more salacious *Stardust,* belonging to the Magna Publications, transfixed the public with its scoops on stars. In addition, scores of film magazines were published in Hindi and the regional languages, particularly the four southern languages of Malayalam, Tamil, Telugu, and Kannada. *Filmi Duniya* and *Filmi Kaliyan,* both Hindi film monthlies, boasted the biggest circulations.

Several vernacular magazines are devoted to cinema and film gossip. According to writer Rachel Dwyer, they tend to be weeklies printed on cheap paper with low production values. Photos are scarce, and when they do appear, they are usually in black and white. These magazines are aimed at a lower-class male market and usually carry advertisements that promise male vigor. Typical of this genre of magazines are *Film City* and *Aar Paar* from Mumbai, and *Kingstyle* and *Filmi Duniya* from Delhi, and they generally have low circulation figures (Dwyer 2001).

Sports magazines include *Sports Weekly* and *Sport World* (from Ananda Bazaar Patrika group), and *Sportstar* (from The Hindu group). One of the many specialized cricket magazines is *Cricket Samrat,* a monthly in Hindi, one of the top-selling magazines.

The growth in the size of the middle classes in the 1980s gave rise to a demand for more specialized newspapers and magazines, such as those covering financial reports: the *Economic Times, Financial Express, Business India, Business Week,* and *Business Standard*. In addition, the post-Emergency era saw the advent of computer magazines such as *Computers Today* and *Dataquest*. Magazines devoted to competitive examinations are also best sellers. One such is *Pratiyogita Darshan*.

In 1987, Ashok Row Kavi, the former *Indian Express* reporter and gay activist, started *Bombay Dost,* India's only gay and lesbian magazine. A sporadic publication, it appears more frequently now that it has found greater financial stability.

The Contemporary Scene

Today, the most striking feature of Indian print media is the sheer diversity of the publications. Newspapers and magazines are printed in each of the eighteen languages and ten different scripts of India. This linguistic variety has ensured that there are no clear national leaders capable of monopolizing the newspaper industry nor any fears of the monopolistic ownership strategies seen among newspaper publishers in the United States, Canada,

Magazine display at an Indian newsstand, 1996. (Jeremy Horner/Corbis)

and Australia (Jeffery 2000). Instead, each language group constitutes a discrete newspaper market characterized by intense competition among the publishers in that language for the top spot.

For instance, the National Readership Survey statistics for 2003–2004 reveal that regional-language dailies have the highest circulation figures in the country. The leading newspaper is the Kanpur-based, Hindi-language *Dainik Jagran*, with multiple editions from seven different cities and nearly 16 million readers. It is closely followed by the multiple-edition Bhopal-based Hindi-language *Dainik Bhaskar*, with 13.5 million readers. The other leading Hindi-language newspaper is *Amar Ujala*, from Agra in the state of Uttar Pradesh. It has a circulation of 8.5 million. But none of these newspapers is known or has much impact outside the Hindi belt of the north-

ern states of Uttar Pradesh, Bihar, and Madhya Pradesh.

Similarly, the Malayalam daily *Malayala Manorama* in Kerala has a circulation of 9 million, and its closest rival, *Matrubhumi*, has a circulation of 7.4 million. Both, like the Hindi-language leaders, are scarcely known outside the communities of Malayalam speakers in Kerala and pockets of the community elsewhere. Two of the other regional-language leaders are the daily *Thanthi* (in Tamil), with a circulation of 8.8 million, and the Telugu-language *Eenadu*, from Andhra Pradesh, with a circulation of 8.1 million.

The only English-language daily in the top ten list of largest circulation is the *Times of India*, published from twelve centers with a combined circulation of 7.2 million. However, although the newspaper is the clear leader in the cities of Mumbai,

Bangalore, and now in Delhi, where it competes with leader *Hindustan Times* for the 2 million readership market, its presence is diminished in the two other megacities of India—Kolkata and Chennai. In Kolkata, the English-language *Telegraph* (with just under one million readers) leads the field, followed by the *Statesman* (400,000 readers). Of the city's Bengali-language newspapers, *Ananda Bazaar Patrika* (over 3 million readers) is followed by *Bartaman* (1.5 million readers).

However, the circulation figures do not indicate the numbers of readers. It is estimated that there are on average around five readers to every newspaper, although writer Robin Jeffery points out that there are eighteen readers to every copy of the Tamil-language *Dina Thanthi* (Jeffery 2000).

The same substantial numbers are reflected among magazine readers, with women's magazines the most widely read genre of magazine. These include *Saras Salil* (Hindi), which has a circulation of nearly 7 million. The magazine is also published in Marathi, Tamil, and Telugu. Another women's interest magazine is *Grihashobha*, with a circulation of 3.7 million in Hindi. It also appears in four other languages—Marathi, Telugu, Kannada, and Gujerati. Also in the women's interest category are the Malayalam-language magazine *Vanitha* (circulation 3.2 million), the Hindi-language *Meri Saheli* (circulation 2.4 million), and *Sarita* (circulation 2.1 million).

The leading English-language magazines for women include *Femina* (published by the Times of India group), *Women's Era*, and *Savvy*. In 1996, foreign magazines for women, such as *Elle* and *Cosmopolitan*, started Indian editions. But after an initial spurt of interest in these international glossies, the circulation figures for both magazines have begun to drop. The only serious magazine for women that consistently explores feminist issues on gender and sexuality without succumbing to the pressures of consumerism and advertising is *Manushi*, edited by the active feminist Madhu Kishwar.

Current affairs is the next most widely circulated genre of magazines. The leading magazine is *India Today*, which appears in several languages. The highest circulation figures are for the Hindi-language *India Today* (4.3 million), with the English-language not far behind (4.1 million). Other magazines on current affairs include *Outlook*, *The Week*, and *Frontline*.

English-language *Filmfare*, from Bennett, Coleman & Sons, which owns the Times of India Group of newspapers, has the highest circulation (2.5 million) and counts among the top ten magazines in circulation. Foreign ownership of newspapers is banned. However, an exception was made for *Readers Digest*, which is also among the top ten best-selling magazines in India.

Issues

Press Freedom

Despite its periodical attempts to muzzle vernacular newspapers, one of the great legacies of the British *raj* in India has been that of a free and robust press. This most remarkable of byproducts of British presence was also one of the most efficient gravediggers of its rule in India.

The struggle for press freedom in colonial India was indirectly related to the struggle between the contrasting ideologies of the two parties in Britain. On the one hand were the Whigs (Liberals), who saw themselves as bringing education and progress (which included freedom of the press) to India; on the other hand were the Tories (Conservatives), who dreaded the progress of education and saw repressive methods as the way to govern India.

When a new Constitution was written in 1950 for an independent India, the freedom of the press was guaranteed in the freedom of expression under Article 19 (1) a. However, there are certain statutory curbs on the freedom of the press mainly through the Official Secrets Act of 1923, the Press and Registration of Books Act of 1867, and the Law of Defamation of 1988. India's first prime minister, Jawaharlal Nehru, was a fierce defender of the freedom of the press as was his successor, Lal Bahadur Shastri. But despite their rhetoric, they used subtle means to control the press, particularly the smaller Indian-language newspapers, a potent force of which the colonial administrator was historically suspicious. These methods included the granting of government advertisements from the DAVP, crucial to the survival of a small publication in the districts and *mofussil*. Another was the allocation of newsprint.

Harassment of the Press

But it was not until the rule of Prime Minister Indira Gandhi that the press was overtly muzzled, and much of the supine print media accepted the restrictions on their freedom of expression demanded by Mrs. Gandhi. But several newspapers did not. And for their defiance they were subjected to persecution, harassment, and vindictiveness on the part of the government—the cutting off electricity to the printing presses, withdrawal of government adver-tising (a significant source of income for most newspapers in India), withholding of newsprint, and the like.

However, some newer magazines, along with a new generation of journalists, have since come into existence and exposed many of the abuses perpetrated by the government. Whereas earlier journalists had been underpaid hacks eager for subsidized accommodation and government hand-outs, the new generation of journalists is self assured, well paid, and not overawed by the power of the government. Their brash, controversial, and even adversarial reporting makes for newspapers that are far more interesting to read.

After the Emergency of 1975–1977, some Indian newspapers and magazines, in particular the *Indian Express* and *The Hindu*, began to run a series of investigations into the kickbacks and bribes received in the defense contracts. They exposed the Swedish company Bofors' defense contracts, the (West) German submarine contracts, and the Fairfax scandals, all of which allegedly pointed to the involvement of Prime Minister Rajiv Gandhi, son of Indira Gandhi, or his subordinates. In an attempt to ward off the investigations, Rajiv Gandhi initiated the Defamation Bill on 29 August 1988, which was passed by the Lok Sabha (the Lower House) without consultation with the various consultative bodies of the press. But seeing the intensity of feelings that the bill inspired from all quarters, including ordinary citizens and eminent jurists, as well as the media, the government decided to withdraw it before it became law.

Violence against the Media

Opposition and secessionist parties and other disgruntled groups can also unleash and orchestrate mob pressure where certain sections of the public, under the guise of the "people's power," decide to take the law into their own hands. Threats by aggrieved persons as well as violent physical attacks on staff and properties of newspapers are not uncommon. The Second Press Commission listed several examples, ranging from threats and abuse—such as those experienced by the editor of the *Indian Express* in 1979 for reporting mass copying and cheating during examinations conducted by Meerut University—to mob attacks, as suffered by the news editor of the *Times of India* and his staff, also in 1979, for reporting the arrest of a city priest for smuggling.

Three newspaper offices were attacked by mobs for reporting an alleged molestation of a female student at the Medical College in Cuttack (Orissa State) in 1981; four newspaper offices were *gheraoed* (surrounded) in Bangalore in 1980 for "misreporting an incident involving the Karnataka State Chief Minister." The worst case was the *gherao* of the offices of *Hind Samachar* in 1981, the burning of the editor Lala Jagat Narain's effigy, and his subsequent murder in 1981 for not supporting the secessionist movement in Punjab (Sarcar 1984). Narain's son was also murdered by Sikh separatists, as were sixty other journalists of the Hind Samachar group of newspapers in the course of their struggle for secession from India.

During the demolition of the Babri Masjid by fanatical Hindu nationalists in 1990, journalists and photographers were attacked and their equipment destroyed to stop them reporting the wanton destruction.

The Case of Tehelka.com

The Indian government has several instruments with which to dissuade the media from close scrutiny of government activities. The most common is that of harassment.

A more recent case was the government's harassment of tehelka.com. In 2001, tehelka.com, a news-based website, exposed the culture of bribe taking at the heart of the Indian Ministry of Defence (MoD). Tehelka set up a bogus company supposedly based in London claiming to sell "thermal binoculars." It tried to get the MoD officials interested in buying them. They were able to meet Jaya Jaitley, head of the Samata Party (also confidante and companion of the Defence Minister George Fernandes) and Bangaru Laxman, secretary of the BJP, the party in government until 2004. They secretly filmed Laxman taking money in exchange for promising help with procurement of defense contracts. Equally, the officials at the MoD were shown as not averse to being plied with alcohol. It was alleged that the services of prostitutes were also eagerly accepted.

There was an outcry when the scandal broke and was carried by the mass media. Faced with the evidence, Fernandes resigned, even though he himself was not shown to be part of the bribe-taking activities, as did Laxman, who clearly was. Jaitley at first accused the journalists of being agents for Pakistan and then raised doubt over the authenticity of the tapes. As part of the investigation, the tapes were sent to a forensic lab in the United Kingdom for examination and were eventually confirmed as genuine. The investigation was stalled for nearly three years, during which time the government, it is alleged, instigated a program of systematic harassment.

In September 2001, editor Tarun Tejpal was charged with "immoral trafficking" (or pimping) for having offered women to the officials. Later the main financial backers of Tehelka were themselves targets of investigations from the customs, police, tax, and anticorruption authorities. The company was ruined. Before the scandal broke, the company had a staff of 120; by 2003 it had just one salaried employee. The investigation was put into cold storage during the BJP-led coalition government that remained in power until 2004. With a Congress-led coalition currently in power, the investigations against the alleged malefactors have been revived and the matter is being investigated by the Central Bureau of Investigation (CBI).

The sensation created by the Tehelka exposé has led to a spate of "hidden camera" investigations as journalists vie to nab an errant politician in a sex or corruption scandal.

Legislative Privileges

The matter of legislative privileges is ambiguous and has not been properly codified in law. Although freedom of the press is guaranteed in the Indian Constitution, the press has no privileges and must therefore operate within the limitations imposed on it by Parliament and state assemblies. Parliament and state legislatures can decide who can be admitted into the press gallery in their august portals for coverage of the day's proceedings. It also has the right to prohibit the publication of these proceedings, particularly those exchanges that have been expunged from the record. It also has the right to punish those violating its privileges and those guilty of contempt.

By and large it is extremely rare for a journalist to be reprimanded by the houses of parliament or the state assemblies. However, powerful political parties with sizeable majorities can misuse the privileges accorded to the legislature to stifle criticism by the press of their behavior. In a few instances press cards have been withdrawn, as in the case R. K. Karanjia, editor of the sensationalist investigative weekly *Blitz*, who was reprimanded for publishing his journalist's report ridiculing an opposition member, Acharya Kripalani, as "Kripaloony." Karanjia had to apologize to the House before his press card was reinstated (Bhatt 1997: 107–108).

Occasionally a newspaper carries exchanges that have been expunged from the records. This can happen in error, as the reporter may be genuinely unaware of the expunction order, which may have been announced much later, long after the journalist has left the press gallery. Lately, legislators have tried to stifle any criticism by invoking legislative privileges. In 1994, Nikhil Wagle, editor of the Marathi newspaper *Mahanagar*, was seen to have violated the privileges of the Maharashtra State legislative assembly when he criticized the fawning tributes legislators paid to a deceased member who had only recently been accused of harboring criminal connections. Wagle was imprisoned for a week when he refused to apologize for his comments (Bhatt 1997).

An even more enthusiastic claimant of legislative privilege is Jayalalithaa, politician, Tamil screen goddess, and one-time costar of the screen god M. G. Ramachandran (generally known as "MGR"), and leader of the All India Annadurai Dravida Munnetra Kazhagam (AIADMK). In 2003, backed by her immense majority, Jayalalithaa got the Tamil Nadu legislative assembly to sentence five senior editors of the august English-language newspaper *The Hindu*, as well as the editor of her political rival DMK's party newspaper *Murasoli*, to a fortnight in prison. On 25 April 2003, *The Hindu* had criticized Chief Minister Jayalalithaa for her high-handedness in an editorial entitled "Rising Intolerance," and *Murasoli* had merely reprinted it.

According to the press, within minutes of the resolution's passage, the police stormed the newspaper offices to arrest the accused for maligning the reputation of Chief Minister Jayalalithaa. But when the news was flashed on television screens across the country, the backlash was immediate. Journalists took to the streets to protest, and both Prime Minister Atal Bihari Vajpayee and Deputy Prime Minister L. K. Advani had to call the state governor for consultations. In the meantime, the Supreme Court granted a stay on the arrests (Ram 2003). In the aftermath of the episode, the Indian Newspaper Society organized a seminar on "Freedom of Press and Legislative Privilege," where several issues—the public accountability of those holding public office, the misuse of the legislative privileges, the removal of the right of legislative assemblies to sentence people to prison, and the increasing intolerance of political parties—were debated. It was finally resolved that the press should not yield to the privileges of the legislature (Imam Ali 2004).

Conclusion

According to a recent report in *The Economist*, there has never been a better time for journalism in India. A strong economy and a bullish stock market have seen enthusi-

asm, both in India and abroad, for investment in fresh news outlets for Indian news media. Consequently there has been a breakdown in the "regional carve-up" of India that many newspapers used to observe. Until a few years ago, most of the big English-language newspapers shared an understanding to stay off each other's turf: the *Times of India* in Mumbai, the *Hindustan Times* in Delhi, the *Telegraph* in Kolkata, and the *Hindu* in Chennai. However the *Times of India* broke up this cozy consensus with a circulation drive in Delhi (*The Economist* 2005). The *Times of India* also launched a new tabloid, the *Mumbai Mirror* in May 2005. The *Hindustan Times* responded by launching a new edition of its paper in Mumbai in July 2005. Meanwhile, in the same month, the owners of Zee TV, and the Hindi-language *Dainik Bhaskar*, the biggest selling newspaper in India, launched *Daily News & Analysis* (advertised as *DNA)* in Mumbai.

One of the biggest areas of concern for the print media, particularly newspapers, in both the English-language and regional-language press, is the growth in television news channels. Market research bureaus insist that the population still prefers the print media to television, with the all-India reach of print media at 25 percent compared with 20 percent for satellite and cable television, and 22 percent for FM radio. However, terrestrial television commands 53 percent of media reach across the country, and in urban areas the reach of terrestrial television is 80 percent, with 46 percent for satellite and cable as well as print media. Print media still commands 51 percent of the total amount spent by companies on advertising, compared with 41 percent for television. But the gap keeps narrowing.

Print media companies have not underestimated the threat of television, and many newspaper companies have begun to diversify into satellite television and private FM radio channels. Ushodaya company, which publishes the Telugu *Eenadu* newspaper, has expanded into television (the ETV channels in regional languages). (The owner, Ramoji Rao, has also constructed film studios in the vicinity of Hyderabad.) Living Media, the publishers of the newsmagazine *India Today*, owns the television news channel Aaj Tak. Bennett, Coleman & Co., which owns the Times of India group of newspapers and magazines and operates Radio Mirchi in Mumbai is looking to expand into television news, while the Ananda Bazaar Patrika group of newspapers provides news content for Rupert Murdoch and the News Corp–owned STAR News satellite channel. Equally, broadcast media companies are teaming up with print media companies to launch new papers, as in the case of Zee TV and the owners of *Dainik Bhaskar*, which launched *Daily News & Analysis* in July 2005 in Mumbai.

Although television channels provide national, international, and regional news, and the newly privatized FM radio channels provide city-centric music and entertainment, local news in local languages will continue to be the monopoly of myriad Indian-language newspapers. Recently foreign media companies have begun to take an interest in the Indian vernacular press. In 2005, the Irish publisher Independent News & Media bought 26 percent of Jagran Prakashan, publisher of the biggest circulation daily, the Hindi-language *Dainik Jagran*. As economic growth spreads gradually to the smaller towns and villages, and the advertisers chase the increased spend-

ing power into the hinterland, the prospect for more and more local or multi-edition regional newspapers looks bright as consumers switch to different media for different spheres of news and information.

A to Z Index

Aj is a Hindi-language nationalist newspaper started in Benares (Varanasi) in 1920. It was the bulwark of the Indian National Congress. Today, *Aj* remains a formidable newspaper in the Hindi-speaking belt of northern India.

Amrita Bazaar Patrika is one of the oldest Indian-owned nationalist dailies; it was founded in 1868 to fight against peasants being exploited by the colonial indigo planters. The newspaper was forced to close down after labor unrest in 1990.

Ananda Bazaar Patrika was started in 1922 and is today the best-selling newspaper in Kolkata. The newspaper group also has several other publications, such as *The Telegraph*, *Sunday*, and *Sports World* in English.

Dainik Bhaskar is the second largest newspaper in India. This Hindi-language paper, started in 1958, is based in Bhopal, Madhya Pradesh, and is published in seven separate editions. In 2005, it started a Mumbai-based English-language newspaper, *Daily News and Analysis*, with the owners of Zee TV.

Dainik Jagran is the largest-selling newspaper of India. The Hindi-language paper, started in 1942 and based in Kanpur, has ten separate editions covering the entire state of Uttar Pradesh.

The Directorate of Audio-Visual Publicity (DAVP) is a government department for government advertising. It places advertisements for public-sector jobs, government tenders, or any other government-related activities in the print media, broadcast media, billboards, and the like.

Eenadu is a best-selling Telugu newspaper started by Ramoji Rao in 1974 in Vishakhapatnam, Andhra Pradesh. Rao now owns several regional-language television channels called ETV, along with a film production center near Hyderabad.

Filmfare was started in 1952 by the Times of India group of newspapers; it was one of the first film "glossies" in English. In 1953, it instituted the Filmfare awards, modeled on the Hollywood Academy awards, allowing the readers to cast their votes to decide the annual winners in all categories.

The Hindu, rated one of the best newspapers in the country, began in 1878 in Madras. In 1905, a lawyer, S. Kasturiranga Iyengar, bought the newspaper and appointed his nephew, S. Rangaswami, as its editor. Rangaswami's vigorous views and powerful writing led to confrontations with the colonial authorities. The newspaper had many distinguished writers as foreign correspondents. Subhash Chandra Bose was its correspondent in Vienna, and V. K. Krishna Menon, later India's defense minister, in London. In 1963 the newspaper was the first in India to create its own air service to fly its newspaper to distant areas. It was also the first to introduce photo type-setting for printing the newspaper. In the late 1980s it also was the first Indian newspaper to invest in high-tech computerized printing in Delhi.

The Illustrated Weekly of India was a best-selling weekly on matters of general interest, published by the Times of India group of newspapers. The magazine reached its golden years under the editorship of novelist, historian, and journalist Khushwant Singh. It shut down in 1985 due to stiff competition from other magazines.

Indian Express is an important multi-edition English-language daily. Backed by its late owner, Ramnath Goenka, it is renowned for its investigative journalism and for having stood up to the bullying tactics of Indira Gandhi.

India Today is one of the best newsweeklies in English. It was started in 1975, the year Mrs. Gandhi declared the Emergency. The magazine today has a circulation of 4.3 million. It is one of the few English-language magazines with editions in many regional languages. Its proprietor, Living Media, also owns the television news channel Aaj Tak and some FM radio channels.

Malayala Manorama is a best-selling Malayalam newspaper based in Kottayam with four other editions in Kerala State. It was founded by K. V. Mappillai in 1904 and became a daily in 1928. It was shut down by the Travancore royal household and reopened only after independence. The *Malayala Manorama Weekly* is also a best-selling magazine. The group started an English-language magazine, *The Week*, in 1982.

The Press and Registration of Books (PRB) Act of 1867 was an attempt by the colonial government to hold publishers and printers responsible for the "seditious" contents of the newspapers. The PRB Act is still in force, with minor amendments to the original law passed in 1867.

Ram Mohan Roy (1772–1833) was a great social reformer and founding father of Indian journalism. He began the great tradition of Indian-language newspapers.

Sakal is the leading Marathi newspaper published from Pune. N. B. Parulekar started it in 1931, and the newspaper became a byword for excellent journalism. He kept the news close to his readers, offering a special column with the daily price of fresh vegetables. The newspaper also challenged the Press Commission efforts to impose a "page-price" schedule and won.

Stardust, the flagship magazine of Magna Publications, a Mumbai-based publishing company owned by Nari Hira, started publication in 1971. The best-selling magazine, formerly edited by pulp fiction writer Shobhaa De, is entirely devoted to film gossip and scandal, and is modelled on the American magazine *Photoplay.*

Tehelka.com is an e-newspaper that ran a sting operation with a hidden camera and caught several senior military officials and politicians accepting bribes, liquor, and the services of prostitutes.

The *Times of India* is the oldest English-language daily in India and has the highest combined circulation for an English-language daily in India today. The company

that owns the publication, Bennett, Coleman & Co., also publishes *Navbharat Times, Maharashtra Times, Economic Times,* and best-selling magazines such as *Femina* and *Filmfare.* However, the *Illustrated Weekly of India,* which was started in 1888, ceased publication in 1985, as did the *Evening News,* when it was unable to compete with Khalid Ansari's *Midday* in Mumbai.

Bibliography and References

Bhaskara Rao, N. "The Newspaper Scene 1998: Miles to Go." *Vidura,* January-March 1999.

Bhaskara Rao, N., and G. N. S. Raghavan. *Social Effects of Mass Media in India.* New Delhi: Gyan Publishing House, 1996.

Bhatt, S. C. *Indian Press Since 1955.* New Delhi: Publications Division, Ministry of Information and Broadcasting, Government of India, 1997.

Coleridge, Nicholas. *Paper Tigers.* London: Heinemann, 1993.

Dwyer, Rachel. "Shooting Stars: The Indian Film Magazine, *Stardust.*" In *Pleasure and the Nation: The History, Politics and Consumption of Public Culture in India.* Edited by Rachel Dwyer and Christopher Pinney. New Delhi: Oxford University Press, 2001.

The Economist. "The Media in India: Popping Corks." 30 July 2005.

George, T. J. S. *The Provincial Press in India.* New Delhi: Press Institute of India, 1967.

Imam Ali, Farwa. "Standing Up for Their Rights." *The Week,* 1 February 2004.

Israel, Milton. *Communications and Power: Propaganda and the Press in the Indian Nationalist Struggle 1920–47.* Cambridge: Cambridge University Press, 1994.

Jeffery, Robin. *India's Newspaper Revolution: Capitalism, Politics, and the Indian-language Press 1977–99.* New Delhi: Oxford University Press, 2000.

———. "Advertising and Indian Language Newspapers: How Capitalism Supports

(Certain) Cultures and (Some) States, 1947–96." *Pacific Affairs* 70 (1) Spring 1997.

———. "Punjab: The Subliminal Charge." *Economic and Political Weekly*, 1–8 March 1997.

———. "Monitoring Newspapers and Understanding the State: India, 1948–93." *Asian Survey* 34 (9) September 1994.

Kesavan, B. S. *History of Printing and Publishing in India*. New Delhi: National Book Trust, 1985.

Lawrence, James. *Raj: The Making of British India*. London: Abacus, 1998.

Mankekar, D. R. *What Ails the Indian Press*. New Delhi: Somaiya Publications, 1970.

Ministry of Information and Broadcasting. *India 2004*. New Delhi: Publications Division, 2004.

———. *Report of the Inquiry Committee on Small Newspapers 1965*. New Delhi: 1966.

Natarajan, S. *A History of the Press in India*. Bombay: Asia Publishing House, 1962.

Padhy, K. S. *The Muzzled Press*. New Delhi: Kanishka: 1994.

Parikh, Jayant, ed. *Press and Journalism: Role and Responsibility in Developing Society*. New Delhi: Commonwealth Publishers, 1998.

Parthasarthy, Rangswami. *Journalism in India: From the Earliest Times to the Present Day*. New Delhi: Sterling Publishers, 1989.

Ram, Arun. "The Hindu: Taking on Muzzle Power." *India Today*, 24 November 2003.

Rao, B. S. S, and B. V. Sharma. "The Regional Press and Political Socialization." *Vidura* 20 (2) 1983.

Sahni, J. *Truth about the Indian Press*. New Delhi: Allied, 1974.

Sainath, P. *Everybody Loves a Good Drought*. New Delhi: Penguin, 1996.

Samaddar, Ranabir. *Workers and Automation: The Impact of New Technology in the Newspaper Industry*. New Delhi: Sage, 1994.

Sarcar, R. C. S. *The Press in India*. New Delhi: S. Chand, 1984.

Sharma, S. K. *Political Communication and Local Newsmedia*. Almora, India: Shree Almora Book Depot, 1992.

Shrivastava, K. M. *Media Issues*. New Delhi: Sterling, 1992.

Spear, Percival. *A History of India: Volume Two*. Harmondsworth, UK: Penguin, 1970.

The Times of India. "Tehelka Tapes to Be Examined." 10 May 2003.

White Paper on Misuse of Mass Media during the Internal Emergency (August 1977). New Delhi: Government of India, 1977.

6
Radio

Radio is the most widespread medium in India. Radio broadcasts can be received by nearly 99 percent of Indian people. In contrast, only 20 percent buy newspapers, and only 60 percent have access to television broadcasts. Radio, also the cheapest means of disseminating information, is generally considered the medium of the masses. There are 209 broadcasting centers, and All India Radio claims that nearly 304 million Indians tune in to the programs on any given day. Battery-operated radios were an important tool in relaying messages to the thousands affected by the tsunami on 26 December 2004, for example, and in providing them with regular updates on missing relatives.

Radio in India is a state-owned monopoly governed by Prasar Bharati, a supposedly autonomous body funded by the government. In 2000, however, the Indian government agreed to privatize some FM channels, a move that has begun to shift the profile of radio broadcasting. Today, the growth of the private FM radio sector is the most significant contemporary development in Indian radio.

History

Radio broadcasting started in the 1920s in colonial India. The first radio program was a private broadcast by enthusiasts in 1924 operating a 40-watt transmitter from the Madras Presidency Club (Rajadhyaksha and Willemen 1999). The station ran for three years. Just seven months after the British Broadcasting Corporation (BBC) began its service in 1927 in the United Kingdom, two radio clubs with private transmitters in Bombay (now Mumbai) and Calcutta (now Kolkata) began a commercial broadcasting service under an agreement with the colonial government of India and inaugurated by Lord Irwin, the viceroy of India. The broadcasts were aimed at the Europeans living in India as well as the thin upper crust of English-speaking Indians. They called themselves the Indian Broadcasting Company.

Indian engineers of the state-run All India Radio (AIR) work on a "phone-in" program at Port Blair, 3 January 2005. Glued to battery-operated radios, survivors in the remote Andaman and Nicobar islands received updates on missing relatives and aid with the help of AIR. (Deshakalyan Chowdhury/AFP/Getty Images)

But by 1930 the company had gone into receivership, and the colonial government was obliged to take control of the service at the insistence of angry license holders and equipment dealers who were stuck with stockpiles of broadcasting hardware (Kumar 2003). The princely states were given the right to install and use their own transmitters and collect the license fees. To ensure that all persons with radio receivers and broadcasting equipment possessed licenses to do so, the government passed the Indian Wireless Telegraphy Act in 1933.

Meanwhile in 1932, the BBC had launched the Empire short-wave radio service from London. Against the backdrop of a growing movement for independence, the British government from its seat of power in London had decided to use the airwaves to wean public opinion away from the Indian freedom fighters. To that effect, a producer with the BBC, Lionel Fielden, and H. L. Kirke, one of the BBC's top engineers, were dispatched to India in 1935 to improve and expand the Indian government-operated system. British strategic, economic, and administrative interests guided this expansion of the radio network. It was hoped that the broadening of the network would increase the potential audience for the London short-wave programs beamed to India.

In 1936, the Indian Broadcasting Company was renamed All India Radio (AIR). Its objective was clear: to inform, educate, and entertain the masses in a manner the authorities thought appropriate. With Fielden as its first-ever director-general, AIR was fashioned along the lines of the BBC. Over the years leading up to Indian independence, oversight of AIR shifted from the Department of Industries and Labor to the Department of Communications and thence to the Department of Information and Broadcasting. After independence it became the Ministry of Information and Broadcasting.

As part of the development and expansion program, a network of six stations was installed—in Delhi, Bombay, Calcutta, Madras, Lucknow, and Tiruchirapalli—along with a complement of eighteen transmitters, six on medium wave and the rest on short wave. All plans for development were put on hold with the declaration of World War II and Japan's subsequent entry into the fray, but radio was an important tool to counter the propaganda being broadcast to the Indian subcontinent by Britain's enemies. Consequently, AIR increased the number of centralized news bulletins. These were broadcast daily in twenty-seven Indian languages to promote the cause of the Allies.

When India gained independence on 15 August 1947, the transfer of power was broadcast live on radio (including Nehru's much quoted speech to the Constituent Assembly about India's "tryst with destiny"). Control of the airwaves passed from colonial hands to the Indian interim government, and the newly independent nation inherited the six radio stations and eighteen transmitters installed by the British. Despite Fielden's efforts, the broadcast coverage at the time of Indian independence was barely 2.5 percent of the country, with less than a quarter million licensed listeners, accounting for just 11 percent of the Indian population. AIR came under the direct control of Sardar Vallabhai Patel, the home minister during the interim government who also had responsibility for the Ministry of Information and Broadcasting.

The authoritarian Patel was renowned for his role in securing the integration of the Indian princely states with his "accustomed vigour and skill" (Spear 1970: 240). He also took their radio stations and placed them under government control. He drew up a plan to extend coverage to a variety of linguistic and geographical areas by building pilot stations with one kilowatt medium-wave transmitters in the state capitals and the border areas. An orthodox Hindu, he also imposed high moral standards on the artists of AIR, which ruled out most of the accomplished courtesans who had adorned the princely courts of north India (Luthra 1986). "With regard to music," writes radio historian David Lelyveld, "the major concern was to replace the system of princely patronage, now clearly dead, and to counterbalance the sources of commercial music, in particular the films" (Lelyveld 1996: 57). By 1950, the number of broadcasting centers had risen to twenty-five; they covered 21 percent of the population and 12 percent of the total area (Baruah 1983).

After the first general elections and the victory of the Congress Party in 1952, B. V. Keskar was made minister of Information and Broadcasting and became its longest-serving minister. An austere Brahmin and devotee of classical Indian music, Keskar made it his personal mission to rescue the general public from the vulgarities of Indian film songs. He was determined to make the elite pleasures of classical music available to the general populace. A purist at heart, he banned the use of the harmonium, a keyboard instrument, on the grounds that it was a hybrid adaptation of a foreign musical instrument. But he saved his particular loathing for Hindi film songs because of the vulgarity of their hybrid Hindustani (a mix of Hindi and Urdu) lyrics and their music, a western-style orchestration that revealed an unabashed amalgam of Indian and Western influences.

The Hindi film industry has always maintained a catholic interest in world music. With the need to provide at least six to eight songs per film, and with over 100 films produced annually in Hindi at that time, the composers raided any musical form they could lay their hands on—Indian and foreign, folk, regional, and classical. From non-Indian sources they cheerfully helped themselves to Mozart, jazz, and Latin American beats. Since the film narratives promoted modernity over traditionalism, the West-inspired musical compositions were entirely suited to the films and were to Indian ears vibrant, exciting, and exotic. Keskar saw it as his duty to rescue the people from such a travesty. He decided to compete with the popularity of film music by setting up a national orchestra, or Vadya Vrinda, with the internationally renowned sitar player Pandit Ravi Shankar as its head. He commissioned Shankar to provide a "light" alternative to the classical broadcasts, and thus a new genre of "light music" was created. Thousands of artists had already been employed by the ministry in a manner not dissimilar to the recruitment of civil servants in other departments, and the light music project was one way to keep them all occupied (Lelyveld 1996).

Film songs were being broadcast on AIR under an agreement between the Indian government and the film producers. In 1952 under Keskar, the practice of announcing the name of the film from which the song was taken was discontinued. It was, reasoned Keskar, tantamount to free publicity for films (Barnouw and Krishnaswamy 1980). Film producers were outraged and broke off negotiations with the Indian government, and film songs were taken off the air. Keskar also discontinued the practice of broadcasting live cricket match commentaries on AIR, on the grounds that cricket was a colonial game and had no place in independent India. In their place, a National Programme of Music was installed. Thereafter, 50 percent of all broadcasts on AIR comprised classical music. The radio was also the outlet for folk music from the diverse regions of India.

During the time Keskar was fighting to keep the baleful influence of film music from polluting the aesthetic sense of radio listeners in India, Ceylon (now Sri Lanka) was starting up its own commercial shortwave radio broadcasts to India. Film songs expelled from the Indian airwaves found a berth on Radio Ceylon, and soon Hindi film music on that channel became prime-time listening for Indians. The highlight of the week was the hit parade, called "Bianca Geetmala." It was broadcast on Wednesdays and sponsored by the multinational Ciba company to promote their brand of toothpaste. Ameen Sayani, brother of Hamid Sayani, who hosted the English-language programs for Radio Ceylon, seduced his listeners with his mellifluous voice, humor, and charm. The program ended with the dramatic announcement, amidst a fanfare of trumpets, of the new top single of the hit parade. "In many northern and central

Indian cities," write Barnouw and Krishnawamy, "that moment found clusters of people huddled around tea shops and other places with radios" (Barnouw and Krishnawamy, 1980: 158). Many remember those moments fondly. Sathya Saran, editor of the women's magazine *Femina*, even kept diaries of the weekly winning songs. "I remember as a schoolgirl sitting glued to the radio with a large diary on my lap, writing down the name of songs, and their listings on the countdown show, as if it were completely necessary to my well being" (*Femina*, January 1, 2004: 128).

A survey of listener preferences revealed that out of ten households with licensed radio sets, nine were tuned to Radio Ceylon and the tenth set was broken (Lelyveld 1996). Keskar, realizing that he could not beat the popularity of Radio Ceylon with his personal preferences, agreed to allow film music back on AIR. In 1957, Vividh Bharati was created, a new service that offered almost nonstop film music broadcasts via two powerful short-wave transmitters from Bombay and Madras. In 1967, the service turned commercial and began accepting commercial advertisements and sponsorship. Today there are thirty-six Vividh Bharati and other commercial stations on AIR. (Also in 1967, television, hitherto under the auspices of AIR, was deemed an important enough medium to be placed under separate management.)

The reign of Keskar was more than just a fight about the imperatives of high and low culture on the airwaves. Although the main concerns of India's First Five-Year Plan (1951–1956) were agriculture, irrigation, and power generation, the development of the radio network, though not a priority, was not totally ignored. Under its auspices several low-power transmitters were either upgraded or replaced by higher-power transmitters. Although the overall number of transmitters remained the same, they achieved far greater coverage, reaching 46 percent of the population and 31 percent of the national geographical area.

Under the Second (1956–1961) and Third (1961–1966) Five-Year Plans, several new high-power medium- and short-wave transmitters were installed. The expansion of the radio services was also implemented through a drive to increase radio ownership in the country. The aim was to use the mass media to usher in modernity and meet the challenges of building a social democracy. Since support for rural communities was a major concern, particularly in matters of farming, farm radio forums based on an experiment in Canada were initiated in 1956, with the help of the UNESCO. The movement was a huge success and expanded. In the 1960s, AIR broadcast advice on high-yielding varieties of rice from its Tiruchirapalli station, which led to a new variety of rice aptly called "Radio Paddy." AIR has thus been credited with helping to usher in the green revolution in India (Kumar 2003).

In the succeeding years, as the cost of transistor radios began to fall, ownership increased exponentially. Transistor radios were also offered as free gifts to men who volunteered for a vasectomy (in keeping with the government's drive to promote family planning) during the 1970s. As the number of transmitters increased, so did the number of listeners. During the infamous years of the Internal Emergency declared by the prime minister, Mrs. Indira Gandhi (1975–1977), the government blatantly used the radio to promote its agenda. There was a clamp down on all dissenting voices, and V. C. Shukla, the minister for Information and Broadcasting, instructed station directors that AIR was not "a forum run by the government to debate on the conflicting ideologies but to make people 'understand' government policies" (Kumar 2003: 2177). All India Radio was soon dubbed "All Indi(r)a Radio" by the listening public.

After the defeat of Mrs. Gandhi and the removal of the Congress government after more than three decades of continuous power, proposals granting autonomy to the broadcast media were circulated. However, all of them were shelved when Mrs. Gandhi returned triumphant after the 1980 election. Against a background of growing violence in the Punjab, Kashmir, and the northeast regions in the 1980s radio, she planned to deploy radio for the purpose of national integration and communal harmony. Any hopes for autonomy of the broadcasting services were firmly quashed. In 1984, radio licenses were abolished, and from that point forward, the funding for radio came from the public purse.

Since then, the issue of autonomy has been raised several times but invariably shelved, either because of a change in government or due to a lack of bureaucratic will. In 1997, the Prasar Bharati, a government-funded body, was set up to oversee the broadcast media and ensure the autonomy of their services. Nevertheless, successive governments have continued to meddle in the composition of its board, half of whose members are appointed by the government. Today AIR remains a centralized bureaucracy disseminating via its expanded network of 210 broadcasting centers what it believes the listening public ought to hear rather than showing any real interest in what they might actually wish to hear. But with the growing competition from television, particularly cable and satellite television, the government has been under tremendous pressure to liberalize the airwaves. If private television channels—even foreign private channels—have been allowed to broadcast to the Indian public, some have argued, why have no Indian private radio channels been granted the same privileges?

In a case brought before it in 1995, the Supreme Court of India delivered a historic judgment by ruling that the airwaves did not constitute the government's exclusive private property. It deemed that the airwaves belonged to the people, and although they could be used for the promotion of the government's political agenda, they also had to be used for promoting the public good. It ordered the government to privatize at least a part of the airwaves. With great reluctance, the government agreed to the sale of some FM frequencies to private entrepreneurs in 2000. But several caveats accompanied the government's agreement to privatize the airwaves. Most importantly, no private FM channels would be allowed to disseminate news, and no foreign direct investment would be allowed in radio broadcasting. One hundred seven frequencies were placed on the market for use in forty cities. But despite the considerable fanfare accompanying this event, only twenty-two private FM radio stations currently operate in fourteen cities. Of these, Sun TV owns four that provide programs in the southern regional languages.

One of the main reasons for the small number of FM channels has been the high cost of the licenses. This was not imposed by the government but stemmed directly from the folly of the private entrepreneurs. Buoyed by the dot-com boom, they entered into a bidding frenzy. When the bubble burst, they discovered that they had entered into a contractual agreement with the government for an annual increase of 15 percent, regardless of earnings. Since advertising revenues in radio are small compared with those in the television or print media, some private FM channels such as Win FM quietly folded. Those that survive are mostly affiliated to media companies.

To recoup the costs of investment and license fees, many of the private FM channels have gravitated toward the most lucrative popular Hindi film and pop music sector. Because they target the same young, urban, educated middle classes to procure advertising revenue, most channels have ended up providing almost identical fare, delivered in the same breezy "Hinglish" (Hindi-English) patter. That these privatized FM channels are indistinguishable was made apparent by DRS, a marketing company survey where listeners to the top three private FM channels—Mirchi, Red, and City Radio—were unable to distinguish between them. According to Anish Trivedi, formerly of Radio Mid-Day: "Unfortunately the radio industry in India doesn't have a choice any more. The fee structure forces it to attract as large an audience as it can get. While there is nothing wrong with this, I feel it limits the scope of the station, in terms of its programming . . . My problem is having to assume that all listeners are idiots" (*Business India* 2003: 14).

The tight control exercised by the state on the production and dissemination of content, on the one hand, and the homogenized fare that is palmed off as entertainment by the privatized channels, on the other, has resulted in the "hegemony of the state and market over broadcasting" (Kumar 2003: 2173). In such a situation, the listening public, both urban and rural, has no say whatsoever in the matter.

Channels and Content

News and music is generally the main fare offered on Indian radio channels. The myriad channels of AIR are divided into five main sections that focus on rural areas (primary channels), cities (FM), the commercial service (nationwide), the nighttime channel (nationwide), and external broadcasts.

The main commercial section of AIR is centered on the thirty-six Vividh Bharati and other commercial stations on AIR. Vividh Bharati, which began in 1957, offers almost exclusively popular film music to the entire nation. News, film, and nonfilm music, talks, discussions, interviews, programs on health, nutrition and hygiene, farming and agriculture, special programs for women and children, sports programs, radio plays, and serials constitute the programming mix that is broadcast on primary channels in the regional languages.

A mix of news and music—in Hindi, English, and regional languages—is the main fare of the nine FM channels that serve the nine major cities (Delhi, Mumbai, Kolkata, Chennai, Bangalore, Panaji, Lucknow, Cuttack, and Jallandhar). They also feature chat shows, help lines, interactive phone-in programs, traffic news, and weather. The four FM II channels in Mumbai, Delhi, Kolkata, and Chennai are largely news-based. Plans for FM radio include forty FM channels that are to be accorded to the education sector in conjunction with the Indira Gandhi National Open University for Gyan Vani (education) channels (*India* 2004).

A group of men in Kashmir, a city situated at the heart of decades of Indian and Pakistan animosity, sit glued to their radio to listen to the two countries battle in a cricket match between India and Pakistan. Srinagar, India, 2004. (Fayaz Kabli/Reuters/Corbis)

A nationwide nighttime program featuring news, music, and sports is broadcast in Hindi, English, and Urdu. The target audience is mostly the Indian male working night shifts.

AIR also features external broadcasts aimed at the neighboring countries and the Indian diaspora in the developed world. The broadcasts are produced in twenty-seven languages—seventeen foreign and ten Indian. The content of the programs is largely news, current affairs, reviews of the Indian press, music, and other subjects of cultural interest.

The most important function of the AIR is the dissemination of news. It provides a total of 364 news bulletins daily. Around half of these emanate from Delhi and are in Hindi. These are then relayed across the country, translated into regional languages and dialects. In addition, forty-five regional news units located around the country produce 187 regional news bulletins. In total, news is disseminated in sixty-four regional languages and dialects.

Critics complain about the dull presentation of the news, and that the language used on AIR is chaste and ornate. The style is stultified and rigid instead of friendly, and as Sayani points out, its broadcasters make "a pronouncement" of everything (Saran 2004: 129). Furthermore, its news coverage is always deferential to the government and avoids all sensitive or controversial issues. Since political power rests in New Delhi and most news bulletins are composed in the capital before being translated into the regional languages and dialects, the news presentation also tends to be very Delhi-centric (A similar pattern of control is visible in radio drama. In AIR's drama contests, regional plays must all be first translated into Hindi and then retranslated into the different regional languages for dissemination.) Consequently, it is commonly perceived that news bulletins pay scant attention to local needs and that local news is rated lower than national news on local radio stations.

Issues

Government Control

The issues of control and autonomy have been at the heart of the debate over radio broadcasting in India. In keeping with the secular and socialist aspirations of the Indian democracy, proponents believed in the nationalization of major businesses, the use of technology for educational purposes, and the creation of a more equitable society. Broadcast media (first radio and then television) were to be managed by the state for the specific projects of education and nation building. News emanated from New Delhi, the seat of power, and commercialization in the media was allowed—but only under the watchful eye of the civil service. Not only did the government wish to mobilize technology to educate the people but also to bring into the national political consciousness a sense of Indian-ness. Government saw the television as a means to connect far-flung rural areas and bring them into the socialistic nation-building project. The fear of cultural invasion and foreign values was always present.

Control of the radio network, at first the monopoly of the British colonial authorities, passed smoothly into the hands of the independent Indian authorities. The Indian government's monopoly stemmed from the Wireless Telegraphy Act of 1933. It was the state that decided to set high moral standards for radio artists and refine the classical tastes of its listeners. It was only when people began to tune their dials to Radio Ceylon that the government capitulated and agreed to provide the listeners choice.

Innumerable studies, reports, committees, and working groups have recommended the decentralization, liberalization, and independence of the broadcast media, but these recommendations have quietly disappeared into the fog of bureaucracy. Although the various commissions and inquiries (Chanda Commission of 1964, the Verghese working group in 1977, the Joshi working group in 1982) were set up over successive decades by different governments to investigate the problems of broadcast media, their findings and recommendations have been quite similar. They have deplored the government's monopoly of the radio and its general disregard for public opinion. They have pointed out that although the radio is a crucial tool in the socioeconomic development of a nation, the government has never bothered to conduct any research to find out what the needs of the people are, particularly in the rural areas that radio is meant to serve. For instance, although the Ranchi Station is located in the tribal belt of Chhota Nagpur, the major content of the broadcasts do not concern the local populace, except for a few snippets of song and drama destined for the tribal community (Kumar 2003).

They have pointed out that political expediency and regional pressures have dictated the development of the network and diverted attention from the development potential of the medium. They have drawn attention to the fact that the monopolistic functioning of AIR has resulted in dull, unimaginative, and routine programs that interest few. They have demanded democratization of the medium so that bureaucratic, overcentralized, and Delhi-centric operations of AIR can be transformed, with more programs emanating from the people whose voices need to be heard. Most importantly, they have pointed to the absence of a coherent communications policy on the part of the government. Moreover, the promises to deploy the radio for education and for communities via community radio have not yet materialized (Kumar 2003).

As is its tendency, the government in India has responded very slowly to these recommendations. Most have been watered down when presented to the houses of parliament for approval, and most have not been passed because changes in government demand that the entire process begin all over again. The Prasar Bharati Bill, aimed at making the broadcast media autonomous of the government, for example, was finally implemented in 1997, seven years after it was passed by parliament. But already its autonomy has been rendered meaningless, with as many as half its board members government appointees, and constant meddling by bureaucrats and their political masters.

On the issue of news, the government is particularly adamant. It has refused to allow the privatized FM channels to broadcast news and news-related programs and has disallowed any direct foreign investment in radio. It points to the threat of "distortion" of the news by irresponsible elements and claims that national integration and maintenance of communal harmony between the various religious groups in India, which is paramount to peace within the nation, could be threatened. The possibility of foreign agencies meddling in Indian internal affairs and spreading false information in order to destabilize the region is another fear of the government. The monitoring of these broadcasts would be, according to the government, difficult.

No doubt these are sensitive areas where irresponsible or malicious reporting can spark religious riots and result in deaths. But even though the concerns of the Indian government are genuine, critics point out that "a combination of broad official guidelines on what constitutes offensive or objectionable material and self regulation by the industry [w]ould suffice" (*Hindu* 2003: 10). Besides, India has been receiving short-wave transmissions from foreign broadcasters such as BBC, Voice of America, and even Pakistani radio for decades.

The government waged a similar crusade against foreign news media on television. Unable to stop the news broadcasts of transnational media companies such as BBC and CNN, the government decided to impose its will on foreign companies seeking to disseminate news in Hindi. It thus pursued Murdoch's STAR TV's news channel with remarkable vigor. Having seen profitability in India rise, STAR News had decided to switch to news services in Hindi. In order to adhere to the government's new guidelines on uplinking, it sought Indian investors for the required 74 percent equity among Indian investors. This led to accusations from rival companies that the company had allowed a plethora of Indian individuals to have a stake in the company but with no real control and that Murdoch would be the dominant influence behind the scenes, as was allegedly the case in its FM Radio City operations. Each night until the dispute was resolved, STAR News, produced in India, had to obtain the Indian government's permission to broadcast for the next seven days via its regional base in Hong Kong. The ritual continued until STAR News found Ananda Bazar Patrika, a Kolkata-based publisher, to acquire the 74 percent stake, and the company won a ten-year license to broadcast its news programs directly from its base in Mumbai (*Economist* 2003).

Conclusion

Since its beginnings in the 1920s, India radio has achieved the much-desired expansion. Today, 99 percent of India's one billion people have access to its broadcasts. But dull programming, unimaginatively conceived by bureaucrats and presented in a stiff and stilted manner, has not endeared it to the listening public. Furthermore, the government is unwilling to give up control of the airwaves, whether it is by allowing the private sector to broadcast news, allowing foreign investment in radio broadcasting, or handing over the power and control of the medium to small rural communities to run their own community radio programming. Moreover, despite the information revolution and the onslaught of transnational media companies via satellite television, the government has still not formulated a coherent communications policy.

One of the future developments could be satellite radio. However, despite its wide

reach, particularly when compared with FM radio, it lacks the ability to provide localized content, which FM radio can deliver. The high cost of receiving sets for satellite radio is also a major concern in India and is likely to play an important role in the popularity of satellite radio with the masses. Cable radio (provided by cable operators) and internet radio do exist in India, but the lack of original content in cable radio and the low numbers of personal computers have so far limited their impact (FICCI 2003).

The government is currently drafting a Convergence Bill to tackle the issue of convergence of telecommunications, information technology, and electronic media.

A to Z Index

All India Radio (AIR) is the national public service radio network under the authority of the Prasar Bharati since 1997, funded by the government of India.

Convergence Bill is a forthcoming bill that will define future government policy on telecommunications, information technology, and broadcasting, and will eventually be presented to the houses of parliament for approval.

Farm Radio Forums is an experiment started under the auspices of UNESCO using radio broadcasting to inform and instruct farming communities on best practices to improve yield.

Five-Year Plans were part of the government's socialist programs to achieve economic growth in India. The government envisaged a growing public sector implementing massive investments in basic and heavy industries. The current Five-Year Plan (2002–2007) is the tenth.

Gyan Vani is an education channel broadcast on both radio and television in collaboration with the Indira Gandhi National Open University.

Internal Emergency refers to a period in 1975 when Prime Minister Indira Gandhi suspended constitutional rights and assumed all powers, imposing a blanket ban on any form of dissent.

B. V. Keskar became minister of Information and Broadcasting in 1952. Educated in Paris and a devotee of Indian classical music, he set about trying to revive Indian classical music on the radio. He is best remembered for having taken popular film songs and cricket commentaries off the airwaves.

Sardar Vallabhai Patel was independent India's first home minister and minister of Information and Broadcasting. He built the modern republic by bringing the princely states into the Indian union.

Prasar Bharati is the supposedly autonomous body created in 1997 to oversee radio and television in India. Prasar Bharati is funded by the Indian government.

Radio Ceylon was a commercial radio station headquartered in Sri Lanka that broadcast popular film songs. Most Indian listeners tuned in to the station to listen to these songs that All India Radio had refused to broadcast.

Vadya Vrinda is an orchestra created by All India Radio under the tutelage of the celebrated Indian musician Ravi Shankar.

Vividh Bharati is the commercial channel of All India Radio, almost entirely dedicated to popular film music.

Bibliography and References

Awasthy, G. C. *Broadcasting in India.* Bombay: Allied, 1965.

Barnouw, Eric, and S. Krishnaswamy. *Indian Film.* New York: Oxford University Press, 1980.

Baruah, U. L. *This Is All India Radio.* New Delhi: Publications Division, Ministry of Information and Broadcasting, 1983.

Business India. "Radio Casualty." 26 May–8 June 2003.

Chatterjee, P. C. *Broadcasting in India.* New Delhi: Sage, 1991.

Economic Times. "Centre Sets Up Committee on FM Radio." 25 July 2003.

Federation of Indian Chambers of Commerce and Industry (FICCI). "The Indian Radio Industry: In Play Mode." In *The Indian Entertainment Sector: In the Spotlight.* Mumbai: KPMG, 2003.

Fielden, Lionel. *Report on the Progress of Broadcasting in India.* Simla: Government of India Press, 1939.

———. *The Natural Bent.* London: Andre Deutsch, 1960.

Government of India. *India 2004: A Reference Annual.* Publications Division, Ministry of Information and Broadcasting, New Delhi, 2004.

———. *White Paper on Misuse of Mass Media during Internal Emergency.* New Delhi: Government of India, 1977.

The Hindu. "Lifeline for FM Radio." 17 August 2004.

Keskar, B. V. *Indian Music: Problems and Prospects.* Bombay: Popular Prakashan, 1967.

Kumar, Kanchan. "Mixed Signals: Radio

Broadcasting Policy in India." *Economic and Political Weekly*, 31 May 2003.

Lelyveld, David. "Upon the Subdominant: Administering Music on All India Radio." In *Consuming Modernity*, edited by Carol A. Breckenridge. Delhi: Oxford University Press, 1996.

Luthra, H. R. *Indian Broadcasting*. New Delhi: Publications Division, Ministry of Information and Broadcasting, 1986.

Mathur, J. C., and Paul Neurath. *An Indian Experiment in Farm Radio Forums*. Paris: UNESCO, 1959.

Ministry of Information and Broadcasting. *Mass Media 2002*. New Delhi: Publications Division, 2002.

———. *Prasar Bharati Review Committee Report*. New Delhi: Publications Division, 2000.

———. *National Media Policy* (A working paper submitted by the parliamentary sub-committee). New Delhi: Publications Division, 1996.

———. *Report of the Expert Committee on the Marketing of Commercial Time of AIR and DD* (Siddhartha Senate Committee). New Delhi: Publications Division, 1996.

———. *Report on Prasar Bharati* (Nitish Sengupta Committee). New Delhi: Publications Division, 1996.

———. *An Indian Personality for Television: Report of the Working Group on Software for Doordarshan*. New Delhi: Publications Division, 1985.

———. *News Policy for Broadcast Media: Guidelines Prepared by Advisory Committee on Official Media*. New Delhi: Publications Division, 1982.

———. *Akash Bharati: Report of the Working Group on Autonomy for Akashvani and Doordarshan*, New Delhi: Publications Division, 1978.

———. *Report of the Committee on Broadcasting and Information Media*. New Delhi: Publications Division, 1966.

Ninan, Sevanti. "History of Indian Broadcasting Reform." In *Broadcasting Reform in India*, edited by Monroe E. Price and Stefaan G. Verhulst. New Delhi: Oxford University Press, 1998.

Page, David, and William Crawley. *Satellites over South Asia*. New Delhi: Sage, 2001.

Pavarala, Vinod, and Kanchan Kumar. "Broadcasting in India: New Roles and Regulations." *Vidura* 38 (3), July–September 2001.

Prabhu, Anupa. "All We Need Is Radio Ga-ga." *Economic Times*, 14 July 2003.

Roy, Devlin. "Why No News Is Bad News." *Economic Times*, 16 July 2003.

Saran, Sathya. "Ruling the Airwaves." *Femina*, 1 January 2004.

Singhal, Arvind, and Everett M. Rogers. *India's Communication Revolution*. New Delhi: Sage, 2001.

Thomas, T. K., ed. *Autonomy for the Electronic Media: A National Debate on the Prasar Baharati Bill*. Delhi: Konark Publishers, 1990.

7

Television

Television is one of the fastest-growing media in India and threatens to dislodge cinema from its status as the most favored national entertainment. After its humble beginnings in 1959 and two decades of unhurried growth, television development suddenly accelerated in the 1980s, as more and more of the country was brought under the umbrella of the national television.

The next leap forward came in 1991, with the arrival of the cable and satellite revolution through the intermediary of STAR TV, beamed from Hong Kong. The growth figures for cable and satellite television are staggering. In 1991, there was, in addition to the five state-owned terrestrial channels, one satellite channel: STAR TV. With the arrival of the Indian-owned Zee TV in 1992, the number of satellite channels had doubled. But within three years there were forty-eight terrestrial and satellite channels, and by 2003 the Indian public had a mind-boggling 224 channels to choose from. With total revenues of INR 111 billion (US$2.5 billion) in 2002, expected to rise to INR 292 billion (US$6.5 billion) by 2007, television provides over 60 percent of the revenues from the entertainment sector (FICCI 2003). Today India is the third largest market for cable subscribers in the world, after the United States and China.

As for the viewers, in 2003 there were 84 million households with access to terrestrial television, of which 41 million households also had access to cable and satellite. Since each household is calculated as consisting of 5.5 individuals, it translates into a potential daily audience of nearly a half billion viewers for terrestrial television and a quarter of a billion viewers for cable and satellite.

History of Indian Television

The Early Years

Indian television began as an experiment in education. On 15 September 1959, the state-owned All India Radio (AIR) inaugurated a pilot TV sta-

A woman carries her television set to safety on 28 December 2004, in Cuddalore, 180 km (112 miles) south of the Indian city of Chennai, which was destroyed when a tidal wave hit two days earlier. (Arko Datta/Reuters/Corbis)

tion with the help of a UNESCO grant. This humble experiment, based in the capital city of New Delhi, was run with a 500-watt transmitter that had a diffusion rate of 25 kilometers. Thanks to this transmitter (obtained from Philips, the electronic giant, at a concessional rate) (Karlekar 1998), AIR began broadcasting 45-minute programs on Tuesdays and Fridays to a small number of state-run schools in the Delhi administrative region. The aim was to mobilize the technology of television to supplement classroom-based instruction, particularly in the field of science (physics and chemistry) at middle and high school levels (Mitra 1993). The enormous success of the experiment led to the Delhi School Television Project, started in 1961, which offered syllabus-oriented lessons in science to middle and high schools in the Delhi area.

Daily telecasting did not begin until 1965, and by then the broadcasts had expanded to one-hour programs. In addition to science education for middle schools, they began to include agricultural programs for farmers in the eighty or so villages surrounding Delhi. They offered advice on crops, fertilizers, and other concerns of the farming communities as well as information and advice on health, hygiene, and family planning. Community television centers were soon set up in villages within reach of these daily broadcasts from Delhi. One of the early enthusiasts of television as a tool for agricultural development was the eminent Indian scientist,

Vikram Sarabhai. He envisaged a national program that would extend the use of television to the entire nation. This, he felt, would promote not just economic and social development in rural areas but would also reach the most inaccessible and least developed areas of the country and bring them into the national consciousness (Mankekar 1999).

The early 1970s saw developments in the infrastructure of television. Advances were made in the production and distribution technologies of television, and local television stations were set up in many metropolitan areas: Mumbai (previously Bombay) had its own television center in 1972; Amritsar and Srinagar in 1973; followed by Kolkata (previously Calcutta), Chennai (previously Madras), and Lucknow in 1975. The early induction of the two border cities of Amritsar and Srinagar, far smaller in size and importance than either Kolkata or Chennai, was to counter the alleged anti-India propaganda unleashed by Pakistani television, whose broadcasts could be received across the border in Indian-administered Kashmir and the Punjab (Mankekar 1999). Repeater stations also proliferated, which brought even small towns under the umbrella of local broadcast facilities. Television, as one expert has pronounced, was producing "a new geography of India" (Mitra 1993: 17).

Broadcasting hours, too, were extended, and by 1972, the Delhi center was telecasting every evening between 6:30 and 10:30 PM. Moreover, as India began to manufacture black and white television sets, the ownership of personal television sets began to increase rapidly, particularly among urban middle-class families. Soon urban household sets outnumbered the commu-

nity sets that had been distributed in the rural areas. It is estimated that by 1970 there were around 22,000 family-owned television sets (Karlekar 1998).

One consequence of the increased urban ownership of television was the pressure to fill the extended hours with programs that were not necessarily educational. Since television programs were sponsored by the Indian government and the studios operated by a handful of engineers who were also program developers, directors, and camera operators (Mitra 1993), the Ministry of Information and Broadcasting had to cast around outside of its ranks to provide entertainment programs. The most convenient material on hand was the vast repertoire of the Indian film industry. Popular Hindi- and regional-language films and film-based programs were quickly used to pad the increased hours of broadcast.

One such film-based program was *Chitrahaar*, a half-hour program that strung together songs from old, and not so old, Hindi films. The success of *Chitrahaar* led to regional versions of the same, with songs from Tamil films, Telugu films, and Marathi films. Thus for much of the 1970s, the modest offerings of Indian television comprised farming programs; information programs and panel discussions on health, hygiene, and family planning; and films and film-based programs.

The Satellite Instruction Television Experiment

In 1975, India embarked on the Satellite Instruction Television Experiment (SITE), which was to have a far-reaching impact on the development of the medium. In May 1974, NASA had launched the Applications Technology Satellite (ATS-6) and posi-

Indian Muslim girls wait for their cultural program to start in the village of Atte Wala Jora, about 35 km (22 miles) southwest from the northern Indian city of Jammu, 21 July 2005. The Indian army sent a television set attached with direct-to-home service to the nomadic village, situated just 800 meters away from the Indo-Pakistan border. (Amit Gupta/Reuters/Corbis)

tioned it at longitude 94° W over the west coast of South America. The purpose of this satellite experiment was to combine advances in communication with spacecraft technology. It aimed to deliver, via space, advanced educational and health services to those parts of the United States where ground facilities were difficult and expensive to establish (for example, remote areas of the Rocky Mountains, Appalachia, and Alaska), causing those communities to be isolated from the national mainstream (Mowlana 1997).

As a result of an agreement between NASA and the government of India's Department of Atomic Energy, at the end of NASA's experiment, ATS-6 was loaned to the Indian SITE program. During the year-long experiment (August 1975–July 1976), 24,000 television sets were installed in 2,330 villages in the six most economically backward states of Bihar, Karnataka, Madhya Pradesh, Orissa, Rajasthan, and Andhra Pradesh, all of which were accessible from the geosynchronous satellite (Agrawal 1984).

Specially prerecorded programs were telecast from a TV station in Ahmedabad in Gujerat State, which was connected to a nearby earth station. The signals were beamed to ATS-6, which had one video and two audio signals. Thanks to the dual audio signals, viewers in two different states could watch the same programs simultaneously, each receiving the audio in its own regional language. SITE programs consisting of education and entertainment were created in the six different languages of the six states and were telecast daily for one and a half hours in the morning and two and a half hours in the evenings. In addition, 355 villages in the Kheda district of Gujerat also received satellite signals on conventional receivers through a rediffusion system (Agrawal 1984).

The objective of this experiment, directed exclusively at rural audiences and children, was to harness the technologies of communications and space for the purpose of education. It aimed to encourage the use of satellite television as an instrument of education both inside and outside the classroom, particularly in the primary grades. It also hoped to show that satellite technology could be used to disseminate information about specific aspects of science, technology, agriculture, health, and family planning. Another objective of the experiment was to demonstrate that this same technology could be used as an instrument of social change and national cohesion. The educational programs received very high ratings in the villages, although the "entertainment" programs comprising mainly folksongs and dances were deemed less interesting (Mowlana 1997).

Some have summed up the SITE program as nothing more than a "hardware success story" (Mowlana 1997: 86); nevertheless, it paved the way for nationwide television and for India's own involvement with satellite communications. By the time the SITE project was concluded, television was deemed an important enough medium to merit its own separate government body. In 1976, television was formally separated from All India Radio, which had hith-

erto overseen its activities, and set up as a discrete entity, Doordarshan (a literal translation into Hindi of the English word *television*). In 1997, the government established Prasar Bharati to oversee the activities of both Doordarshan and All India Radio and to ensure their autonomy.

Mrs. Gandhi: The "Tele-visionary"

Indira Gandhi, prime minister of India from 1966 to 1977, and again from 1980 to 1984, has been credited with ushering in the satellite age in India. As a one-time minister for Information and Broadcasting, she recognized the power of a nationwide television program emanating from New Delhi and its potential for image building and political gain in a democracy. The first three prime ministers of India are characterized thus: "Nehru was a visionary, Lal Bahadur Shastri a revisionary, and Indira Gandhi a televisionary" (Johnson 2000: 151).

In 1980, when Mrs. Gandhi returned to power after a hiatus of two years, she made sure that television was given due attention in the government's policies and programs. Her advisers had seen the possibilities of nationwide television during the SITE program and were determined to connect the entire country to a diffusion center, controlled by the central government and located in New Delhi.

First of all, she approved the expansion of the system. Accordingly, the government worked out a comprehensive scheme that ranged from installation of hardware to training of personnel and software production. A special allocation of nearly INR 1 billion (US$22.2 million) was earmarked for the expansion of the system under the Sixth Five-Year Plan (1980–1985). In 1982, the first Indian satellite INSAT1-A was launched (by the space shuttle *Challenger*), followed by a second satellite INSAT1-B in 1983. Television was expanded to provide primary coverage (55dbW signal) by installing twenty-six high-power transmitters and 112 low-power transmitters in combination with the INSAT1-B satellite. According to S. S. Gill, then the director general of Doordarshan, the aim was to build "a transmitter a day" (Mankekar 1999: 60). In 1984, Doordarshan started a second channel from New Delhi.

Mrs. Gandhi also effected two major changes: the first was the transition to color television and the second, the introduction of a National Program emanating from New Delhi and broadcast to the entire nation every evening. Licenses to own television sets along with the license fees were also scrapped in 1984. Henceforth, television was to be funded entirely from the public purse.

The transition to color was achieved with much pomp and enthusiasm. It heralded the start of ASIAD, the Asian Games, held in Delhi in 1982. The state wished to exploit the public relations opportunity that the international event offered by showing the Indian electorate that Mrs. Gandhi's government "could produce results." It was also an opportunity to show the world that "India was no longer a nation beset with poverty and unemployment" but could take its rightful place "among the most modern nations of the world" (Mankekar 1999: 56). The enormous success of the Asian Games confirmed to Mrs. Gandhi the immense potential of television as a medium to reach mass audiences.

Some political watchers have argued that Mrs. Gandhi's quest for a public relations coup was a sign that her power base had become shaky, and with the national elections looming, she was eager to exploit the potential of television for political propaganda (Mankekar 1999). But there were other pragmatic reasons for the government's enthusiasm for the switch to color. Indian engineers had by now mastered the relevant technology, and color television sets were already rolling off the production lines in India. Furthermore, television set manufacturers around the world had fully switched to color, making replacement of black and white production equipment or acquisition of spare parts more difficult (Mankekar 1999).

The year of the Asian Games was also the year of the inauguration of *National Programme* relayed from New Delhi. *National Programme* was a two-hour program of news (produced in New Delhi) and entertainment (produced in New Delhi and other metropolitan centers) relayed to the entire nation beginning at 8:40 every evening. The two-hour sequence, in Hindi and English, followed the local programming in the regional languages. It began with the evening news in Hindi and included various nationalist programs such as tele-biographies of national leaders and heroes of Indian independence, dramatizations of anticolonial struggles, serials based on works of different regional writers of India, and programs on the folk culture and flora-fauna of the different regions of India.

The purpose of *National Programme* was to disseminate the government's version of the daily news from the capital. Much of the news concerned the activities of the prime minister (and sometimes members of the cabinet), always shown in a positive light. Each news bulletin invariably opened with news of the prime minister and showed her dressed in beautiful saris. The rest of the cultural entertainment programs were concerned with creating a national consciousness and forging a national identity. According to S. S. Gill, director general of Doordarshan, *National Programme* aimed at "bringing Indian viewers onto a common national platform for at least a small segment of the total transmission time" (Mankekar 1999: 66). For several critics, however, the construction of "Indianness" that Doordarshan projected was predominantly a "Hindu-Hindi" one (Mitra 1993: 135). In other words, the programs from New Delhi privileged the North Indian, Hindi-speaking, Hindu identity and marginalized the rich assortment of the multi-ethnic, multi-religious, and multi-cultural regional identities that comprised the nation.

Thanks to the government's strenuous efforts to expand television, the network that had served only 15.2 percent of the population in 1980, by the end of 1984 served an estimated 50 percent of the population (Pendakur 1989). This was a remarkable achievement for the creaking Indian bureaucracy mostly famous for moving at a snail's pace in executing its well-meaning plans.

As television expanded, programs increased and ownership of television sets rose dramatically. Hitherto, importation of television sets had been restricted, and most Indians had to make do with black and white sets. But because Indian manufacturers were unable to cope with the dramatic rise in the demand for color television sets, import restrictions were eased just before the Asian Games in 1982. It is estimated that about one million television sets were imported in 1982, and the number of television sets owned in the country rose from a few thousand to five million in less than two years (Pendakur 1989).

One of the most poignant ironies of Mrs. Gandhi's push for television expansion and color was that her own death and funeral rites were some of the earliest pieces of dramatic news to be beamed across the country. In 1984, Mrs. Gandhi was assassinated by two of her Sikh security guards. Her death triggered riots in Delhi where, according to official figures, 2,717 people (mainly Sikhs) were killed by mobs, with the alleged assistance of the Congress (I), so named after Mrs. Gandhi's first name, Indira (Rajadhyaksha and Willemen 1999).

The Mother of All Soap Operas

The legacy left behind by Mrs. Gandhi was one of an expanding television network owned and controlled by the government. But, by the year of her death, the original emphasis on education was already shifting to entertainment. The number of community television sets in rural areas had been very quickly overtaken by personal television sets in the towns and cities. The new breed of urban middle-class owners, who were beginning to experience the joys of cars, refrigerators, and other "white goods," demanded more entertainment and less education. Even during the early days of Indian television, owners of black and white personal television sets avoided the educational programs, switching on only to watch the news, the weekly films, and other film-based programs. The rapid extension of ownership among the middle classes brought pressure on Doordarshan to provide more entertainment programs.

To balance the competing demands of entertainment and education, a compromise was sought in the form of the "pro-development" serial, which would uphold the obligations of a public service organization to educate as well as to entertain. The importation of foreign serials was not a real option. A few American serials such as *I Love Lucy* and films by Charlie Chaplin were being imported, but importation was restricted because of a shortage of the hard currency demanded by international distributors. Furthermore, there were genuine fears among the political and cultural elites that the importation of foreign serials would invite cultural values alien to the Indian ethos and contaminate the "purity" of Indian culture. To forestall such cultural colonization by the West and maintain an unsullied Indian identity, it was necessary to create indigenous serials that would reflect the hopes, fears, and anxieties of the young, independent republic that was India.

The first Indian "prodevelopment" serial was *Hum Log*, which enjoyed unprecedented success. The serial had 157 episodes and ran for seventeen months during 1984 and 1985. It sought its inspiration from Mexico's Televisa. In 1969, Televisa producer Miguel Sabido had produced a Peruvian telenovela called *Simplemente Maria*. It was an inspiring saga about a young woman, Maria, who sews for a living, educates herself, and then rises from the slums to wealth, literacy, and success. Although the story was replete with romance, melodrama, and emotional tension, it also touched upon the fears and anxieties of a people confronting modernity. It wove into its narrative women's issues such as family planning, women's rights, and education (Mankekar 1999). *Simplemente Maria* was a televisual phenomenon all over Latin America, and each week an entire continent held its collective breath for the next installment of Maria's life. Such was the power of the serial that it made going to school fashionable in Lima,

and the ruling military junta of the time rescheduled meetings so they would not miss any episodes (Thomas 2003).

Miguel Sabido participated in a workshop held in India on how population control could be encouraged through educational yet entertaining narratives, and the result was *Hum Log*. The serial concerned the family of Basesar, an alcoholic carpenter who lives with his extended family of parents, wife, and five children in a two-room tenement. According to Purnima Mankekar, who has written extensively on Indian television,

> *Hum Log* was didactic: it aimed at informing and persuading viewers about the importance of family planning (Basesar is miserable because he has more children than he can support); the evils of alcohol (the entire family suffers because of Basesar's fondness for drink); the scourge of dowry (the eldest daughter, the plain Badhki, is rejected by prospective in-laws because her parents cannot afford a "decent" dowry for her); the ills that befall young women who venture outside the protective control of their families (the second daughter, Majhli, defies her parents by going to Bombay, where she is sexually exploited); the importance of women's education (Badhki rails against her parents for not allowing her to study further, while the perky youngest daughter, Chutki, is determined to become a doctor and thus avoid the fate of her two older sisters). (Mankekar 1999: 110)

Each episode ended with a moral instruction delivered by the veteran Hindi film actor Ashok Kumar, who also responded to letters of viewers commenting on the story lines or advising characters on how to solve the latest crisis in their lives (Mankekar 1999). *Hum Log* was broadcast on *National Programme* and reached all corners of the Indian network. With just one channel available to viewers, entire districts resounded with its sound track and resembled a mass congregation for a modern-day sermon on secular morality.

Writing about the run up to the making of *Hum Log*, Mankekar says: "First, Gill went to Bombay to persuade professionals in the Hindi film industry to produce his serial. When he found no takers, he hired Shobha Doctor, advertising professional, to produce the serial and commissioned anthropologist S. C. Dube to write a paper on the 'negative and positive family values in the India family.' Corporations such as Food Specialities Ltd. met the serial's costs. A popular journalist, Manohar Shyam Joshi, was hired to write the script for the serial. Joshi came up with a formula that kept hundreds riveted to their television screens week after week" (Mankekar 1999: 72).

Hum Log was also the trigger for the commercialization of Indian television. "Commercialization," in the lexicon of Doordarshan, has a very particular meaning: it refers to the availability of sponsorship for programs in a network entirely owned and controlled by Doordarshan, itself funded and overseen by the Indian government through its Ministry of Information and Broadcasting. According to scriptwriter Joshi, it was only when the script was fully prepared and work was about to begin that Doordarshan realized it had no studios to film the serial. At that point it had no option but to contract with an independent producer, who in turn financed the programs by selling advertising time. And that, according to Joshi, "was the starting point of commercialization in Indian television" (Joshi 2002: 59). A limited amount of commercial sponsorship had in fact been allowed on Doordarshan since 1983, but most of this sponsorship by private companies was for film-based programs, as these were deemed the most popular.

The success of *Hum Log* secured the future of soap operas on Indian television, and even more importantly, of indigenous serials. By 1987, forty Indian-made serials had been telecast on Doordarshan (Mankekar 1999). Even today, Indian-made serials attract more viewers and advertising, both on terrestrial and cable and satellite networks, than do American or Australian soap operas shown on Indian television. Although the educational ethos was quickly diluted by the demands of urban viewers for entertainment, most soaps still adhered to social and developmental themes. *Rajani* (about a woman campaigning for the rights of the citizens); *Buniyaad* (also written by Manohar Shyam Joshi, about the trauma experienced by families who were victims of partition in 1947); *Nukkad* (about the urban working classes); and *Tamas* (about Hindu-Muslim rivalry in the shadow of the partition of the country into India and Pakistan) were some of the serials that followed *Hum Log* and were extremely popular with the viewers. The success of these serials immediately aroused the interest of the Hindi film industry, which witnessed the emigration of talent from cinema to television. In a few years time, veteran directors from the silver screen were to deliver the two greatest successes of Indian television.

The Soap Opera of the Gods

By the mid-1950s, soap operas (known as "serials" in India), films, and film-based programs were the most popular programs, attracting increasing amounts of sponsorship and advertising revenue.

Other daily features included news, sports, talk shows, and quiz shows. Within two years of the last episode of *Hum Log* came a completely new kind of soap opera: the mythological serial. Although devotional films based on the ancient Indian epics of the *Ramayana* and the *Mahabharata* have always been perennial favorites in Indian cinema, this was Doordarshan's first attempt to serialize them.

The *Ramayan* screened its first episode on *National Programme* on Sunday, 25 January 1987, and the serial ran for seventy-eight weeks. It was produced and directed by Ramanand Sagar, a veteran of the Hindi film industry. Although the *Ramayana* is attributed to the sage Valmiki, there are many regional versions of the epic. The one chosen for Doordarshan's production was mostly based on Tulsidas's *Ramacharitamanas*, a seventeenth-century devotional glorification of Lord Rama, the protagonist of the epic. (To distinguish between the serials and the epics, the serials shall henceforth be referred to as the *Ramayan* and the *Mahabharat*, and the epics as the *Ramayana* and the *Mahabharata*, a practice espoused by some academics.)

A synopsis of the story is as follows: Rama, the eldest son of King Dasharath, is exiled to the forest for fourteen years, thanks to a foolish vow made by his father to his third and favorite wife, Kaikayi. Both Rama's wife, Sita, and his brother, Lakshman, follow Rama into exile. The grief of separation from Rama kills the father. Kaikayi's son, Bharat, is crowned king, which is what his mother had always wanted. But Bharat refuses the crown and instead, in a symbolic act, places his brother Rama's sandals on the throne.

In the forest, Ravana, the king of Lanka, abducts the beautiful Sita. Rama then fights Ravana with the assistance of an army of monkeys and rescues Sita. When Rama, Sita, and Lakshman return to Ayodhya at the end of the term of exile, Rama assumes the throne. However, rumors begin to surface about Sita's chastity while she was in Ravana's custody. Pregnant with Rama's twins, she is nevertheless banished from the kingdom and finds refuge in a hermitage. There she gives birth to twin boys who vindicate her honor when they grow up. Rama forgives her and invites her back home, but Sita refuses. In the epic, she is the daughter of the earth, and the earth opens to take Sita back into its embrace.

As with all epics, there are many subplots and digressions contained within the tale. Thanks to the director's film background, the serial was filmed in Hindi with extravagant costumes, lavish sets, and opulent visuals. Although emotional, melodramatic, and overwrought, it was designed to move the viewer to feelings of devotion for Lord Rama. For many, the weekly episode was a religious moment, a time for devotion. Academics point out that many bathed and purified themselves, even lighting oil lamps and incense sticks (symbolic acts of worship) in front of the television set, prior to viewing the serial. Some have argued that the revival of Hindu nationalism and the election victory of the rightwing Hindu-nationalist Bharatiya Janata Party (BJP) in the regional and national elections from 1991 onwards can be traced back to the success of this serial.

The second epic to be screened on Doordarshan's *National Programme* was the *Mahabharat*. It was directed by another veteran Hindi film director, B. R. Chopra, and its production was as gaudy, garish, opulent, and extravagant as the *Ramayan*—and even more popular. The *Mahabharata* epic is made up 83,000 couplets divided into eighteen cantos. It is longer than the *Ramayana*, the Bible, and Homer's *Odyssey*. It was serialized in ninety-three episodes from September 1988 to July 1990.

The central story concerns a fratricidal war between cousins—the Pandavas on the one hand and the Kauravas on the other. The blind king Pandu has five sons from three wives who comprise the Pandava clan. Pandu's brother Dhritarashtra has a hundred sons who comprise the Kaurava clan. The oldest brother of the Pandavas is Yudhistira, whose fondness for gambling makes him recklessly stake and lose his kingdom, his brothers, and his wife, Draupadi, to the Kauravas in a rigged game of dice. The injustices and humiliations inflicted upon the Pandavas (such as the disrobing of Draupadi, in the grand council in front of the elders) lead inexorably to war, which ultimately annihilates both families in the Mahabharata war fought on the great Indo-Gangetic plain.

Both epics form part of the Hindu consciousness, and references to their episodes sprinkle everyday life and speech. However, the two epics are fundamentally different. The *Ramayana* is a morality tale inhabited by idealized characters—Rama is the ideal king, his wife the ideal woman, his brother the ideal brother, and even the villain is an idealized example of villainy. As an epic it offers guidance on what constitutes good and evil, and what upholds righteousness. In contrast, flawed and tragic characters people the *Mahabharata*. No one is perfect. The wrong doers have poignant moments of goodness and the heroes have critical weaknesses that move events inexorably towards the tragic war. The epic holds in its heart a complex but deeply antiwar narrative and condemns the destructive nature of war.

Most critics, who had already sharpened their pencils for a frenzy of acerbic barbs and clever writing, panned both epics. They sneered at the advertising *shakti* (power) in *bhakti* (devotion) and sought amusing alliterations in "mythology, make-believe, and *masala*" and "devotion, *dharma* (righteousness), and drama" to describe the serials. But while the intelligentsia dismissed them as pure kitsch, the serials found an immense and devoted following among the general public.

At first the advertisers showed little interest in sponsoring the serials. But once they realized that almost the entire nation, particularly the urban middle class, was mesmerized by the weekly renderings, they promptly queued up to advertise their products during its transmission. *Ramayan* represented a milestone in the history of commercial sponsorship on Doordarshan, generating spectacular revenues for the network and out-grossing all concurrent programs. The *Mahabharat* outdid even the record-breaking revenues of *Ramayan*. According to a newspaper poll, nearly 92 percent of Indian television viewers watched the *Mahabharat* (Mitra 1993).

The success of these serials established the mythological/devotional genre as a permanent feature of Indian television—so much so that the genre, which originated in cinema, has been entirely appropriated by the little screen and has virtually ceased to exist in popular Hindi films. But the genre has not remained the monopoly of

Doordarshan. When satellite television arrived in India in 1991, the new channels lost no time in offering their own daily devotional and mythological serials.

The Arrival of Satellite Television

The arrival of commercial satellite television in India dates back to 1990, when AsiaSat1 was launched. It was the first privately owned satellite communication network covering all of Asia, and its owners were a consortium led by three firms: the Hong Kong–based Hutchinson Whampoa, Britain's Cable & Wireless, and China's CITIC Technology Corporation. The northern and southern geographical extents of AsiaSat1 covered thirty-eight countries, from Egypt in the west to Japan in the east. The southern footprint of AsiaSat1 covered the entire Indian sub-continent. In 1991, STAR TV was launched as a joint venture between Hutchinson Whampoa and its chairman, Li Ka-Shing. Since STAR (an acronym for Satellite Television Asian Region) is an English-language network, Hutchinson Whampoa gambled on being able to attract the English-speaking elite communities of Asia by offering them high-profile Western programming. The venture was to be funded by the advertising dollar, with multinational firms vying to sell luxury products and services to this niche market (Barraclough 2000).

But even before the arrival of STAR TV and the other satellite and cable networks, an informal, illegal, and unregulated form of cable network was already operating in India. Cable had begun unofficially in India in 1984, spreading from tourist hotels to apartment blocks and finally to individual households. Videocassette players, linked centrally to a cable network, fed the networks (hotels, a few apartment blocks, and individual households) by subscription, and by May 1990 there were 3,450 such cable networks. In the four major Indian cities—Delhi, Mumbai, Chennai, and Kolkata—over 330,000 households had been cabled, forming an audience of 1.6 million (Ray and Jacka 1996).

In 1991, cable networks that had equipped themselves with satellite dishes gained free access to STAR TV and its BBC and CNN channels. The first real challenge to the Doordarshan's news monopoly came with CNN's broadcasts of the Gulf War in January 1991. This kind of access to a foreign war zone within the comfort of one's living room increased the Indian public's interest in cable networks. The death of Prime Minister Rajiv Gandhi, son of Indira Gandhi, in 1991 was the first time Indians witnessed a major national tragedy live on a foreign TV network (Lahiri 1995).

An Indian audience consisting largely of the English-speaking, urban middle classes became the news networks' avid viewers. STAR TV also brought to the urban living rooms the fiendishly complicated lives of *The Bold and the Beautiful*, and the Indian public was transfixed by the big hair, greed, and glamour of its characters. According to one enthusiastic reporter, "The mundane (TV) set has suddenly turned into an incredible [T]echnicolor dreamboat" (Rahman 1992: 74).

Nevertheless, Hutchinson Whampoa's earlier dream of an advertising windfall failed to materialize, and in 1993 Rupert Murdoch's NewsCorp purchased 64 percent equity in STAR TV. Since then, NewsCorp's share has grown to 100 percent ownership of STAR and a 26 percent share in the cable company Hathway.

In 1991 STAR's package of four channels initially offered news, sports, MTV, and

A squatter area along the Yamuna River in New Delhi contrasts with the satellite dish offering pirated TV to the residents in Delhi. Easy access to satellite transmissions has made television widely available to Indians regardless of their economic status, 12 December 1997. (T.C.Malhotra/Getty)

general entertainment. Although most of the programs beamed from its Hong Kong headquarters were "a motley mix of second hand soaps, unfamiliar sports such as ice hockey and American football, and even heavy metal music" (Rahman 1992: 74), Indian viewers, starved of information and entertainment, were transfixed by its sheer novelty.

At first STAR targeted the urban, educated, middle-class viewers. It offered special introductory rates for advertisements on its channels, which cost a quarter of the price of advertisements on Doordarshan. Small local companies advertising greeting cards, shoes, and fire extinguishers jostled with multinationals to sponsor U.S. programs such as *The Cosby Show* and *Murphy Brown*, which, together with *Santa Barbara* and *The Bold and the Beautiful*, had become primetime viewing. In fact, *The Bold and the Beautiful* became *the* conversation topic in urban Indian society. Dinner parties were rescheduled to allow aficionados the pleasure of the broadcasts.

STAR also conducted research on its audiences and found that Indians tended to stay at home rather than head for the hills or the countryside on weekends, unlike viewers in the western countries, so they quickly revamped their lackluster weekend schedules (Rahman 1992). Within six months, subscribers to STAR TV had jumped from 400,000 to 1.2 million, an increase of over 200 percent. By the end of the year India had become the largest national audience for STAR TV, a phenomenon that astonished its executives in Hong Kong. However, STAR TV's audience, large as it was, constituted just a fraction of Doordarshan's, which in 1992 stood at around 125 million in the urban areas and around 75 million in the countryside (Rahman 1992).

Exactly a year after the arrival of STAR, a second satellite channel emerged: the Indian-owned Zee TV. It was the brainchild of Subhash Chandra Goel, whose other business ventures include an amusement park. Zee leased the same transponder as STAR in October 1992 and initially benefited from its association with the glitzy Hong Kong–based company. Zee TV began a daily broadcast of three hours in Hindi and was an instantaneous success with the vast middle classes, whose appetite for entertainment had already been whetted by STAR. The biggest advantage that Zee offered was that its programs were in Hindi, spoken and understood by more than 40 percent of the population, compared with STAR TV's English-language programs, appreciated only by the thin upper crust of urban elite.

Once Zee TV had established itself as an Indian channel, it sought to augment its character and substance. It appointed Kamlesh Pandey, writer of Bollywood blockbusters such as *Beta* (Indra Kumar, 1992), *Saudagar* (Subhash Ghai, 1991), and *Tezaab* (N. Chandra, 1988), as head of programming. Zee TV boldly ventured into areas that had studiously been avoided by Doordarshan and STAR TV. It offered programs such as *Shadi Ya?*, a twenty-six-part series that explored issues such as sex after marriage, adultery, domestic violence, male insecurity, and marital rape, and it openly discussed the hitherto taboo subjects at the end of each episode (Jain 1993). *Shadi Ya?* was made by the controversial woman film director Aruna Raje, maker of the Hindi film *Rihaee* (1988). Less contentiously, Zee produced programs such as *Tol Mol Ke Bol*, an Indian version of *The Price Is Right* game show and regularly screened popular Indian films.

Zee TV also provided the venue for teleplays, telefilms, and soaps that had been rejected by Doordarshan. Producing for Zee provided a welcome relief from the bureaucratic hurdles placed by Doordarshan, and producers got confirmation for their programs in two days rather than the two years they had to wait with Doordarshan. Urban Indians with cable and satellite connections soon began abandoning both STAR TV and Doordarshan to watch Zee TV. By 1993, the channel had the highest viewing figures among cable and satellite viewers: 58 percent as compared with 16 percent for STAR Plus (STAR's entertainment channel).

Immediately Murdoch bought a 49.9 percent stake in Asia Today Limited (ATL), the broadcaster of Zee TV, signaling a major shift in STAR's strategy. Murdoch felt that in order to attract the non-English-speaking sectors of Asian societies, the new broadcasters needed to enter into partnerships with the producers of popular local programming, which targeted specific linguistic and cultural groups. Thus the strategy of "narrowcasting" was born (Barraclough 2000). The purchase was a marriage of convenience. STAR got access to a Hindi channel over the region, and Murdoch's executives could use this opportunity to un-

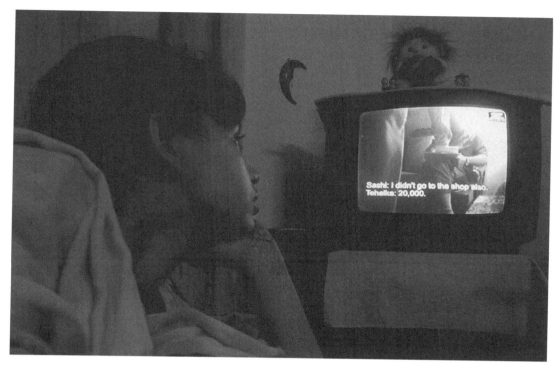

A Bangladeshi student watches a broadcast of Tehelka.com's video on Indian satellite television channel Zee TV in Dhaka. Bangladeshis saw the video for the first time when it was aired on the Zee Network on 22 March 2001. (Jewel Samad/AFP/Getty Images)

derstand Indian conditions better before striking out on their own. Zee got access to NewsCorp's expertise and professionalism as well as its international markets and channels in the United Kingdom, Europe, and North America. However, the synergy lasted just a few years.

The Great Television Scramble

Soon, the rest of the leading global media companies—Sony, TNT, ESPN, Disney, and CNBC—were all operating in India via cable and satellite. Indian viewers also saw a wave of Western programming delivered by transnational media companies such as MTV and Discovery, in addition to BBC World and CNN International. Within a few years, Indian-owned companies such as Sun TV, Asianet, ETV (Eenadu Television),

Sahara, and SABe, joined the great television scramble and began competing for transponder space and for viewers by offering programs in Hindi and regional Indian languages.

It was the proliferation of Indian-language channels offering local programs and, in some cases, local versions of Western programs that characterized the next stage of the cable and satellite revolution. Major regional-language television companies, such as Sun, Alpha (owned by Zee), Sahara, and ETV, staked out the territory that had been ignored by the transnational and national networks. Sun TV, owned by Kalanidhi Maran, a government minister after the 2004 elections and grandnephew of the Tamil nationalist party, DMK, president Muthuvel Karunanidhi, became the most popular Tamil-language channel. It quickly overtook Doordarshan's local Chennai channel, which had hitherto operated without any competition at all. Sun TV soon expanded into other southern regional languages—Udaya TV in Kannada, Gemini TV in Telugu, Soorya TV in Malayalam—and in the late 1990s launched a second channel in Tamil. Today Sun TV has twelve channels operating in all of the four southern states of Tamil Nadu, Andhra Pradesh, Karnataka, and Kerala.

Asianet is the leading Malayalam-language channel. It caters to Malayalis in Kerala state as well as those working overseas in the Gulf states. Zee TV, too, started regional-language channels called Alpha TV in Marathi, Bengali, Gujerati, and Punjabi. Currently Zee has a total of sixteen channels in Hindi and regional languages and is poised to increase them. ETV, owned by Ramoji Rao (often known as the "Murdoch of the South" because of his ownership of newspapers and television channels) and based in Hyderabad has twelve regional-language channels. Sahara, a media, housing, aviation, and para-banking conglomerate owned by Subrata Rai, is a largely news-based network, aiming to provide news channels in almost every regional language of India.

When STAR TV realized that its mainly U.S.-originated programming was reaching a tiny, though wealthy, urban audience, it began subtitling Hollywood films and dubbing popular U.S. soaps into Hindi, and airing them on STAR Plus. In 1996, five years after its initial broadcast, STAR Plus began telecasting programs in Hindi. In 1999, it claimed nineteen million viewers. Since 2003, STAR has begun broadcasting entirely in Hindi, unleashing a cutthroat competition with Zee, Sun, Sony, and Doordar-

shan. In 2003, STAR Plus had the highest viewership among all the cable and satellite channels (ET Intelligence Group 2003).

However, none of the cable and satellite channels can compare with the reach of the state-owned Doordarshan, which operates a three-tier system—national, regional, and local—and has one of the largest terrestrial networks in the world. It has twenty-three channels and operates in twelve regional languages. It has a nationwide reach of 90 percent and covers all twenty-eight states and the seven Union Territories of India. In absolute figures, Doordarshan still has the largest total number of viewers in the country.

Cablewallahs *and MSOs*

Satellite television is delivered to Indian viewers uniquely by cable. The arrival of satellite television created a completely new problem for the authorities. For a country known as the land of "license *raj*" because of its rule by licenses, India had totally failed to foresee the advent of cable and to regulate for it (*Economist* 2000). Although dish reception is legal with licenses, cable redistribution is technically against the law. By an archaic Indian Telegraph Act of 1885, it is against the law to dig across a road and lay cables without the permission of the Telecom Commission. To bypass the law, cable operators simply ran their lines over the streets and through the branches of trees and lampposts. Hampered by the lack of resources and an equal lack of will to police such a phenomenal growth of these rudimentary networks, the Telecom Commission is reported to have quietly given up on the matter (Chan 1997). Thus the cable and satellite revolution in India was conducted by unorganized bands of cable operators who simply set up satellite dishes at one end, ran a few spaghetti-like wires over lampposts, beamed programs, and collected the money at the other end (*Economist* 2000).

A good system requires higher investment, and better cables mean greater expense. Over the years, local operators with the financial muscle to upgrade their equipment consolidated their position, swallowing up the small operators who, in turn, either ceased to exist or became franchisees or subcontractors. These larger operators, known as multi-system operators (MSOs), began to act as middlemen who took signals from the broadcasters and passed them on to the local *cablewallahs* (cable operators). *Cablewallahs* interface with viewers, collecting payment and installing connections. At one stage, the number of such *cablewallahs* was said to be between 60,000 and 70,000, but with consolidation it has since dropped to around 30,000 (*Economist* 2000).

However, even fifteen years after the arrival of cable and satellite television, the system in India is still relatively primitive. Because of the high cost of satellite dishes, satellite channels in India reach viewers mostly through cable networks. A broadcaster uplinks signals, which are received by satellite dishes. Since few in India own a satellite dish, MSOs invest in dishes and receive the signals; they then convert them through modulators; these signals are amplified every 250 meters by cable lines and delivered to the homes of subscribers.

The major MSOs are InCableNet, owned by the Hinduja brothers, SitiCable owned by Zee, the *Hindustan Times* newspaper-backed IITL, and Sumangali Cable Vision, owned by Sun TV. Meanwhile, STAR TV has invested in Hathway. These major MSOs account for more than 80 percent of all cable connections in the four major cities of Mumbai, New Delhi, Kolkata, and Chennai. Smaller cities and towns are serviced by independent MSOs. Industrial houses and even multinationals are now showing great interest in the cable industry.

Doordarshan's Response

At first Doordarshan had no response to the satellite onslaught. As an unchallenged monopoly for over three decades, it never had to contend with competition and was uncertain how to react. It took comfort from the fact that STAR TV (initially exclusively in English) and Zee TV were restricted to entertaining the urban elite and continued to broadcast its standard programs, which had never found much favor with its captive viewers.

In 1993, commentator Amit Agarwal wrote in despair:

> As for the programs they've dug out, they're a sure cure for all insomniacs. Some samplers: The Music Channel had a program on folk dances from Bangladesh in the afternoon preceded by folk dances from Himachal Pradesh in the morning the other day. The Business and Current Affairs Channel has repeat shows of *Parakh*, *Tana Bana* and *Business Baatein* followed by—hold your breath—*Carry On Behind*, from the risqu[é] comedy series. The Enrichment Channel is like a multiple dose of Valium with programs on Employee Grievance Handling and the Jat Regiment, followed by one on the Border Roads Organisation. And the Sports Channel's menu contains ancient shows—Asiad 1982, Asiad 1986 and Flying Sikh Milkha Singh. (Agarwal 1993: 47)

Doordarshan had problems that made it difficult to respond to the satellite onslaught. It was run by the inflexible, unimaginative bureaucrats affiliated with the Ministry of Information and Broadcasting, which made any quick changes impossible. Furthermore, as a public service broadcaster, it had to honor its responsibilities to inform and educate rather than just entertain the nation. Its board of aging civil servants, unable to decide whether to increase public service broadcasting and hand over the second channel (DD 2) to universities or to lease it to private production companies and meet the cable and satellite challenge head on, prevaricated for several years. It finally opted for the latter.

Moreover, allegations of corruption at Doordarshan relating to the allotment of serials as well as labor problems were regularly reported in the press. In one case it was alleged that Doordarshan's northeast channel, headquartered in Guwahati in the state of Assam, was known to place a board outside its office announcing the unofficial commission (or bribe) rate (generally between 20 and 30 percent of the total fee) for approving programs for the channel. "Lethargy, inefficiency, corruption, cynicism and sterility of ideas mark this bureaucratic wasteland," wrote M. Rahman in disgust in *India Today* (Rahman 1992: 33).

However, Doordarshan did eventually respond by exploiting the one great advantage it had over the new arrivals—its extensive reach: Doordarshan's INSAT satellite footprint covered 90 percent of India. The big transnational companies had completely ignored the regional viewers, so Doordarshan increased the number of regional transmitters and regional-language satellite channels. In 1984, it had already introduced four entertainment channels

(DD Metro) in Mumbai, New Delhi, Kolkata, and Chennai on its terrestrial network, where independent producers could buy time. DD Metro was meant to appeal to the smart urban viewers and offered entertainment programs in English, Hindi, and the local language. These four channels were interlinked by satellite in 1997, so that the four cities could watch one another's programs.

Despite the onslaught by commercial cable and satellite channels offering round-the-clock entertainment, Doordarshan has remained resilient, even though it continues to broadcast public service programs that are so unattractive to advertisers and commercial television. In 2000, Doordarshan inaugurated Gyan Darshan, an educational channel along the lines of the Open University. More recently Doordarshan decided to rectify its battered image of a down-market, ungainly dinosaur by hiring a public relations firm to develop its image and brand. It has tried to improve its presentation by improving sets, professionally training anchors, and amending its programs to take account of viewers' preferences and the market.

Programs

General Entertainment

Although the results of surveys published by the Federation of Indian Chambers of Commerce and Industry (FICCI), the *Economic Times*, and other newspapers and magazines, tend to vary, they all agree that the regional channels and general entertainment in Hindi garner over 80 percent of the total viewership and comprise the largest segment of the market. The programs include primetime soaps, quiz shows, music contests, comedy programs, and talk shows. STAR TV's Star Plus channel, which now broadcasts entirely in Hindi, leads the field in entertainment, with forty-five of the nation's top fifty programs, followed by Sun TV, Gemini TV, Sony Entertainment, ETV, and Zee TV (ET Intelligence Group 2003).

The most-watched category of the general entertainment is the soap opera. At any given time, every broadcaster in Hindi and the regional languages has at least one and often more soaps. They are generally about extended families, with the struggle for power among various members of the extended family dominating the action. Central to these conflicts are the vicious power struggles between the mother-in-law (*saas*) and the daughter-in-law (*bahu*). Since most Indians, both in the cities and villages, live in extended families with several generations cohabiting under one roof, these soaps find great resonance with audiences. These *saas-bahu* struggles are epitomized in long-running soaps such as STAR TV's Hindi-language *Saas Bhi Kabhi Bahu Thi*. Others include *Kahani Ghar Ghar Ki* (STAR), *Des Mein Nikla Hoga Chand*, *Kkoi Dil Mein Hai*, and *Kkusum* (Sony). The leader of the pack is *Kyunki Saas Bhi Kabhi Bahu Thi*, which, in order to keep ahead of the rest, must come up with ever more innovative and daring ideas. For example, its production company, Balaji Telefilms, was the first to decide to shoot some its episodes in Australia.

The soaps target female audiences, and most run only on weekdays. Drawing on unrestrained feminine greed and ambition, first introduced to Indian viewers by *The Bold and the Beautiful*, screened by STAR TV in the early 1990s, Indian soaps are intense family dramas. "Television clearly loves the new nasty who seduces husbands, steals boyfriends, exchanges babies and manipulates mothers-in-law," writes critic Kaveree Bamzai (Bamzai 2003b: 74). So popular are negative female characters that when the serial *Des Mein Nikla Hoga Chand* began to slide in the ratings, director Aruna Irani allegedly decided to expand the predatory female's role. The series' subsequent rise to the ranks of the top fifteen television shows was proof that nasty women have the best ratings.

The soaps concentrate on affluent, urban, unhappy Indians and unfailingly narrate incidents of rape, divorce, and extramarital relationships. "A good soap asks for the impossible," says television's top writer Manohar Shyam Joshi, who invented the genre with *Hum Log* and *Buniyaad*. "It must be high drama which can masquerade as reality" (Chandra 1996: 103). In the once squeaky clean *Saas Bhi Kabhi Bahu Thi*, Tulsi, the mother-in-law, vows to avenge her pregnant daughter, who was recently raped by her son-in-law and framed her boyfriend for a murder he did not commit; in *Kkoi Dil Mein Hai*, the recently widowed Kajal is forced by the family to marry her brother-in-law, whom she once loved, but he is now married to her best friend; in *Kkusum*, Garv finds that a one night stand with Kali, whom he once loved, leaves her pregnant, and that now he really loves his wife, Kali's stepsister; and in *Tanav*, everyone lives unhappily ever after—Mrs. Malik has a boy toy, her husband is sleeping with his secretary, her stepdaughter has discovered that her lover is married, and her son, who is gay, has AIDS. Adultery, ambition, AIDS, murder, madness, seduction, betrayal, impotence, rage: these are the subjects that are advanced on a transfixed Indian public (Chandra 1996).

Manohar Shyam Joshi despairs of the contemporary soaps: "Earlier the episode would climax with a stirring dialogue. Now it closes with a slap, a shriek, and a cuss word" (Bamzai 2004: 88).

In 2003, as an antidote to the surfeit of *saas-bahu* dramas, Sony introduced a new serial called *Jassi Jaissi Koi Nahin*. Its central character, Jassi, is an earnest but clumsy secretary with braces in her teeth and thick spectacles. The series was a surprise hit, because the ugly duckling role is said to have reassured hundreds of ordinary-looking girls about their self worth. Secretaries frequently invite Mona Singh, the actress who plays Jassi, as guest of honor to their events. Story-wise, it also leaves open the possibility for Jassi to turn into a beautiful swan. To capture the mood of the nation, the Indian postal services have even commemorated a new postal cover and cards in her honor. Imitations of *Jassi Jaissi Koi Nahin*, such as *Yeh Meri Life Hai*, *Saakshi*, and *Dekho Magar Pyar Se* have not been as successful as the original.

Quizzes and game shows are also extremely popular on Indian television. The most successful was *Kaun Banega Crorepati?*, an Indian version of *Who Wants to Be a Millionaire?* that aired in the late 1990s and was hosted on STAR by a mature Amitabh Bachchan, the biggest star of Hindi cinema. The program is said to have revived the fortunes of the faltering channel. Attempts by other channels to replicate the success with other film stars were not effective, pointing to the newness of format and charisma of the superstar for the extraordinary success of the program.

In 2004, Sony and STAR TV's music channel, Channel V, both launched Indian versions of *Pop Idol* with a celebrity panel of judges. Ten Indian cities competed to find a winner on Channel V's *Super Singer*, while Sony's *Indian Idol* limited the search to the four major cities. Music contests have been popular on Indian television for over a decade. *Antakshari*, where each contestant has to sing a song beginning with the final syllable of the previous singer's lyrics, first began on Zee TV in 1993 and has maintained a loyal audience ever since. In 1995 the channel started a second musical contest, *Sa Re Ga Ma*.

In addition to programs on the various general entertainment channels, the two major channels dedicated to music are MTV and Channel V. Initially MTV broadcast only western music but found that the only way to penetrate the Indian market was to offer Indian (and Indian film–based) music. International music now constitutes just 2 percent of all music on Indian television, with 98 percent devoted to Indian music delivered by young male and female DJs who speak "Hinglish," a Hindi-English patois most popular with the young. The two channels have revolutionized Indian music and created a whole new genre of Indipop, sung in Hindi, English, and Hinglish. They have also fueled a boom in the music videos market.

Other primetime programs on Indian-language channels include Simi Garewal's interviews with stars and celebrities and Sanjeev Kapoor's cookery program, *Khana Khazana*.

Detective action series, such as *Ak . . . tion Unlimited Josh*, are largely imitations of *Miami Vice* featuring muscular men fighting crime. They are aimed to interest male audiences driven away by *saas-bahu* fatigue incurred by the daily dose of extended family traumas. In an Indian version of *Crimewatch UK*, the city police de-

Indian film lyricist, screenplay writer, and poet Javed Akhtar (left), singer Ila Arun (center), and actress Mandira Bedi (right) pose for photographers at the launch of Sony Entertainment Television's new show *Fame Gurukul* in New Delhi, 5 May 2005. After the success of its talent search *Indian Idol*, Sony Entertainment Television is all set to replicate the reality TV drama with another music competition, *Fame Gurukul*, based on the internationally successful Spanish format, *Operacion Triunfo*. (Raveendran/AFP/Getty Images)

partments describe certain crimes that have been actually committed and seek public assistance in solving them. Current comedy programs feature writer, director, and producer Aatish Kapadia, whose work includes *Khichdi* and its sequel *Instant Khichdi*. Kapadia is also behind the program *Sarabhai vs. Sarabhai* and *Main Office Tere Angan Ki*, whose titles are spoofs on Hindi films and plays. Other popular comedy programs include *Office Office* and *LOC*. A new channel entirely devoted to comedy, called Smile TV, came on air in 2004.

Indian television also offers at least three imitations of *Sex and the City: Dil Kya Chahta Hai* on STAR TV, *Kuchh Love Kuchh Masti* on Sahara, and *Kabhi Haan Kabhi Naa* on Zee TV. In general, however, copies of western soaps are not particularly popular. An early imitation of *Friends*, remade on Zee TV as *Hello Friends*, failed to excite the public. Reality TV such as *Big Brother* has not yet been attempted but no doubt will be soon.

Major companies that provide the content for general entertainment on television include Balaji Telefilms, Cinevista Communications, Padmalaya Telefilms, Sri Adhikari Brothers, Pritish Nandy Communications, Ronnie Screwvala's UTV, and Crest Communications.

Entertainment in English, including films, is largely provided by Zee English, Zee MGM, STAR World, STAR Movies, HBO, AXN, and Hallmark and constitutes just under 2 percent of the total viewership in India. National Geographic and Discovery channels usually dub their programs into Hindi.

Hindi films attract around 4 percent of total viewership on Indian television. Doordarshan as well as all cable and satellite channels screen feature films in Hindi and in regional languages. There are also channels dedicated to screening Hindi films, such as B4U, Zee Cinema, and Sony Max. Independent cable operators who are not affiliated with MSOs often offer a film channel with films in Hindi, English, and regional languages as a "goodwill gesture" to their subscribers. These screenings are mostly without authorization and include the screening of pirated videos. Some are even said to offer soft porn films late at night.

News and News-Based Programs

The rise of dedicated news and news-based channels is a recent phenomenon on Indian television. After decades of total control by Doordarshan on the dissemination of news throughout the nation, the cable and satellite networks first opened the doors to foreign news channels after STAR began broadcasting to India in 1991. But it was not long before the cable and satellite networks began to provide national, regional, and local news in regional languages. Today, news channels in Hindi and the regional languages attract the largest percentage of news viewership.

In 2005, there were 32 dedicated news channels offering news and news-based programs, ten of them in English, and the rest in Hindi and all the major languages of India. Of these, ten channels have recently come on air, including channels that offer business news in Hindi, such as Zee Biz, Videocon, CNBC-TV18, and NDTV. An additional twenty Indian channels are preparing to enter the market. The planned new arrivals include one produced by Bennett, Coleman & Co. (owners of the English-language newspaper *Times of India*) and Reuters.

The most successful news channel is the Hindi-language Aaj Tak, owned by Living Media India, Ltd., which also owns the news magazine *India Today*. The company's success can be attributed to its decision to woo the small businesses that had previously been shunned by advertisers as too insignificant or down-market. In doing so, it broke advertising records and showed that dedicated news channels could be lucrative business. The success of Aaj Tak encouraged other broadcast companies to start news channels in regional languages.

Zee News and STAR News are the next most-watched news channels. STAR News became a serious contender in the business of news services when it switched its services to Hindi in 2003. Until then its Hindi news service was provided by NDTV, a company that previously provided a weekly roundup of news and events for Doordarshan. NDTV is now an independent 24-hour news channel in Hindi. Aaj Tak and NDTV have both started a new English-language service called Headlines Today and NDTV 24x7, respectively. The increased competition among the news channels has resulted in attractive packaging and high production values. The English-language Headlines Today, for instance, is said to have trained its newscasters with CNN (Bamzai 2003a).

Indian Prime Minister Manmohan Singh observes proceedings during the India Economic Conclave 2005 organized by CNBC-TV18 business news television channel in New Delhi, 13 January 2005. Awaaz, India's first consumer channel, was launched at the CNBC-TV18 Indian Economic Conclave. (Prakash Singh/AFP/Getty Images)

Sun TV has dedicated news channels in Tamil and English, Udaya TV in Kannada, and Asianet in Malayalam. It will soon have two new channels in Telugu and Malayalam. Sahara Samay, which already has four dedicated news channels, is set to roll out another thirty-one city-centric news channels. English-language transnational news channels available in India are CNN and BBC World. CNBC has also launched an Indian channel, CNBC India.

Doordarshan's national and regional channels also carry news in Hindi, English, and most regional languages. Although Doordarshan is the front-runner in the news channels stakes by virtue of its ter-

restrial monopoly and access to 51 percent of the nation's households, its presentation is perceived as progovernment and dull. In 2004, Doordarshan inaugurated two new, dedicated channels to broadcast live all proceedings in the Lok Sabha and Rajya Sabha, the lower and upper houses of the Indian parliament. It is hoped that the election in 2004 of several former film stars to Parliament might evoke greater interest in watching the Indian legislators at work.

According to the survey published in the *Economic Times*, the cable and satellite news channels' share of viewership, which was just 2 percent a few years ago, has risen to 6–7 percent (ET Intelligence Group

Indian cricket star Sachin Tendulkar speaks to reporters at a promotional event for a sports shoe company in Mumbai, 12 August 2004. (Shyam Sunder/Reuters/Corbis)

2003). Advertising revenues have accordingly increased, too. News channels corner 14 percent of the total television advertising revenue. The reason for this disproportionate share of revenue is the perception that the genre mainly attracts men, who are the decision-makers for the purchase of high-value goods in most families. Also, news viewers are often perceived as the opinion formers of the nation. Advertisers therefore consider them a significant emerging market.

Sports Channels

Cricket dominates sports in India, and it is the most important game on television. To many, cricket inspires a religious fervor akin to that inspired by that other religion of India: cinema. No other sport generates the same nationwide interest and excitement.

The yearlong calendar of cricket matches in India and abroad dominates the intense bidding war for the rights among sponsors for the matches. There are a variety of inter-regional matches, but more important are the test and one-day international (ODI) matches played among the handful of cricket-playing nations of the world. The most important of all these matches are without doubt the World Cup matches and any match that features India playing Pakistan. They command the highest fees for advertising—about $25,000 for a 10-second spot (as compared with $2 million for the Super Bowl in the United States).

Because of India's abysmal international performance in most sports other than cricket, the national interest in sports channels is not as great as elsewhere in the world. However, field hockey, tennis, and football are growing in popularity. The new Indian sports stars, such as Sania Mirza in tennis and Narain Karthikeyan in Formula One racing, are beginning to emerge on the international stage and may spur more broadcasts of these sports on Indian television.

STAR Sports, Zee Sports, Doordarshan's DD Sports, and ESPN are the main sports channels in India.

Religious Channels

Religious and mythological soaps have been a perennial feature on Indian television, and all channels have at least one (but usually several) such series on air at any given time. Recently the major religious serials were *Shree Ganesh* and *Shree Krishna* on Sony, *Ma Shakti* on STAR Plus, *Jai Ganesh* on Zee TV, *Brahma Vishnu Mahesh* and *Sati Savitri* on SABe, *Draupadi* on Sahara, with Doordarshan's *Ramayan* and *Mahabharat* repeated on Zee and Sony, respectively. In 2004, the toughest fight for audiences was between Sony's *Devi* on the goddess Durga and *Sarrthi* about Lord Krishna from STAR Plus.

In addition to the religious and mythological serials, nine channels have emerged over the last five years entirely devoted to spreading the word of God. These are *Aastha, Sanskar, Maharishi, Om Shanti, Maa TV, Sadhna, Jagran* (sponsored by Zee TV), GOD (a Christian channel based in Jerusalem), and Quran TV (for Muslims). The competition among the seven Hindu channels is intense, particularly since many offer similar fare of devotional music, religious discourses, astrology, celebrations of religious festivals, and sometimes fundraising projects, and programs about the work of nongovernmental organizations. They all cater to an older audience,

but the battle for the hearts and minds of younger viewers is always on. Most of the channels depend on a handful of male and female speakers: Sant Morari Bapu, Guru Maa, Sukhbodhanandji, Sudhanshu Maharaj, Asaram Bapu, and the more cosmopolitan Jaya Rao.

Children's Television

An emerging television market is that for children's programs. There are currently six major channels for children: Cartoon Network, Nickelodeon, Splash, Animax, POGO, and Hungama, with the imminent arrival of a seventh, Walt Disney International. Children's programs constitute nearly 10 percent of the broadcasts on Indian television, and nearly 70 percent of these programs feature cartoons.

Sony's Animax, Turner International's POGO, and UTV's Hungama started broadcasting in January 2004. Hungama, an Indian channel launched by UTV with the intention of broadcasting original programs for children as well as interactive game shows made entirely in India, is an entirely new phenomenon and is being watched with great interest by the other media companies. UTV and its owner, Ronnie Screwvala, who produces television programs for Doordarshan, STAR TV, Gemini, Vijaya, and Sun TV, are also involved in the production of Hindi films. For Hungama, UTV has created a governing body entirely made up of children who offer advice on programming (John 2004).

Overseas Distribution of Indian Programs

Indian programs on cable and satellite are popular among the 20 million Indian expatriates living in North American, Europe, Africa, and Southeast Asia. The Zee network, along with Sony, has been the prime mover in the international arena. Sony was the first channel from the subcontinent to be launched in the United States, where the Ethnic American Broadcast Company (EABC) distributed it on the DirecTV DTH platform (Joshi 1998). Zee beams transmissions to Fiji, the United Kingdom, and mainland Europe, as well as South Africa. It also reaches out to immigrant Indians in Asia and Australia. The network has expanded into a 24-hour telecast in the United States, from its previous two-hour daily broadcast. Former Indian tennis champion Vijay Amritraj owns the downlinking and distribution rights in North America for Doordarshan's international channel, DD India. Recently the Israeli cable network, Hot, launched a free channel called "Hot Bombay," dedicated to Bollywood films.

The international broadcasts include Indian programs and sometimes programs specially made for the immigrant population overseas, which constitutes an important revenue and target for advertising (Joshi 1998). So lucrative is the overseas market that many Indian programs such as the musical quiz-cum-singing contest *Sa Re Ga Ma* are shot in the United States and the United Kingdom with Asian audiences.

The Future of Television in India

In November 2000, the government opened the doors to companies wishing to invest in DTH (Direct to Home) technology. Both STAR (via its company Space TV) and Zee have staked a claim in the market for DTH. However, a FICCI report finds that many companies consider the start-up and rolling costs (including the high fees de-

manded by the government) of DTH as too high. Companies are also uncertain as to whether Indian consumers will be interested in DTH as yet. Zee TV intends to explore the option of HITS (Headend in the Sky) involving encryption of scores of different channels in one headend (a feat made possible by digital compression), which is uplinked to a satellite (the headend in the sky) and then transmitted directly to consumers (FICCI 2003).

The government has placed a number of conditions upon companies applying for a license, and at present there are twenty-two licenses that must be acquired from the various ministries (including the Ministry of Defense and the Department of Telecommunications) between the initial letter of intent and the final DTH license. Foreign investment in a DTH company is restricted to 49 percent of the total equity, and cross-holding by media companies, both Indian and foreign, is restricted to 20 percent. Similarly, a DTH broadcasting company can hold only 20 percent of equity in a broadcasting and cable company. Other obligations include the establishment of an earth station that uplinks in India and adherence to the Indian Program and Advertisement Codes. All content provided by the DTH platform, irrespective of source, must pass through common encryption and conditional access systems, and although the company is allowed to use foreign satellites, those using Indian satellites will be given preferential treatment (FICCI 2003).

Doordarshan intends to use state-owned telecommunication service providers such as BSNL and MTNL and lease four transponders for Ku-band transmission, which will allow it to access the 200,000 or so households that lie in remote, inaccessible mountainous and border regions. Door-darshan, which has around 90 percent of coverage of the geographical territory of India, hopes to capture the remaining 10 percent that lie outside the reach of the terrestrial television. It aims to start with twenty new channels and increase them to sixty within a year.

Issues

Cable Operators and the CAS Act

India is probably the only country in the world where satellite and cable television are delivered to the consumer without an addressable system involving set-top boxes and smart cards. Instead, the entire delivery sector remains largely unorganized. Broadcasters beam their content, which is downloaded by satellites owned by multi-system operators (MSOs), who lay down cables. Local cable operators or *cablewallahs* own the "last mile" of the cable and distribute it to subscribers' homes, delivering nearly a hundred channels for around INR 175–250 (US$3–$5) a month, making India's cable rates among the lowest in the world. *Cablewallahs* go from door to door collecting the monthly subscriptions for the agreed bouquet of channels. If the household desires a program not in the package, then an extra payment is required.

This informal organization of the marketing and delivery of satellite television via cable is chaotic and creates a litany of problems for all concerned: the subscribers, the broadcasters, the MSOs, and apparently even the *cablewallahs*. Subscribers complain that *cablewallahs* offer an indifferent service, that the pictures they receive are often of poor quality and

blurred, and that the *cablewallahs* are frequently rude and insolent. Furthermore, subscribers cannot choose their local cable operator because *cablewallahs* often divide territories among themselves and operate an informal cartel. As a consequence of such monopolistic trade practices by the *cablewallahs*, subscribers can be subject to arbitrary increases in subscription rates (*Economist* 2000).

Cable operators also determine the choice of channels. For a flat fee, they offer a clutch of programs, regardless of whether the viewer desires them. For example, if a non-Gujerati-speaking family lives in an area of Gujerati speakers in Mumbai, then Gujerati programs will form part of the subscription package. Programs in the non-Gujerati-speaking subscriber's language of choice would cost extra. Furthermore, subscription rates vary according to the locality: a subscription package costs more in the wealthy district of Malabar Hill in Mumbai than the same package costs in the slums of Dharavi. *Cablewallahs* thus decide rates according to their perception of a locality's ability to pay. Consumer organizations in towns and cities across India have filed numerous complaints against local cable operators for their contravention of the Monopolies and Restrictive Trade Practices (MRTP) Act.

Broadcasters complain that MSOs grossly underreport the subscriber base and MSOs accuse the cable operators of passing on very little of the subscription revenue collected. It is estimated that a quarter of the annual revenue of India's cable TV industry comes from advertising and the rest from subscriptions. MSOs and broadcasters accuse the *cablewallahs* of underreporting the number of subscribers and pocketing around 90 percent of the subscription revenues—leaving MSOs with just 5–6 percent and broadcasters about 4–5 percent of the total sum collected (*Economist* 2000). Other estimates place the figures at 15 percent for the broadcasters and 20 percent for the MSOs, with the rest taken by the cable operators.

The broadcasters complain that such an imbalance in the redistribution of revenues collected forces them to depend heavily on advertising to recoup their lost earnings. They also accuse the *cablewallahs* of piracy and even murder. The MSOs, who see themselves as pioneers operating in a market of low incomes, poor technology, and excessive regulation, complain that they provide the money for hardware and maintenance in exchange for the revenue that the local operator is supposed to hand over. Disputes between the broadcasters and MSOs, and between MSOs and their franchised *cablewallahs* can lead to disruption or suspension of service, leaving the hapless consumer with no pictures.

In 2003, STAR and the Sun TV–owned multi-system operator SCV had a very public falling out over the matter of payment defaults and underreporting of subscribers in Chennai. Each side mounted vigorous campaigns against the other in the print media. STAR TV took its channels off SCV, and Hathway (in which STAR has a substantial stake) blocked Sun TV's programs (Govardan 2003). Around the same time in Mumbai, a host of broadcasters including STAR and Sony switched off their channels to InCableNet for nonpayment of dues. Frequent disputes between broadcasters and MSOs often lead to the interruption of transmission to subscribers. Many local cable operators simply resort to stealing signals from neighboring networks to prevent

a blackout of transmission and keep their subscribers happy.

For their part, the much-maligned *cablewallahs* accuse broadcasters of overestimating viewer figures in to order to impress advertisers and blame them for raising prices unreasonably and blacking out channels when the cable operators object. They complain that MSOs don't invest in better equipment that would provide the extra channels demanded by irate customers. The *cablewallahs* blame the customers for wanting new channels but refusing to pay more for them. In their own defense the *cablewallahs* explain that their own energies are spent in fighting off competition and constantly replacing bad and stolen equipment. They complain that in a cutthroat market infiltrated by the criminal underworld, where competitors practice cable cutting and amplifier stealing, they are often operating at a loss (*Economist* 2000).

Many of the financial dealings surrounding cable delivery are cash transactions, and the large amount of money circulating in the industry has, it is alleged, attracted the attention of the underworld. As for the government, the lack of organization has meant that the state loses tax revenue (entertainment tax, service tax, and so forth). Pilferage of entertainment tax revenues is substantial: *cablewallahs* often include the tax in their subscriptions but do not issue government authenticated receipts for the tax collected.

Government's Response

The cable and satellite invasion of the 1990s caught the Indian government napping. Decades of government monopoly over radio and television broadcasting meant that it had no comprehensive broadcasting policy to restrain and guide the media. In fact, the Telegraph Act of 1885 was still being used to guide the government's broadcast policy. A gradual realization that it had been completely overtaken by technology prompted the government to start thinking about formulating a more relevant broadcast policy.

At first the government's response was contradictory. On the one hand, the former Information and Broadcasting minister K. P. Singh Deo told Parliament that India must give a fitting response to the "cultural invasion" by foreign satellite channels, and called upon Indian advertisers not to support "anti-India propaganda" on these channels (Agarwal 1993). At the same time the Minister of State for External Affairs Salman Khursheed told CNN, "we embrace the foreign networks and would like their co-operation in projecting the correct picture of India" (Agarwal 1993:47).

In 1995, the government passed the Cable Television Networks (Regulation) Act, which legalized the cable operations of the 70,000 or so *cablewallahs* (whose numbers have since fallen to around 30,000). The Cable Act was intended to legalize the mushrooming of cable networks all over the country and curb the "cultural invasion" of the unregulated broadcasts. The fear of anti-Indian broadcasts from sources inimical to national interest, as well as undesirable advertisements by tobacco and liquor companies beamed to viewers without any censorship, were matters of grave governmental concern. Furthermore, the government deemed that subscribers of satellite and cable networks as well as programmers and cable operators were not aware of their responsibilities and obligations in respect of the quality of service, use of material protected by copyright, ex-

hibition of uncertified films, and the broad framework of the laws of the land as stipulated by the Cinematograph Act of 1952, the Copyright Act of 1957, and the Indecent Representation of Women (Prohibition) of 1986.

The Cable Television Networks (Regulation) Act tried to make the programming and advertising code of Doordarshan applicable to all foreign cable and satellite channels. It required *cablewallahs* to register with the authorities and made it mandatory for them to carry Doordarshan's channels, DD1 and DD2. As for the foreign channels, the Indian government had no direct control over those that did not uplink from India and therefore could not force them to comply with the laws of the land. However, the government could enforce the law by imposing fines on Indian companies that placed offensive advertisements on foreign networks. In some cases, the government tried to go after Indian advertisers on foreign channels and local cable operators over whom authority could be exercised.

The government ordered the *cablewallahs* to monitor content by switching off any program that violated the programming or advertising codes. As one bureaucrat declared: "When Pakistan TV started showing an objectionable program on Kashmir during the lunch break of a cricket match, some alert operators switched it off immediately. We want programs and ads not conforming to our codes to be stopped on a regular basis" (Rahman and Agarwal 1993: 48). Another bureaucrat explained: "Cable operators should not show anything which violates the code. For instance, STAR TV channels [from Hong Kong] carry liquor ads. We cannot allow that. Some explicit MTV songs violate guidelines. Nudity is out. And, of course, a communal program [one that demonizes a particular religious community] is objectionable. The new codes for cable TV will only be more liberal versions of existing codes for AIR and Doordarshan" (Rahman and Agarwal 1993: 48).

Despite these brave words, the Cable Act changed very little. Cable operators refused to police the airwaves, pointing out that they had no control over the programs and advertisements on satellite channels and they could therefore not be held responsible for any violations (Rahman and Agarwal 1993). They continued to show pirated films and lay wires randomly without obtaining permission from civic bodies. They also continued to show programs that violated both the programming and advertising codes.

In 2003, the Indian parliament passed the Cable Television Networks (Regulation) Amendment Bill, which introduced amendments to the Cable Act of 1995. Referred to as the Conditional Access System (or the CAS) Act, it sought to regulate the chaotic world of cable operators, multi-system operators, and broadcasters, and to rectify their malpractices such as poor service, rising prices, and underreporting of subscribers. The act made it mandatory for every cable operator to transmit (or retransmit) programs from pay channels through an addressable system involving the use of a set-top box, smart cards, and subscriber management systems. However, with the change in government after the 2004 elections, implementation of the CAS Act has been quietly buried. Intense lobbying by the big satellite companies, afraid that the increased costs incurred by set-top boxes and smart cards might turn subscribers away from pay channels to free-to-air channels and lead to a loss in their advertising revenues, is said to have been behind the move to scuttle plans to put the act into effect.

Piracy and Plagiarism

The two major problems that plague Indian television are piracy and plagiarism. Piracy mostly concerns the dissemination of cinematographic works on the cable networks without obtaining the cable rights to do so. Independent cable operators are commonly the ones who practice this kind of piracy rather than those franchised with the large MSOs. In addition to the satellite channels that are delivered by the local cable operators, many independent local operators run an extra cable channel showing the latest film releases of both Bollywood and Hollywood. Local operators offer this as a personal goodwill gift to their customers in the face of growing competition from the larger MSO-affiliated cable operators. Most of the films are shown via their own video players, with videos usually borrowed from video libraries or bought from retailers. Sometimes cable operators screen pirated videos of the latest Indian and American films within days of their release in the cinemas. The "goodwill" channel screens a minimum of four films per day, but many screen films throughout the day. The consequences of cable piracy are widespread and damaging. The loss of revenue to film producers, theater owners, video shops, and the government is substantial, the latter through loss of taxes from theaters and legitimate video shops.

Plagiarism is widespread in Indian cinema as well as television, and it usually goes undetected overseas. Even when detected, it is rarely pursued through the Indian law courts. Many quiz and game shows are reproduced in India without permission or even acknowledgment. In one case a few years ago, the U.S.-based entertainment companies TIYL Productions California, Ltd., and Ralph Edwards Productions filed a suit against New Delhi Television, Ltd. (NDTV), and Zee Telefilms, Ltd., claiming that the TV series *Jeena Isi Ka Naam Hai* was a copy of their popular program *This Is Your Life* (TIYL). TIYL was unaware of the copycat program in India until it was about to grant a license to the BBC for telecasting the program in India. While researching the market, it learned that a similar program was already on the air. In fact, Zee TV had telecast thirty-five episodes of the Indian version on Indian TV as well as over its Zee network in the United Kingdom and the United States.

Because few overseas companies seek to take the copycats to court, the Indian television industry, which has always "borrowed" ideas with impunity, was astounded when best-selling Anglo-American author Barbara Taylor Bradford slapped a plagiarism suit against Sahara TV in May 2003. The channel had planned a much-hyped opening of a new multi-million rupee soap, *Karishma—A Miracle of Destiny* starring Karishma Kapoor, one of the leading actresses from Bollywood. Bradford claimed that the serial was an unauthorized copy of her popular novel *A Woman of Substance*, which chronicles the metamorphosis of Emma Harte from a servant girl into head of Harte Enterprises, a financial empire. *Karishma* has Devyani, a domestic servant, rise to head Devyani Enterprises, a financial empire.

What surprised the Indian producers most was Bradford's determination to bring the case to court to receive ade-quate compensation. In the cutthroat business of primetime television, most suspect that rival channels had alerted Bradford to the matter and encouraged her to pursue the channel for compensation. However, most writers for television could barely disguise their delight. They hoped a victory for Bradford would give them an opportunity to present their own original scripts. Said screenwriter Anurag Kashyap, "I have so many original scripts no producer wants to touch. They prefer

Bollywood star Karishma Kapoor speaks about her television debut in the soap opera *Karishma—A Miracle of Destiny* during a media gathering in Bombay, 18 August 2003. India's highest court dismissed a petition in early August, filed by New York–based best-selling author Barbara Taylor Bradford, to stop the telecast of the soap opera, which the writer said was copied from her novels. (Reuters/Sherwin Crasto/ Corbis)

to play safe, making remakes of Hollywood hits. Hopefully this case will force Indian producers to buy the right of films and books before copying them" (Shedde 2003). Unfortunately for the purveyors of original scripts, the Indian courts ruled in favor of Sahara TV.

Not all acts of plagiarism involve the overseas companies. Before *Karishma*, another case of plagiarism involving Zee TV was brought before the Supreme Court. In this case, Sundial Communications, a media company, had accused Zee TV of stealing its original idea for a 52-episode series called *Krishna Kanhaiyya*. The series was about a matriarch concerned about discord in her extended family who seeks advice from an orphan (the child god Krishna in disguise) on how to resolve those problems. Zee TV, they alleged, had used the very same idea in their series *Kanhaiyya* (*Times of India* 2003).

Conclusion

The most impressive feature of Indian television has been its exponential growth. Despite a late start, television is now the fastest growing area of entertainment in India, and the forecast for Indian television, particularly regional television, is one of continued growth. As penetration of terrestrial, cable, and satellite television into the rural areas increases, the regional sector is expected to grow considerably.

There are a total of 192 million households in India—56 million in urban areas. Of these, 43 million receive terrestrial television, with 27 million households also subscribing to cable and satellite networks. There is therefore scope for growth in urban areas, particularly in cable and satellite television connectivity.

There are 136 million rural households, of which only 39 million receive terrestrial television and 13 million have cable and satellite connections. Cable and satellite penetration in regional hinterlands, away from the main commercial capitals, is particularly low, and the scope for growth in the rural areas is tremendous. However, growth in television connectivity in the hinterland will depend on improved infrastructure, particularly the availability of electricity in the rural areas.

The way forward toward greater organization of the cable networks may come through MSOs such as InCableNet and Siti-Cable, who are keen to offer households and businesses broadband Internet connections through cable television. They are therefore seeking to improve the communications infrastructure by upgrading the networks, sometimes even the "last mile," which cable operators usually control (*Economist* 2000).

Direct to Home (DTH) technology has been discussed as the future for television in India. DTH refers to the distribution of satellite and cable channels using digital technology in Ku Band, which provides signals directly to the subscriber's premises. The biggest advantage of DTH technology is that it renders the role of the cable operator redundant. Digital technology and signal compression also create savings on transponder services while allowing for greater numbers of channels. However the more expensive addressable system and aerial dish required for DTH result in increased costs for the subscriber, a very important consideration in mass media diffusion in India (FICCI Report 2003).

A to Z Index

All India Radio (AIR) is what the government-owned radio broadcasting system is known as in English; it is known as Akashvani in Hindi and the regional languages.

Amitabh Bachchan (1942–) is the biggest star ever of the Hindi screen. In the 1990s, after a spectacular film career, the megastar was heading for equally spectacular financial ruin. At that point, Bachchan was offered the job of hosting, on STAR TV, the first Indian version of *Kaun Banega Crorepati?* (*Who Wants to Be a Millionaire?*). The program was a hit and revived the fortunes of Bachchan.

Bharatiya Janata Party (BJP) is the main right-wing Hindi nationalist party, which formed a coalition government in 1999 after the Congress Party was defeated.

Cable Access System (CAS) is a cable television technology. In order to organize the cable distribution system, the BJP government decided to introduce an accessible system. The 2003 Act that required the accessible set-top box was called the CAS. However, the CAS was never fully implemented, and the government changed after the general elections in 2004.

Cablewallahs are cable operators. In India, most satellite channels are delivered by a cable system. The local cable operator (known as a *cablewallah*) delivers the satellite program to the house of the subscriber by cable on behalf of the multisystem operator, who receives the satellite signals. He also signs up subscribers, collects the dues, and carries out maintenance on the "last mile" of the cable, which he owns. Transactions with the *cablewallah* are usually in cash, and many fear the infiltration of the criminal underworld into the operations.

Chitrahaar was a highly popular half-hour program on Doordarshan that strung together film clips of song-and-dance sequences. It was a precursor to the music video and the MTV programs now being broadcast, except Chitrahaar had no video jockey or commentary. The regional centers copied the program and broadcast song-and-dance sequences from the regional-language films.

B. R. Chopra (1914–) is a film director who migrated from the studios of Lahore (now in Pakistan) to those of Bombay (Mumbai), where he directed several hit films, including the salacious rape-revenge drama *Insaaf ka Tarazu* (1980) based on the Hollywood film *Lipstick*. In 1988, he was invited to direct a serialized version of the Indian epic, the *Mahabharata*. The audience drew 75 percent of the urban population and over INR 10 million (US$225,000) per episode in advertising (Rajadhyaksha and Willemen 1999).

Communal program: The word "communal" within the Indian context refers specifically to a religious community: either Hindu or Muslim. A communal program is therefore one that disseminates ideas (or prejudices) that adherents of one religious group may harbor about the other. The memory of the violence during the partition of India, which displaced millions on either side of the border, is still strong in north India, and broadcasters generally avoid communal programs.

Direct to Home (DTH) refers to the distribution of satellite and cable channels using digital technology in Ku-band that provides signals directly to the subscriber's premises through an accessible system.

Hum Log was the first Indian soap opera. It combined entertainment with education on the socials evils that plague modern urban societies.

Karishma—A Miracle of Destiny was a serial that was meant to mark a shift to television for screen star Karishma Kapoor. It ran into controversy just before it was scheduled to go on air. Rivals allegedly alerted the British writer Barbara Taylor Bradford to the blatant plagiarism of her popular novel *A Woman of Substance*. In court, the judge acquitted the producers.

Kyunki Saas Bhi Kabhi Bahu Thi, an important, long-running serial—a popular Hindi domestic drama about extended families and their fraught relationships—was the prototype for most of the soaps that followed in Hindi and all the regional languages.

License *raj*: Under the quasi-socialist principles that governed Indian political and economic thought until 1991, the government disbursed licenses for the manufacture of goods to ensure that only those products deemed fit and useful by the state were produced. Wags thus commented that the British *raj* (rule) had given way to the "license *raj*."

Multi-system operators (MSOs) are cable companies. Most satellite broadcasts in India are delivered by cable to the viewers. The MSOs receive the signals from broadcasters and pass them via their cables to the subscribers through the intermediary of the local cable operator, who owns the "last mile" of the cable.

National Programme, an all-India television program broadcast every evening in Hindi from New Delhi, commanded total respect from the various television centers, which frequently interrupted regional programming to air the program containing news, views, and music.

Prasar Bharati is the governing body for Doordarshan and All India Radio. Although it claims to be independent, it is financed by the government, which also appoints the members to its board.

Prodevelopment programming consists of television serials created with the aim of social development. Started in South America, the model, which combines entertainment with education, was considered worth pursuing by public television broadcasters such as Doordarshan.

Ramanand Sagar (1917–) is a one-time journalist and writer turned Hindi film director and producer after migrating from Lahore (now Pakistan) after partition. In 1986 he directed the epic *Ramayan*, the first-ever religious serial to be broadcast on television. A total of ninety-one episodes were aired on Sunday mornings over a period of two years, and each episode drew unprecedented numbers of viewers.

Satellite Instruction Television Experiment (SITE) was an experiment in the use of television and space technology for the purposes of education. It was pursued for a year in 1975 in India.

Bibiliography and References

Agarwal, Amit. "Doordarshan: Five Flew over the Cuckoo's Nest." *India Today*, 15 September 1993.

———. "Doordarshan: Bollywood or Bust." *India Today*, 30 April 1993.

Agrawal, Binod C. "Satellite Instruction Television: SITE in India." In *World Communications: A Handbook*, edited by George Gerbner and Marsha Siefert. New York: Longman, Inc., 1984.

Bamzai, Kaveree. "Reality Check." *India Today*, 22 November 2004.

———. "The New Face of News." *India Today*, 28 April 2003a.

———. "Mean Queens." *India Today*, 7 April 2003b.

Barraclough, Steven. "Satellite Television in Asia: Winners and Losers." *Asian Affairs* 31, October 2000.

Butcher, Melissa, *Transnational Television, Cultural Identity and Change: When STAR Came to India*. New Delhi: Sage 2003.

Chan, Joseph Man. "National Responses and Accessibility to STAR TV in Asia." In *Media in Global Context: A Reader*, edited by Annabelle Sreberny-Mohammadi, Dwayne Winseck, Jim McKenna, and Oliver Boyd-Barrett. London: Arnold, 1997.

Chandra, Anupama. "Script Writers: A Flourish of the Pen." *India Today*, 31 January 1996.

Economist. "The Wiring of India." 27 May 2000.

ET Intelligence Group. "The ET Television Survey, 2003: It's a Home Theatre, It's a Multiplex, It's a TV." *Economic Times*, 26 September 2003.

Federation of Indian Chambers of Commerce and Industry (FICCI). *The Indian Entertainment Sector: In the Spotlight.* Mumbai: KPMG, 2003.

Govardan, D. "Crossed Signals." *Economic Times*, 8 April 2003.

Government of India. *India 2004: A Reference Annual.* Publications Division, Ministry of Information and Broadcasting, New Delhi, 2004.

Jain, Madhu. "Shadi Ya? Scenes from a Marriage." *India Today*, 28 February 1993.

John, Sangeeta. "Switched On." *The Week*, 3 October 2004.

Johnson, Kirk, *Television and Social Change in Rural India.* New Delhi: Sage, 2000.

Joshi, Manohar Shyam. "Mother of Soaps." *The Week*, 29 December 2002.

Joshi, Namrata. "Satellite Channels: Westward Bound." *India Today*, 10 August 1998.

Karlekar, Hiranmay. "Media: The Mirror and the Market." In *Independent India: The First Fifty Years*, edited by Hiranmay Karlekar. Delhi: Oxford University Press. 1998.

Lahiri, Indrajit. "Indian Broadcasting 1947–1994." In *Rasa: The Indian Performing Arts in the Last Twenty-five Years*. Calcutta: Anamika Kala Sangam, 1995.

Mankekar, Purnima. *Screening Culture, Viewing Politics: An Ethnography of Television, Womanhood, and Nation in Postcolonial India.* Durham and London: Duke University Press, 1999.

———. "Television Tales and a Woman's Rage: A Nationalist Recasting of Draupadi's Disrobing." In *Feminist Television Criticism: A Reader*, edited by Charlotte Brunsdon, Charlotte, June D'Acci, and Lynn Spigel. Oxford and New York: Clarendon Press, 1997.

Merchant, Khozem. *The Television Revolution: India's New Information Order.* Reuters Paper No. 54, unpublished monograph. Oxford: Green College.

Ministry of Information and Broadcasting. *Indian 2004.* New Delhi: Publications Division, 2004.

———. *Mass Media 2002.* New Delhi: Publications Division, 2002.

———. *Prasar Bharati Review Committee Report.* New Delhi: Publications Division, 2000.

———. *National Media Policy* (a working

paper submitted by the parliamentary subcommittee). New Delhi: Publications Division, 1996.

———. *Report of the Expert Committee on the Marketing of Commercial Time of AIR and DD* (Siddhartha Sen Committee). New Delhi: Publications Division, 1996.

———. *Report on Prasar Bharati* (Nitish Sengupta Committee), New Delhi: Publications Division, 1996.

———. *An Indian Personality for Television: Report of the Working Group on Software for Doordarshan.* New Delhi: Publications Division, 1985.

———. *Akash Bharati: Report of the Working Group on Autonomy for Akashvani and Doordarshan.* New Delhi: Publications Division, 1978.

Mitra, Ananda. *Television and Popular Culture in India: A Study of the Mahabharat.* New Delhi: Sage, 1993.

Mowlana, Hamid. *Global Information and World Communication: New Frontiers in International Relations.* London: Sage, 1997.

Pendakur, Manjunath. "New Cultural Technologies and the Fading Glitter of Indian Cinema." *Quarterly Review of Film and Video* 11, 1989.

Prospect. "In Fact." May 2004.

Rahman, M. "The New TV Superbazaar: Now at Your Fingertips." *India Today*, 15 November 1992.

Rahman, M., and Amit Agarwal. "Cable Bill: Ominous Signals." *India Today*, 15 September 1993.

Ray, Manas, and Elizabeth Jacka. "Indian Television: An Emerging Regional Force." In *New Patterns in Global Television*, edited by John Sinclair, Elizabeth Jacka, and Stuart Cunningham. New York: Oxford University Press, 1996.

Shedde, Meenakshi. "Script of Success: Steal but Do Not Get Caught." *Times of India*, 18 May 2003.

Thomas, Bella. "What the Poor Watch on TV." *Prospect*, January 2003.

Times of India: "High Court Will Rule on which 'Kanhaiyya' Is Real McCoy." 25 March 2003.

8
Cinema

Cinema is the most important form of popular entertainment in India. With an annual production of 800–1,000 films, India is the world's largest producer of films, and this wealth of production informs all aspects of Indian cultural life.

The centrality of Indian cinema to Indian lives cannot be overemphasized. Songs from films account for around 66 percent of the music industry's revenues. Feature films, film songs, interviews with films stars, and other industry-based programs are an important feature of terrestrial and cable television. Films provide sartorial guidance in matters of dress, and clothing designers vie to design for feature films and for stars attending celebrity events. Women seek inspiration from films for their styles. For

A giant billboard advertising a movie stands in the street, Chennai. (Hans Georg Roth/Corbis)

Bombay, now known as Mumbai, is referred to as Bollywood because it is the moviemaking capital of India. India is the worldwide leader, by far, in the quantity of movies produced, and watched, each year. Cinemas are generally packed to capacity, especially when the films are new releases of American classics, such as *Jurassic Park*, or Hindi classics that star famous Indian filmstars like Shashi Kapoor and Shabana Azmi. (Lindsay Hebberd/Corbis)

example, the all-time hit Hindi-language film *Hum Aapke Hain Koun!* (Sooraj Barjatya, 1994), described by many as no more than an extended wedding video, transformed the nation's wedding attire. Music played on national days is mostly patriotic songs from films, while devotional songs from films serve on religious festivals. Even folk singers and dancers have started adapting songs and dances from films in their performances, while cabaret shows at dance bars adopt film song-and-dance routines in their entirety.

The Indian film industry is fragmented into several regional film-producing centers scattered across the country. Films are made in all eighteen official languages, with even an occasional film in classical Sanskrit. However, the majority of films are produced in two main centers: Mumbai (formerly Bombay) and Chennai (formerly Madras). The Mumbai-based film industry produces between 150 and 200 films a year and is now routinely referred to in the media as "Bollywood." These films are in Hindi and follow a standard formula made up of familiar storylines elaborated by six to eight spectacular song and dance extravaganzas and comic subplots. The emotions are overstated; a grandiloquent, melodramatic narrative style is much preferred to quiet realism.

Bollywood films have the largest national following because Hindi, spoken in a variety of dialects by around 400 million people of northern and central India—40 percent of the population—is the national language. Furthermore, because Hindi originates from Sanskrit, as is the case with the regional languages of western (and some parts of eastern) India, it is also understood (in varying degrees) by a majority of Indians living in those regions.

Chennai is home to films made in the southern Indian languages of Tamil and Telugu, spoken in Tamil Nadu (of which Chennai is the capital) and the neighboring state of Andhra Pradesh, respectively. However, with the building of new state-of-the-art studios such as Ramoji Studios, in Hyderabad, Andhra Pradesh is also becoming an important film-making center. Southern India has a vibrant film culture, and around 150–200 films are made annually in Tamil and Telugu each. But because familiarity with the south Indian languages is restricted to just four southern states (which account for 20 percent of the national population), the films do not have the same pan-Indian following enjoyed by the popular Hindi cinema.

Such is the all-pervasive cultural influence of Indian films on the Indian populace that even the mighty machine of Hollywood, which has laid low many national cinemas of the world, has been unable to make a dent in the Indian market. Hollywood films constitute between 5 and 10 percent of total film revenues in India (Kheterpal 2003), although recent strategies to dub some American blockbusters into Hindi have improved prospects for the major distributors.

The dissemination of Indian cinema beyond India's national borders also mounts a small but significant challenge to the global hegemony of Hollywood. Historically, Indian films have been popular in all of south Asia (Pakistan, Bangladesh, Nepal, and Sri Lanka) and much of Southeast Asia (Indonesia, Malaysia, and Thailand). Indian cinema is also an important feature of cultural life in nations with large, long-established Indian populations, such as South Africa, Mauritius, and Fiji. Thanks to India's close political and commercial ties with the Soviet Union and the East European states during the Cold War, Indian films were regularly exported to the region. Not only have Indian films been regularly shown in Egypt and North Africa, but also in Israel, East Africa, and sub-Saharan Africa, where they have influenced the development of modern Hausa films and videos in Nigeria (Adamu 2004). The migrant Indian workers in the Gulf States constitute an important market for Indian films in the Middle East, and with an estimated 20 million persons of Indian origin living in the United States, Europe, Australia, and elsewhere, the Indian film industry has begun to recognize that the Indian diaspora is a valuable market for its products. In total, Indian films attract a global audience of 3.6 billion, as compared with 2.6 billion for Hollywood films (Perry 2002). In recent years, Indian films and films based on Indian subjects have caught the attention of some American and European distributors. The commercial success of films such as *East Is East* (1999), *Bend It Like Beckham* (2002), *Monsoon Wedding* (2001), *The Guru* (2002), and *Bride and Prejudice* (2004) has shown that there is an international interest in "ethnic" themes.

Popular Hindi Cinema

In the blockbuster *Naseeb* (Manmohan Desai, 1981), the character played by Amitabh

Scene still from *Monsoon Wedding*. (Mirabai Films/Delhi Dot Com/The Kobal Collection)

Bachchan, one of the biggest stars of the Hindi screen, says: "Hindi films are really very simple. Boy meets girl, boy rescues girl from a sexual assault in a magnificent fight scene, the two fall in love, sing many songs and live happily ever after. The audiences get their money's worth and go home happy." What Bachchan is referring to, of course, is the familiar story, a central feature of the formula that lies at the heart of the popular Hindi film. This hackneyed plot is emotionally enacted by stars and stretched, with the help of six to eight song-and-dance extravaganzas, spectacular fights, and comic subplots, into nearly two hours and forty-five minutes of unabashed cathartic release.

Plot

The familiar plot, which can be varied with countless combinations and permutations, goes like this: A handsome but poor man meets a rich and beautiful woman. The two fall in love, but the young woman's father refuses to let them entertain any thoughts of marriage, having already chosen the totally unsuitable son of his friend or business partner as his future son-in-law. However, in the course of the film the father's abysmal judgment becomes apparent when his choice of husband for his daughter is uncloaked as either an evil man or an impostor intent on defrauding the credulous father, whereas the poor man turns out to be the embodiment of virtue. The father acknowledges the error of his ways and welcomes his daughter's choice into the family.

Obviously, family relationships and kinship obligation play an important role in such stories. A father who must be obeyed, a widowed mother, often blind or lame and sometimes both, who must be looked after—these elements create the tensions necessary to endanger an early and smooth conclusion of the romance.

Sometimes family relationships form the dominant theme of a film, with the romance relegated to the subplot. These films dramatize the strains and pressures of modern life on the extended Hindu family when it is confronted by modernity in the form of an emancipated young bride. The "modern" newcomer disrupts the family's harmonious existence by refusing to honor the traditional family hierarchy and nearly causes a family breakup. The situation is saved in the nick of time when an exemplary member of the household awakens the young bride to the dangerous foolishness of her behavior. (Indian television advertisements often parody such "family breakup and reunion" stories. An advertisement for a cement company shows two brothers who have a falling out erect a wall dividing the ancestral property. However, after a melodramatic reconciliation they find that they are unable to break down the wall because of the excellent quality of the cement.)

A perennial favorite of the family drama is the "lost and found" theme first explored in G. Mukherji's *Kismet* in 1943 and which came into its own in the 1970s. Two brothers (or sisters, as in Ramesh Sippy's 1972 hit *Seeta Aur Geeta*) are separated at birth—by a natural disaster (floods, earthquakes), an accident (usually involving trains), or by the abduction of one child by a villain. Both grow up in the same city, unaware of their blood ties. One becomes a flashy gangster while the other is a hardworking policeman. When it eventually falls to the policeman to shoot the gangster in the line of duty, kinship is suddenly recognized—a birthmark, a pendant, a longlost sepia photograph—and the brothers

embrace, then set off to bring to justice the arch villain, usually the man the gangster used to work for.

These story lines are completely familiar to the spectators. As critic Ashis Nandy has pointed out: "The Bombay film story does not generally have an unexpected conclusion, it only has a predictable climax. It bases its appeal not on the linear development of a story line but on the special configuration which the film presents of many known elements or themes derived from other movies, or . . . from familiar traditional tales" (Nandy 181: 90).

The central conflict in the stories involves notions of good and evil, the Hindu concept of *dharma* (duty, righteous action), kinship ties, and social obligations (Thomas 1985). Popular Hindi films have incorporated many of the formal conventions of the popular theaters that flourished before the arrival of cinema in India. In the *Ram Lila*, popular theater in north India, for instance, episodes from the epics are performed at festival time to audiences who are completely familiar with the stories of the god Rama. The pleasure lies as much in the performance and the spectacle as in revisiting a familiar and well-loved episode. The interest thus lies in "*how* things will happen rather than *what* will happen next" (Thomas 1985: 130; emphasis in the original).

Emotion

The familiar narrative serves to provide openings for the exploration of emotions as well as songs, dances, and spectacle. Critic Kaveree Bamzai writes: "If there is one thing Bollywood cannot be accused of, it is lack of passion. Even its worst movies have a seat-of-the-pants chutzpah and a spontaneity that probably springs from the fact that dialogues mouthed by the actors were written just a minute ago. In Bollywood they don't act, they feel. They don't sing, they yodel. They don't dance, they whirl" (Bamzai 2004: 62).

The affective principle is of utmost importance in the cinematic experience. The emphasis on emotion finds its origins in the *Natyashastra* (ca. second century AD), a scholarly treatise on the classical Sanskrit stage attributed to Bharata, who documented an elaborate theory of *rasa* (the *essence* of emotions). Although the classical Sanskrit stage fell into decline in the eighth century AD, certain essential features were incorporated first into the popular theaters that survived it and later into the popular urban theaters of the late nineteenth and early twentieth centuries and thence into popular Indian films. The exploration of the entire range of emotions identified by Bharata within a single film has led the popular Hindi films to be labeled *masala* (mixed spices) movies. Violence and spectacle are blended with romance, comedy, and pathos. And it is not enough to simply convey these emotions— they must be powerfully overstated. Melodramatic overstatement is a "crucial stylization" of the Bombay film, for it strives to be "convincing as a spectacle by exaggeration," posits Nandy, citing the case of a disgruntled film critic who complained that whenever a clock strikes in Indian films, it always strikes twelve (Nandy 1981: 90).

Songs and Dances

Even more important than the exaggerated emotion is the presence of songs. Each film has six to eight songs, although *Indrasabha* (J. J. Madan, 1932) is said to have contained seventy-one songs (Kabir 1991). Songs and dances in dramatic perform-ances were an established convention in the classical Sanskrit theater; in the popular theaters such as *tamasha*, *nautanki*, and others; as well as in the urban popular theaters such as the Parsi theater that flourished in the nineteenth and twentieth centuries. Until recently, any Hindi film without any songs was immediately categorized as an "art film" and not for the consumption of the broad mass of film-going populations. The importance of music in popular films can be gauged by the fact that the music director (composer and arranger) has his or her name appear early in the roll of credits and alongside those of the producer and director on the massive, hand-painted billboards that advertise the films. (Stars are never identified by name on billboards and publicity materials—the affectation being that the public recognizes them just by looking at them.)

The success of the first talkie, a musical called *Alam Ara* (A. Irani, 1931) and a direct transfer from the Parsi stage, determined the future of the Hindi film as a musical. According to film historians Barnouw and Krishnaswamy: "The Indian sound film, unlike the sound film of any other land, had from its first moment seized exclusively on music drama forms. In doing so, the film had tapped a powerful current, one that went back some two thousand years" (Barnouw and Krishnaswamy 1980: 69).

During the silent era, film screenings were accompanied by live music played by a small group of musicians. Indian musical accompaniment was provided for Indian films and western musical accompaniment (usually piano) for imported films. Sometimes the musicians also provided sound effects such as the galloping of horses or the crash of thunder, and sometimes narrators would translate the "title cards" and explain the intricacies of the plot.

The songs in the early talkies were taken from folk as well as classical traditions. The microphones used for sound recordings were still fairly primitive and had to be kept stationary in order to reduce noise disturbances. This severely restricted the movements of the actors (Skillman 1986). To muffle the whirring sound of the camera, it had to be buried under mattresses. Then a single microphone would be directed at the actor/singer while the small group of musicians sat outside the camera frame and provided accompaniment. The actor/singer was usually unable to move without upsetting the balance between voice and accompaniment and consequently the scene had to be shot in a single take with the singer rooted stiffly to one spot (Kabir 1991). Sometimes orchestras were hidden behind trees and bushes. Some were even suspended from trees to help the singer hear the notes clearly.

The increasing importance of songs forced producers to hire singers even if they were unable to act, since that failing was considered a lesser evil than actors unable to sing. However, R. C. Boral (1903–1981) soon solved the problems of microphones, singers, and musical accompaniments by prerecording the songs with professional singers and then having the actors to lip-synchronize on screen when the songs were played back during shooting (Skillman 1986). These singers came to be known as "playback" artists and became celebrities in their own right. The most famous playback singer is Lata Mangeshkar, who has over 25,000 songs to her credit in a career that has spanned over half a century. Playback liberated the actors to dance and whirl, and elaborate

Popular Bollywood star Shilpa Shetty (center) dances with co-stars during the shooting of a song sequence for her new thriller *Khamosh*, or *Quiet*, in Bombay, 2004. (Sherwin Crasto/Reuters/Corbis)

song-and-dance routines (known as "item numbers") became an essential feature of popular Indian films. The sylvan settings, which began as a technical necessity, became a time-honored convention of the Hindi film song, and the elite press regularly satirized the alacrity with which actors "run around trees" during song and dance sequences.

Hindi film songs have an existence far beyond the screen. They are played over loudspeakers during religious festivals and national celebrations. Bands belt them out as wedding processions make their leisurely way across crowded streets; beggars singing on commuter trains have a repertoire of the latest hits. Even the performers of "folk" songs that were once borrowed and adapted by music directors for the screen have started performing the screen versions of their own songs. Some radio stations are dedicated entirely to film songs, and a substantial proportion of MTV's broadcasts to India comprise Hindi film songs.

The song-and-dance sequences are devised as visual pageants with exotic dancing, lavish costumes, grand settings, and spectacular landscapes. Many are contrived as dream sequences, thus permitting dizzyingly frequent changes of costume and location. The song-and-dance sequences grant the actors permission to "express the inexpressible" and the viewers to indulge in the pleasures of looking. Most importantly, they provide the stars a chance to display their physical beauty and exhibit themselves as pure objects of desire to be visually devoured by fans.

Genre

The formulaic unfolding of Hindi films defies generic classifications. Ever since the establishment of its major studios, Hollywood has catered to its global audiences by organizing the production and marketing of its films around "genres" (musicals, thrillers, comedies, and so forth), each genre with its own distinctive "system of orientations, expectations and conventions that circulate between industry, text and subject" (Neale 1980: 19). This system has enabled the industry to predict audience expectations, guide the audience's viewing, and cater to the preferences of varied audiences (Cooke 1985), and such an arrangement is commercially viable because studios calculate their profits by an averaging of total profits. In contrast, there is little genre differentiation in the current Hindi

film industry. Most films belong to the "omnibus" genre characterized by a romantic plot, melodramatic renditions, song-and-dance extravaganzas, unrelated subplots, and narrative digressions.

The origins of the omnibus genre lie in the historical evolution of the Hindi film and in the manner in which films are made in India, where most producers are "independent" and where, unlike Hollywood, there are no longer any corporate studios left.

History

Beginnings   India's fascination with cinema dates back to the very early days of filmmaking. The Lumière brothers opened their cinematograph on 28 December 1895 in Paris. Six months later their emissary, Maurice Sestier, on his way to Australia, stopped off in Bombay to screen his collection of short films. The screening for British residents in India, some Europeans, and a few Anglicized Indians was held at Watson's Hotel on 7 July 1896. It was an unprecedented success. Further screenings were then hurriedly arranged for even bigger crowds at the larger Novelty Theatre.

Overnight an enthusiastic audience had been created, and by 1897 the regular screening of imported European and American films had begun. The first decade of the twentieth century was abuzz with film-related activities. British residents and Indians imported filming equipment to make their own films—short features that included comic gags, operas, sports events, and other documentaries chronicling local events (Barnouw and Krishnaswamy 1980). Indian entrepreneurs embarked on a theater-building spree. The greatest of them all was J. F. Madan (1856–1923), who by the 1920s controlled about 100 out of the 300 theaters. Madan's agreements with overseas film companies led to a virtual monopoly of imported films in the country (FICCI 2003). He established an integrated film production-distribution-exhibition empire that would dominate the Indian subcontinent for the next three decades. Abdulally Esoofally (1884–1957) set up a network for the exhibition of films—not just in India, but also in the other British colonial territories of Singapore, Sumatra, Java, Burma, and Ceylon (Barnouw and Krishnaswamy 1980).

The Silent Era   The first Indian feature-length film was *Raja Harishchandra*. Made in 1912 by D. G. Phalke (1870–1944), it retold the famous story from Hindu mythology of King Harishchandra and his willingness to sacrifice everything in the pursuit of the truth. The film was 3,700 feet long; when screened with a hand-cranked projector, it lasted approximately fifty minutes. It is said that the inspiration for this first Indian film came from the film *Life of Christ* by the French director Alice Guy (Gaumont, 1906), which was screened as a Christmas feature in Bombay in 1910. Film historian B. V. Dharap points to an article written by Phalke in November 1917 where the filmmaker states:

> While the life of Christ was rolling before my physical eyes, I was mentally visualising the Gods, Shri Krishna, Shri Ramachandra, their Gokul and their Ayodhya. I was gripped by a strange spell. I bought another ticket and saw the film again. This time I felt my imagination taking shape on the screen. Could this really happen? Could we, the sons of India, ever be able to see Indian images on screen? (Dharap 1985: 35)

Phalke liquidated his assets and traveled to London to learn filmmaking. He bought some filmmaking equipment and returned to India to enlist the help of his wife in the making of *Raja Harishchandra*. Phalke, an art school graduate and photographer for the Archaeological Department of the colonial government of India, was also an amateur magician, and he incorporated the cinematic tricks and special effects of the celebrated Georges Méliès (1861–1938). The effort was met with unabashed enthusiasm. The Méliès tricks lent themselves spectacularly to the depiction of the miracles and divine interventions that abound in stories from Hindu mythology. Suddenly these mythological gods and kings, so familiar to ordinary Hindus, came alive on the cinema screens. Phalke's film was such a success that it is said that he carried away his nightly box office collections in huge mountains of coins piled high on a bullock cart (Barnouw and Krishnaswamy 1980).

Thereafter, all of Phalke's films were based on stories from Hindu mythology. Other filmmakers followed in his footsteps, and the "mythological" was the first-ever genre of Indian cinema. Gradually historical and social themes began to find a place in the array of films. A total of 1,331 silent films were made in India (Rajadhyaksha and Willemen 1999). Most of these have perished, but the few that survive are stored at the Film Archives in Pune (formerly Poona). Although Indian audiences showed a clear preference for Indian themes, only 15 percent of the total number of films released in India in 1926–1927 were Indian films. The rest were foreign films, mostly imported from the United States (Barnouw and Krishnaswamy 1980). However, these percentages would change with the arrival of the "talkies."

The Advent of Sound   The arrival of the talkies proved a serious challenge for the film industry. With its linguistic diversity, India would need to make films in different regional languages and risk fragmenting the vast national market into smaller, less lucrative regional ones. The first talkie, *Alam Ara* (A. Irani, 1931) was made in Mumbai in Hindustani, a mixture of Hindi and Urdu. The film was a remake of a popular Parsi theater production with spectacle, songs, and dances. The film was a great success, and musical fantasy as a genre, already prevalent in the theater, seemed to show the way forward for film producers.

The advent of sound necessitated the construction of sound studios and the switch to indoor shooting. Scores of studios sprang up in the major cities. Lahore (now in Pakistan), Mumbai, Kolkata (formerly Calcutta), and later Chennai became major film centers. By the end of the 1930s, nearly one hundred studios, big and small, were involved in film production. Those that survived the struggle to remain solvent adopted the Hollywood model, controlling the production, distribution, and exhibition of films. This vertical integration allowed for investment in equipment and technologies, and for economies of scale. But studios also needed theaters for exhibition, and Madan, controling over a third of the existing 300 theaters, exercised a near monopoly. Since his theaters exclusively screened imported (mostly American) films, only bigger studios had the muscle needed to get their Indian films screened (FICCI 2003).

Three major studios emerged during the frenzied activities of the 1930s that would greatly influence the future of Indian cinema: New Theatres in Kolkata, Prabhat (in Kolhapur and later Pune), and Bombay Talkies in Mumbai.

New Theatres   In 1931, B. N. Sircar, an engineer by profession, had just completed the construction of a theater for a client when he decided to build one for himself in Kolkata. He equipped it with a first-class studio and provided the talented group of Bengalis he had gathered around him with everything they could possibly need to work creatively. This was the start of New Theatres. One of the directors to achieve fame and recognition soon after the establishment of the studio was Debaki Bose (1898–1971). His first success, *Chandidas* (1932), was based on the life of the eponymous sixteenth-century poet-saint. Bose's liberal use of devotional songs and music perfectly suited the requirements of the religious theme. His later films were also based on religious or mythological themes; the most famous were *Puran Bhagat* (1933) and *Seeta* (1934). The latter was the first Indian film screened at an international film festival.

However the greatest sensation to emerge from New Theatres was P. C. Barua (1903–1951), an Assamese prince whose production of *Devdas* (1935), based on a novel by the renowned Bengali litterateur Saratchandra Chatterjee, overwhelmed the nation. Made in two versions—Bengali and Hindi—it tells the tale of Devdas, the dissolute son of a rich, feudal landowner, who takes to drink when his childhood sweetheart is married off to another. So moving were the melancholic songs and the tragic dénouement that "virtually a generation wept over *Devdas*" (Barnouw and Krishnaswamy 1980: 80). The film has been remade several times in different languages. The most recent remake in 2002 was an extravagant blockbuster in Hindi by Sanjay Leela Bhansali. It starred Shah Rukh Khan and Aishwarya Rai, the reigning king and queen of Bollywood. Barua directed both of the original versions but starred only in the Bengali one. Like his protagonist, he

Devdas, by director Sanjay Bhansali, is the most expensive (US$12 million) Indian film ever made, with opulent sets, period costumes, and melodious music. Since its release the movie has broken records. Even after several weeks, the movie tickets were hard to get. The film's original costumes are part of a traveling exhibition, and will be auctioned in London. A whole range of *Devdas* brand products were launched in the market. The film is an adaptation of the novel written in 1901 by Saratchandra Chatterjee. The coveted role is played by the leading Bollywood actor Shah Rukh Khan with former Miss World Aishwarya Rai. This photograph shows a rare hand-painted billboard of *Devdas*, painted by the artist Vaidya in central Bombay, 12 July 2002. (Noshir Desai/Corbis)

died of drink (but not of melancholy) at the age of 48.

Most of the later films made by New Theatres were drawn from literary sources, and the audiences usually associated New Theatres with sophisticated, intellectual music dramas.

Prabhat   For New Theatres in Kolkata, competition was to come from Prabhat studios in Poona. Originally established in Kolhapur in Maharashtra State in 1929, the studio shifted to Poona in 1933. Like New Theatres, Prabhat began by making mythological and devotional films. The most influential personality to emerge from this studio was the actor-director V. Shantaram (1901–1990). His first film, made in Marathi (the regional language), was *Ayodhyache Raja* (1932), which once again explored the life of the same King Harishchandra that made Phalke famous. In 1936, Shantaram's associates S. Fatehlal (1897–1964) and V. G. Damle (1892–1945) made a devotional film, *Sant Tukaram*, on the life of the eponymous seventeenth-century poet-saint. The film won an award at the Venice Film Festival, the first international award for an Indian film. Many consider it the finest Indian film ever made. It is part of the library of films screened in villages by the Maharashtra State Government's mobile film unit.

Shantaram quickly moved away from the mythological genre and began to explore social issues. As was the practice of the day, he made two versions of his films—in Marathi and Hindi. His most famous films were *Kunku/Duniya Na Mane* (1937), which examined the issue of older men taking younger wives, and *Shejari/Padosi* (1941), which explored Hindu-Muslim relationships. Soon Prabhat became known for its social themes. Not only were the films ideologically bold for the times, they were also innovative in their use of camera, music, and song, which was to influence later directors serving as apprentices at the studio.

Bombay Talkies   The third major studio in the 1930s was Bombay Talkies, set up by Himansu Rai (1892–1940). Rai had worked in Britain and Germany, but economic depression and the rise of fascism in Germany had forced him and his actress wife, Devika Rani (1907–1994), to return to India, accompanied by a few German technicians. They set up Bombay Talkies in Mumbai and proceeded to make three films a year. These were generally sophisticated, lightweight romances in Hindi directed by Rai with Devika Rani as his leading lady. The studio occasionally produced a film with a "social message," such as *Achhut Kanya* (1936), which explored a doomed romance between a high caste Brahmin man and a woman from an "untouchable" caste.

Rai ran his studio with a paternal authoritarianism. Only university graduates were eligible to join and all recruits—from leading actor to clapper boy—were accorded equal status. They all received a monthly salary and worked fixed hours. Bombay Talkies was renowned for its excellent sound system. It was famed for the excellent care it offered its workers (canteen, health care, and free education for the children) and its revolutionary, caste-free egalitarianism. According to film historians Barnouw and Krishnaswamy: "It was known that at Bombay Talkies all company members, of whatever caste, ate together at the company canteen. It was even said that top actors, on occasion helped clean floors . . .

All this was part of the legend of the role of Bombay Talkies" (Barnouw and Krishnaswamy 1980: 103). Many famous directors of the post-independent films received their early training at Bombay Talkies.

In addition to these three major studios, smaller studios included Minerva Movietone. It was founded in 1936 by actor-director Sohrab Modi (1897–1984), often compared to Sir Laurence Olivier. He specialized in historical films and "misogynistic psychodramas" (Rajadhyakasha and Willemen 1999: 150). Wadia Movietone was established in 1933. It produced Fairbanks-inspired stunt films featuring their star performer, "Fearless" Nadia (1910–1994), allegedly of Greek and Welsh origin. "Nadia of Wadia" delighted her audiences with dramatic rescues from moving trains, runaway cars, and wild horses.

War and the Struggle for Independence   The studio era was an exciting period in the development of Indian cinema. It laid the foundations for a powerful nationwide industry, trained a whole generation of actors, directors, and technicians, and created an enthusiastic but discerning audience all over the country. And now that films were written and produced entirely in Indian languages, Hollywood films ceased to dominate the screen.

The outbreak of World War II, in which India was an unwilling participant, drastically changed the film industry. Scarce film stock was rationed out by the colonial government to a few established studios, which had to reciprocate by dedicating at least one film in five to the subject of the war effort. Such films were rarely popular with the audiences, and many directors found ways to circumvent the order. Director V. Shantaram made an "anti-Japanese" film, *Dr Kotnis Ki Amar Kahani* (1946) by setting it in China and recounting the tale of an Indian doctor who helped the communist forces fight the Japanese invaders. It was possibly the only war effort film to find favor with the Indian public.

The war years were also a period of intense political activity that continued until India gained independence from British colonial rule in 1947. There was strict censorship of political content in cinema, and films that ridiculed British soldiers, government officials, the police, and others were immediately banned. Not willing to risk their capital by having their films banned, yet wanting to capture the nationalist patriotic fervor of the time, some producers resolved their dilemma by reviving the historical and mythological genres. In *Sikander* (Sohrab Modi, 1941), a brave Indian king repels Alexander the Great's attempts to conquer the country, which provided several occasions for rousing speeches on the need for national freedom and Indian independence. In *Ram Rajya* (Vijay Bhatt, 1943), the epic battle between the god Rama and Ravana (a struggle between good and evil in the *Ramayana*) came to signify India's struggle against the evil colonizer. Even in *Kismet* (G. Mukherjee, 1943), a crime thriller, a rousing song warns Germans and Japanese soldiers to stay clear of India. However, the cinematic rendition of the song left few doubts about which foreign power the lyrics implied. The film was a huge success, thanks in no small measure to the song, and ran for nearly three and a half years in Calcutta.

Other producers responded to the censor's strictures by creating an Indian character who caricatured British mannerisms. Wearing a tailored suit and carrying a hat, he was either ridiculed as a buffoon who disdained Indians as "damn fools" or demonized as a villain. Needless to say, the nationalist hero in Indian attire usually got the better of him.

Still other directors began slipping in patriotic symbols. In *Anmol Ghadi* (Mehboob, 1945), a character opens a magazine with a picture of Subhash Chandra Bose, founder of the outlawed Indian National Army, on its cover. In courtroom dramas, pictures of Mahatma Gandhi adorned the walls instead of the British monarch. The censors lost no time in removing these images, but occasionally a few did manage to slip past the scissors. Barnouw and Krishnaswamy write:

> Film producers now took to the casual introduction of Congress symbols into films. On the wall, in the background, one would see the Gandhian motif, the spinning wheel, signifying defiance of the economic pattern of the empire. In a store there would be a calendar with Gandhi's portrait; in a home, a photograph of Nehru; on the sound track, the effect of a passing parade, with a few bars of a favorite Congress song. Often such symbols had no plot reference; but in theaters they elicited cheers. As war began, British censors ordered the scissoring of such shots. After 1942, when Gandhi was again imprisoned—along with a number of Congress leaders—no photograph of Gandhi was allowed on screen, no matter how incidentally. (Barnouw and Krishnaswamy 1980: 124)

Beginning of the Formula The war years necessitated an expansion of defense-related industries and thus fueled a spurt in economic activity. Rapid industrialization required more workers and put extra money into circulation (Barnouw and Krishnaswamy 1980). More and more young men left the countryside to find work in these new industries, thereby increasing the population of the cities and increasing the number of avid film spectators. The reduced marine traffic between Britain and India led to a scarcity in essential commodities and resulted in a flourishing black market. Much of the untaxed profits found their way into film production, marking the beginning of a long and covert relationship between money laundering and film finance, a relationship that has, over the decades, further strengthened.

With large amounts of cash from black marketeers eager to plow their money into films, new independent producers entered the business of making movies. Not wishing to be encumbered with the overheads of maintaining a studio and a permanent staff, they set up production companies and began to entice actors, musicians, singers, and cameramen away from the studios with very large sums of money. Producers had long known the marketing value of a "star." Placed in sylvan settings where romance blossomed, the stars sang soulful songs and engendered a fan following among the audiences. By promoting the beauty, talent, and charisma of stars, producers created a commodity that would lure audiences to the cinema in droves. A simple story, usually a romance that would exalt the star, was hurriedly concocted. In the process, the crucial role of the screenwriter was completely devalued. Unencumbered by the steep overheads of maintaining a studio with hundreds of employees on the payroll, the new independent producers made handsome profits.

Within a decade, the established studios ran into difficulties. Some folded quickly,

and others, like Bombay Talkies, managed to survive by renting out their studios to the new, independent producers. The collapse of the studios was also accelerated by the demise or decline of the dominant central figures around whom many of these studios were built (for example, Shantaram at Prabhat and Rai at Bombay Talkies).

With extra money in circulation, the number of producers kept increasing. By the mid-1940s, thanks to mass migration from villages to the cities to take advantage of the increased prospects of work in the factories, mills, and docks, audience figures, too, had doubled. However, government controls over scarcity materials, such as those required for construction of theaters, resulted in no new theaters being built to accommodate the growth in the number of films and spectators (Barnouw and Krishnaswamy 1980). With an oversupply of films and a scarcity of theaters, distributors and exhibitors began to dictate terms to producers. They began to influence the kinds of films that were being made. Exhibitors had identified certain stars, and certain kinds of songs and dances as crowd pleasers and demanded that producers deliver these features if they wished to have their new films screened.

Romantic stories (with complicated family relationships to provide emotional tension), highlighting stars, songs, dances, and spectacle, became the order of the day, and remained so for several decades thereafter.

Independence and After   The film industry celebrated the independence of India with a spate of films about freedom fighters and nationalist martyrs. But nothing could dispel the gloom of the partition of the country into two nations—India and Pakistan—and the horrific violence that ensued between the Muslims and Sikhs on the one hand and the Hindus and Muslims on the other. Partition also had a very direct impact on the Hindi film industry. Lahore, a major city and film-producing center in the northwest of undivided India, became part of West Pakistan. As a result, hundreds of Hindu directors, producers, actors, musicians, lyricists, singers, and technicians made their way to Bombay film industry, enriching it with their immense talent.

In eastern India, Bengali cinema headquartered in Calcutta was badly hit when it lost half its Bengali audience to East Pakistan (now Bangladesh). Films had now to be exported to the new country and then re-imported subject to all kinds of levies and tariffs. As studios in Calcutta began to fold, an exodus of talent to Bombay took place.

Meanwhile in Bombay, the studio owners tried desperately to save their studios from the unstoppable rise of the "independent" producers. They sought government intervention and assistance, and proposed the creation of a film-financing institution involving commercial lending agencies, including banks. A corporate structure was proposed in an effort to protect the studios from unfair competition, and established public figures were drafted to lend credibility to their efforts. However, the government of a newly independent India had more pressing concerns and did not view the film industry as a priority investment area (FICCI 2003). It did, however, see the potential of the film industry as a revenue earner. Thus films became subjected to steep entertainment taxes, a feature of government policy that persists even today. State governments levy entertainment tax; levels vary but average 45 percent of the price of a ticket across the country.

The Golden Age of Hindi Cinema The arrival in Bombay of talented filmmakers from the different studios of India gave new vigor and confidence to the bustling Hindi film industry and has led many film historians to label the 1950s as the "golden age" of Hindi cinema. It was an age of great actors such as Dilip Kumar, Raj Kapoor, Dev Anand; actresses such as Nargis, Meena Kumari, and Madhubala; composers Naushad Ali, Salil Chaudhary, and Ravi;

On 17 May 2003, Indian actor and director Dev Anand received the Lifetime Achievement Award for Indian Cinema at the fourth International Indian Film Academy Awards (IIFA) at the SunDome in Johannesburg. Legendary actor and Bollywood filmmaker Dev Anand received the 2003 Dadasaheb Phalke award, the prestigious accolade given by the Indian government for lifetime contributions to the cinema. The 80-year-old actor-producer-director is one of the few surviving legends of the pre-Partition era. Durban, South Africa. (STR/AFP/Getty Images)

and lyricists Sahir Ludhianvi, Majrooh Sultanpuri, and Shakeel Badayuni. Never again was the city to witness such a glittering assembly of talent in the Hindi film industry.

Four directors dominated the decade: Mehboob Khan, Raj Kapoor, Bimal Roy, and Guru Dutt. All four had served as apprentices in the major studios and had shown themselves to be open to the influences of Hollywood and the major film movements in Europe, which they duly incorporated into the now established formula film that was the signature of the Hindi film factories.

Mehboob Khan (1904–1964) The early films of Mehboob Khan portray an idiosyncratic blend of Islam and Marxism. Only in his later films did he embrace the extravagant flourishes of Cecil B. De Mille. His early films examine issues surrounding extreme poverty (of which he had firsthand experience as a young boy when his mother struggled to feed him and his siblings) and the plight of women under patriarchy. *Roti*, made in 1942, is a whimsical but stark denunciation of capitalism and human greed. Mehboob's most celebrated work is *Mother India* (1957), which has often been described as a left-wing *Gone with the Wind*. A remake of his earlier film *Aurat* (1940), it recounts the tale of an abandoned peasant woman as she struggles to keep her children alive in the wake of famine. The narrative unfolds against a backdrop of the nation's transition from primitive farming to modern mechanized agriculture, and while the denunciation of exploitation of peasants is robust, the production itself is extremely lavish. His other films, such as *Najma* (1942), *Andaz* (1949), and *Anmol Ghadi* (1945), explore the claustrophobic world of women and the tragedy of those who try to escape it. An ardent supporter of Nehru's socialist programs, Mehboob died within a day of Nehru's death.

Raj Kapoor (1926–1988) Four generations of the Kapoor family have found fame and fortune in the Hindi film industry. Raj Kapoor's father, Prithviraj Kapoor, was a well-established stage actor in Lahore, where he established Prithvi Theatres (1944–1960) and where he was the star actor and director. To keep the theater company solvent, he accepted roles in films as well. With his sons Raj, Shammi, and Shashi Kapoor, and his grandsons Randhir and Rishi Kapoor and great granddaughters Karishma and Kareena Kapoor, he spawned a great acting dynasty.

Raj Kapoor began work as a stagehand at his father's theaters. He later trained with Bombay Talkies, and by the age of twenty-two, he had established his own production company, R. K. Studios, and directed his first film, *Aag* (1948), in which he also played the leading role. Unusually handsome, with blue eyes, his screen persona was influenced by Hollywood actors such as Ronald Coleman, Clark Gable, and Charlie Chaplin. His early films tackle urban issues of unemployment and homelessness—serious themes that were examined not didactically but entertainingly, with lively songs and love scenes. *Awara* (1951) was an instant hit, not just in India, but also in the Soviet Union. It was said to be Chairman Mao Zedong's favorite film. With *Shri 420* (1955), Raj Kapoor established himself as the darling of the masses.

His later films—*Jis Desh Mein Ganga Behti Hai* (1960), *Sangam* (1964), *Satyam Shivam Sundaram* (1978), and *Ram Teri*

Ganga Maili (1985)—showed a greater preference for eroticism than socialism. In his lifetime, Kapoor acted in over seventy films and produced about seventy features.

Bimal Roy (1902–1966) Scion of a rich landowning family, Bimal Roy began his directorial debut at New Theatres in Kolkata with the Bengali film *Udayer Pathey* (*Hamrahi* in the Hindi version, both 1944). He moved to Mumbai in 1950. After working briefly with Bombay Talkies, he set up his own company, Bimal Roy Productions, where he made thirteen films in eleven years (Rajadhyaksha and Willemen 1995).

Roy was best known for his social themes, which depicted the injustices of the *zamindari* (landowning) system, as in his classic film *Do Bigha Zameen* (1953). Other memorable films were *Madhumati* (1958), about the exploitation of tribal communities; *Sujata* (1959), about the Hindu caste system; and *Bandini* (1964), about the freedom struggle. He also remade P. C. Barua's *Devdas* in Hindi with the reigning star of the time, Dilip Kumar, in the title role. Roy was one of the few Indian cineastes to be able to combine his own political ideology with the Indian box office requirements of romance, songs, dances, and melodrama. His cinematic style reveals the influence of the Italian neorealist directors.

Guru Dutt (1925–1964) No other popular director has attained the cult status that has been accorded to the actor-director Guru Dutt, who committed suicide at the age of 39. A trained dancer, he worked as actor, choreographer, and assistant director at Prabhat studios before setting up his own production company. He experi-mented with a large variety of genres—romances, comedies, and adventure films. His most celebrated films were *Baazi* (1953), a gangster film noir; *Pyaasa* (1957), about a poet who decries the corruption of society; and *Kaagaz ke Phool* (1959), about the decline of a major studio. The latter flopped at the box office, a failure that Dutt took so much to heart that he refused to acknowledge his next film *Chaudhvin Ka Chand* (1960). It was a romance set in a traditional Muslim family and became a huge box office success. This was followed by yet another hit, *Sahib Bibi Aur Ghulam* (1962), a haunting unraveling of a feudal Bengali landowning family.

The 1960s and the Arrival of Color
Color processing equipment was not imported into the country until the 1960s. When Mehboob Khan's *Aan* (1952) was shot in 16mm Gevacolour and blown up in Technicolor, it was the first successful transition from black and white to color in India (Rajadhyaksha and Willemen 1995). Color film encouraged lavish sets. Initially the prohibitive cost of color forced some directors to film only a few scenes (usually the ones that lent themselves to spectacle) in color. In K. Asif's spectacular romantic historical, *Mughal-e-Azam* (1960), recently re-colored and re-released by his son and greeted with warm tears of nostalgia by audiences, the famed "hall of mirrors" song-and-dance number is in color while much of the rest of the film is in black and white.

The 1960s was the decade of romance. The formulaic film had by now come into its own, particularly since color cinematography encouraged outdoor shooting in the magnificent landscapes of Kashmir and the Himalayas, bringing home to the urban audiences the splendors of the natural scenic beauty of the Indian subcontinent. In *Jungalee* (S. Mukherjee, 1961) the Elvis-inspired, quiff-sporting protagonist undertakes a trip to Kashmir, where he meets a young woman. The two spend a substantial part of the film cavorting in the snow singing lively songs of love. When the scenic beauty of Kashmir was exhausted, producers moved to exotic locales in Switzerland, Hawaii, and elsewhere. Film titles such as *Love in Tokyo* (1966), *Singapore* (1960), or *Around the World in Eight Dollars* (1967) became commonplace. Despite the allure of seeing their favorite stars in color, the spectators remained a capricious bunch. The majority of films lost money, a small percentage broke even, and a smaller percentage made money. But it was the elusive possibility of hitting the jackpot that kept investors and producers eager to keep making films.

The love of romantic scenes shot in "exotic" foreign locations such as Switzerland and France has strengthened over the decades and spawned an entire tourist industry specialty: Indian tourists travel to sites where certain successful films have been shot with the fervor of religious pilgrims. To capitalize on this lucrative industry, many delegates from foreign tourist offices have travelled to India to encourage Indian producers to shoot films in their countries.

The Angry Young Man   The romance of the 1960s was to change dramatically with the arrival of a new team of screenwriters. Salim Khan and Javed Akhtar (known as Salim-Javed) replaced the romantic hero with the angry young man. In *Zanjeer* (Prakash Mehra, 1973), their first commercial success, the lean, mean, and angry hero who would rather fight than romance the leading lady was inspired by Clint Eastwood. The image of the introverted avenger popularized by Amitabh Bachchan was to dominate the screen for the next fifteen years. It also briefly brought back the screenwriter, devalued by the independent producers of the previous decades, as an important figure in the film-making process.

New technology allowed cinematographers greater scope for spectacular violence (blood spurts, neck breaks, and so forth) and created a new function—that of the fight composer, the person who choreographed these spectacular fight sequences. His job was to add choreographed bone-crunching fight sequences to the narrative. Gory spectacle in disused warehouses and colorful cabaret dances in the sleazy, smoke-filled bars frequented by the hero replaced the mellifluous love songs set in natural scenic beauty.

One way of increasing the visual pleasures of the film was to have multiple lead actors ("heroes") who, when not romancing their respective women in snow-covered mountains, flower-filled parks, or in the throbbing strobe lights of dance floors, were spectacularly fighting off multiple villains. Thus was born the "multi-starrer." One such multi-starrer was Ramesh Sippy's *Sholay* (1975), often described as a "curry western," and one of the highest grossing Hindi films of all time.

The 1970s also revived the "lost and found" stories about separated twin brothers, which permitting the reigning star to play double roles in the film and offered the spectators the visual treat of, as one film publicity poster famously announced, "twice the star for the price of one."

Art Films and the Parallel Film Movement   The decade of the 1970s also signalled the arrival of "art" films or "parallel" cinema, a movement that had, in fact, already begun with Satyajit Ray. Dispensing with the formula film world of stars, songs, and spectacle in favor of serious realistic themes, these small-budget films targeted the more discerning filmgoer.

Satyajit Ray (1921–1992), the celebrated director, brought to Indian cinema international recognition and status of the kind it had never before enjoyed. Born in Kolkata, Ray studied at Nobel laureate Rabindranath Tagore's Shanti Niketan. In 1947, he started a film society, which introduced him to the cinemas of post-war Europe and the Soviet Union. When Jean Renoir (1894–1979) came to film *The River* (1951), Ray was able to observe the French director at work. Inspired by what he saw, he bought the film rights to the Bengali novel *Pather Panchali* by Bhibhutibhushan Bannerji and wrote out a complete screenplay in Bengali. But finding a producer proved to be almost impossible. Dismayed that the film had no songs or dances, producers flatly turned it down. In desperation Ray sold his personal belongings and began to shoot a few scenes. When the money ran out, he turned to the state government of West Bengal, which, surprisingly, agreed to finance the venture. It was, many historians and economists agree, the best investment ever made by a government body in an artistic field.

Shot in natural surroundings on a very tight budget and with a musical score by Ravi Shankar, *Pather Panchali* (1955) is a simple, realistic, and exquisite document on the childhood of a boy named Apu. A great success in West Bengal, it was initially unknown outside the state. An official entry at the Cannes Film Festival that year, it was voted the "best human document." The film also set a new record for the longest running film at New York's Fifth Avenue Cinema. After his success with *Pather Panchali*, Ray completed the trilogy on Apu's life with *Aparajito* (1956) and *Apur Sansar* (1959).

The success of the trilogy marked the beginning of a career in filmmaking that spanned thirty-five years, during which Ray experimented with several genres— comedy, literary adaptations, adventure, musical fantasy. His only non-Bengali film was *Shatranj Ke Khilari* (*The Chess Players*, 1977), where he used the reigning stars of Bombay's film world. Although the greatest influences on Ray's filmmaking style were the Italian neo-realists from whom he also learned to make films on a shoestring budget, his view of the world was always unique and distinctive.

The legacy of Ray encouraged young filmmakers of the 1970s to experiment with new forms. The establishment of the Film and Television Institute of India (FTII) in 1961 and the creation of the Film Archives in 1964 had already spawned a new generation of professionally trained directors and technicians. Many of these were absorbed into the film factories of Bombay and Madras. But some wished to experiment with alternative forms of cinematic expression, even though raising funds for such experimental endeavors proved nearly impossible. Although the state-funded Film Finance Corporation (FFC) set up in 1960 was amalgamated with the state-funded Indian Motion Pictures Export Corporation (IMPEC) to form the National Film Development Corporation (NFDC) in 1980, it provided only a few opportunities for newcomers to finance low-budget films.

Two new films financed by the FFC heralded the start of a wave of art films: Mrinal Sen's *Bhuvan Shome* and Mani Kaul's *Uski Roti*, both made in 1969. *Bhuvan Shome*, a comic satire on bureaucrats tells how a principled but heartless officer sacks his junior, only to be charmed by the latter's vivacious peasant wife during a chance encounter at a duck shoot. Kaul's experimental *Uski Roti* is based on a Mohan Rakesh short story about a young woman who walks several miles each day to deliver her bus driver husband his midday meal. One day her sister is sexually assaulted, and she is late. Her husband drives off in a huff, and uncertain of his intentions, she remains rooted there until nightfall.

Despite the excitement about the new trends in cinema, art films never found it easy to find distributors or exhibitors. Most remained confined to the film-club circuit and, in some cases, to their cans, never having been screened. While some like Mani Kaul and Kumar Shahani made largely incomprehensible experimental films, others such as Shyam Benegal made realistic films but shunned the dream-like fantasy and the song and dance routines of the popular Hindi cinema. Benegal's first film, *Ankur* (1974), and later *Nishant* (1975) treated the theme of peasant exploitation by the feudal landowning classes. Interestingly, Ramesh Sippy's curry western blockbuster *Sholay*, made the same year, also touched on a similar theme of rural exploitation, neatly pitting Bollywood's vision of the world against that of the artists.

Directors such as Basu Chatterjee (*Sara Akash*, 1969; *Piya Ka Ghar*, 1971) and Basu Bhattacharya (*Teesri Kasam*, 1966; *Anubhav*, 1971) mostly worked within the constraints of the conventions of the popular Hindi film but toned down the excesses of emotion and spectacle, replacing the implausible stories with more realistic ones. Theirs was not a world of separated twins reunited by chance encounters, but a middle class world of university lecturers, office clerks, and retired postmasters trying to come to terms with life. Songs were sometimes given realistic motivations, such as a radio broadcast or a record playing. Such films offered more refined entertainment for the urban middle classes.

The cinema of the 1970s could thus be divided into four categories:

1. The mainstream popular film with its familiar plots, overstated emotions, spectacular fights, and songs and dances, which dominated the screens.
2. The emotionally restrained and "sober" stories narrated in a more realistic fashion while retaining the songs (but dispensing with the grand choreography of dances), as exemplified by the films of Chatterjee and Bhattacharya.
3. The realistic films that completely dispensed with fantasy, songs, and dances, as seen in the works of Benegal and Sen.
4. The experimental art films where directors such as Kaul and Kumar Shahani (*Maya Darpan*, 1972) experimented with the formal devices of cinema itself.

Although the art film movement failed to take off, it had nevertheless created an opening for a new kind of cinema. The decade of the 1970s was an exciting time for Indian cinema, with a variety of cinemas and diversity of genres not seen since the 1930s.

The Gloomy Decade of the 1980s

The decade of the 1980s was a gloomy period for the film industry. The violent spectaculars and multi-starrers of the 1970s had run their course by the mid-1980s, and Indian filmgoers had had enough of testosterone-fueled actors. Besides, Amitabh Bachchan and others who embodied the genre were starting to gray and lose their appeal.

In 1983, when Amitabh Bachchan suffered a near-fatal accident during the shooting of *Coolie* (Manmohan Desai, 1983), millions of fans gathered weeping outside the hospital and prayed for his recovery. Yet within a few years, Bachchan's high-profile films began to flop at the box office—*Mard* (Manmohan Desai, 1985), *Sultanat* (Mukul Anand, 1986), *Agneepath* (1990), *Khuda Gawah* (1992). The worst was *Mrityudaata* (1997), which ruined Bachchan's production company, Amitabh Bachchan Corporation Limited (ABCL).

The high cost of crowding major stars into a single film led to correspondingly huge losses, and overruns in time schedules due to stars working in several films concurrently added to the huge cost overruns. Of the 132 films made in 1983, only seventeen were reported to have recovered their costs. In 1985, only one in eight films recovered its costs (Pendakur 1989).

In contrast, the success of tragic romances such as *Qayamat Se Qayamat Tak* (Mansoor Khan, 1988), about doomed love between children of feuding families, or romantic comedies like *Mr. India* (Shekhar Kapur, 1987), *Tridev* (Rajiv Rai, 1989), *Ram Lakhan* (Subhash Ghai, 1989), and *Maine Pyar Kiya* (Sooraj Barjatya, 1989)

heralded the return of romance and the dawn of a new era of directors and actors. In particular, it marked the emergence of stars Salman Khan, Aamir Khan, and Shah Rukh Khan, three stars who continue to dominate the screen today.

The financial outlook for the industry in the 1980s was further dampened by the video boom and with it, video piracy. Besides, by the 1980s television too had begun to make its presence felt.

Competition from Television

The expansion of television in the 1980s was a major blow to the Hindi film industry. Although television made its first appearance in 1959 (largely as an experiment in educational development), daily telecasting did not begin until 1965. Initially, the broadcasts were just an hour long and geared toward educating farmers on agricultural matters. The shift in the fortunes of television was a consequence of Prime Minister Indira Gandhi's personal vision. Mrs. Gandhi astutely recognized that the medium could be harnessed to showcase the government's achievements to the vast nation. The inauguration of the Ninth Asian Games held in Delhi provided the appropriate occasion to herald a new era of television entertainment in color. A *National Programme* broadcast from New Delhi was also introduced, providing the central government a platform from which to address the entire nation.

Thanks to the temporary lifting of restrictions on the importation of television sets, ownership multiplied six-fold, from 2.7 million in 1984 to 12.5 million in 1986 (Rajadhyaksha and Willemen 1999). The first government-sponsored serial, *Hum Log*, that ran for nearly a year and a half (1984–1985) had a large part of the Indian nation fascinated by the trials and triumphs of the family of Basesar, the alcoholic carpenter. This serial was promptly followed by a 57-part serialization (1987–1988) of the Hindu epic *Ramayana*, which proved to be an unprecedented hit in the history of television. This, in turn, was immediately followed by a 93-part serialization of another Hindu epic, the *Mahabharata* (1988–1990). Both mythological serials were made by well-established Hindi film directors Ramanand Sagar (*Ramayan*) and B. R. Chopra (*Mahabharat*).

In 1991, the arrival of satellite television from Hong Kong's STAR (soon after bought by Rupert Murdoch) resulted in a television revolution. Within a decade there was an explosion of choice, with over 100 regional and international channels available to the Indian viewers. The success of television had a negative impact on attendances in the cinema halls.

Hindi Cinema in the 1990s

Hindi cinema survived the spread of television by focusing on what the small screen could not offer—spectacle. The biggest hits of the 1990s were *Hum Aapke Hain Koun!* (Sooraj Barjatya, 1994) and *Dilwale Dulhaniya Le Jayenge* (Aditya Chopra, 1995), both celebrating engagement ceremonies and wedding preparations. In the former, an "extended wedding video," romance takes place in the sheltered atmosphere of a blissfully harmonious extended family. The first half of the film explores the delights of a wedding engagement, the actual wedding ceremony, and the joy of children. The only drama occurs halfway through the film, when the wife falls down the stairs of her mansion and dies. The family elders decide that the younger sister (Mad-

huri Dixit) must marry the widower so that the children may grow up in a loving atmosphere. Unfortunately, unbeknown to the family elders, the young woman loves the widower's younger brother who reciprocates her sentiments. But while the latter is willing to sacrifice his love for the sake of his brother and the greater good of the extended family, the young woman and her Pomeranian dog are not. However, all ends well when the dog (as a messenger of the god Krishna) exposes the romance to all concerned and the lovers are married. Such was the success of the film—and in particular its costumes—that copies of saris worn in the film were being sold in far off outposts of Indian populations such as Singapore and Fiji.

Chopra's *Dilwale Dulhaniya Le Jayenge* assiduously follows the formula of the classic Hindi romance. The only concession to changing times is that the lovers are members of the Indian diaspora, or "NRIs" (nonresident Indians). The first half is concerned with sight-seeing and romance in the snowy Swiss Alps while the second half focuses on preparations for a wedding—that of the young woman Simran (Kajol) to a man of her tyrannical father's choice. The unmitigated success of these two films with extended scenes of wedding celebrations engendered a flurry of copycat films replete with the finery of the wedding saris and other costumes.

The decade of the 1990s also saw the emergence of a new genre of romantic films set against a backdrop of political turmoil. These were pioneered by Mani Rathnam, who began his career in southern Indian films. *Nayakan* (1987) is a *Godfather*-like narrative on the Mumbai underworld, with a style that marries Coppola and MTV. *Roja* is set in the political turmoil of Kashmir, where a newly wed woman searches for her husband, abducted by the Kashmiri militants. Made in Tamil, it was dubbed into Hindi for a wider release. The controversial *Bombay* (1995) was Rathnam's first foray into the world of Hindi cinema. It concerns a romance between a Hindu man and a Muslim woman set in Mumbai, a city that had just suffered bombings perpetrated by Muslims in 1993. Thereafter Rathnam made *Dil Se* (1998), where a journalist (Shah Rukh Khan) falls in love with a female terrorist (Manish Koirala). The film is better remembered for the song "*Chaiyya chaiyya . . .*" Rathnam's more recent film, *Yuva* (2004), is about modern-day angst and Indian youth.

A new genre of lowbrow comedy was born when director David Dhawan teamed up with actor Govinda in films like *Aankhen* (1993), *Raja Babu* (1994), *Coolie No. 1* (1995), *Biwi No. 1*, and so on. The success of the Dhawan-Govinda duo was based on Govinda's ability to dance and mouth the bawdy double entendre of the lyrics; some, such as "*Sarkailo khatiya . . .*" were called obscene. Govinda (who confessed to being inspired by Dada Kondke, a veteran artist of *tamasha*, the popular Marathi theatrical tradition whose bawdy humor found great success on the Marathi screen) won a seat in Parliament in 2004.

In the 1990s the major American distribution companies began to dub Hollywood blockbusters into Hindi. In 1994 *Jurassic Park* (Steven Spielberg, 1992) was dubbed and made INR 120 million (US$2.6 million), an impressive figure considering that the market for American films was still small. Other films have followed the trend— *Cliffhanger* (1992), *Aladdin* (1992), *Speed* (1993), *True Lies* (1994), and *Twister* (1996) (Rajadhyaksha and Willemen 1999), although none of the later films were able to replicate the success of *Jurassic Park*.

Dubbing American films is not without its problems. In *Jurassic Park*, unable to find the Hindi language word for "dinosaur," the translators settled on "*badi chipakli*" (big lizard). Since Hindi films rarely have sexually explicit dialogue or abusive language, a sexually graphic description is briskly translated as "cheating in examinations" (D'Souza 2004).

Contemporary Hindi Cinema *Lagaan* (Ashutosh Gowarikar, 2003) is a landmark film of contemporary Hindi cinema. Set in colonial India, it combines the excitement of a cricket match with the fight for freedom from colonial tyranny. Representatives of the British colonial government challenge the poor peasants of a village to a cricket match, promising that they will waive the onerous taxes they have just imposed if the villagers win the encounter. The film then explores the villagers' successful efforts to rise to the challenge. By combining the three central passions of Indians—the nation, cricket, and song-and-dance spectacles, the film made history at the box office. It was nominated for an Academy Award in 2003 for Best Foreign Film in the United States (but failed to win) and was sportingly reviewed by *Wisden*, the cricket journal in the United Kingdom.

The success of *Lagaan* provoked a spate of patriotic films set in colonial India or at the time of Partition. The colonial theme also offers opportunities for European actors, either as the oppressor or as a love interest. In the past, an Indian actor in a blond wig and riding boots was sufficient to portray the British colonial. However, since the success of *Lagaan*, the European actor is the sine qua non of the new patriotic films such as Subhash Ghai's *Kisna* (2005) and Ketan Mehta's *1857—The Rising* (2005). The latter, which deals with the Indian Rebellion against the British in 1857, was partly financed by the U.K. Film Council. Patriotism is also the theme of Gowarikar's more recent *Swades* (2004), about an Indian-born NASA scientist who returns to India and dedicates his skills to the "upliftment of the motherland."

Building on the patriotic theme are the "war" movies. In the aftermath of the 1999 Kargil confrontation with Pakistan, J. P. Dutta's *LoC Kargil* (2004) put the conflict on celluloid. His earlier film *Border* (1997), also about a border conflict with Pakistan, was a surprise box office hit. Some of the patriotic/war films in 2004 have been Gaurang Doshi's *Deewar*, Anil Sharma's *Ab Tumhare Hawale Watan Saathiyon* (the title is from the lyrics of a 1964 war film, *Haqeeqat*, by Chetan Anand), and Farhan Akhtar's *Lakshya*.

In the same year as *Lagaan*, its lead actor, Aamir Khan, was also the star of Farhan Akhtar's *Dil Chahta Hai*, a multistarrer about urban youth and the new consumerist lifestyles. The success of *Dil Chahta Hai* was significant because it marked the emergence of a completely new phenomenon—that of "new" Bollywood. Hitherto, films were made by bearing in mind a heterogeneous spectatorship, one that spanned both the rural and urban constituencies. What *Dil Chahta Hai* did was to break free from the rural viewers by concentrating on the urban audiences. It was a film about love—for women, for cars, for consumer goods. And it actively promoted a lifestyle not available to the ru-

ral areas. The film indicated changing times and tastes.

Three important and concurrent developments contributed to the growth of the "new" Bollywood films. First, the economic liberalization of the 1990s had led to the rapid growth and enrichment of the urban middle classes. Although the economic policies undoubtedly improved the lives of rural Indians, it was the urban classes that benefited most from the government's policies. These growing numbers of middle-class Indians were interested not just in the standard Bollywood blockbusters but also in new kinds of entertaining films.

Second, in 1998, the government granted cinema the status of an industry, entitling it to institutional finance. Although the initial enthusiasm for bank loans was small, it now constitutes 33 percent of all film financing. Those companies that have taken up the offer of bank loans for film production have tended to be mainly small and middle-sized entertainment companies that have begun producing new kinds of films catering to the growing middle class eager for new varieties in entertainment. At the same time, certain state governments, such as the government of Maharashtra, decided to grant tax relief for the construction of new multiplex cinemas. These new cinemas have tended to be in the towns and cities providing entertainment companies with the opportunity to develop new idioms in cinema targeting niche audiences. Since the start of the new millennium, the number of screens has multiplied. The higher-cost ticket engenders a more exclusive social environment consisting of genteel audiences. The new theaters also offer a better viewing experience, bringing the middle classes back to the cinemas.

The sudden surge in new kinds of film is

A heavily garlanded poster created in the Rajkamal Arts Studio hangs on the facade of the Majestic Theatre. Bangalore, Karnataka, 2004. (Joseph Khakshouri/Corbis)

the most telling feature of the new Bollywood. On the one hand films such as *Lagaan*, *Devdas* (Sanjay Leela Bhansali, 2002—the twelfth version to date of the classic), and *Munnabhai MBBS* (R. Hirani, 2003) continue to entertain both urban and rural India. On the other hand, new films—such as Madhur Bhandarkar's *Chandni Bar* (2001), a gritty film about a woman who survives by dancing in a bar; Anant Balani's *Jogger's Park* (2003), about a friendship between a retired judge and a feisty young single woman; Gustad Kaizad's *Boom* (2003), about the underworld and the modeling world; Nagesh Kukunoor's *Hyderabad Blues* (1998), about an Indian who returns from the United States to find himself a stranger in his own homeland; Dev Benegal's *Split Wide Open* (2001), about the lives of four

disparate people; Mahesh Dattani's *Morning Raga* (2003), about a tragedy that draws together three characters through the theme of music; and Vishal Bhardwaj's *Maqbool* (2003), an adaptation of Macbeth set in Mumbai's underworld—are all a result of new audiences willing to watch new kinds of films.

Issues

Film Finance   One of the biggest issues confronting the Hindi film industry is the unorganized manner in which films are financed. Formal contracts are rare, and where they do exist they are considered neither important nor legally binding. Thanks to the archaic and slow-moving legal system, a dispute can take decades to come to court. Most of the transactions that take place among producers, distributors, exhibitors, music companies, actors, and directors are informal, based on mutual understanding, and leave no paper trail. Figures reported are rarely true. Films that have done average business, for example, are often trumpeted as box office hits, and the seven trade magazines invariably offer differing versions of a film's commercial performance. Besides, there is no finished script before a film begins shooting, nor is there a detailed shooting schedule.

In most cases, the production of a film proceeds thus: A producer announces a project and, producers being highly superstitious creatures, chooses (with the help of astrologers) an auspicious moment to inaugurate the film shooting. A *mahurat* (religious ceremony) is performed during which the first frame (usually of the family deity or some lucky mascot) is shot. Actors, directors, chief guests, and even cameras associated with the project are garlanded and sweets distributed. The film, which is yet to be made, is then sold to distributors.

The distribution business is regional and fragmented. Six distribution territories cover the entire domestic market—Mumbai, Delhi/Uttar Pradesh, North India/East Punjab, Central India, the Eastern Circuit, and the South. The entire overseas market constitutes a single territory. Each regional territory has its own set of competitors, and very few business houses have a large-scale, cross-regional presence (Kheterpal 2003).

Distributors bid for the rights to a specific territory and pay an advance of 25–30 percent of the agreed price at the start of the project. Another 20–25 percent is paid as the production progresses. The outstanding balance is paid on delivery of the completed film (Kheterpal 2003). The producer mobilizes these funds to start the project. The secrecy and lack of transparency within the business obscure the actual transacted figures, and most figures are at best "guesstimates." The financial muscle of the distributors gives them considerable say in the casting and treatment of a film. As conservative businessmen, they prefer to repeat the same successful actors and the same tried and tested formulas in new ventures, often urging directors to include a particular feature (gypsy dance, cabaret number, comic actor, and the like) that has been a success in a previous film. With substantial sums at stake, the industry is averse to new ideas, new plots, new stars, or any feature that has not already proven its worth at the box office.

The producer also sells the music rights of his film to recording companies. Songs are recorded well before the film starts shooting (and in some cases well before a screenplay has even been written), and these are then slotted into the narrative—sometimes the plot is even altered to accommodate the songs. The cassette revolution of the 1990s initiated an unprecedented demand for film songs on cassettes, and songs from films have always dominated the music market. Even today they constitute approximately 66 percent of total music sales.

Over the years, as more and more music labels have entered the market, the bidding for the rights to a film's music has become frenzied. Some producers have been able to recover 40–60 percent of their costs through the sale of music rights (FICCI 2003). However, in 2002, the high cost of acquisition, exacerbated by the devastating effects of music piracy, the rise of FM radio stations, and the possibilities for digital downloading of music, drastically reduced the profits of the music industry, which in turn has drastically lowered its bids to film producers.

Consequences of an Unorganized Market The consequences of the unorganized and fragmented nature of the industry have been far reaching. It has deeply entrenched the *formulaic film* with its predictable plots, spectacular and erotic song-and-dance numbers, and comic subplots. Only a well-established star actor or director can exert the muscle of his box office credentials to push for change in this matter, but few star actors or directors are willing to risk their careers to force change onto the film industry.

In the absence of any interest in original stories, the Hindi film producers are not at all averse to lifting stories from Hollywood films. These stories are then transposed into an Indian context and Indianized by subjecting them to the classic formula treatment. Frank Capra's 1934 classic *It Happened One Night* was copied, not once but twice, becoming *Chori Chori* by Anant Thakur in 1956 and *Dil Hai Ke Manta Nahin* by Mahesh Bhatt in 1991. Professor Abdalla Uba Adamu at the Center for Hausa Studies in Kano, Nigeria, in his research on Nigerian cinema compiled a list of the scores of Hollywood films that have been ripped off by Hindi film producers, which in turn have been ripped off by Hausa producers, the latter unaware in many cases of their Hollywood origins. The list shows that Martin Scorcese's *Cape Fear* (1991) became *Darr* (Yash Chopra, 1993); *Dead Poets' Society* (Peter Weir, 1989) became *Mohabbatein* (Yash Chopra, 2000); Khalid Mohammad's *Tehzeeb* (2004) is inspired by Ingmar Bergman's *Autumn Sonata* (1978), and so on. In no case was the original source ever acknowledged. Adamu quotes director Sanjay Gupta, who shrugs off the accusations of plagiarism: "I wouldn't mind admitting I borrow ideas from Hollywood films. But I don't call it plagiarism—I call it 'inspiration.' And there's nothing wrong with being inspired. Every piece of art, be it books, music or film, derives its inspiration from another. What is originality anyway? It's the art of concealing the source" (Adamu 2004: 36).

Because the hegemony of the formula film has resulted in the accretion of the "omnibus" genre, it has led to the eroding of generic variety. The *loss of generic variety* has its origins in the rise of the independent (freelance) producer and the "formula" film. Whereas the studios of the 1930s could average out their profits over several films, for the new breed of independent producers in the 1940s, every project was a "one-off" commercial gamble and a one-time opportunity for a quick sale to territorial distributors to recoup their investment (Pendakur 1990). The overriding concern with securing high returns on investment led to an increasing need to depend on tried and tested plot lines, established actors with proven box office successes, and spectacular song-and-dance routines.

Furthermore, Indians generally view films with their families, and it is not unusual to see twenty members of an extended family colonize a corner of the auditorium. Under the circumstances, the commercial advantages of the *omnibus genre*—where romance, spectacle, comedy, melodrama, violence, pathos, and heroism are all inscribed into a single film—are substantial. Unlike Hollywood, which fragments its audience and caters to their varied interests and expectations through generic differentiation, the omnibus genre of the Hindi film divides the film into segments, and caters to the different constituencies of its heterogeneous audiences by dedicating each segment to a particular constituency—a sad episode full of pathos for women who like to weep; erotic dances for the male or female erotic gaze; choreographed violence with graphic blood spurting for the young adolescents and adults; slapstick comedy for the children; and so on. Instead of fragmenting its audiences and thereby its revenues by catering to varied expectations through generic differentiation, the individual, one-off producer amalgamates the varied pleasures of different genres into a single film (Kasbekar 2001). To control such a disparate agenda in a single film is extremely difficult and requires dexterous handling, and to the uninitiated, the producer's "something for everyone" intention gives an impression of a lack of focus.

The capriciousness of the filmgoing public also makes the business of film financing extremely volatile. It is estimated that 5 to 10 percent of Hindi films make money, and about 15 to 20 percent break even, while the rest lose money. According to the figures for the year 2000, only twenty-one films made profits out of a total of 230 films released that year. The industry lost INR 3 billion (US$66.6 million) on gross revenues of 39 billion (US$866.6 million) (FICCI 2003). The shortage of film theaters (estimated at 13,000 for the entire country) has also prevented the marketing and exhibition of nonformula or alternative films.

Another consequence of the unorganized market and the extreme conservatism of the film producers and directors is the *refusal to take any risks* by making films without stars. Currently the top three male stars (Aamir Khan, Shah Rukh Khan, and Salman Khan) have held their perch for more than fifteen years. Stars are a known commodity and function as brands. The anxiety surrounding casting new actors is that, unlike stars, they do not draw audiences to the theaters. Over the last two decades, most newcomers to the Hindi film have been promoted by their families, who are already in the film business—Abhishek Bachchan, son of superstar Amitabh Bachchan; Sanjay Dutt, son of star couple Sunil Dutt and Nargis; Saif Ali Khan, son of the Nawab of Pataudi, who captained the Indian cricket team, and Sharmila Tagore, star of the 1960s–1970s; Akshaye Khanna, son of 1970s star-turned-politician Vinod Khanna; Sunny Deol, son of 1970s superstar-turned–Member of Parliament Dharmendra; Karishma Kapoor and her sister Kareena Kapoor, great-granddaughters of Prithviraj Kapoor, granddaughters of Raj Kapoor, and daughters of Randhir Kapoor and his actress wife Babita, star of the 1970s. In addition, Aditya Chopra, star director of *Dilwale Dulhaniya Le Jayenge*, is the son of Yash Chopra, stalwart director of Hindi films (*Deewar*, 1975; *Dil To Pagal Hai*, 1997). Farhan Akhtar is the son of lyricist and screenwriter Javed Akhtar, one half of the screenwriting duo Salim-Javed, and Salman Khan is the son of Salim Khan, the other half of the screenwriting duo.

Those who aspire to act in Hindi films but do not possess a star pedigree gain a foothold by being successful models, winners of international beauty contests—such as Aishwarya Rai (Miss World, 1994) and Sushmita Sen (Miss Universe, 1995)—or television stars. Shah Rukh Khan, one of the top three actors today, found his way to the screen via television and theater, while John Abraham is a well-known model.

Another consequence of the manner in which films are financed in Bollywood is that they *rarely take up contentious subjects*. The political system is, for instance, rarely overtly challenged. In 1976, Amrit Nahata made *Kissa Kursi Ka*, a political satire on the Internal Emergency declared by Mrs. Indira Gandhi in 1975, during which she rounded up the opposition leaders and had them imprisoned. The film explores the rape of a nation through a symbolic rape of a woman. The film became a cause célèbre when henchmen of Mrs. Gandhi's son Sanjay destroyed the film negative. Nahata remade the film in 1977, but by then Mrs. Gandhi's Congress Party had lost the election and a new government was in power. Nahata himself later joined the Congress Party and disowned the film (Rajadhyaksha and Willemen 1999).

In other matters of censorship and morality, profanity is completely unacceptable. The few mildly abusive terms in the film dialogue are confined to "bastard" and "bloody fool," usually uttered in English. Since cinema-going is a family activity, any obscenity would immediately restrict the viewing to a mature audience, thus decimating the film's commercial potential. Similarly, nudity and sex are avoided—at least overtly. Instead, actors and actresses get drenched in sudden, unseasonal downpours that reveal their body forms, and sing erotic songs accompanied by suggestive dance movements, providing the Indian alternative to the Hollywood bedroom scene.

Occasionally producers get into trouble for having crossed the lines of "decency." In 1993, an erotic song and dance sequence from *Khalnayak* containing lyrics, which began: *Choli ke peeche kya hai...?*

("What lies beneath my bodice?"), was condemned as "obscene" by a Delhi-based lawyer who claimed that the song had a corrupting influence on his young son (Bhardwaj 1993). He charged that the film was unfit for general viewing, even though the producer disingenuously protested that the answer to the question in the lyrics was: "Dil!" (My heart!).

In the 1950s, the leaders of independent India considered on-screen kisses an "un-Indian" activity even though they were quite uncontentious in Indian films made during the colonial government. Censors frowned upon such un-Indian behavior and lost no time in cutting them out of films. To avoid delays at the censors, particularly when producers had financed the films with money borrowed at very high (40–60 percent) interest rates, the song-and-dance number was deployed as a strategic substitute for erotic titillation. A decade ago censors began allowing on-screen kissing, but so successful had been the stratagems and subterfuges to circumvent the moral police of the previous decades that only a few producers and actors have taken up the opportunity. Some films, however, market themselves as "daring" adult material. These are normally low-budget ventures that hope to recruit their investment by the publicity they generate. Karan Razdan's *Girlfriend* (2004) is supposedly an exploration of lesbianism and managed to create a stir for portraying a sexual act between two women. Bal Thackeray, the chief of the quasi-fascist Shiv Sena party, whose henchmen attacked theaters where the film was being screened, condemned the notion of lesbianism as "not part of Indian culture." (Raval 1998: 80).

The most far-reaching consequence of the unorganized nature of film financing has been the *entry of the Dubai-based Indian underworld*. The association between film finance and money laundering is almost as old as Hindi cinema itself. The burgeoning film industry had always offered an easy route for laundering gains from the flourishing black market in India during World War II. Thereafter the route remained open for all kinds of illegal gains from gold smuggling or untaxed profits of local businesses. The unorganized nature of film production and distribution was a convenient method for laundering large sums of money through the financing of films. The story of the gold smuggler Haji Mastan (who prefers to call himself a "businessman") was even the subject of a film in the 1970s.

The falling revenues in the 1980s and the resulting reluctance of distributors to concede to the high advances demanded by producers opened the gates for greater involvement of the underworld in film production. The 1980s also marked the meteoric rise of Dawood Ibrahim Kaskar, son of a humble policeman. Once a minor gang member, today he controls a large conglomerate with operations in Dubai, Pakistan, Nepal, and India of both legal and illegal businesses estimated at INR 70 billion (US$1.5 billion) (Chengappa and Raval 2003). The activities of his numerous syndicates are wide ranging and include gold smuggling, gambling, drug trafficking, video and music piracy, money laundering, gun running, and extortion. He also harbors a passion for Hindi films and cricket. Many film stars used to frequent his parties in Dubai and accompany him to cricket matches in Sharjah.

It is the lucrative overseas distribution territory that is of greatest interest to Dawood's criminal syndicates. Forced to flee from India to escape the Mumbai police and rival gangs after a shootout in 1985, Dawood was said to control his empire from Dubai, where he took refuge. His financial interests in Hindi films are allegedly controlled by "Chhota" ("Little") Shakeel, based in Pakistan. Despite several requests for his extradition to India, the UAE government had refused. The reasons were two-fold: firstly India has no extradition treaty with the UAE, and secondly, when in the past Dubai had requested the extradition of an Indian national on criminal charges, the Indian government had refused to comply.

Dawood's investment in films in the 1980s was a timely lifesaver to film producers and directors. Many struggling and aspiring film personalities begged him for help in keeping their careers alive, and with so many film personalities beholden to him, he and his acolytes began to wield great power within the industry. Journalists M. Rahman and Arun Katiyar have highlighted the curious phenomenon whereby Sudhakar Bokade, an airport cargo-handler, had suddenly turned into a film producer, as had Dinesh Patel, a garment shop owner (Rahman and Katiyar 1993). Even more curiously some directors and actors seemed never to be short of work despite a string of flops at the box office. For many in the volatile business of film production seeking the help of the criminal underworld seemed a safe way of guaranteeing their careers.

However, in 1991, the economic liberalization policies introduced by the Indian government included lifting restrictions on the importation of gold and making the Indian currency fully convertible. These policies made a severe dent in some of Dawood's smuggling and *hawala* (illegal

Bollywood film financier and diamond merchant Bharat Shah gestures as he sits in his car outside a Mumbai court. The court sentenced Shah to a year in jail for hiding information from police. Mumbai, 2003. (Roy Madhur/Reuters/Corbis)

money transfers that leave no paper trail) operations. His syndicates then expanded into extortion and protection rackets. Successful actors, producers, and distributors began to receive death threats if they did not pay up the large sums of protection money demanded. Director and composer Raakesh Roshan, father of current heartthrob Hrithik Roshan, suffered a near-fatal shooting (the bullet is said to have missed his heart by a few millimeters) after refusing to pay the money demanded by gangsters.

Since then a large number of similarly threatened film personalities have either paid up or requested police protection. In 1997, Gulshan Kumar, the audiocassette "king" of India, was gunned down in broad daylight. It was alleged that Abu Salem, once Dawood's henchman and now his rival, had executed the murder at the request of Nadeem Saifee, part of the film music-composing duo Nadeem-Shravan. Saifee was, it is alleged, annoyed that Gulshan Kumar had frozen him out of the recording business. Saifee has taken refuge in the UK, which has refused to extradite him to India.

The extent of the underworld's involvement in Mumbai's film world came to light in 1993 when Mumbai experienced a series of bombings that targeted several buildings of symbolic importance such as the Mumbai Stock Exchange and the Air India buildings. The bombings that killed 257 people, maimed 713 others, and destroyed property worth millions were claimed as retaliation for the destruction of the Muslim Babri Masjid mosque in Ayodhya in 1992. The explosives used were traced to Pakistan and the Mumbai-based family of gangster "Tiger" Memon. Dawood's associates in India as well as some Mumbai film personalities were also implicated.

During the police investigations into the bombings, an AK-56 assault rifle was recovered from the residence of Sanjay Dutt, a leading star of Bollywood and son of star parents the late Sunil Dutt (Member of Parliament) and Nargis. Dutt denied possessing the weapon while at the same time making arrangements to dispose of it. With extraordinary timing, Dutt's arrest came just a few days before the release of his film *Khal Nayak* (Subhash Ghai, 1993), where he played a gangster seeking to destabilize India through terrorist activities. Dutt was charged and imprisoned for two years. In 2001, Bharat Shah, an important financier of Hindi films for 30 years, was also accused of having links with the underworld. It was stated that at any point of time he had around INR 1.5 billion (US$33.5 million) invested in films (Desai 2003).

It was to wean the industry away from their dependence on "black" money and the criminal underworld that the Indian government granted film production the status of an "industry" in 1998, a move that entitles producers to seek institutional finance and tax rebates.

Piracy   The problem of piracy is the biggest single threat facing the Indian film industry. However, because of the informal and secretive nature of the film industry, there are no estimates regarding the extent of the menace. The video boom of the 1980s, so called because of a sudden increase in the number of households possessing VCRs, made a deep dent in the profits of the Hindi film industry. Cheap pirated versions of new releases hit the markets within days of a new release. In small towns, video parlors offered viewers daily showings of the latest films within days of their theatrical release in the big cities. As to the operations of these video parlors, Pendakur writes:

> An entrepreneur would acquire a 20-inch color television set and a VCR, place it in a hall that could hold 50 to 100 chairs, and show feature films in various languages from 9.00 AM until 2.00 the next morning. These video cafes, reminiscent of storefront theaters of the early 1900s, mushroomed in cities, towns, and villages all over India within a very short time. (Pendakur 1989: 71–72)

Traditionally, a video release is deferred until eight to twelve weeks after a film's release in the theaters, but countering the menace of piracy has brought forward the release date to four to six weeks after its cinema release. Over the years, the damage wreaked by piracy has increased due to improved VCRs and DVDs that offer better quality. Furthermore, the declining prices of both VCR and DVD players have increased the number of households that own the products (Kheterpal 2003). Like Hollywood, Indian distributors are now trying for a blanket weekend release in theaters across the country in order to maximize ticket sales before the video pirates cream off potential viewers.

While terrestrial and satellite television channels do not show pirated films, cable operators (those who deliver the "last mile" of satellite channels to private homes), often set up a separate channel that screens pirated versions of the latest films. This is offered as a goodwill gesture to their patrons to compensate for frequent breakdowns due to faulty cables and abrupt blackouts during disputes with the multi-system operators from whom they acquire their satellite programs.

Music piracy, which affects not just music companies but also the entire film industry because film songs constitute a substantial proportion of music sales, is estimated at around 40 percent of the market by the music industry (FICCI 2003). High government taxes on the sale of cassettes make authorized music cassettes more expensive than the pirated ones. Moreover, patrons of pirated cassettes make further savings when they buy compilation cassettes of all the best songs from the latest film releases. These pirated cassettes are compiled each week or each month, depending on consumer demand.

Controlling piracy is a difficult task. The police see it as a victimless crime and prefer to focus their meager resources on more serious crimes. Even when an arrest is made, the judicial process is extremely slow, and by the time the case reaches court it could be several years after the event. However, the government and police have pledged their support in fighting piracy, and taxes on cassettes have been reduced.

Conclusion

The social and economic changes occurring in Indian society have created a more discerning middle class that desires greater variety than what the hegemonic film factories have been offering so far. The growth of new and better cinemas and new technologies is already beginning to manifest small but significant changes within the film industry.

Banks are now willing to offer loans to production companies as long as they guarantee transparency of process and provide detailed budgets, scripts, and production schedules. The proportion of organized funding—from banks, IPO funds, venture capital, and other "organized" sectors of the money markets—has increased from 4 percent in 2001 to 33 percent in 2003 (Singh 2004). But old habits die hard, and the bigger film producers continue to maintain their relationships with moneylenders, and a large proportion of sums earmarked for film production by the IDBI and other banks has not been taken up.

Although the volume of traditional, unorganized funding of films by debt financiers at high interest rates has decreased, it still constitutes the major source for the financing of films. The new sources of funding have been more popular with the new, small-, and mid-sized film companies catering to the niche market created by the growth of multiplex cinemas in the big cities than with the big banners of the commercial industry. In 2003, thirty-three firms attracted corporate funds of INR 1.76 billion (US$39 million). Many of these firms have links to television companies and are making films with middle-sized budgets.

Since the start of the millennium, the number of screens in Mumbai has increased. In 1980 there were 6,368 permanent and 4,024 touring cinemas in all of India (Rajadhyaksha and Willemen 1995). Later figures place the total number of cinemas at 12,387. Of these, nearly two-thirds are located in southern India, which accounts for just over 20 percent of India's total population. The need to address the lack of theaters available for the Hindi cinema moved the state government of Maharashtra to offer a three-year tax holiday for the construction of multiplex theaters in the state. The owners of 130 single-screen cinema halls in Mumbai promptly went on strike, but the government held firm.

By 2002, nearly twenty-five new multiplex screens were completed and another sixty awaited completion (Kheterpal 2003). The new multiplex screens offer more comfortable seats and an improved viewing experience, but at a higher cost. These higher-cost cinemas, coupled with the lifestyle boutiques and shopping malls, offer the urban middle classes a more congenial environment for consumerism. On the distribution side of the film industry, the new theaters have loosened the stranglehold of distributors and exhibitors over producers, allowing smaller budget films to gain a foothold.

The new multiplex screens have also allowed American distribution companies to achieve a bigger presence in the Indian market, and the increase of multiplex screens has been matched by an increase in dubbed versions of Hollywood films. Nevertheless, box office revenues from Hollywood films constitute less than 5 percent of all Indian films and 10 percent of the main stream Hindi film market (Kheterpal 2003).

As for the criminal underworld, until the terrorist attacks on the United States on 11 September 2001, Dawood remained untouchable in Dubai. But Dawood was subsequently found to have had links through *hawala* (illegal international money transfers) to drug trafficking as well as gun-running activities in Afghanistan with Al-Qaeda and even Osama bin Laden. It was alleged that he has donated funds to the organization and helped its members to escape the country (Chengappa and Raval 2003). In 2003, Dawood was declared a "global terrorist" by the United States, and Dubai, wishing to improve its global image, asked the myriad gangs operating from that haven to leave the country.

Some from Dawood's gang have sought refuge in Pakistan and Europe, while the remaining have been extradited to India where they await trial. Abu Salem, Dawood's one-time henchman and the alleged killer of music baron Gulshan Kumar, who had sought refuge in Portugal, has also been extradited to India. Dawood is said to divide his time between Pakistan and Southeast Asia, the base of his erstwhile colleague and now rival "Chhota" Raja. Since 2004, the extortion rackets and demands for money from the film industry are said to have declined.

The lucrative market comprising the Indian diaspora has started to have an effect on the Hindi film industry and its film narratives. The global success of Indian directors, Indian subject matter, and even Indian-made films has boosted the confidence of filmmakers in Mumbai. M. Night Shyamalan, the Indian-born director whose Hollywood production *The Sixth Sense* in 1999 delivered sensational box office returns, followed his success by making *Unbreakable*, *Signs*, and *The Village*. Other directors of Indian origin to deliver global box office successes are Gurinder Chadha (*Bend It Like Beckham*) and Ugandan-born Mira Nair (*Monsoon Wedding*).

The Indian media categorizes such cross-cultural products as "crossover" films. Chadha specializes in stories about growing up in the Indian diaspora, with *Bhaji on the Beach, Bend It Like Beckham,* and her most recent adaptation of Jane Austen in *Bride and Prejudice.* Nair also chooses Indian subjects, as in *Salaam Bombay,* about street urchins in Mumbai; *Mississippi Masala,* about racist attitudes among Indians overseas; and *Monsoon Wedding,* about an Indian wedding in Delhi. Her film adaptation of William Makepeace Thackeray's *Vanity Fair* was her first move away from an Indo-centric theme, although it must be remembered that Thackeray was born in Calcutta.

The exploration of Indian themes in British and American films and television and on the stage has provided international opportunities, not only for Indian film stars such as Aishwarya Rai, Naseeruddin Shah, and Om Puri but also for composers A. R. Rehman and Anu Malik (*Bride and Prejudice*), choreographer Farah Khan (*Bombay Dreams* and *Vanity Fair*), and designers such as Manish Malhotra (*Vanity Fair*).

The success of the Bollywood film *Lagaan* in India as well as the interest it raised in the United Kingdom and the United States, where it was nominated for an Academy Award in the Best Foreign Film category in 2001, has given the Indian film industry confidence to consider a global markets for their products. In 2004, *Shwaas,* a low-budget film in Marathi, was entered for an Academy Award nomination. Actress Aishwarya Rai and director Ashutosh Gowarikar have been members of the jury at the Cannes Film Festival. Indian producers looking for sales, co-productions, and financial backers have started scouring international film festivals and related events.

With so many changes in the offing, the future of Bollywood, unlike that of its for-mula-packed emotion-charged films, is certainly not predictable.

Films from the South

If Mumbai is the bustling center for the production of Hindi films, then the other major center of film activity is Chennai (formerly known as Madras), which has been the center for Tamil, Telugu, Kannada, and Malayalam films. Unfortunately, due to linguistic restrictions, these films do not enjoy a pan-Indian market. But this fact has in no way dampened the enthusiasm for film production. Although the smaller states of Karnataka and Kerala now have their own local film-producing centers, Chennai still remains the biggest center for most film production and post-production activity in southern India.

The importance of Chennai as a film-producing center stems from the political organization of the states. Under British colonial rule, the Madras Presidency comprised much of the southern region with the exception of the princely states of Hyderabad, Mysore, Travancore, and Cochin. During those years, its capital city, Madras, was the center of commercial activity. Major studios such as AVM, Gemini, and Vijaya were established there, producing films in the four southern languages as well as in Hindi. In 1956, nine years after Indian independence, the Indian states were reorganized along linguistic lines. The Madras Presidency along with the autonomous princely states became the four southern states: the predominantly Tamil-speaking state of Tamil Nadu with Madras as its state capital; the predominantly Telugu-speaking state of Andhra Pradesh with the city of Hyderabad as its capital; the pre-

A giant billboard advertising a movie stands on a street in Madras, ca. 1985–1995. (Hans Georg Roth/ Corbis)

dominantly Kannada-speaking state of Karnataka with Mysore as its capital; and the Malayalam-speaking state of Kerala with Trivandrum (earlier known as Tiruvananthapuram) as its capital.

The total population of the four southern states is approximately 200 million and constitutes about 20 percent of the Indian population. Nearly two-thirds of the national total of 13,000 theaters are located in the four southern states, and the state of Kerala has the largest ratio of theaters to population. The largest numbers of films are produced in Tamil and Telugu, which attain an annual average of 170 in each language, most of them made in Chennai. Thus as many films are produced in Telugu each year as in Hindi and in Tamil, and film production in these three languages com-

prises over half of the total number of films produced in India. About seventy films are produced each year in both Kannada and Malayalam and are now mostly made in the states of Karnataka and Kerala, respectively. Thanks to the Gulf boom in the 1970s and 1980s and the paychecks sent home to Kerala by economic migrants to the Gulf States, the number of films in Malayalam peaked in 1985 at 136 films. In contrast, Kolkata, once a pioneer in Indian film production and a major film center, now makes less than fifty films a year in Bengali.

Like the commercial Hindi cinema, the south Indian films are mainly melodramas about romance and family relationships enacted by stars and embellished by songs, lavish spectacle, and comic subplots. In fact, in the Tamil and Telugu films the melodramas are even more elaborate and complicated than in Hindi films, the emotions more heightened, and the suffering more intense. Songs play as important a part in south Indian films as in those from Mumbai, and some South Indian composers such as A. R. Rehman and Ilyaraja have an enthusiastic national, and even international, following. As for spectacle, the choreographed fights and stunts inspired by the Hong Kong–Chinese films are generally very well executed; in the domain of choreographed dances, Tamil films began to "out-Bombay Bombay" quite early on in their evolution. The production of the Tamil film *Chandralekha* (S. S. Vasan, 1948), with its lavish dances, some of them performed by scores of dancers on giant drums, is a case in point.

With well-organized, giant studio complexes such as AVM, Gemini, Vijaya, and now Ramanaidu Studios and Ramoji Film City, and more theaters per population, the cinema in the south is economically very robust. But the southern cinema suffers from a distribution severely restricted by language limitations. Hindi cinema benefits from an audience that comprises more than 40 percent of India's population, whereas the combined total of southern films caters to only 20 percent of the Indian populace. Since the 1990s, south Indian cinema, just as with cinemas all over India, has been feeling the effects of increasing competition from satellite and cable television.

The four southern cinemas are different from one another, and each has a particular defining characteristic that has been crucial to its development. The most important aspect of Tamil cinema has been the successful mobilization of the medium by the DMK and the AIADMK, political parties that have formed the government since 1967 and have been responsible for five consecutive chief ministers from the film world. Although Andhra Pradesh, too, ended up with a film-star politician and chief minister, it has been the business acumen and commercial skills of its entrepreneurs that has defined its cinema. Unable to compete with the industrial production of the Tamil and Telugu films, the smaller states of Karnataka and Kerala have been at the forefront of the "new" Indian cinema, one that eschews stars and formula to offer more personal cinematic visions. In doing so they have won acclaim in the arthouse circuits in India and at international film festivals abroad.

Tamil Films and the Cinema of Politics

As in Bombay, the first film screenings in Chennai were of film shorts made by the Lumière brothers. R. Venkaiah, a Telugu entrepreneur and distributor of films who died in 1941, soon began to import European and American silent films. He also screened the silent films that were being made in India and in doing so introduced southern India to the pleasures of cinema. Venkaiah is well known for rigging up an ingenious device by attaching the projector to a gramophone record, which allowed him to screen films accompanied by music, giving the impression of synchronized sound. He was also the first Indian to build cinemas in Madras—the Gaiety, the Crown, and the Globe. R. N. Mudaliar (1885–1972) is credited with the first silent film, *Keechaka Vadham* (1916), made in the south with Tamil, English, and Hindi intertitles.

Although Madras eventually became the film capital of the south, the city was a relative latecomer to the art of filmmaking. The first Tamil talkie, *Kalidas* (H. M. Reddy), on the life of the great Sanskrit poet and playwright was not made until 1931. The film was shot in the studios of Bombay. Chennai had no studios equipped for sound films and the two leading languages of the south were for some years the focus of mighty struggles between the studios of Bombay and Calcutta. Many of the studios in these cities made films in Tamil or Telugu for the southern market. Producers in Madras also undertook trips to these centers in the north to make films in Tamil and Telugu.

In Calcutta, Tamil films were the preserve of the East India Film Company, and south Indian producers regularly organized junkets to the city. On the first such junket, K. Subrahmanyam (1904–1971) took sixty-five people, rented a house for all of them for three months, and rented a car to shuttle them to and from the East India studio. The studio supplied all technical personnel, including its editor. The films made were huge financial triumphs, and soon other producers joined the three-monthly exodus to Calcutta or Bombay (Barnouw and Krishnaswamy 1980).

Tamil and Telugu films continued to be made in Bombay, Kolhapur, and Calcutta until 1934, when the construction of sound studios began, not just in Madras but also in Salem and Coimbatore. With the availability of local studios, junkets to the north were abandoned. Instead, technicians from the various studios in Bombay, Kolhapur, and Calcutta made their way southwards to make films. Once Madras had its own technicians, the link with the northern studios was severed. Thereafter, it was never dependent on Bombay or Calcutta for its movies. The film industry laid down its

roots in Madras, which quickly took charge of film production not just in Tamil and Telugu, but also in Kannada and Malayalam.

As elsewhere in India, the early films had mythological or devotional themes, with stories from the epics and religious literature or on the lives of saints. These were followed by social themes exposing the plight of Hindu widows or the excesses of the caste system. It was around the 1940s that the DMK film emerged, a completely new, unique kind of propagandist fare that would transform Tamil cinema and create a political cadre of film personalities.

The DMK and the AIADMK   The origins of the DMK lie in the Justice Party (also known as the South Indian Liberation Federation) established in 1917. During the national freedom struggle spearheaded by Mahatma Gandhi, a parallel movement for a separate state independent of the north pioneered by the Justice Party had begun to take effect in the south. Its central ideological plank was anti-Brahminism.

Brahmins were historically priests and interpreters of the Sanskrit religious texts and sanctioned the legitimacy of regimes in the eyes of the heavenly gods and earthly men. They held the highest caste in the fourfold hierarchy of the caste system and were historically identified with the Aryans who, long before the first millennium, had invaded the south, marginalized the local inhabitants, established their culture over an older Dravidian civilization, and pushed the conquered Dravidian peoples into the lower castes. The caste system remained relatively impervious to political change and foreign conquests over the centuries. Although Brahmins constituted less than 3 percent of the population of the state of Tamil Nadu, they held a very privileged position in Tamil society. Even under British colonial rule, the caste system was upheld and government positions and special privileges went exclusively to the Brahmins (Barnouw and Krishnaswamy 1980).

The Justice Party sought justice for the non-Brahmins of the south. However, according to the film critic Chidananda Das Gupta, it was not the lumpen poor who were the party's main concern. Instead it was the emerging educated, wealthy, non-Brahmin Tamil middle classes who were fighting for the same privileges enjoyed by the Tamil Brahmins. One of the leading figures of the movement was E. V. Ramaswamy Naicker (1879–1973), respectfully referred to as "Periyar" ("the great one") and who initially belonged to the Congress Party. Like Gandhi, Periyar was entirely opposed to the Brahmin suppression of the lower castes, particularly the *harijans* (the "untouchable" castes). However, when Periyar found segregated eating arrangements for children at a school managed by the Congress Party, he left the party in 1925 to form the Self Respect Movement. The arrival of Periyar with his Self Respect Movement radicalized the Justice Party, and its new ideology was summed up by Charles Ryerson as "no God, no religion, no Gandhi, no Congress and no Brahmins" (Rajadhyaksha and Willemen 1999: 91).

The Brahmins were also identified with Sanskrit, the language of Aryan classical and sacred literature. The southern Brahmins were disdainful of the local Tamil language, preferring to modify it with a Tamil that was lexically embellished with Sanskrit words. As the movement to impose Hindi on the whole of India even before independence from Britain began to gather pace in North India, the anti-Brahmin movement of the south immediately rallied around an anti-North, anti-Hindi, and anti-Sanskrit principle. The Justice Party's anti-Congress stance also made it an ally of the British. It supported the British war effort and in return was given plenty of succor by the colonial British. Periyar's newspaper was subsidized by the colonial government, and when Periyar sought secession from independent India he was given the opportunity to meet opponents of Gandhi, such as the Muslim leader Mohammad Ali Jinnah and the *dalit* leader Babasaheb Ambedkar, to demand an independent Dravidian state (Das Gupta 1991).

However, Periyar's alliance with the colonial British rule alienated many Tamil people. With the imminent prospect of the Congress Party forming the first government after independence, C. N. Annadurai (1909–1969), Periyar's lieutenant, moved a motion to rename the Justice Party the Dravida Kazagham (DK) in 1944. When Periyar declared that 15 August 1947, India's day of independence, was a day of mourning for Tamilians for not having achieved his dream of a separate Tamil state, Annadurai distanced himself from the remarks. The 1949 DK party conference chose Annadurai (or "Anna" as he was respectfully referred to) as successor to the now seventy-year-old Periyar. But when Periyar demanded that his new twenty-nine-year-old wife succeed him, Annadurai broke away from the DK to form the Dravida Munnetra Kazagham (DMK) (Das Gupta 1991). As leader of the DMK, he diluted the anti-Brahminism and antireligious politics of Periyar and concentrated on anti-Hindi, anti-North, and anti-Congress rhetoric instead.

In 1967, Annadurai, playwright and a screenwriter for Tamil films, won the elections for the state legislature and became chief minister. On his death two years later, M. Karunanidhi (1924–), his protégé and also a screenwriter, succeeded him. In 1972, M. G. Ramachandran ("MGR"), the greatest star of the Tamil firmament and a DMK supporter, was expelled from the party for indiscipline. Undeterred, MGR founded his own party—the "Anna" DMK, which he declared would be more faithful to the great man's legacy than his anointed successor. The party was later formally registered as the All India Annadurai Dravida Munnetra Kazagham (AIADMK).

He deployed the DMK's own propaganda techniques against the DMK and won the elections. With the support of the much-hated Congress Party he become chief minister in 1977, a post to which he was elected three times until his death in 1986. Thereafter MGR's wife, Janaki, also a film star, briefly held the post of chief minister before the elections returned Karunanidhi and the DMK. Since then the DMK and the AIADMK have been bitter rivals. Between 1991 and 1996, Jayalalithaa (1948–), MGR's co-star and member of his AIADMK was chief minister. In 1996, she was defeated by Karunanidhi and the DMK, and had to devote much time to fighting off allegations of corruption.

The DMK Film   In the 1940s, the DK used the performing arts to disseminate its message across the region. Just as the Indian People's Theatre Association (IPTA), the cultural arm of the Communist Party, had deployed poetry, songs, and plays in the 1940s to spread the Communist gospel among the far-flung populations, the DK artists spread their message through poetry, songs, and plays before mobilizing the cinema to propagate their ideology. An-

nadurai wrote radio plays, short stories, novels, and poems. He invited intellectuals to join the movement and held literary and political conferences to elicit their participation (Rajadhyaksha and Willemen 1999).

His mobilization of the film medium for political propaganda came just as he formed the DMK party. His first film script, *Velaikkari* in 1949, was based on his stage play, and its success led to five other screenplays including *Nallathambi* (also in 1949) and *Sorgavasal* (1954). In 1954, his novel *Rangoon Radha* was adapted for the screen by M. Karunanidhi.

The intention of the movement was to establish the Brahmin as a negative symbol and the non-Brahmin (or the Dravidian) as a positive one. Furthermore, the aim of the movement was to create a distinct and unique Tamil identity based on the past greatness of the Tamil people and the Tamil language, idealized into a "Utopian vision of a casteless pre-Aryan society" (Das Gupta 1991: 203).

However, the DMK artistes were not the first to make anti-Brahmin films. K. Subrahmanyam (who had pioneered the junkets to Calcutta and elsewhere) had made *Balayogini* (1936), the first Tamil film that exposed the plight of Hindu widows. In the film, a Brahmin widow and her little daughter are turned out of the family home and forced to seek shelter in the house of a low-caste servant. The film incensed the powerful Brahmin community. As film historians Eric Barnouw and S. Krishnaswamy (son of the director) have explained: "Brahmin widows are expected to shave their heads, wear only white saris—always covering their heads—and live a life of austerity and seclusion. The sight of a widow was a bad omen. The sight of a widow on screen was a defiance of taboo on a grand scale (Barnouw and Krishna-swamy 1999: 114).

In the aftermath of the film, a group of Brahmins conferred in the city of Than-javur and roundly declared the director (himself a Brahmin) an outcaste. Unde-terred and defiant as ever, Subrahmanyam made *Bhakta Chela*, a devotional film about a saint from the *harijan* caste of "untouchables." His other social films in-clude *Seva Sadan* (1938) and *Thyagab-hoomi* (1939)—the former a Gandhian story about prostitution and the latter about a Brahmin who breaks Hindu taboos and allows *harijans* to enter the temple and seek shelter from a hurricane, for which he is duly punished.

But Subrahmanyam's perspective was that of a Gandhian who believed in social reform, whereas the DMK's motivation was directly political. The DMK pressed the all-embracing genre of melodrama for politi-cal propaganda. Its first foray into film was announced with *Nallathambi* (Krishnan-Panju) and *Velaikkari* (A. S. A. Sami), both written in 1949 by C. N. Annadurai. In the first, a feud between two members of a family over ancestral property sets the scene for the elaboration of the DMK's po-litical program. In *Velaikkari*, a son is de-termined to avenge the death of his father, driven to suicide by rapacious landlords and moneylenders. *Sorgavasal* (A. Kasil-ingam, 1954), also written by Annadurai, is about the trials and tribulations of a court poet and his sister, who cannot marry the man she loves and goes mad after being raped by a king.

The early DMK films followed certain cardinal principles: they deployed an elab-orate story that incorporated members of extended families in rural areas who be-came victims of scheming Brahmin temple priests and usurers, whose casteism and greed decimated the family; the melodra-matic plot inevitably culminated in a court-room scene where the victim argued his case with passion and eloquence, some-times for over thirty minutes, against the exploitation of the poor by the privileged caste of Brahmins; it was in flowery rheto-ric. Annadurai excelled in flowery rhetoric and was celebrated for his "chaste" Tamil—a Tamil denuded of all "foreign" Sanskrit words, and his gift for alliteration in Tamil won applause in the cinema halls. Sales of the cassettes of the film dialogues were as brisk in the markets as for the songs. According to Sivathamby, the argu-ments were so radical and heretical that they posed a threat to the very foundations of Tamil rural society (Sivathamby 1981). So worried were the producers about the atheist tirade against God in *Vellaikkari* that they appended a title card at the end of the film affirming that there was only one God and one community (Rajadhyak-sha and Willemen 1999).

Many of Annadurai's films deployed the symbols and iconography of the DMK. Just as the Hindi films had taken to casually in-serting banned Congress Party symbols in the background to elude the colonial cen-sors, the DMK films introduced black and red party flags or an image of the rising sun, the symbol of the movement, into the background, although there was no ban on doing so.

The word *Anna*, which means "big brother," a reference to Annadurai the party leader, was often used as in the following:

Man 1: The night is dark.
Man 2: Don't worry! The rising sun will soon
    bring light and good fortune.
(Audience: wild cheers and applause)

Or:

He: Believe me sister!
She: I do, Anna, I do! The whole land
   believes in you, and will follow you.
(Audience: wild cheers and applause)

In the casual selection of a sari:

She: I always like a black sari with a red
   border.
(Audience: wild cheers and applause)

Two people lost in a forest:

Man 1: Should we turn north?
Man 2: No, never! South is much better.
(Audience: wild cheers and applause)
   (Barnouw and Krishnaswamy 1980:
   179–180)

So noisy was the applause that greeted these Dravidian injections that producers unconnected with the movement began to use the symbols. They too wanted the applause and the cheering. Actors found it quietly prudent to associate themselves with the DMK movement (Barnouw and Krishnaswamy 1980).

It has been alleged that Annadurai's scripts were modeled on Hollywood films and that *Nallathambi* recalls Frank Capra's *Mr. Deeds Goes to Town* (1936), and *Sorgavasal* resembles Rouben Mamoulian's *Queen Christina* (1933), while *Rangoon Radha* (1956) recalls George Cukor's *Gaslight* (1944) (Rajadhyaksha and Willemen 1999).

"From Stars to Czars"   The DMK films were exceedingly popular, and they made Sivaji Ganesan (1927–), a party worker and stage and screen actor par excellence, into a star. Ganesan, however, drifted away from the DMK and found a huge fan following playing a wide range of roles. M. G.

Ramachandran (1917–1987), popularly known as "MGR," also a stage actor and a party worker, became the new face of the DMK films. MGR had one of the most successful careers in the history of cinema and acted in total of 292 films. In his early films he played a swashbuckling hero, modeled on the screen personae of Douglas Fairbanks and Errol Flynn. He joined the DMK in 1953 after playing the lead role in *Manthiri Kumari* (1950), directed by the American Ellis Duncan and written by screenwriter and future chief minister M. Karunanidhi. The film is a period costume drama wherein the evil Brahmin priest's son commits crimes by impersonating the dashing general (MGR), who is also the paramour of the princess. The priest's son marries a minister's daughter who tries to reform him but is forced to kill him in self-defense. His father, the Brahmin priest, then kills her.

The arrival of MGR also marked a shift in the propaganda films made by the DMK from courtroom-based impassioned arguments designed to convert the public to its cause to a focus on the hero as the sole vehicle of the party's ideology. In the later films MGR invariably played the saintly subaltern: peasant, fisherman, or urban working-class hero, an association that was to play a crucial part in his subsequent political career. Unusually for a film star from the south, he never played a divine incarnation. However, this did not stop his own deification after his death, when a temple dedicated to him was built on his funeral grounds. It is said that over two million fans and citizens turned out for his funeral procession.

As chief minister, MGR was accused of pursuing recklessly populist policies and of heavy-handed intimidation of the press. Interestingly, neither Annadurai nor MGR did any favors to the Tamil film industry. The only contribution by Annadurai to cinema was a reduction in the entertainment tax levied by the state government on the sale of film tickets. MGR as chief minister tried to ban the political film *Thaneer Thaneer* (K. Balachander, 1981), which exposed the corrupt nexus between politicians and police when drought-stricken villagers, unable to get the help of the politicians to get water, decide to boycott the elections. (The success of *Thaneer Thaneer* led to another political film by K. Balachander, *Achamillai Achamillai* in 1984.)

NTR MGR was not the only film star to become head of a state legislature. In Andhra Pradesh, N. T. Rama Rao (1923–1996) also rose to the post of chief minister. The life of NTR, as he was generally referred to, is the stuff of soap operas. A farmer's son, NTR received his first break in films in 1949 with L. V. Prasad's *Mana Desam*, a melodrama that combined romance and patriotism. The film exulted in the newly won independence but bemoaned the speed with which the people had forgotten Gandhi.

NTR became a star to be reckoned with when three of his lavish melodramas produced by Vijaya Studios—*Patala Bhairavi*, a folklore fantasy; *Malleeswari*, a grandiose romance set in an imperial past; and *Pelli Chesi Choodu*, a multi-starrer romantic melodrama about three couples who do not love the persons they are supposed to—became consecutive box office successes.

However, the enduring image of NTR that was to help him in his political career was his association with director K. Kameshwar Rao, who specialized in "mythologicals." These were stories from the epics, the

Puranas, or the lives of gods, and NTR ended up playing the god Krishna seventeen times in his film career. NTR further encouraged the image of a "living god" by receiving devotees outside his home after director P. Pulliah's *Shri Venkateshwara Mahatayam* in 1960, in which he played the presiding deity, Lord Venkateshwara, of the Tirupati temple, one of the major temples of India, and performed all kinds of miracles on the screen (Rajadyaksha and Willemen 1999). In all, NTR acted in 262 films. Although he played in other genres such as folklore fantasies, melodrama, and vigilante cop films, it was his association with the divine that set the stage for his election to the highest post of the state of Andhra Pradesh.

According to the critic Chidananda Das Gupta, early in 1982 NTR was asked if he would like to play Bhramendra Swami, a sixteenth-century astrologer who had predicted that a man with a painted face would rule Andhra. "But that's me!" NTR is said to have exclaimed on hearing about the prediction (Das Gupta 1991: 221), and within weeks he had formed the Telugu Desam Party with the declared aim of protecting the "self-respect" of the Telugu people. That same year Telugu Desam, whose ideology was built on the pride in language, culture, and simple sons of the soil of Andhra Pradesh, won the state elections, unseating the Congress Party that had governed the state for nearly twenty-five years. The film that had engineered his political career was *Shrimad Virat Veerabhramendra Swami Charitra* (1984), with NTR directing himself in the title role.

Like MGR, NTR introduced several populist and unworkable measures. He also tried to muzzle the critical press. With his love for the theatrical, NTR took to wearing saffron robes, worn by Hindu monks as a sign of renunciation of worldly desires. He was expelled from the party by his son-in-law in 1995 and died in 1996. But the Telugu Desam Party remains an important player in Andhra Pradesh politics. It is said that there were even bigger crowds at NTR's funeral than at MGR's a decade earlier.

Fan Clubs   A key feature in the political power of MGR and NTR was the fan club, many of which are active in south Indian cinema. Estimates of the number of fan clubs for MGR vary between 800 and 20,000 (Dickey 2001), although Das Gupta places it at 27,000 with a membership of 1.5 million (Das Gupta 1991). There is no doubt that these highly organized and mobile fan clubs played a crucial role in the election of both the stars. The highest number of fan clubs today are for the current Tamil film stars Rajnikant and Kamalahaasan, but neither can match the numbers reached by MGR.

Fan clubs adherents tend to be urban, poor, overwhelmingly male, and largely devoted to male stars (Dickey 2001). They express their devotion by whistling, cheering, and clapping at the screen when the star first appears on screen. Their cheering is of extreme importance. MGR fans heckled the Kannada film star Manjula for having slapped MGR in a film even though all she had done was what the script had demanded (Das Gupta 1991). Fans turn up at opening shows, distribute posters promoting their idol, and sing his praises, eulogizing his generosity, humility, and other virtues that are relevant to the construction of an ideal person as viewed by the working class male in the south.

In a display of rival fan power, when Nagarjuna, a major star of the Telugu screen since the 1990s, in a scene from *Varasudu* (E. V. V. Satyanarayana, 1993) held Krishna, a former star who plays his father in the film, by the collar, there was widespread protest from Krishna's fan clubs. Large advertisements had to be placed in newspapers explaining the significance of the scene to the disgruntled public (Rajadhyaksha and Willemen 1999). In another film directed by E. V. V. Satyanarayana, the fans of the current Telugu megastar Chiranjeevi threatened to immolate themselves if the film *Alludu Majaaka* (1995), in which he plays a stellar role, was banned as demanded by women's and students' groups (Rajadhyaksha and Willemen 1999). The banning action had been called because of the sexually explicit dialogues and the flirtation of the hero (Chiranjeevi) with his mother-in-law.

The Entrepreneurial Spirit of Telugu Cinema

One of the decisions taken by NTR that had a direct impact on Telugu cinema was the "slab" system of taxation. The level at which the entertainment tax can be set remains the prerogative of individual states. In most states, it is set on the sale price of each film ticket, and the national average stands at 45 percent. NTR replaced the collection of tax per ticket sale with a slab system levied at a fixed rate per cinema hall regardless of the number of tickets sold. This meant that exhibitors had to make certain that the cinemas ran at full houses for each show. To achieve this, the producers resorted to the time-honored strategy of making formulaic films with well-known stars and lots of spectacular songs and fights. Experimentation in Telugu film was made unaffordable and thus extremely rare.

The need to deliver successes has also put extreme stress on the current Telugu stars: Chiranjeevi, Mohan Babu, Vishwanath, Nagarjuna, and Balakrishna. The latter is NTR's youngest son and in June 2004, he was charged with shooting a film producer and his assistant at his residence with his wife's revolver. The argument was allegedly over a film that flopped at the box office. However, the seriously injured persons withdrew their allegations, turned hostile to the prosecution, and the case was eventually thrown out of court for lack of evidence.

One of the most remarkable features of both Telugu and Tamil cinemas has been the entrepreneurship of its pioneers. Andhra Pradesh did not come into existence until the linguistic reorganization of the states in 1956. Consequently the early Telugu entrepreneurs set up their studios in Madras, the commercial and political capital of the Madras Presidency.

R. Venkaiah was one of the first Telugu entrepreneurs to start an entire network for the exhibition of silent films in the south, and he was the first Indian to build cinemas in Madras. In his theaters—the Gaiety, the Crown, and the Globe—he screened Hollywood and European films as well as the silent movies made in different parts of India. He sent his son, R. S. Prakash (1901–1956) to study filmmaking in the studios of England, Germany, and the United States. On the son's return, Venkaiah set up in Madras the Star of the East studio, also known as the Glass Studio because of its glass roof. As exhibitor, director, and producer, Prakash helped to assemble some of the early pioneers of Telugu cinema and set into motion an industry that today makes the second-largest number of films in India.

The first Telugu talkie, *Bhakta Prahalada*, was directed in 1931 by H. M. Reddy, a Telugu who also directed the first Tamil talkie, *Kalidas*, in the same year. Both films had all the characteristics of early Indian cinema—they were like stage plays, which is not surprising since they were taken from the repertoire of the Telugu Surabhi Theatres, and made on mythological and classical themes, respectively. Some of the Surabhi stage actors, including the male lead in *Kalidas*, spoke their dialogue, not in Tamil, but in Telugu (Rajadhyaksha and Willemen 1999).

Several other studios and production companies were set up during the 1930s, not just in Chennai but also in Rajahmundry (Durga Cinetone in 1936) and Vishakapatanam (Andhra Movietone in 1937). Many were short-lived because of a lack of funds and technicians (Srihari 1985), but others managed to survive and thrive. Vel Pictures, one of the first sound studios in the south, set up by P. V. Dasu in 1933, lasted only a few years, while others, such as Shobhanachala Studios, built by the rajah of Mirzapur in 1941, are still in business. In the 1970s the leading stars of the Telugu screen, NTR and A. Nageswara Rao, started their own studios, Ramakrishna and Annapoorna, while the star Krishna set up Padmalaya.

The 1940s was a decade when the studios in Bombay, Poona, and Calcutta, unable to compete with the savvy independent producers elsewhere, were closing down. In total contrast, film production companies in the south were consolidating their positions and studios were being set up at an astonishing rate. The most important of these studios were Gemini, AVM, and Vijaya.

Gemini Studios, established by S. Srinivasan (known by the abbreviated version S.

S. Vasan), first began as a distribution company for K. Subrahmanyam of the Madras United Artistes Corporation (which later became the Motion Picture Producers' Combine, a joint enterprise formed by several south Indian film producers). In 1941, a fire broke out at an uninsured studio owned by the Combine. With infighting already having set in among the various producers, it was sold very cheaply to S. S. Vasan, who rebuilt as it Gemini Studios. One of the initial successes of Gemini was *Chandralekha* (1948), released in both Tamil and Hindi. It was a huge and lavish spectacle on a scale never before seen in India, and it made the entire nation gasp. Vasan, always an astute businessman, made repeated attempts to invade the Hindi film market but could never replicate in the north the success he enjoyed back home.

A. V. Meiyappan Chettiar (1907–1979), who began as a distributor for Odeon (a German phonograph company), ended up one of the biggest film moguls in India. He set up *AVM Studio* in 1947, where he introduced the industrial production of films in several languages—Tamil, Telugu, Kannada, and even Hindi—and placed on his payroll directors to work in each of these languages. He also pioneered the practice of dubbing films so he could capture the entire south Indian market. Today, more than a third of the films screened in Andhra Pradesh are dubbed from Tamil and other languages. Several of the DMK propaganda films were made at AVM studios.

The genesis of *Vijaya* can be found in Rohini Pictures, set up in 1937 by H. M. Reddy (1882–1960), who had made the first talkies in the south. At Rohini, Reddy had assembled the pioneering screenwriters and directors of Telugu cinema. In 1939, B. N. Reddi (1908–1977), a professional accountant and founder of the BNK printing press, and who had helped H. M. Reddy set up Rohini Pictures, transformed it into Vauhini Pictures, a production company, and in 1946 it also became a film studio. A few years later, B. N. Reddy, an investor as well as studio manager at Vauhini, and Chakrapani, a screenwriter, set up an independent production unit called Vijaya Pictures, which soon took over the entire Vauhini company, which came to be known as the Vauhini-Vijaya complex. It was one of the biggest studios in all of Asia and had the most elaborately equipped studios of India (Rajadhyaksha and Willemen 1999).

All three studios made repeated attempts to penetrate the all-India market through Hindi films. The strategy they adopted was to remake successful Tamil or Telugu films into Hindi versions with stars from the Hindi screen. But despite occasional forays, the Hindi film market has remained too volatile for any of them to make a serious dent.

Since the 1990s, Telugu film production has started moving out of Chennai (formerly Madras), thanks to the new Ramanaidu Studios and Ramoji Film City. The latter is a world-class facility set up in 1999 by the press baron Ramoji Rao just outside Hyderabad, the capital of Andhra Pradesh. With its fully automated, air-conditioned, and dust-free film laboratory, its state of the art technology, and its advanced digital post-production facilities, it points the way for the future of Indian cinema and confirms the entrepreneurial and business acumen of the men connected with Telugu cinema.

Genres Driven by the studios, the Telugu film factories in Chennai carefully divided the market into select genres. Experimentations were few and far between, and much of the filmmaking was conducted in an organized, industrial manner.

Mythological films constituted the major genre of Telugu cinema and prevailed as a genre for much longer than elsewhere in India. For the Telugu entrepreneurs, the mythological was a safe bet, since it guaranteed a devoted and devotional audience. The prolonged popularity of the mythological genre in Telugu cinema was, according to some, a consequence of the low levels of education, literacy, and political awareness in Andhra Pradesh (Sankaranarayanan 1995). According to the 2001 census, Andhra Pradesh has a population of 75 million and its literacy rate stands at 61 percent, which is lower than the national average of 65 percent. The population is largely rural and conservative, and the existence of a feudal landowning system and rigid caste hierarchy has helped keep Andhra Pradesh one of the backward states of India. (In 1999, the ex-Chief Minister Chandrababu Naidu [son-in-law of NTR] tried to drag it into the twenty-first century by attempting to turn it into an information technology hub, but the largely rural voters voted the government out of power in the 2004 elections.) Just as the genre was assumed to be finally dying out, the success of *Ammoru* (Kodi Ramakrishna, 1995), with computer-assisted special effects for miracles and divine interventions, revived the mythological as the perennial favorite of Telugu cinema.

After the mythological films, Telugu cinema soon added to its production the *reformist melodrama* with films that advocated some kind of social reform. The "social" genre, aimed at highlighting some form of social evil and advocating its reform, was the outcome of the ban on political films under the British colonial govern-

ment. H. M. Reddy, who had already pioneered the talkies in the south with the first Tamil and Telugu talkies, inaugurated his production company, Rohini Pictures, with *Grihalakshmi* in 1938. Its convoluted plot has a respectable doctor fall in love with a dancer. Infatuated with her, he takes to drink and throws his wife out of the house. The wife goes mad after a fight with the dancer and the doctor is ruined, financially and socially. The film was also important because it was the first time that Telugu actors, accustomed to the grandiose literary delivery style in mythologicals, spoke in colloquial Telugu (Srihari 1985).

The commercial success of the reformist genre led to a sudden spate of similar films such as *Malapilla* (1938) about a girl from the "untouchable" caste who falls in love with a Brahmin man. Made by G. Ramabrahman, it was dedicated to the Maharaja of Travancore, who had passed a law allowing all castes access to temples (Rajadhyaksha and Willemen 1999). Ramabrahman became infamous for his next film, *Raitu Bidda* (1939), about a peasant who borrows money from a moneylender but does not vote for the moneylender's landlord patron in the elections. It revealed the power politics played by the feudal landowning classes. The film was banned following protests from the landlords in Nellore and Madras. The royal families of Bobbili and Venkatagiri threatened the film producer with lawsuits, and copies of the film were publicly burned (Rajadhyaksha and Willemen 1999).

In the same reformist genre was *Malli Pelli* (Y. V. Rao, 1939) about widow remarriage. A six-year-old girl is married off to an old man who dies immediately, leaving her a widow. Her conservative father tries to force her to live the austere life of a widow but she refuses. She eventually meets and falls in love with a young man who, defying tradition, marries her and rescues her from her living hell. B. N. Reddi at Vauhini Pictures also took up the theme of widow remarriage through a love triangle in *Sumangali* (1940), where the leading man prefers to wed the widow rather than a young unmarried woman. The film that was to redefine the genre was a reformist film with a socialist message, *Rojulu Marayi* (T. Chanakya, 1955). It was quickly remade into Tamil as *Kalam Maripochu*, with Gemini Ganesh in the lead role. It tells of a peasant (A. Nageswar Rao) who takes on the might of a feudal landlord with a substantial landholding and forces him, thanks to a helpful police force, to redistribute it among the peasants.

The social reform genre transmuted into a more stridently *political genre* concerned with the people's struggle for empowerment and these films were dubbed "red" films because of the prolonged Naxalite (ultra left-wing groups associated with the activities of the Marxist-Leninist Communist Party) activities in the state of Andhra Pradesh and elsewhere. Examples of the red film are *Yuvatharam Kadhilindi* (Davala Satyam, 1980), *Rangula Kala* and *Daasi* (1983 and 1988, both by B. Narasinga Rao), and *Erra Sainyam* (R. Narayanamurthy, 1994). In *Rangula Kala*, the romantic painter becomes politicized, thanks to his Marxist journalist friend and the tragedies that befall his working-class friends. In *Daasi*, set in the countryside where landlords still exact their feudal rights, a servant girl is made pregnant by a landlord and then forced to have an abortion by the landlord's wife. *Osey Ramulamma* (1994), directed by the veteran commercial director Dasari Narayana Rao

(1947–), made the commercial viability of slickly produced red films apparent.

The *folklore* or *fantasy genre* has for decades been the speciality of Telugu cinema. The folklore genre came into its own with the success of *Balanagamma* (C. Pullaiah, 1942), which is about a woman who keeps her virtue for twelve years, from the time she is abducted by a demon until her rescue. Another folklore film was *Ratnamala* (P. S. Ramakrishna Rao, 1947), in which a young princess is tricked into marrying a young boy prince. She rescues him from the kidnappers, but the gods have to descend from the heavens to sort out the age difference. The plot of another fantasy, *Rakshrekha* (R. Padmanabhan, 1949), is as follows: a princess is determined not to marry until fairies bring the prince of a neighboring country into her bedroom. They fall in love and marry, but another celestial fairy also loves the prince, and she abducts him and sends him home once a week. Pregnant but accused of infidelity because of the absent husband, the princess flees the palace, only to be kidnapped. Disguised as a man, she escapes her kidnappers and finds that she is the object of devotion of another princess, whom she "marries." The film starred several leading actors of the Telugu screen and was a great hit.

Other fantasies followed with similar fairy tales or pseudo-historical and mythological stories. The most successful of these, *Patala Bhairavi* (K. V. Reddi, 1951), was made by Vijaya studios and broke all box office records. The story was akin to a children's fairy tale, but the production was extravagant and lavish. A sorcerer wants to offer a handsome young gardener to the goddess as a human sacrifice so that she may grant all his wishes. The gardener, who incidentally loves the princess of the kingdom, has to overcome several trials and traps before he can overcome the sorcerer. He then turns the tables and offers the sorcerer as the sacrifice to the goddess, who grants him unimagined wealth, and he marries the princess. The film enhanced the persona of NTR, who played the lead role of the gardener.

The fantasy genre remains an annual favorite among the Telugu filmgoers, as is evidenced by the success of *Bhairava Dweepam* (Sangeetham Srinivasa Rao, 1994), with the lead role played by NTR's son Balakrishna, and *Yamaleela* (S. V. Krishna Reddy, 1994).

The Telugu *family melodrama* was a speciality of L. V. Prasad. In *Samsaram* (1950) a newly wed couple's happiness is decimated by the arrival of the extended family—the man's mother, sister, and brother-in-law—who proceed to wreck the harmony of the household. The film pits the man's filial duty toward his mother and family against his own personal happiness. Prasad's *Shavukaru* (1950), made for Vijaya a few years before *Patala Bhairavi*, was an elaborate rural melodrama with a complicated story: the cohesion of a village is threatened by a falling out between a rich moneylender and his friend, the village chief. Their children, who are young adults, are supposed to marry, but the marriage is called off. A fight between the village chief's son (played by NTR) and the village elder's son also exacerbates the feud and lands them both in jail until the end, when all misunderstandings and enmities are resolved.

The family melodrama developed a subsidiary branch in the "mother-in-law" films, where aggressive women such as mothers-in-law (or arrogant wives) are punished by the male protagonist. These include *Donga Mogudu* (A. Kondandarami Reddy, 1987), *Attaku Yamudu Ammayaki Mogudu* (A. Kondandarami Reddy, 1989), *Bobbili Raja* (B. Gopal, 1990), and *Gharana Mogudu* (K. Raghavendra Rao, 1992). However, when a public outcry resulted from the sexual innuendoes in the exchanges between the male protagonist and his mother-in-law in *Alluda Majaaka* (E. V. V. Satyanarayana, 1995), the genre lost its appeal.

A new genre that recast classical arts in a light, popular fashion was created in the 1980s with K. Vishwanath's *musical melodrama Shankarabharanam*, about a classical singer/teacher and his chaste relationship with a beautiful dancer who happens to be a prostitute's daughter, a relationship that brings him into disrepute. The dance theme is exalted by the Kuchipudi dance style of Andhra, and the film pits Andhra culture against the rest of Indian culture. In *Malleeswari* (1951), a royal court dancer (P. Bhanumathy) falls in love with a sculptor but can't marry him because of her superior status. The sculptor sets off to improve his lot in the world but comes back to the court. When the queen discovers their secret she has them sentenced to death, but the king, who has seen the dancer dance for her beloved in the rain, pardons them.

The success of the film encouraged Vishwanath to make a sequel—*Sagara Sangam* (1983)—on the classical arts and the teacher/disciple relationship, starring the Tamil megastar Kamalahaasan. Other films in the "native" revivalist vein included *Megha Sandesa* (D. Narayana Rao, 1983) and *Ananda Bhairavi* (Jandyaia, 1983), about a classical dance competition, *Sitara* (Krishna Vamsy, 1984), *Rudraveena* (K. Balachander, 1988) starring Chiranjeevi, *Mavichiguru* (S. V. Krishna Reddy, 1996), and *Sindhooram* (Krishna Vamsy, 1997).

The success of *Khaidi* (A. Kondandarami Reddy, 1983) launched the career of Chiranjeevi as well as the genre of the *vigilante* film. Kondandarami Reddy repeated his success with Chiranjeevi in *Mutha Mistry* (1992), where a vegetable market worker protects the market from property developers who are in cahoots with politicians. Female vigilante films, many of them starring Vijayashanthi, include *Pratighatana* (T. Krishna, 1985), *Kartavyam* (A. Mohan Gandhi, 1990), *Street Fighter* (B. Gopal, 1995), and *Police Lockup* (Kodi Ramakrishna, 1993).

There have been a few art films in Telugu. The three most famous are Gautam Ghose's *Maa Bhoomi* (1979), Mrinal Sen's *Oka Oori Katha* (1977), and Shyam Benegal's *Kondura/Anugraham* (1977). Ghose and Sen are Bengali directors, and although Benegal is from Hyderabad, he is better known for his films in Hindi.

The careers of Ram Gopal Verma (1961–) and Mani Rathnam (1956–) (both of whom now work in Hindi cinema) began in the south. Mani Rathnam's films are generally dubbed into Telugu. These two directors introduced to southern screens the slick, violent action in films about gangsters (*Shiva* by Varma in 1989) and campus romances such as *Geetanjali* (Rathnam, 1989) that combined love, action, and spectacle. Eleti Chandra Sekhar, whose *Aithe* (2003), about an underworld criminal who needs to escape to Dubai and decides to gather four people to hijack a plane, won a film award. He attributes his inspiration to Rathnam and Varma.

The last decade has been difficult for Telugu cinema. High-budget spectacles have done badly at the box office, and the lack of successes among blockbuster films has had a demoralizing effect on the Telugu film industry. Attendance has been falling due to television (three TV stations are devoted exclusively to Telugu cinema), DVDs, and other systems delivering home entertainment.

The New Kannada Cinema

Kannada cinema has grown up under the shadow of Tamil and Telugu films. Kannada films used to be produced in Madras, and remakes of successful films in Tamil and Telugu were quite common. Often the large Tamil and Telugu studios would finance the production of mythologicals, folklore fantasies, melodramas, and comedies in Kannada, which would then be processed in their studios in Madras.

It was the arrival of the theater personalities—Gubbi Veeranna and B. R. Panthulu—that really set the Kannada cinema on the road. Both were from different theaters of the Company Natak, local theater companies set up at the beginning of the twentieth century. Inspired by the success of the Parsi theater, they combined the new staging of plays as seen on the English stage in India with traditional local and folk forms of performance. Stories from folklore, history, fantasy, or the epics were staged in proscenium theaters with painted sets, lavish costumes, and footlights—just like in the English theaters touring in India.

It was not until 1966, when the Karnataka State government decided to subsidize Kannada films made in the state that Kannada cinema began to forge a distinct identity for itself. The government also halved the entertainment tax levied on the sale of film tickets. These incentives encouraged a small but important body of art-house films that heralded the new Kannada cinema, a movement that began in 1970. In a move to further assist the local filmmakers, the Karnataka government decided in 2004 to prohibit films made outside the Karnataka State from being screened in the state for the first six weeks after its release elsewhere in India. This decree effectively stopped all Hindi, Telugu, Malayalam, and Tamil films from finding immediate release in the city and led to protests by distributors and exhibitors, particularly those in the cosmopolitan city of Bangalore, India's fourth largest metropolis, who found themselves with no new films to screen.

History   The players from the Company Natak who moved into movies often filmed the plays from their repertory with great success. One of the prime movers of the Kannada cinema was Gubbi Veeranna (1890–1972), stage actor and owner of a theater company. Veeranna laid the foundations for Kannada cinema: he established a film company, the Gubbi-Karnataka Production Company, with investment from A. V. Meiyappan of the powerful AVM studios. He later set up a distribution company and bought a theater for the purposes of exhibition. At first his films were remakes of his successful stage plays made by outside directors whom Veeranna invited to make films in Kannada. Later he added mythologicals to his list of productions.

The first truly "Kannada" film made entirely with local talent was *Bedara Kannappa* (H. I. M. Simha, 1954). The film, which launched the extraordinary film career of Rajkumar, belonged to the folklore genre about gods banished from heaven who come down to live on the earth as humans and endure untold hardships.

The other eminent figure from the early years of Kannada cinema was B. R. Panthulu (1911–1974). Like Veeranna, Panthulu was also a stage actor and owner of his theater company. When he moved to film, he acted in several films that had been successfully staged by his theater company. Panthulu has been associated with a wide variety of films, from low-budget "socials," such as *Samsara Nauka* (1936) and *School Master* (1958), to lavish costume spectaculars starring the Tamil megastars MGR and Sivaji Ganesan, such as *Veerapandiya Kattaboman* (1961) and *Ayirathil Oruvam* (1965), both concerned with Indian heroes and their rebellion against the British.

Panthulu's assistant, Puttanna Kanagal (1933–1985), was an important figure of the Kannada cinema of the 1960s and 1970s. His unusual films have been considered precursors of the new Kannada cinema that emerged in the 1970s. Kanagal was preoccupied by the plight of women trapped in patriarchal family systems. Sexual repression, hysteria, and insanity are recurring themes in his elaborate psychological melodramas. In *Bellimoda* (1967), an heiress finds that her fiancé breaks off their engagement when her mother bears a baby boy who will now inherit the family fortune; in *Gejje Pooje* (1970), a woman escapes the brothel to save her daughter from a fate similar to her own, only to find that respectability is elusive and that she cannot escape her destiny; in *Sharapanjara* (1971), the hallucinations of a pregnant woman land her in an asylum, and when she is released, her husband and friends refuse to accept that she is not insane, so she returns to the ward; in *Ranganayika* (1981), a stage actress marries but finds she cannot resist the urge to return to the theater, which offers her release. She escapes her marriage to tread the boards again but is divorced by her husband, who also takes custody of her son. Years later, when she discovers the man she is having an affair with is her own son, she kills herself.

Another precursor of the new Kannada cinema was the director N. Lakshminarayan, who died in 1991. Lakshminarayan made films on social themes, often with a tragic ending. In *Nandi* (1964), he explores a father's efforts to cope with a deaf-mute son, who dies just when the father has learned to speak with him in sign language; *Uyyale* (1969) examines the life of a wife who is neglected by her professor-husband; in *Mukti* (1970) the protagonist discovers a dark secret from his late father's past and discovers with horror that the woman he loves is his half-sister; and in *Abachurina Post Office* (1973), a village postman who reads out letters to illiterate peasants finds that he must leave the village because his mother-in-law has been eavesdropping and gossiping about the content of those letters.

One of the biggest stars of Kannada cinema was Rajkumar (1929–), who made 200 films, or about 25 percent of the total film production in Kannada. He retired at the age of sixty-five to become a producer. A child actor for Company Natak theaters, Rajkumar got his film break with *Bedara Kannappa* (1954). Over his three-decade-long career, he played not just the usual genres of mythological and devotional films on the lives of gods and saints, but also many contemporary melodramas and the occasional imitation of James Bond on the Kannada screen. The costume dramas set during the great Dravidian kingdoms of the seventh-century Pallavas or the fourteenth-century kingdom of Vijaynagaram were the basis for his attempts to enter into politics. He claimed a distinct identity for Karnataka and drew on an atavistic past. He was active with a group that insisted on Kannada being learned by all inhabitants of Karnataka, a move that led to riots and many deaths. Horrified by the violent turn of events, he withdrew from active politics. In 2000, Rajkumar was abducted by the infamous bandit and elephant poacher Veerappan and released after 108 days for an alleged ransom of INR 400 million (US$9 million). The bandit was shot dead by the police in 2004.

The inspiration for the new Kannada films came from the emerging modernist Kannada literature or the *navya* movement, which reached its apotheosis in the late 1960s (Rajadhyaksha and Willemen 1999). One of the protagonists of this literary movement was U. A. Anandamurthy, whose novel *Samskara* became the first cinematic adaptation that heralded the new Kannada cinema.

Directed by Pattabhi Rama Reddy, *Samskara* (1970) examines the hypocrisy and religious bigotry of the Brahmins. When Naranappa, a heretical meat-eating, alcohol-drinking Brahmin, dies of the plague in the arms of his low-caste mistress, no member of the Brahmin caste wants to perform his funeral rites. His mistress approaches a young Brahmin scholar (Girish Karnad) to take up the task. The scholar ends up having an affair with the mistress. He is overwhelmed with guilt and undertakes a journey to contemplate the esoteric Sanskrit scriptures. He returns with the conviction that there is more to the meaning of life than mere obscurantism and agrees to undertake the funeral ceremony. The film faced stiff opposition from Brahmins but managed to get a censor certificate, thanks to efforts of the Information and Broadcasting minister in New Delhi,

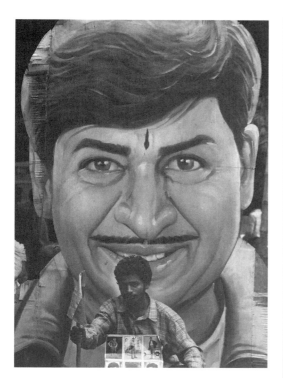

K. Nagaraj, an ardent fan of kidnapped superstar Rajkumar, stages a hunger strike in front of a huge cut-out of the actor in Bangalore, 9 August 2000. Rajkumar had been abducted by Koose Muniswamy Veerappan, southern India's most wanted outlaw. (Reuters/Savita Kirloskar/Corbis)

and went on to win several national awards.

Samskara set the tone and style for the new Kannada cinema of the 1970s. Most of these new films were based on new Kannada fiction and its anti-Brahminism. All the new films examined similar subjects: rural life, obscurantist Brahmin orthodoxy, the caste system, widowhood, the exploitation of the poor, and death. *Vamsa Vriksha* (1971), co-directed by Girish Karnad and B. V. Karanth, examines the consequences of a Hindu widow's remarriage when she is denied custody of her son by her late husband's family; in Karnad's *Kaadu* (1973),

when a man begins an affair with a woman in the neighboring village, hostility between the two villages culminates in violence and death; B. V. Karanth's *Chomana Dudi* (1975), based on a novella by Shivrama Karanth, follows the tragic disintegration of Choma, who belongs to the untouchable caste, when he cannot pay back his loan to the landlord; Karnad's *Godhuli* (1977), made in Kannada and Hindi, made the question of cow slaughter—taboo in Hindu society—the bone of contention between a western-educated Indian and his American wife; in Girish Kasarvalli's *Ghatashraddha* (1977), a child widow who becomes pregnant, attempts suicide, and has an abortion, is ostracized and sent into exile to live alone in the forest with no further human contact; M. S. Sathyu, who won critical acclaim with an Urdu film, *Garam Hawa* (1973), about a Muslim family caught in the aftermath of the partition of India, returned to his Kannada roots to make *Kanneshwara Rama* (1977), about a local outlaw who challenges the British government and is hanged for it; Karnad's *Ondadandu Kaladalli* (1978) is an "action" film based on the ancient martial arts tradition of south India and an homage to Japanese director Akira Kurosawa; T. S. Nagabharana's *Grahana* (1979) is about the dilemma faced by members of a particular group of low-caste Hindu who, thanks to an arcane ritual, become Brahmins for a fortnight each year. One of their members dies during the ritual, and the question that arises is what caste funeral rites is he entitled to?

In the 1980s, the second generation of the new Kannada films moved away from the rural stories of caste-based exploitation of men and women to the issues of the urban centers. The tone was set by P. Lankesh's first film, *Pallavi* (1976), about a young woman who marries her boss and is then accused by her former love, now being chased by the cops, of letting him down by choosing financial security over idealism. Kasarvalli won the nation's highest award for *Tabaranna Kathe* (1987), about an ordinary municipal employee who tries to get his provident fund released from the Kafkaesque maze of Indian bureaucracy so that he can treat his diabetic wife. His next film, *Mane* (1989), made in Kannada and Hindi, explores the trials and triumphs of a young couple who move to the big city to escape the suffocating control of their extended rural families. Nagabharana, who eventually moved into mainstream commercial films, adapted novelist R. K. Narayan's story *The Financial Expert* to make *Banker Margayya* (1983), about a smooth-talking entrepreneur whose son usually ends up ruining all his get-rich-quick ventures. In 1990, Sathyu made *Santha Sishunala Sharefa*, starring Girish Karnad, about a mystic poet-saint. The film had a strong anti-orthodoxy slant (Garga 1996).

Prema Karanth, one of the few women filmmakers in Kannada, made a single foray into feature filmmaking before settling on making documentaries. Karanth came to cinema after directing children's theater and assisting her husband (B. V. Karanth) and other Kannada directors in their film ventures. *Phaniyamma* (1982), based on a book by M. K. Indira, is about a child widow who endures the cruel treatment meted out to widows in orthodox Hindu society. However, as she grows to adulthood, she begins to defy society by assisting a woman from an "untouchable" caste in childbirth. Later she stands by another young widow who refuses to submit to the cruelties of the orthodoxy.

The flood of art-house films made in Kannada in the 1970s petered out in the later decades, despite increases in the subsidies and grants made by the Karnataka government to promote Kannada cinema. A few directors, however, have continued to make new kinds of films. The most prolific has been Girish Kasarvalli. His recent film *Dweepa* (2002) concerns an environmental issue that pits economic development against the need to save forests and natural species. The issues are unraveled through the story of a village that finds it is going to be submerged to make way for a dam. All the families except one move away from their ancestral homes. The film then explores the tragedy of displacement and the trials that surround the lone family as it lives marooned on the island with the rising waters of the dam surrounding their land. The film won the President's Award, and Kasarvalli became only the third Indian filmmaker after Satyajit Ray and Mrinal Sen to have won the prize four times.

Cinema in Kerala

As was the case with the new Kannada cinema, the art-house films that began to emerge from Kerala from the 1960s had a tremendous impact on the proponents of the new Indian cinema.

As a state, Kerala has very distinctive features informed by a unique history and political evolution. At 90 percent, it has the highest literacy rate in the whole of India. With 1,300 screens for a population of 32 million, it also has the highest ratio of film theaters to population, creating the space for greater varieties of cinemas to co-exist in the Malayalam film market. As a society it has a multi-religious composition, with Hindus, Christians, and Muslims.

Historically, the kingdoms of Travancore and Cochin have been more progressive than elsewhere in India, with reform-minded maharajas, a modern social and economic infrastructure, and a legal system inspired by nineteenth-century Europe (Thoraval 2001). They introduced universal suffrage and education for all. Furthermore, they did away with much of the obscurantist Hindu orthodoxy so widespread in the rest of southern India and made Hindu temples open to all castes. This enlightened historical development no doubt contributed to the establishment of Communist governments that were democratically elected and have been in and out of power in a variety of alliances since 1957.

As with the other southern states, Kerala came into existence after the reorganization of Indian states along linguistic lines in 1956 and was slow to embark on film production, remaining content to watch films made in Madras and Bombay. A silent film, *Vigatha Kumaran*, made by J. C. Daniel in 1928, qualifies as the first Malayalam film, thanks to the fact that its inter-titles were in the Malayalam language. The second film, *Marthanda Varma*, directed by P. V. Rao and based on a book by C. V. Raman Pillai, is of significance because it is one of the few films from that era that remains completely intact. The film, completed in 1931, was screened only once because the producer had failed to obtain the film rights for the book from the publishers, who sought an injunction after its first screening and took possession of the only copy. It was never screened again until 1994, when the National Film Archives of India allowed its use at the first film festival of Kerala (Pillay 1981).

With the arrival of the talkies, Kerala became entirely dependent on Madras and Bombay. For the studio barons in Madras, Kerala was a market just waiting to be conquered and controlled. The studio barons began to finance Malayalam films with local actors. Technicians from the studios in Madras were dispatched to Kerala to assist with their making, and the films were then brought back to their studios in Madras for processing. The first Malayalam talkie, *Balan* (1938), was directed by S. Nottani and produced by T. R. Sundaram of Modern Theatres in Salem; *Gnanambika* (1940), also directed by Nottani, was made at Newtone Studios in Madras; *Prahladan* (1941), directed by K. Subrahmanyam, was shot at Gemini Studios. The latter was a story from the Hindu epics, whereas both *Balan* (which had twenty-three songs) and *Gnanambika* concerned the evil designs of wicked stepmothers who wish to harm the children of the husbands' late wives.

During these years, Tamil cinema, despite its theatrical style, continued to find a ready audience in Kerala, primarily because of a shortage of Malayalam films. Telugu films, too, found favor with the people in Kerala for their sentimentalism and family dramas, while extravagant production values with stars, expensive sets, music, and dance were the selling points of the Hindi films. However, as the number of local films produced increased, Malayalam cinema began to find its own voice and an infrastructure began to be built.

Already by 1935 networks were in place in the big cities for the distribution and exhibition of Tamil, Hindi, and Telugu films. In 1949, P. J. Cherian was the first native from Kerala to embark on film production with *Nirmala* (P. V. Krishna Iyer, 1948). Film archivist P. K. Nair maintains that this is the first film made and completed in Kerala, though others award that distinction to

Velli Nakshatram (Felix Beyis, 1949), which was made at the new Udaya Studios set up in 1947 in Allepey by distributor K. V. Koshy and Malayalam film director Kunchako. Whatever the case, Udaya Studios soon made its mark with a string of box-office successes and became a household name.

Ten films were made in Malayalam in the 1940s, and it was only in the 1950s, when the state of Kerala was created, that Malayalam cinema acquired a momentum and an identity of its own. In 1951, the mayor of Tivandrum built Merryland Studio in his city and modeled it on S. S. Vasan's Gemini Studios in Madras. The proprietors of Udaya and Merryland used their studios for their own productions, while private producers without studios continued to go to Madras. Kunchako (1912–1976) specialized in political thrillers, melodrama from literary sources, and mythologicals, whereas Subrahmanyam, after building Merryland, tried his hand at directing and made about fifty films (mainly melodramas and mythologicals) in twenty years.

In the 1950s, *Navalokam*, *Thiramaala*, *Newspaper Boy*, and *Neelakkuyil* were some of the notable Malayalam films. The latter (1954), co-directed by Marxists P. Bhaskaran and Ramu Kariat, is the story of a Brahmin who outrages his fellow caste members by adopting his illegitimate son by an "untouchable" woman on her death. *Newspaper Boy* (1955), made by a batch of film students headed by P. Ramdas, is about an adolescent orphan who must single-handedly feed his younger brothers and sisters. It succeeded, according to the critics, in presenting characters and situations drawn from everyday life with feeling and simplicity (Pillay 1985).

The 1960s mark the beginning of the rise of star actor Prem Nazir (1928–1989), who is said to have acted in over 600 films in a career that spanned thirty years. He is featured in the Guinness Book of Records for the highest number of films for an actor anywhere in the world.

The 1970s were also a decade of exponential growth of Malayalam cinema, and film production jumped from 33 films in 1966 to 123 films in 1978 to 136 in 1985. Since then, numbers have fallen, averaging about 70 films a year. Most of the growth in the 1970s was the consequence of the influx of Gulf money—paychecks sent home by millions of people from Kerala who emigrated to work in the Gulf States. Most of the money was invested in real estate, industry, and fisheries, but some made its way to the film industry in the form of loans. It was known as "blade" money to indicate the extortionist interest rates charged by the moneylenders (Rajadhyaksha and Willemen 1999).

The director most closely associated with the film boom and the "blade" companies of the 1970s is the prolific (seven or eight films annually) I. V. Sasi (1948–). His work generally features scripts by Marxist writer T. Damodaran, with whom he made a series of political melodramas on the scandals in Kerala politics in the 1980s. Sasi also specialized in vigilante films with the actor Mammooty in the stellar roles. These portray a heroic individual fighting and overcoming an oppressive system by resorting to extralegal means. In *Avanazhi* (1986) an honest cop (Mammooty) is blamed for the murder of a student who has died in police custody. Sasi's films include fast-moving action, plenty of violence, and a complicated plot that moves at a dizzying pace. *Avanazhi*'s sequel, *Inspector Balaram* (1991), chronicles the further investigations of the honest cop (always Mammooty) into the corruption that is allowed to proliferate thanks to effete liberal laws and state institutions. *Vartha* (1986) has the owner of a newspaper (Mammooty again) launch a crusade against the forces of corruption, and *The City* (1994) revisits the same grounds as *Avanazhi*, ending with a climactic fight between rival gangs that are then wiped out by the honest cop.

Sasi's most (in)famous work was *Avalude Ravukal* (1978), a poignant but sexually explicit love story featuring an orphaned brother and sister. It became notorious when it was screened nationwide in a dubbed Hindi version, re-titled *Her Nights*, and for some time thereafter, Malayalam films were synonymous with "soft porn" in the rest of India. The association of Malayalam films with soft porn that Sasi introduced has now become the exclusive prerogative of the Malayali star Shakeela, and currently nearly a third of the Malayalam films feature her (Thoraval 2001).

The other successful partnership in Malayalam popular cinema has been that of actor Mohanlal with director Priyadarshan, whose range included comedies, lavish musicals, and psychological and tragic melodramas. His most famous films are *Thalavattam* (1986), about a mentally disturbed man (Mohanlal) in an asylum whose romantic feelings for a nurse are scotched when the father of the nurse, who is also the owner of the asylum, has him lobotomized. In *Chithram* (1988), a spirited young woman pretends to be married to a lovable con artist (Mohanlal) to save her fortune from falling into the wrong hands. The two, who pretend to be man and wife, eventually fall in love, but in the end, the con artist's past catches up with him and

he is sent to the gallows. However, *Kilukkam* (1988) is a light-hearted romantic caper featuring an heiress running away from her tormentors, and the tourist guide (Mohanlal) and his sidekick photographer who rescue her (Thoraval 2001).

New Malayalam Cinema   Malayalam cinema first attracted national attention with Ramu Kariat's *Chemmeen* (1965). Based on a popular novel by T. S. Pillai, its theme is chastity. A fisherman's daughter loves a Muslim trader but is unable to marry him. Instead she is married to another fisherman. When her husband goes out to sea, the young woman has an affair with the trader and her husband dies at sea. The film explores the age-old belief among fishing communities that the safe return of the fishermen who go out to sea depends on the chastity of their women. *Chemmeen* won national awards and international attention.

Five years later, P. N. Menon made *Olavum Theeravum* (1970), about a trader who loves a young woman and endeavors to earn enough so that they can live comfortably when they are married. Unfortunately the woman's greedy mother marries her off to a rich man. The trader leaves the village and the young woman commits suicide. In 1973, M. T. Vasudevan Nair made *Nirmalayam* about a village oracle whose services are no longer needed by the community and whose family begins to fall apart. In a heightened finale, he kills himself as he performs his last ritual dance in front of the goddess, whom he has served his entire life.

These three films set into motion the flowering of art-house films that have today become the defining quality of Malayalam cinema and captured the interest of art-film lovers across the nation. Several directors contributed to this flowering, many of them graduates of the Film and Television Institute of India (FTII) in Pune. However two personalities remain central to this new movement. They are Adoor Gopalakrishnan and G. Aravindan.

Adoor Gopalakrishnan   Adoor Gopalakrishnan (1941–) is a graduate of the FTII and formed the Chitralekha Film Cooperative in 1965 together with other FTII graduates to provide the opportunities to make "personal" films in a commercial world. Chitralekha was intended as a production-cum-distribution organization and later added a laboratory and training facilities.

Gopalakrishnan's films are about the social and political changes in Kerala with the erosion of a matriarchal system and the rise of a competitive world conventionally coded as masculine, the impact of technology, and so on (Rajadhyaksha and Willemen 1999). Travancore's delayed entry into the nationalist mainstream and its sudden transformation from a feudal state ruled by Dewan C. P. Ramaswamy Aiyer into one run by a Communist Party of India (CPI) government created the break in Kerala's history that animates Gopalakrishnan's films (Rajadhyaksha and Willemen 1999).

The Chitralekha co-operative produced his first film, *Swayamwaram* (1972). An unconventional film in both style and content, it examines the plight of an unmarried couple living in a small town and coping with the hostility of its inhabitants as they descend into financial penury. The film ends with the death of the man and the woman pregnant and facing an uncertain future. His next film, *Kodiyettam* (1977), named after a performing style of theater in Kerala, is about the coming of age of a village simpleton who observes life as it unfolds around him. Central to his world are a weak-willed lorry driver and a lonely widow who cannot cope with her exploitative partners and eventually commits suicide. The young boy also begins to understand that women are human beings in their own right, not just nurturers and providers.

Elippathayam (1981), considered by many to be his best, it is an elegiac fin-de-siècle kind of film about a man, a relic of the disintegrating feudal state, who cannot come to terms with modernity and retreats, rat-like, into his sewer—an ancestral home that is slowly disintegrating. The parasitic brother's three sisters portray three different reactions to his behavior—the oldest fights for her share, the second succumbs to his tyranny and remains like a slave, and the third defies him by eloping with her lover. The film won acclaim both in India and abroad (Garga 1996).

The story told in *Mukhamukham* (1984) spans two discrete decades: the first, 1945–1955, just before the CPI won the elections in Kerala; the second, a decade later, when the CPI has split into two. A trade unionist successfully resists mechanization and saves factory jobs but has to go underground when the head of the factory is killed. In his absence he becomes the icon for the party and the trade union movement. A decade later he emerges from hiding, an alcoholic and a broken man. Interestingly, he finds that the party has also fragmented. In his sorry state he becomes an embarrassment to his fellow trades unionists. When he is mysteriously murdered, his iconic state is seamlessly resurrected (Garga 1996). According to critics Ashish Rajadhyaksha and Paul Willemen: "The film . . . shifts the entire critique into one where the mass culture generated by incomplete capitalist growth merges with the rhetoric of left activism, the whole masking what the director suggests to be the major problem: the absence of a valid indigenous culture able to define the terms of its engagement with capitalist systems" (Rajadhyaksha and Willemen 1999: 466).

Anantaram (1987) is a study in alienation and angst. It is narrated in two interwoven stories—one real and the other a fantasy—by the protagonist, a young man. The only link between the existences is the desire for a particular kind of woman. *Mathilukal* (1989) is based on an autobiographical story by political prisoner Basheer and concerns the relationship between him and a woman imprisoned for murder. The two have never seen each other but still manage to communicate. On the day they have set up a meeting, Basheer finds that he is released and cannot make the appointment. In 1995, Gopalakrishnan made a history of Kerala since independence for the Japanese broadcasting company NHK. *Kathapurushan* sees the events after independence unfold through the life of the young man Kunjunni and his family members. The last film by Adoor Gopalakrishnan is *Nizhalkuth* (2002), about a hangman who at first is a firm believer in the death penalty but experiences growing doubts that in the end prevent him from doing his job.

G. Aravindan   The other great figure of the new Malayalam cinema was G. Aravindan (1935–1991), a caricaturist most famous for his cartoon series *Cheriyamanushyanum Valiyalokavum* (Little Men and the Big World) and its central character, the middle-class Ramu, who takes life too seriously. The films of Aravindan are lyrical, mystical, beautiful, and contemplative but sometimes incomprehensible. In *Uttaranayanam* (1974), his first film, Aravindan surveys the corruption that has seeped into post-independence India and wonders if the sacrifices of his father and his friends, all freedom fighters, have been in vain. Unable to get a job and provide for his mother and grandmother, he escapes into the mountains and, thanks to a wise old woman, learns the true innocence that exists in nature (Garga 1996).

In Aravindan's next venture, *Kanchana Sita* (1977), he takes the epic *Ramayana* and transforms it into a contemplation on righteousness (epitomized by Lord Rama) and the healing power of nature (Sita), before Rama merges into nature. Interestingly he drew on the Ramachenchus, a tribal community living in the state of Andhra Pradesh who claim direct descent from Lord Rama, to play the parts. *Thampu* (1978), shot in black and white, narrates the arrival and brief sojourn of a circus in a small village in Kerala. The excitement of the arrival of the circus fractures the dull monotony of everyday life in a village, which returns to emptiness when the circus folds up its tent and moves on to the next village. *Kummatty* (1979), a children's film, draws on folklore and tells of a magician storyteller who comes to a village. The children, entranced by his tales, are turned into animals. He restores them all before departing, but one little boy who has been turned into a dog and chased away by the villagers misses the moment and remains a dog. The villagers try all kinds of remedies to bring him back to human form but fail. Finally the magician returns and restores the boy (Garga 1996).

Estheppan (1980), a film on religious mysticism, is about a Christ-like figure that defies definition. The fragmented narrative seems to question whether a human being is ever a real and knowable creature. A similar concern surrounds *Pokkuveyil* (1981), when a mental asylum inmate's life is reconstructed through a series of flashbacks. Jealousy and stark passion are the themes of *Chidambaram* (1985), when the chief supervisor at a farm returns with a bride. The wife is attracted to the cowherd, and the supervisor, unable to bear the jealousy, hangs himself. When the cowherd embarks on a pilgrimage to Chidambaram to expiate his guilt (though there is no indication of adultery), he encounters the woman. In *Oridathu* (1986), all kinds of problems beset a village with the arrival of electricity. Aravindan made *Vastruhara* (1990) just before his sudden death. A government servant has the task of selecting refugees from Bangladesh for resettlement in the Andaman Islands. One of the persons seeking to be resettled is his widowed aunt from Kerala.

Two independent-minded Malayalam filmmakers who died early were John Abraham and P. A. Backer.

John Abraham (1937–1987) was an intense and individualistic filmmaker. During his brief film career (he died at the age of 49) he made four films. The first, *Vidyarthikale Ithile* (1970), he dismissed as a compromise with the film industry. His second film, *Agraharthi Kazhuthai* (1978), was made in Tamil and is a comic rendition of Brahmin orthodoxy. A professor adopts a donkey as a pet. Ordered by the college principal to get rid of it, he takes it to his village, but his fellow Brahmins kill it. Fearing the wrath of God, they decide to make amends by erecting a temple to the donkey. The film is said to pay homage to *Au Hasard Balthazar* (1965) by

the French new-wave director Robert Bresson. In *Cheriyachante Kroota Krityangal* (1981) a feudal autocrat must pay for his crimes as the forces of change catch up with him.

Abraham started a film movement called the Odessa Collective (named after a famous scene in Eisenstein's *Battleship Potemkin*) with a group of people who wanted to make personal films. Its first production was *Amma Ariyan*, a film entirely financed by small individual contributions of INR 2–10 from ordinary people. The maximum contribution allowed from any individual was INR 500 (US$11). *Amma Ariyan* (1986) centers on the suicide of an ex-revolutionary. His comrades identify his dead body and travel together to inform his mother of his death. The film is like a wake and is told in a series of memories of the dead boy and the revolution that failed. The eventual picture that emerges from each memory is confusing and contradictory. Abraham was posthumously awarded the National Award for the film.

P. A. Backer (1940–1993) was an assistant to Ramu Kariat before producing P. N. Menon's *Olavum Theeravum* in 1969. He was part of John Abraham's Odessa Collective, and his first film ran into problems with the censors. *Kahani Nadi Chuvannappol* (1975) is a love story between a radical political activist who has been declared a criminal by the police and a young woman. The man is killed and the woman reads about it in the press. The censors pulled the film during the Emergency declared by Mrs. Indira Gandhi (Rajadhyaksha and Willemen 1999). Most of Backer's films center on women. *Chuvanna Vithukal* looks at the hardships of life as an older sister becomes a prostitute to help her younger sister have a better life—in the end it all seems to have been in vain. His next film, *Manimuzhakkum* (1976), is about the confusions created by religion when a young boy born a Hindu but raised by a Christian is later adopted by a Hindu. He finds himself rejected by the Hindu women for being too Christian and by the Christian women for being too Hindu. *Sanghganam* (1979) tells of a young man looking for a leader who, in the end, realizes he must take responsibility for his own actions (Thoraval 2001; Garga 1996).

T. V. Chandran, who played the lead role in Backer's *Kahani Nadi Chuvannappol*, was deeply influenced by it, and history is a central theme in his films. His debut film was *Krishnakutty* (1980), followed by *Alicinte Anveshanan* (1989), *Ponthan Mada* (1993), and *Ormakalundayirikkanam* (1995). *Ponthan Mada* looks at the friendship between the low-caste Ponthan, who has been a mute witness to the vicissitudes of history, and an absent, westernized aristocrat who has come home after decades. History is also the concern of *Ormakalundayirikkanam*, starring Mammooty. It is about life in a small community, set against the background of the abrupt removal from power after two years of the democratically elected Communist government by the Congress Party in power in New Delhi, under Jawaharlal Nehru.

Like Chandran, Shaji Karun is one of the new generation of Malayalam filmmakers keeping alive the tradition of new cinema. A cinematographer for Aravindan and an FTII graduate, his first film, *Piravi* (1988), garnered several awards. The story concerns a son's disappearance during the Emergency (1975–1977) declared by the prime minister, Mrs. Indira Gandhi. The father patiently awaits his son's arrival and goes daily to the bus station to get news of him. His daughter discovers that her brother has died of torture. The father moves from hope to despair to hallucination as he begins to believe that his son is still alive and living with him. Another study in grief is *Swaham* (1994), where the death of the breadwinner begins the family's descent into poverty. To add to the tragedy, the young son is trampled to death in a stampede outside an office where crowds have gathered to enlist in the army. In *Vanaprastham* (1999), a Kathakali actor (Mohanlal) finds that his wife is more in love with his stage personality than his true self and in despair he kills himself. Karun's recent film *Nishad* (2002), in Hindi, is about a mother's fears for her son who is an officer in the Indian Air Force.

One of the promising young directors of Malayalam cinema is Murali Nair, whose first feature film, *Maranasimhasanam*, won him the prestigious Camera d'Or at the Cannes International Film Festival in 1999. A black comedy, it tells about a poor peasant who steals a few coconuts and finds he is sentenced to death. A newly imported electric chair from the United States is going to be tried out on him, and the occasion soon acquires the breathless excitement of a circus. The peasant's successful execution heartens senior government officials to resolve to get a loan from the World Bank to import more of these wonderful machines. His second film, *Pattiyude Divasam* (2001), also has darkly comic undertones, as a dog gifted by a king to a peasant begins to destroy the happiness of the villagers. In Nair's recent film *Arimpara* (2003), the protagonist is a man living in rural Kerala who finds one day a wart developing on his chin. Initially everybody, including his wife, finds it attractive, but as it gets bigger it begins to enslave the man as he finds himself abandoned by his family and friends.

Conclusion

More than half of the films made in India come from the combined total of the south Indian films. The four regional cinemas have characteristics that are particular to their respective regions, yet thanks to the practice of dubbing films into other south Indian languages initiated early by the studios in Chennai, each of the southern regions is also familiar with films from their neighboring states. South Indian films dubbed into Hindi have never been very popular in northern markets, however. Many of the powerful studios set up just as the studios in Mumbai and Kolkata were being closed attempted to make inroads into the northern markets but never really found it financially viable.

In addition to piracy and the spiraling costs of a star-driven industry, the biggest threat to the commercial cinema in south India comes from television, which has seen exponential growth since the 1990s. Multiple channels broadcast in each of the four languages of the south, and several channels are entirely devoted to cinema. As a result, commercial cinema is currently operating under very difficult circumstances. Some states, such as Karnataka, have taken the unprecedented step of placing moratoriums on screening non-Kannada films for a few months and initiating other measures to protect the local film industry from intense competition from the neighboring states. These efforts have led to protests and strikes by distributors and exhibitors. In the meantime, the film indus-

tries must rethink their strategies in order to cope with the various challenges to their hegemony. However, with the growth of new studios with state of the art technology in Hyderabad and elsewhere, the prospect of films with better production values is bright.

The art-house films of Karnataka and Kerala today lead the way for the development and flowering of a new alternative cinema, one that is personal and thought-provoking, different from the formulaic and escapist commercial cinema. The construction of new cinema multiplexes in Mumbai and elsewhere, and the burgeoning, cosmopolitan middle classes in the major Indian cities, now offer the best opportunity for these regional art-house films to obtain commercial release in all the major cities of India.

A to Z Index

Farhan Akhtar (1974–) wrote and directed *Dil Chahta Hai* in 2001, marking the arrival of the new Bollywood films. Son of screenwriters Javed Akhtar and Honey Irani, Akhtar's second film, *Lakshya* in 2004, is set in Kargil, the area of a recent military skirmish between India and Pakistan. He also wrote the lyrics in English for Gurinder Chadha's *Bride and Prejudice* (2004).

C. N. Annadurai (1909–1969) was a Tamil screenwriter and ideologue who propagated the DMK message through his films and became the first DMK chief minister of Tamil Nadu.

K. Balachander (1930–) is a director and producer of films in Tamil, Telugu, Kannada, and Hindi who made mainly social melodramas but gained all-India fame for his political films: *Thaneer Thaneer* (1981) and *Achamillai Achamillai* (1984).

Balakrishna (1960–) is the Telugu superstar and son of late N. T. Rama Rao (NTR) recently embroiled in the shooting of two colleagues. The case was dismissed due to lack of evidence.

Dev Benegal (1969–) studied filmmaking in New York and is known for his cinematic adaptation of Upamanyu Chatterjee's novel *English, August* (1994), a satire on Indian bureaucrats. His next film, *Split Wide Open* (2001), about four disparate lives, is considered a more mature piece of work.

Madhur Bhandarkar (1967–) started as assistant with Ram Gopal Verma and became famous as director of *Chandni Bar* (2001), about a woman's fight for survival as a dancer in a bar, and *Page 3* (2005); he became infamous for allegations of sexual misconduct by starlet Priti Jain.

Chiranjeevi (1955–) made his early films with director K. Balachander but gained his Telugu superstar status with the violent gangster and vigilante genres in A. Kondandarami Reddy's films.

Vidhu Vinod Chopra (1955–) is an arthouse director who moved to mainstream Hindi films. He directed *Parinda* in 1989, and later *1942: A Love Story* in 1994, and *Mission Kashmir* in 2000. He produced the hit comedy *Munnabhai MBBS* in 2003.

Devdas (Sanjay Leela Bhansali, 2001): In this twelfth and most lavish version of Sarat Chandra Chatterjee's novel, Devdas (Shah Rukh Khan) takes to drink when his father refuses to let him marry his childhood sweetheart because she belongs to a lower caste than he. Paro marries a widower and moves away, while Devdas takes a mistress but pines away and dies.

Dil Chahta Hai (Farhan Akhtar, 2001): Three young men seek to live the easy consumerist life in Mumbai. But their lives change when Akash (Aamir Khan) and Sameer (Akshaye Khanna) fall out over Sameer's newfound love Tara (Dimple Kapadia), an alcoholic divorcee. Hailed as a new kind of Bollywood film, it clearly defines the urban consumer as its target audience rather than the urban-rural spread sought by the old Bollywood producers.

Sivaji Ganesh (1927–) was a star Tamil actor who acted in Annadurai's DMK films, then moved on to join the Congress Party before joining Janata Dal and finally starting his own political party. Together with MGR, he dominated Tamil cinema. He was considered by most to be a better actor but a worse politician than MGR.

Ashutosh Gowarikar (1960–) started as a small-time actor in films. His first major achievement was *Lagaan* with Aamir Khan in 2001. His next film, *Swades* (2004), about a NASA scientist who returns to India to help rural communities, was less well received. He was named as a member of the jury at the 2005 Cannes Film Festival.

Kamalahaasan (1954–) is a Tamil superstar and superb dancer who has also played in Malayalam and Telugu films. He later modeled his career along the lines of Robert de Niro, playing unusual characters, many of them in the style of the Sicilian mafia.

Prema Karanth (1936–) is a director who moved to cinema after working in children's theater. She made *Phaniyamma* (1982), which was very well received by critics and fans of art-house films, and moved to making documentaries thereafter.

Girish Karnad (1938–) is a playwright, actor, and director of art-house films in Kannada and is part of the group of filmmakers who kick-started the new Kannada cinema with *Samskara* in 1970. Karnad was also a success in a few Hindi films.

Shaji Karun (1952–) is an FTII graduate and Malayalam director and cameraman for Aravindan and other Malayalam directors. His debut film, *Piravi*, was about a father's patient wait for a dead son; his last film was in Hindi, *Nishad* (2002), about a mother's fears for her son.

Director of new Kannada art-house films, **Girish Kasarvalli** (1949–) won the President's award four times, most recently for *Dweepa* (2002).

Aamir Khan (1965–) is one of the top three stars of Bollywood, along with Salman Khan and Shah Rukh Khan. He shot to fame with *Qayamat Se Qayamat Tak* in 1980. His superstardom came with *Lagaan* (2003) and *Dil Chahta Hai* (2003), very different films released the same year. He is known to be very choosy about his roles and, unlike most other actors, prefers

to concentrate on just one or two roles at a time. His recent films include *1857—The Rising* (2005), where he plays a rebel leader.

Farah Khan (1962–) is a dance choreographer with nearly 100 films to her credit. The daughter of B-film-maker Karmuddin Khan, her first film was *Jo Jeeta Wohi Sikander* in 1992. She moved to direction with *Main Hoon Na* in 2004, starring Shah Rukh Khan. Farah Khan choreographed the dances for Andrew Lloyd Webber's musical play *Bombay Dreams*.

Shah Rukh Khan (1965–), one of the top three stars of Bollywood, began his acting career on stage. He moved to "art" films, such as Mani Kaul's *Idiot* in 1991, before beginning his steep ascent into stardom. He also has a production company with his star colleagues called Dreamz Unlimited.

Nagesh Kukunoor (1968–) is an engineer from the United States who moved to filmmaking with the low budget *Hyderabad Blues* (1999). At first, his distributor had to give tickets away free to get an audience, but the film went on to became one of the highest-grossing low-budget films in English. His later films include *Bollywood Calling*, *Rockford*, and a sequel to *Hyderabad Blues* (2004).

Madhumati (Bimal Roy, 1958): Devendra (Dilip Kumar), on an official tour of a distant district, has to take shelter in an abandoned house. There he relives his previous incarnation as Anand, a manager of a timber estate who falls in love with Madhumati (Vyjayanthimala), a member of a tribal community being exploited by Ugra Narain (Pran), Devendra's boss.

Maine Pyar Kiya (Sooraj Barjatya, 1989): After returning from the United States, Prem (Salman Khan) falls in love with Suman (Bhagyashree), the daughter of his father's childhood friend. But his father, having risen in the world, would prefer Prem to marry the ambitious daughter of his business friend.

Mammooty (1953–) is the Malayalam star of the 1980s mainly known for his films with I. V. Sasi and his vigilante genres; he has also acted in art-house films such as *Mathilukal* (1989).

A. V. Meiyappan (1907–1979) was the movie mogul who set up AVM studios in Chennai and introduced industrial production of films in three south Indian languages as well as in Hindi.

Mohanlal (1962–), a Malayalam film star who often played comic roles, has worked closely with Malayalam director Priyadarshan and has played in art-house films such as Aravindan's *Vastruhara* (1990).

Mother India (Mehboob, 1957): In this left-wing *Gone with the Wind*–type film, Radha (Nargis), a peasant woman, is abandoned by her disabled husband. She struggles to raise her starving children and fights off the advances of moneylender Sukhilala, who is willing to help her out if she sleeps with him. But Radha survives the ordeal with her honor in tact. Many years later her son Birju (Sunil Dutt) abducts Sukhilala's daughter, but Radha shoots her own son dead to preserve the honor of womankind.

Munnabhai MBBS (Vidhu Vinod Chopra, 2003) is a comedy that brings together the medical profession and the criminal underworld. A lovable crook (Sanjay Dutt) must become a doctor and uses the only (crooked) methods he knows to achieve this, with hilarious consequences.

Nagarjuna (1959–) is one of the top Telugu stars and son of superstar A. Nageshwar Rao. He shot to fame with Mani Rathnam's *Geetanjali* and Ram Gopal Varma's *Shiva*, both made in the same year.

Murali Nair (1966–) is an art-house Malayalam film director. His debut film *Maranasimhasanam* (1999), a black comedy, won an award at Cannes; his latest film *Arimpara* (2003) is another black comedy about a wart that enslaves a man.

Pyaasa (Guru Dutt, 1957): Vijay (Guru Dutt) moves in with a poor prostitute, Gulab (Waheeda Rehman), one of the few persons to recognize his true worth as a poet. When Vijay is mistakenly presumed dead, Gulab publishes his poems from her meager savings. He is an instant success but cannot abide the bourgeois hypocrisy. He renounces the society of the chattering classes and takes Gulab with him.

Aishwarya Rai (1973–), the first Indian winner of the Miss World title, in 1994, moved to films by first acting in regional films, an interest she still maintains, as seen in her association with director Rituparno Ghosh's *Choker Bali* in 2003. She is currently the most important female actor of the Hindi screen and played a leading role in the lavish production of *Devdas* in 2002. She was voted the most beautiful woman by *Hello* magazine, beating Julia Roberts, Catherine Zeta-Jones, and Nicole Kidman for the title. After *Bride and Prejudice*, she found an opening in foreign ventures and has signed with the elite William Morris agency. She appeared with Meryl Streep in *Chaos* (Coline Sevreau, 2006).

Rajkumar (1929–), a Kannada superstar who has acted in 200 films, entertained political aspirations before settling on producing films that promoted his sons. He was kidnapped by the bandit and elephant poacher Veerappan in 2000 and released for an alleged ransom of INR 400 million (US$1 million).

Rajnikant (1950–), a bus conductor before becoming a Tamil superstar, is known and loved for his trademark trick of tossing a cigarette into the air and catching it with his teeth.

N. T. Rama Rao (NTR) (1923–1996) was a Telugu star who played in some 260 films and rose to be chief minister of Andhra Pradesh. He returned briefly to acting and directing after he lost his seat in the elections.

M. G. Ramachandran (MGR) (1917–1987) was the greatest star of the Tamil screen, with nearly 300 films to his credit. He went on to become the chief minister of Tamil Nadu, a post he held for nine years.

A. R. Rehman (1966–) is India's foremost contemporary composer. He started with Tamil and Hindi films and broke through with Mani Rathnam's *Roja* (1992). Ram Gopal Verma's *Rangeela* and Rathnam's *Bombay* (both 1995) made him an all-India star; he composed the music for Andrew

Lloyd Webber's stage musical *Bombay Dreams*.

Sholay (Ramesh Sippy, 1975): Veeru (Dharmendra) and Jai (Amitabh Bachchan) are two lovable crooks hired by Thakur, a retired police officer (Sanjeev Kumar) to avenge the annihilation of his family by the outlaw Gabbar Singh (Amjad Khan). This "curry western" about bounty hunters is a loving homage to "spaghetti westerns" and Clint Eastwood.

S. S. Vasan (1903–1969) was a producer and director of Tamil films; he made several attempts to conquer the Hindi film market. Owner of Gemini Studios, he is best known for the first ever super-spectacle, *Chandralekha* (1948), which he dubbed into Hindi, a first for a Tamil film.

Ram Gopal Verma (1961–) was a civil engineer and later director of Telugu films who turned to mainstream Hindi films. His successes include *Rangeela* (1995) and *Satya* (2000). He has now revived the erstwhile horror and thriller genres with *Bhoot* (2001), *Murder* (2003), and *Company* (2005), the latter about the gangster Ibrahim Dawood's outfit, known as D-Company.

Note

Some parts of this chapter first appeared in "An Introduction to Indian Cinema" in *An Introduction to Film Studies*, edited by Jill Neimes and published by Routledge in 1999.

Bibliography and References

Adamu, Abdalla Uba. *The Song Remains the*

Same: Media Parenting and Construction of Media Identities in Northern Nigerian Muslim Hausa Home Videos. Unpublished monograph. Kano, Nigeria, 2004.

Bamzai, Kaveree. "Lost in Translation." *India Today,* 25 October 2004.

Bannerjee, Shampa, and Anil Srivastava. *One Hundred Indian Feature Films: An Annotated Bibliography.* New York: Garland Publishing, 1988.

Barnouw, Erik, and S. Krishnaswamy. *Indian Film.* Oxford: Oxford University Press, 1980.

Basu, Siddharth, Sanjay Kak,and Pradip Kishen. "Cinema and Society: A Search for Meaning in a New Genre." *Indian International Centre Quarterly* 8 (1) 1981.

Bhardwaj, Praveena. "Dirty Dancing?" *Filmfare,* September 1993.

Bhaskaran, Theodore S. *The Eye of the Serpent: An Introduction to Tamil Cinema.* Madras: Affiliated East West Press, 1996.

———. *The Message Bearers: Nationalist Politics and the Entertainment Media in South India, 1880–1945.* Madras: Cre-A, 1981.

Bhattacharya, Rinki. *Bimal Roy—A Man of Silence.* New Delhi: Indus, 1994.

Chakravarty, Sumita S. *National Identity in Indian Popular Cinema 1947–1987.* Austin: University of Texas Press, 1993.

Chatterjee, Gayatri. *Awara.* New Delhi: Wiley Eastern, 1992.

Chengappa, Raj, and Sheela Raval. "Getting Dawood." *India Today,* 3 November 2003.

Chopra, Anupama. *Dilwale Dulhaniya Le Jayenge: The Making of a Blockbuster.* New Delhi: HarperCollins India, 2003.

Cooke, Pam, ed. "Genre." In *The Cinema Book.* London: British Film Institute, 1985.

Das Gupta, Chidananda. *The Painted Face: Studies in India's Popular Cinema.* New Delhi: Roli, 1991.

David, C. R. W. *Cinema as a Means of Communication in Tamil Nadu.* Madras: Christian Literature Society, 1983.

Desai, M. S. M. Interview with film journalist, Mumbai, 2003.

Dharap, B. V. "Dadasaheb Phalke: Father of Indian Cinema." In *70 Years of Indian Cinema,* edited by T. M. Ramachandran. Bombay: CINEMA India-International, 1985.

Dhareshwar, Vivek, and Tejaswini Niranjana. "*Kaadalan* and the Politics of Resignification: Fashion, Violence and the Body." *Journal of Arts and Ideas* 29, January 1996.

Dickey, Sara. "Opposing Faces: Film Star Fan Clubs and the Construction of Class Identities in South India." In *The History, Politics and Consumption of Public Culture in India,* edited by Rachel Dwyer and Christopher Pinney. New Delhi: Oxford University Press, 2001.

———. *Cinema and the Urban Poor in South India.* Cambridge: Cambridge University Press, 1993.

———. "The Politics of Adulation: Cinema and the Production of Politicians in South India." *The Journal of Asian Studies* 52 (2) 1993.

Dirks, Nicholas. "The Home and the Nation: Consuming Culture and Politics in *Roja*." In *The History, Politics and Consumption of Public Culture in India,* edited by Rachel Dwyer and Christopher Pinney. New Delhi: Oxford University Press, 2001.

D'Souza, Marcellus. "*Voice Over: Dubbing Hollywood's Big Business, but It Also Kills the Mood.*" *Economic Times,* 1 June 2004.

Dwyer, Rachel. *All You Want Is Money, All You Need Is Love: Sex and Love in Modern India.* London: Collins, 2000.

———. *Yash Chopra.* New Delhi: Roli, 2002.

Dwyer, Rachel, and Christopher Pinney, eds. *The History, Politics and Consumption of Public Culture in India.* New Delhi: Oxford University Press, 2001.

FICCI (Federation of the Indian Chambers of Commerce and Industry). *The Indian Entertainment Sector: In the Spotlight.* India: KPMG, 2003.

Garga, B. D. *So Many Cinemas: The Motion Picture in India.* Mumbai: Eminence Design Pvt. Ltd., 1996.

Gopalakrishnan, Adoor. *Face to Face— Mukhamukham.* Translated by Shampa Bannerjee. Calcutta: Seagull Books, 1985.

———. *The Rat Trap—Elippathayam.* Translated by Shampa Bannerjee. Calcutta: Seagull Books, 1985.

Gopalakrishnan, V. S. "Four Decades of Tamil Films." *Filmfare*, April 1962.

Gopalan, Lalitha. *Cinema of Interruptions: Action Genres in Contemporary Indian Cinema.* London: British Film Institute, 2002.

Guy, Randor. *Starlight, Starbright: The Early Tamil Cinema.* Chennai: Amra Publishers, 1997.

———, ed. *History of Tamil Cinema.* Madras: International Film Festival of India, 1991.

———. "Tamil Cinema." In *70 Years of Indian Cinema (1913–1983)*, edited by T. M. Ramachandran. Bombay: CINEMA India-International, 1985.

———. *B. N. Reddi: A Monograph.* Pune: NFAI, 1985.

Hardgrave Jr., Robert L. *When Stars Displace the Gods: The Folk Culture of Cinema in Tamil Nadu.* Austin: University of Texas, 1975.

———. "The Celluloid God: M. G. R. and the Tamil Film." *South Asian Review* 4, July 1971.

Hardgrave Jr., Robert L., and Anthony C. Neidhart. "Film and Political Consciousness in Tamil Nadu." *Economic and Political Weekly*, 1 January 1975.

India 2004: A Reference Annual. New Delhi: Publications Division, Ministry of Information and Broadcasting, Government of India, 2004.

Iyer, Lalita. "Real Life Shooting," *The Week*, 20 June 2004.

Kabir, Nasreen Munni. *Indian Film Music.* Unpublished monograph. London, 1991.

Kasbekar, Asha. "Hidden Pleasures: Negotiating the Myth of the Female Ideal in Popular Hindi Cinema." In *The History, Politics and Consumption of Public Culture in India*, edited by Rachel Dwyer and Christopher Pinney. New Delhi: Oxford University Press, 2001.

Katyar, Arun. "Obscene Overtures." *India Today*, 15 January 1994.

Kaul, Gautam. *Cinema and the Indian Freedom Struggle.* New Delhi: Sterling Publishers Private Limited, 1998.

Kesavalu, V., ed. *Impact of MGR Films.* Madras: Movie Appreciation Society, 1989.

Kheterpal, Sunir. *The Indian Motion Picture Industry: A Structural and Financial Perspective.* Mumbai: Rabo Finance Private Limited, 2003.

Madras Institute of Development Studies. *Workshop on Tamil Cinema Dossier, Tamil Cinema: History, Culture, Politics.* Madras 1997.

Menon, Murali. "The Other John." *Sunday Times of India*, 30 May 2004.

Micciollo, Henri. *Guru Dutt.* Paris: L'Avant-Scène du Cinema, 1979.

Nair, P. K., ed. *Fifty Years of Malayalam Cinema.* Trivandrum: Filmotsav 1988 and Kerala State Film Development Corporation, 1988.

Nandy, Ashis. "The Popular Hindi Film: Ideology and First Principles." *India International Centre Quarterly* 8 (1) 1981.

Neale, Stephen. *Genre.* London: British Film Institute, 1980.

Niranjana, Tejaswini, and S. V. Srinivas. "Managing the Crisis: *Bharateeyudu* and the Ambivalence of Being Indian." *Economic and Political Weekly*, 31 (48) 30 November 1996.

Oomen, M. A., and K. V. Joseph. *Economics of Indian Cinema.* New Delhi: Oxford and IBH Publishing, 1991.

Pandian, M. S. S. "Tamil Cultural Elites and Cinema: Outline of an Argument." *Economic and Political Weekly* 31 (15) 13 April 1996.

———. *The Image Trap: M. G. Ramachandran in Film and Politics.* New Delhi: Sage, 1992.

———. "Parashakti: Life and Times of a DMK Film." *Economic and Political Weekly* 26 (11–12) March 1991.

Pendakur, Manjunath. "New Cultural Technologies and the Fading Glitter of Indian Cinema." *Quarterly Review of Film and Video* 11, 1989.

———. "India." In *The Asian Film Industry*, edited by John A. Lent. Bromley: Christopher Helms, 1990.

Perry, Alex. "Queen of Bollywood." *Time*, 27 October 2003.

Pfleiderer, B., and L. Lutze. *The Hindi Film: Agent and Re-agent of Cultural Change.* New Delhi: Manohar, 1985.

Pillay, P. R. S. "Malayalam Cinema" In *70 Years of Indian Cinema (1913–1983)*, edited by

T. M. Ramachandran. Bombay: CINEMA India-International, 1985.

Prasad, Madhava. *Ideology of the Hindi Film: A Historical Construction.* Delhi: Oxford University Press, 1998.

Radhakrishnan, M. G. "All Eyes on Lal." *India Today*, 22 September 2003.

———. *Malayalam Cinema: 50 Years.* Bombay: Sahrudaya Film Society, 1989.

Raghavendra, M. K. "Southern Indian Cinema after 1947: Trends and Thematic Concerns." In *Rasa: The Indian Performing Arts in the Last Twenty-Five Years*, edited by Chidananda Dasgupta, Calcutta: Anamika Kala Sangam, 1995.

Rahman, M., and Arun Katyar. "Underworld Connections." *India Today*, 15 May 1991.

Rai, Amit. "An American Raj in Filmistan: Images of Elvis in Indian films." *Screen* 35 (1) 1994.

Rajadhyaksha, Ashish. "Neo-traditionalism." *Framework* 32–33. London, 1986.

Rajadhyaksha, Ashish, and Paul Willemen. *Encyclopaedia of Indian Cinema.* New Delhi: Oxford University Press, 1999.

Ram, Arun. "Remake Ripples." *India Today*, 25 October 2004.

———. "Flop Show." *India Today*, 19 May 2003.

Ramachandran, T. M., ed. *70 Years of Indian Cinema (1913–1983).* Bombay: CINEMA India-International, 1985.

Ramakrishnaiah, M. V., and H. H. Narahari Rao. *A Glimpse of Kannada Cinema.* Bangalore: Suchitra Film Society, 1992.

Rangoonwalla, Firoze. *Indian Cinema: Past and Present.* New Delhi: Clarion, 1982.

Raval, Sheela. "I Added Petrol." *India Today*, 21 December 1998.

Regional Cinema. Hyderabad: Secunderabad Film Society, 1983.

Reuben, Bunny. *Mehboob: India's de Mille.* New Delhi: Indus, 1994.

Robinson, Andrew. *Satyajit Ray: The Inner Eye.* London: Andre Deutsch, 1989.

Ryerson, Charles. *Regionalism and Religion: The Tamil Renaissance and Popular Hinduism.* Madras: The Christian Literature Society, 1988.

Sandow, Raja. "The Memoirs of Raja Sandow." *The Movie Mirror* 2 (7/8) 1928.

Sankaranarayanan, Vasanthi. "The Star Politicians of the South." In *Rasa: The Indian Performing Arts in the Last Twenty-Five Years*, edited by Chidananda Dasgupta. Calcutta: Anamika Kala Sangam, 1995.

Sastry, K. N. T. *L. V. Prasad: A Monograph.* Delhi: NFAI/Wiley Eastern, 1993.

Singh, Gurbir. "Bollywood Catches India Inc's Fancy, Gets Rs.176cr Funds in '03." *Economic Times*, 16 March 2004.

Sivathamby, Karthigesu. *The Tamil Film as a Medium of Political Communication.* Madras: New Century Book House, 1981.

Skillman, Terri. "The Bombay Hindi Film Song." In *Yearbook for Traditional Music 1986.* New York: International Council for Traditional Music, 1986.

Slingo, Carol J. "The Malayalam Commercial Cinema and the Films of Mammooty." *Asian Cinema* 5 (1) 1990.

Srihari, Gudipoodi. "Telugu Cinema." In *70 Years of Indian Cinema (1913–1983)*, edited by T. M. Ramachandran. Bombay: CINEMA India-International, 1985.

Srinivas, V. S. "Film Culture, Politics and Industry." In *Seminar* 525, April 2003.

———. "Devotion and Defiance in Fan Activity." In *Making Meaning in Indian Cinema*, edited by Ravi S. Vasudevan. New Delhi: Oxford University Press, 2000.

———. "Gandhian Nationalism and Melodrama in the '30s Telugu Cinema." *The Journal of Moving Image* 1 (Autumn) 1999.

Thomas, Rosie. "Indian Cinema: Pleasures and Popularity." *Screen* 26 (3–4) 1985.

———. "Sanctity and Scandal in Mother India." *Quarterly Review of Film and Video* 11, 1989.

Thoraval, Yves. *The Cinemas of India.* New Delhi: Macmillan India, 2001.

Vaidyanatahan, T. G. "Kannada Cinema." In *70 Years of Indian Cinema (1913–1983)*, edited by T. M. Ramachandran. Bombay: CINEMA India-International, 1985.

Vasudev, Aruna. *The New Indian Cinema.* Delhi: Macmillan India, 1986.

Vasudevan, Ravi. "The Melodramatic Mode and

the Commercial Hindi Cinema." *Screen* 30 (3) 1989.

———. "Shifting Codes, Dissolving Identities: The Hindi Social Film of the 1950s as Popular Culture." *Journal of Arts and Ideas* 23–24 (January) 1993.

———. "Bombay and Its Public." In *The History, Politics and Consumption of Public Culture in India*, edited by Rachel Dwyer and Christopher Pinney. New Delhi: Oxford University Press, 2001.

Velicheti, Rajeev. "Women, Violence and Telangana: Changing Constructions in Telugu Cinema." Unpublished paper. Hyderabad: Anveshi/Subaltern Studies Conference, 1993.

Venkatnarayan, S. *NTR: A Biography*. New Delhi: Vikas, 1983.

9

Cricket

"Every nation has a preoccupation," wrote the cricket writer, Vijay Barve, in 1971. "In China, it is Mao; in Latin America, it is Revolution; in India, it is cricket" (Barve 1971, quoted in Guha 2002: 328). But while China and Latin America have overcome their love for Mao and guns, India's obsession with cricket continues unabated.

How cricket, the slow, stately, and quintessentially English game with roots in a cold and damp island thousands of miles away, could have been so successfully transplanted into the hot, dusty, and crowded playing fields of noisy India has been an enigma to most sociologists, social historians, cricket writers, and all other fellow travelers of the sport. But whatever its reasons, it remains India's national sport with a mass following as considerable as that of cinema, and cricketers jostle with film stars to be the nation's reigning deities. Important cricket matches bring the machinery of government and business to a halt as unprecedented numbers of blue- and white-collar workers take sick leave to watch the matches either in person at the stadiums or on television. The audiences for cricket matches reach hundreds of millions, and it is estimated that during the cricket match series held in March-April 2003 between India and its arch-enemy, Pakistan, the total number of viewers watching on television per day exceeded the entire population of Europe (*Prospect* 2004).

There are just a handful of cricket-playing nations around the world, all of them former British colonies. The major cricketing countries are the West Indies, England, South Africa, Pakistan, India, Sri Lanka, Australia, and New Zealand, while Kenya, Zimbabwe, Canada, and Bangladesh represent the less important teams. Most of these former British colonies have very little in common other than their love for cricket, which has been described as the "invisible cord" that binds these Commonwealth nations together.

History of Cricket in India

The origins of cricket are blurred but it is assumed that some form of a game resembling cricket was played in the English countryside around the thirteenth century. By the fifteenth century it had gained in popularity, and by the seventeenth century rules governing the sport were formulated. The first cricket match was played in Sussex in 1697. In eighteenth-century England, the game became gentrified with players dressing in lace shirts and knickerbockers, and bowling underarm. By the nineteenth century, the sport had acquired "gentleman" players and aristocratic patrons who introduced an "elaborate ritualisation" and even created a lofty ideology around the concept of "amateurism" (Nandy 2000: 4–5). The sport made its way into the playing fields of the public schools of Eton and Harrow where it was injected with Victorian values.

Cricket, seen as a quintessentially masculine activity, was considered "the most powerful condensation of Victorian elite values . . . It expressed the codes that were expected to govern all masculine behaviour: sportsmanship, a sense of fair play, thorough control over the expression of strong sentiments by players on the field, subordination of personal sentiments and interests to those of the group, unquestioned loyalty to the team" (Appadurai 1998: 91–92). It is said that Reverend James Pycroft encapsulated the spirit of the game in 1851 when he declared that breaches of unwritten rules were "not cricket." For example, it is not cricket to dispute the umpire's decision or to claim an opponent is out when you know he is not, or to disturb someone's concentration by swearing at him. And, although players of contemporary cricket routinely defy all these unwritten rules of the sport, the notion of voluntary decent behavior, which has reached far beyond the field of play, remains defined by it (*Economist* 2000a).

The sport and its philosophical baggage was introduced to the Indian subcontinent by British colonels and popularized by the British Army. Soon the game became one of the central activities at that great bastion of British social life in India—the "Club." The Club or *gymkhana* was, as cricket historian Ramachandra Guha points out, the refuge of the expatriate British. There amidst its all-white members, the expatriate could take comfort in English food and English entertainment and escape for a few hours from the dirt, chatter, smells, people, and chaos of India (Guha 2002).

Gymkhana is an Anglo-Indian word incorporating both the English gymnasium or gymnastics and the Hindustani *gend khana*—a "ball house" or racquet house. In the *gymkhana* the British whiled away the time indulging in tennis, billiards, rifle shooting, whist, and cricket. Many were devoted to cricket, as was the Calcutta Cricket Club founded in 1792, the first of its kind outside England (Guha 2002). However, it was Bombay (now Mumbai) not Calcutta (now Kolkata) that was to establish itself as the cricket capital of India, and unlike its pastoral origins in England, cricket in India was to remain an exclusively urban form of recreation.

The British had never intended to impart the intricacies of the game of cricket to the Indians. It was after all *their* game, which *they* played in the safety of *their* clubs. In Bombay, it was played at one end of the esplanade or *maidan*, a large open space outside the city fort area that had been cleared to provide a range of fire in the eventuality of a French attack. The inquisitive inhabitants of Bombay watched the British indulge in their sport, and the Parsis (or Parsees) first decided to imitate this

The 1st British Royal Welch Fusiliers Cricket Eleven, during their service in India, 1 January 1888. (Hulton Archive/Getty Images)

new and exotic form of recreational sport by improvising with makeshift equipment. They used umbrellas for cricket bats, chimney pots for wickets, and a ball sewn together from rags (Guha 2002).

Parsis and the Parsi Gymkhana

The Parsis or Zoroastrians are a small, entrepreneurial community originally from Persia who had landed on the west coast of India in eighth century AD seeking refuge from the invading Muslim Arabs. In India they adopted the Gujerati language and mode of dress while continuing to practice their religion freely. As a minority, with a population that was diminishing at an alarming rate (and continues to do so today), the Parsis saw collaboration with the

colonial British not only as a useful conduit for business contacts but also as a bulwark against the hundreds of millions of Hindus and Muslims.

The seriousness and skill with which the Parsis pursued the sport can be gauged by the fact that in 1848 they formed the Oriental Club (later to became the Young Zoroastrian Club) and within the next decade there were around thirty more such Parsi clubs dotted around Bombay. Many of these clubs received financial assistance from the newly rich, successful Parsi entrepreneurs. In 1877, they invited the Bombay Gymkhana, the *pukka*, all-white club that had established itself on one end of the maidan, to a cricket match. The normally disdainful British agreed to play; an acceptance lubricated no doubt by the offer of Sir Cowasji Jehangir to pay for the furnishings of the Bombay Gymkhana's clubhouse pavilion. For Sir Cowasji it was a shrewd business move made in case he needed to ask for future concessions from the British colonials (Guha 2002).

At the first such cricketing encounter, the Parsis put up a stout resistance but were no match for their English counterparts. Undaunted they persevered at the game and within a decade they were heartened enough by their progress to undertake a visit to England in 1886 to play the smaller clubs and teams—a trip that was unfortunately both a financial and cricketing disaster.

Meanwhile a long-running conflict over the use of the *maidan* raged between the amateur cricketing enthusiasts and the British Army's polo teams who used the same grounds for a polo match twice a week. When the polo teams played, they wrecked the myriad carefully nurtured pitches. A long correspondence between Shapoorji Sohrabjee, a chronicler of Parsi cricket, and the Bombay Gymkhana followed. Finally, in 1887, the Bombay Presidency decided to allocate a plot of land further north of the city in newly reclaimed land by the sea, and the Parsis financed and built their own Parsi *gymkhana* there (Guha 2002). By now the Parsis were deemed to have sufficiently improved their performance on the cricket pitches to undertake another tour of England in 1888, this time with far better results. According to cricket writer Mihir Bose, the Parsis, used to the disdain and the condescension of the British in India, were genuinely surprised by the civility and courtesy with which they were received by the English in England (Bose 2002).

When a team of English cricketers undertook a tour of India in 1889–1890 to play the all-white English gymkhanas that were dotted around the Indian subcontinent, one match was earmarked for Parsi Gymkhana in Bombay. It took place in January 1890, and was the first important cricketing event in India. At the match, not only did the Parsis win against the visiting team, but they also inflicted the visiting team's only defeat of the tour.

Bose describes the carnival atmosphere that surrounded the victorious day: "Some 12,000 people—a 'variegated Oriental crowd' . . . gathered to watch the match. Along the maidan, *shamianas*—Indian-style marquees—were erected to house the glittering members of society. There were Parsee priests present in their ceremonial dress invoking the assistance of their prophet Zoroaster and, as one observer noted, 'dark-eyed daughters of the land for the first time mustered strongly.'" And when the Parsis won: "One of the leaders of the community felt it was the greatest Parsee show since they had been beaten by the Arabs in the battle of Navahand [in AD 641], a defeat which led to their exile in India. Parsee women garlanded the victors and the Parsee rich of Bombay held lavish parties. It was as if a people, which had lost its country in a battle long ago, had suddenly rediscovered itself on a cricket field" (Bose 2002: 26).

Many British expatriates watching the developments from their armchairs in the clubs saw ominous signs for the Empire in the cricket matches between the Indians and the British. "While the British may appear to be as firmly in our Indian saddle as ever, it is well that we should win and not lose whatever matches we play the natives," wrote one. "For we rule in India by conquest, by strength, by prestige and we cannot afford that these bonds of empire should be loosened even through the medium of so trivial an affair as a game of cricket" (quoted in Guha 2002: 113).

However, Lord Harris, the cricketing governor of Bombay (1890–1893), who had allowed the match to proceed and had even called the Parsi team to lunch, deemed that the sport would aid Britain's "civilizing mission" in its colonies. In this Lord Harris was simply concurring with the Victorian middle-class views about the character-building virtues of cricket. It would thus serve as a means of "solidifying the bonds of empire, lubricating state dealings between various Indian 'communities,' which might otherwise degenerate into communal (Hindu/Muslim) riots and implanting English ideals of manliness, stamina and vigour into Indian groups seen as lazy, enervated and effete" (Appadurai 1998: 93). Furthermore, the sport was going to epitomize the triumph of a superior culture over an indigenous one, and it would hopefully make the native more grateful for colonial rule. Once the colonial government had decided to redeem the natives through the Victorian virtues embodied in the game of cricket, the sport began to be encouraged at Indian universities, colleges, and schools.

Triangulars, Quadrangulars, and Pentagulars

Meanwhile the Hindus of Bombay, spurred by the example of the Parsis, started their own cricket clubs, the first being the Bombay Union Cricket Club in 1866. Soon other clubs followed, and like all things Hindu, membership to these clubs was segregated along caste lines. And since caste is also defined by region, the clubs bore names like the Gowd Saraswat Brahmin Club, the Kshatriya Cricket Club, the Gujerati Union Club, the Maratha Club, and the Telugu Young Cricketers (Guha 2002). Not all Hindus were enamored of the British sport, and many decried the newfound craze for cricket among the urban youth, condemning it as a form of subservience to foreign culture and values. But this did not in any way diminish the Hindu enthusiasm for the sport and in due course, after the usual supplications to the concerned government authorities, the Hindus were allotted a plot of land, next to the Parsi Gymkhana, where, with the assistance of prosperous traders and other rich patrons, the Paramanand Jivandas (or PJ) Hindu Gymkhana, named after its principal benefactor, was established in 1892.

By now the matches between the Parsi Gymkhana and the Bombay Gymkhana had become annual events. With the arrival of the Hindu Gymkhana fielding an all-Hindu team in 1907, the event became the "Triangular." A few years later in 1912, when the Islam (or Muslim) *gymkhana* was founded, it too joined the league and the tournament became the "Quadrangular." Twenty-five years later, in 1937, the Quadrangular became the "Pentangular" when a team called "the rest" made up of the religious minorities (Indian Catholics, Indian Jews, Anglo-Indians—that is, mixed-race Indians—and so forth) was constituted.

The tournament was divided along religious lines. Consequently it was extremely competitive, as the various religious communities regrouped around their teams to cheer them on. In the beginning, the matches were free but soon spectators were charged a fee to watch. The matches eventually became extremely commercial, garnering the *gymkhanas* and clubs huge revenues through ticket sales. The matches were played through the decades of the 1910s, 1920s, and 1930s, and continued until the winter of 1945–1946 before succumbing to the political realities of religious violence and the partition of India.

The Quadrangular matches during the 1920s were the highlight of the cricketing calendar and confirmed Bombay as the cricket capital of the subcontinent. Each year as the tournament approached all of Bombay went cricket crazy. The sporting competition, fueled by political and commercial rivalries among the three religious communities and intensified by the deep religious divisions that existed in the city, rendered these matches the most exciting events in Bombay.

The 1920s marked the glory years of these matches. Teams were chosen strictly along religious lines. At first the Hindu and European players were required to be residents of the Bombay Presidency, but later this requirement was waived and the four (and later five) communities could field players from anywhere in India. What was at first an urban contest limited to the city of Bombay had grown into a de facto national tournament with national talent streaming along religious and racial lines into the five teams—British, Parsis, Hindus, Muslims, and "the rest."

Crowds thronged to the encounters in the *maidan* and the number of spectators grew from 15,000 to 20,000, then 30,000, and later 40,000. When the matches ultimately ceased in the 1940s, it was estimated that nearly 50,000 spectators attended these annual events. It is also estimated that the matches made around INR 150,000 (US$3,500) in annual profit, no mean sum in those days (Majumdar 2004a). There were commentaries in the English language on All India Radio. The English language and the vernacular presses delivered considered opinions and homilies on the intricacies of the game, the cricketing tactics of the teams, and the failures and successes of individual players—all of which helped to popularize the game with the city residents.

With such a huge spectatorship, successful players became stars overnight and were showered with the unrestrained adulation of Bombay cricket fans. At the time, the cricketing stars of Bombay included Palwankar Baloo (from the untouchable caste); the brilliant batsman C. K. Nayudu, a stylish man with film star looks and the sartorial elegance to match; Lala Amarnath, the fiery northerner; Vinoo Mankad;

Indian cricketer Lala Amarnath (1911– 2000) during the All-India tour of England on 30 April 1936. Amarnath played for India between 1933 and 1953. (A. Hudson/Topical Press Agency/Getty Images)

Mushtaq Ali; Vijay Merchant; Wazir Ali; and Vijay Hazare. Many of the star players of the Quadrangulars and the later Pentangulars continued to dominate Indian cricket well into the 1950s.

The matches also highlighted the curious anomalies of cricket in Bombay, where the most cosmopolitan Indian city thrived on the most communal of sporting rivalries, and the most foreign of games had been most successfully indigenized and "vernacularized" (Appadurai 1998). Elsewhere in the country, there were a myriad of cricket clubs sponsored by the Indian princes, business houses, banks, railways, universities and colleges, and other organizations. In fact, many of the stars of the Quadrangulars and Pentangulars were in the employ of the Indian princes who sported heterogeneous teams with players of all faiths and even a few English players.

But few of the matches organized by these other teams generated the same sporting thrills as the communal Quadrangulars—and later the Pentangulars— driven as they were by intense "Hindu prejudice, Parsi social snobbery, Muslim insularity and British racial superiority" (Guha 2002: 307). In fact, encouraged by the financial and sporting successes of the Bombay fixtures, Karachi, a port city like Bombay and now in Pakistan, inaugurated its own Pentangulars, while Lahore, in the northwest and now also in Pakistan, hosted a Triangular played by Hindus, Sikhs, and Muslims.

The Princes

A substantial contribution to the development of Indian cricket was made by the patronage of the Indian princes. During the *raj*, the princes ruled approximately a third of the country, while the rest was under direct British rule and divided into eight provinces. The size and wealth of these princes differed enormously. Some, like the maharajas of Mysore and Kashmir, reigned over very large, rich kingdoms. The Nizam of Hyderabad, then one of the richest men in the world, ruled over a kingdom that was bigger in size than France; while the state of Bhadwa with a population of 1,401 had a ruler who worked as a railway guard before he ascended his throne (Bose 2002).

It was the rulers of the middling states who saw cricket as a means of establishing closer links with the aristocracy in Britain and the colonial government in India, the latter being their de facto overlord. The very large states did not have to bother with cricket (although some like the Maharaja of Kashmir did), as their sheer size and wealth provided them with adequate political weight, while the very small states were really too poor to indulge in the sport even if they wanted to.

The princes who embraced cricket as a means of political advancement often hired English coaches to train their teams, and many Indian princes took to playing the game in their idiosyncratic, princely ways. Some were able players; others showed no traces of talent, which did not in the least deter them from playing. Guha cites the example of the Maharaja of Kashmir, who enjoyed batting but completely disregarded the other aspects of the game. Consequently when his team was playing he would remain in his prayer room awaiting a telephone message indicating that it was his turn to bat. Thereupon, "a car, still a rarity in India, brought the Maharaja to the ground, where pads and gloves were reverentially put on him by his valets. The Maharaja would walk on the pitch, his hands on his helpers' shoulders. The bowlers were instructed and paid to bowl a series of slow long hops and full tosses, deftly aided by fielders' feet across the boundary line. In time the scorer would announce that the Maharaja had reached his century" (Guha 2002: 106).

Ranji

One of the greatest batsmen of all time, not just of Indian cricket but of the game of cricket itself, was HH Sir Ranjitsinhji Vibhaji, Maharaja Jam Saheb of Nawanagar (1872–1933), generally known as Ranji. He was the first cricketer of Indian origin to achieve international greatness and immortality. However Ranji was a resolute Anglophile—he never played cricket for India and always considered himself an English cricketer. Hence all his achievements were exclusively in England. In fact, he exerted himself very little either for Indian cricket or for his Nawanagar subjects. According to his biographer, Mario Rodrigues, Ranji's taxation and personal expenses were the highest among the princely states while his spending on education and public health was among the lowest (Rodrigues 2003).

Social historians have offered a variety of explanations for the enigma that was Ranji and his sycophantic cultivation of all things English (Nandy 2000; Rodrigues 2003). Ranji was the adopted son of the heirless Jam Saheb of the tiny state of Nawanagar, and his claim to the throne was always very tenuous. Educated at the Rajkumar College in Rajkot that was traditionally patronized by the Indian princes, Ranji went on to study at Cambridge and play cricket for the university. After Cambridge, Ranji played for Sussex County. As the fame of his extraordinary cricketing skills spread, it opened doors to the highest social circles in England and imperial Britain began to fawn over the exotic prince whose cricketing skills were now becoming legendary. In 1897, he dedicated a book on cricket, *The Jubilee Book of Cricket*, to Queen Victoria to celebrate the sixtieth year of her reign.

Ranji, according to the critic Arjun Appadurai, was the quintessential and living trope of an "Oriental" form of cricketing skill. He was seen to bring a peculiarly Indian genius to batting. He represented the "glamorous obverse of the effeminacy, laziness and lack of stamina that many colonial theorists thought Indians represented." Thus, in him "wile became guile, trickery became magic, weakness became suppleness, effeminacy was transformed into grace. This Orientalist glow, of course, had a great deal to do with Ranji's impeccable social credentials, his total devotion to English institutions (all the way from college to Crown), and his unswerving loyalty to the empire" (Appadurai 1998: 96–97).

Whether his enthusiasm for all things British was evidence of astute political expediency motivated by the fact that his was a disputed title remains an enigma. In any event, his loyalty to Britain paid off and his accession to the throne was achieved thanks to the interference of the colonial connections and the British Resident (Rodrigues 2003). Later, during the freedom struggle, Ranji remained steadfastly loyal to the Empire. His opposition to the nationalist movement was a political move to save himself and his tiny kingdom from being absorbed into the Indian state, which, more than fifteen years after his death, it eventually was.

Baloo

Cricket touched the lives of both the great and the small in India. While Ranji frequented the rarefied circle of British aristocrats, a more humble genius (and Ranji's contemporary) was being nurtured in the all-white Poona Club where Palwankar Baloo, an untouchable by caste, was a groundsman. In his spare time he made a little extra money by bowling to those keen on getting in some batting practice. Word of Baloo's extraordinary bowling talent had reached the conservative Brahmins of Poona (now Pune), which created a dilemma for them—should they invite Baloo to play in their matches against the British and thereby have a good chance of victory against the supercilious British or should they uphold caste prejudices and risk defeat and disdain while such precious talent lay wasted? After much discussion, they reached a compromise: they invited Baloo to play on their team as long as the caste taboos were maintained between games. Thus he did not have meals in the company of the other players, he drank his tea from a separate container, and he used separate facilities located outside the pavilion (Guha 2002). But, his spectacular bowling performance was heralded all over Poona, and his low caste origins made him a hero of the social reformers.

Eventually Baloo made his way to the Bombay matches where, ironically, his struggle for recognition and equality among the Hindus (he was never officially made captain of the team despite being the best and most senior player) mirrored the Hindus' struggle for parity with the British.

Meanwhile, the social and political success that Ranji enjoyed with the British aristocracy and the representatives of the *raj* through his cricketing skills encouraged other princes to emulate his strategy. And like all things to do with the Indian princes, their competition to own the best teams, to captain "national" teams on tours of England, and to curry favor with the British were rife with intrigue, vicious backstabbing, and betrayal. The most prominent and generous of the princely patrons of cricket was the priapic Bhupendra (or Bhupinder) Singh, Maharaja of Patiala, whose exploits in the bedroom, rather than on the cricket pitches, have been the stuff of legends. His polo team had already enhanced the reputation of Patiala and brought him great political benefit, and the magnanimous maharaja decided to extend his patronage to cricket as well. He had several Indian and British cricketers on his payroll; he employed English coaches (usually retired English professionals) to train him and his other players; and he often sponsored the Marylebone Cricket Club (MCC) tours to India.

One such tour was the 1926–1927 MCC tour of India. During the tour, the visitors played English clubs as well as the various maharajas' teams. Impressed by the talent of players such as C. K. Nayudu and others, many of them stars of the Quadrangular and Pentangular but also part of royal cricket teams, further tours were contemplated. But cricket in India was still a diffused and unorganized affair. It was thereupon decided that a central governing body for the sport was required and in 1928 the Board of Control for Cricket in India, which would oversee the disparate cricket teams scattered across the country, was duly created. It would act as a supervisory body arranging foreign tours and would speak for Indian cricket. And naturally, the maharajas would be the captains of these touring teams to England, even if they were never the best players.

The 1930s Onward

In the 1930s, away from the indolent maharajas and their sycophantic coteries, Mahatma Gandhi's efforts to push for Indian independence intensified. A civil disobedience movement began and there were strikes in many cities. The colonial government tried to use tough repressive measures, and, by the end of the 1930s, 60,000 people were jailed. Throughout the 1930s, political turmoil led to frequent cancellations of the communal cricket matches in Bombay. In other parts of the country, such as Karachi in northwest India, where the effects of the civil disobedience movement were not so strongly felt and where the communal riots were, at least initially, less violent, the matches continued unhindered.

In 1932, while Gandhi languished in jail, the Indian cricket team toured England under the captaincy of the maharaja of Porbandar, who is said to have owned more Rolls Royce cars than scored runs on the playing fields (Guha 2002). They played the first Test (a Test match is an official match between two countries played over five days with each team generally playing two innings) between India and England at Lord's in London. India was completely outplayed despite fine performances by C. K. Nayudu and Wazir Ali. Unfortunately, two Indian princes, K. S. Duleepsinhji, the nephew of Ranji, and the Nawab of Pataudi, who were playing for England at the time and who could have made a difference to the Indian side, had refused to play for India.

Meanwhile in India another cricketing body was in the process of being created. In 1933, the Cricket Club of India (CCI) was established along the lines of the MCC that had been founded in London towards the end of the eighteenth century and was the highest cricketing authority in England. The aim of the CCI was to promote the game and make it popular throughout India by encouraging it at schools and colleges and arranging for coaching. In July 1934, the Board of Control for Cricket set out to establish an interprovincial and secular tournament along the lines of the English County Championships. The Maharaja of Patiala donated a trophy, named after the great cricketer, Ranji, who had died in 1933. The first Ranji Trophy matches were inaugurated in the winter of 1934–1935 and the contestants were the dozen or so teams that had registered with the CCI.

The establishment of the secular Ranji Trophy was a direct challenge to the Quadrangular matches and the hegemony of Bombay as the cricketing capital of India. Faced with such a threat, the temporarily suspended Quadrangular was immediately reinstated in 1936, much to the delight of cricket fans. Furthermore, All India Radio decided to broadcast a live ball-by-ball commentary during these matches throughout the tournaments. Cricket had now become a mass spectacle.

The Ranji Trophy matches were to compete head-on with the Quadrangular and later Pentangular matches, particularly since from 1937 onward they were played at the same venue, the CCI's Brabourne Stadium, the first stadium built specifically for cricket in India. Although it was named for the departing British governor, Lord Brabourne, the maharajas, notably the maharaja of Patiala, and other rich Indian patrons, had raised most of the money for its construction.

The Quadrangular became the Pentangular in 1937. The first Pentangular matches were played in Bombay, with a new team comprising "the rest," a group consisting mainly of Christians but also adherents of any faith followed by Indians that was not covered by the Hindus, Muslims, and Parsis. However, the Hindu team withdrew over a rather petty pecuniary altercation between the Bombay and the PJ Hindu gymkhanas, so a truly five-way match did not take place until the following year.

In 1938, war broke out in Europe, but, like World War I, when India had remained largely untouched, this war did not disturb the progress of cricket within India, although it did put a stop to the tours of England. In the political domain, there was more disagreement between the Indian National Congress (INC) and the British colonial government, particularly since the British viceroy had declared India's unconditional support for the war effort without consulting its leaders. There were fights within the INC and also between the INC and the Muslim League, leading to civil unrest, police firings, deaths, and the jailing of the leaders of the INC, including Gandhi.

In 1942, Gandhi launched the Quit India movement and in the increasingly volatile political situation and growing animosity between the Hindus and the Muslims, and the INC and the Muslim League, the Pentangular was canceled, but it was back on track by 1943. The matches were now the platform for new stars such as Vijay Merchant and Vijay Hazare. During the 1944–1945 tournament played against a background of intense political tensions be-

The vice-captain of the Indian cricket team, V. M. Merchant. He holds the record score in India of 359 not out, May 1946. (Raymond Kleboe/Picture Post/Getty Images)

tween the Hindus and Muslims in many parts of India, the Pentangular match final between the Hindus and Muslims in Bombay was very closely fought and extremely thrilling.

By 1946, the war had ended and demands for the creation of a separate Pakistan, emboldened by the Muslim League's victories in the regional elections, were growing. There were public meetings, demonstrations, strikes, and many outbreaks of violence. In Bombay, although the Pentangular was played during the winter of 1945–1946, the tournament was dying on its feet. With violent rioting and thousands being killed in some parts of India, attendance for matches at the

Brabourne Stadium dropped drastically as the fear of violence and communal conflagration in the streets kept the fans away.

India became independent in 1947 and the independent state of Pakistan was created. The Pentangular arranged along religious lines was never played again. In its place, the secular Ranji Trophy became the focal point of zonal competition with heterogeneous teams. But the crowds that had flocked to the Pentangular were conspicuously absent, confirming that it was religious competitiveness that had given early Indian cricket its edge and commercial interest.

Post Independence

After independence, India became an official Test playing nation and joined the circuit of tours to and from other cricketing nations. Between 1932 and 1947, India had played a total of seven Test matches all against England; between 1947 and 1957 it played forty-two Test matches, not counting the fifteen unofficial Tests against visiting Commonwealth sides; and during the decade of the 1960s India played fifty-two Tests against teams from England, Pakistan, the West Indies, and New Zealand (Bose 2002). Never before had the Indian fan seen such an array of international cricketing talent.

Before 1947, Bombay was the capital and the very center of Indian cricket. With the end of the Pentangular, and the rise of the Ranji Trophy matches, a process of dispersion began and new centers for cricket developed in other parts of India. In the winter of 1934–1935, when the Ranji Trophy was inaugurated, the various teams belonging to princes, businesses, banks, provinces, and presidencies that had registered with the CCI were allowed to compete. In 1956, the Indian government restructured the provinces along linguistic lines and the old presidencies, provinces, and royal fiefdoms were replaced by new states. In cricket, these new states were granted their own teams but the older teams were allowed to carry on despite the demise of the geographical entities that they represented.

In Mumbai, the *gymkhanas* abandoned their religious proclivities and became secular and cosmopolitan, and from 1949 onward they began accepting members of all faiths. At the same time, the center of cricket moved northwards from the *maidan* in south Mumbai toward Dadar and Shivaji Park, once suburbs of the city but now at the heart of the metropolis. In the winter of 1961–1962, the Board of Control for Cricket in India started a zonal competition with six competing teams in each zone and the winners qualifying for the Duleep Trophy, named after K. S. Duleepsinhji, the cricketer nephew of Ranji who had died young of an illness.

Although cricket had by now established firm roots in India, there was still the occasional nationalist politician who decried the Indian love of the game as a vestige of outdated colonialism. The attempts of B. V. Keskar, the new minister of Information and Broadcasting, to remove live commentaries of cricket matches and all popular film songs from the airwaves in a determined bid to "improve" the tastes of ordinary Indians, proved short-lived. Already in 1946, he was questioning whether cricket would not "Quit India" with the British (Keskar 1946). For many nationalist politicians, the continued popularity of the sport provided a convenient political platform to harangue the general public. Many cricket historians have recounted the story of Ram

Indian skipper Ajit Wadekar and teammate B. S. Chandraserhar wave to cheering crowds at the Oval after India won the Test series against England, 24 August 1971. (Central Press/Getty Images)

Manohar Lohia, the socialist member of Parliament who hectored people in cafés on India's continued mental enslavement to the British through the game of cricket, only to stroll outside and check on the latest Test score at one of the neighboring cigarette kiosks, which usually had transistor radios blaring live commentary on the matches (Bose 2002; Guha 2002).

However, despite the increased number of matches and tournaments, India (like Pakistan and New Zealand) was, at the time, really a second-rate cricketing country—the top national teams being those of England, Australia, and the West Indies. (South Africa was later excluded from this elite group as a result of the sporting ban imposed in 1970 by the Commonwealth and other world bodies for its apartheid policies.) This was to change in 1971 with India's dramatic and comprehensive wins over England and the West Indies. Suddenly India had been catapulted from the second rung into the top league of cricketing nations. The world, it seems, had woken up to India's cricketing prowess and for the first time since the first Test matches were played between England and India, the English began sending their best team on tour to India.

It was also in the 1970s that the world of cricket was to witness a new phenomenon—the one-day match. As already mentioned, on international tours, cricket was played in a series of five-day matches in two innings for each side. Despite the six-day events (there was one rest day between the five days), it was always possible for a match to end in a draw. However in the newly introduced one-day match, each side played just one inning of fifty "overs" each, which meant that the match ended the same day and a result was guaranteed. The one-day cricket match transformed the slow and stately game into something fast, exciting, and dramatic.

In 1977, international cricket witnessed the arrival of the Australian magnate Kerry Packer. Having failed to win the rights to televise the England-Australia Tests, Packer organized a rival cricket circuit called the World Series Cricket, with teams comprising stars players poached from the national teams of England, Australia, Pakistan, and the West Indies. Indian players were unaffected although there were rumors that the great Indian batsman, Sunil Gavaskar (one of the best players of all times), was approached. Thanks to Packer, the world of cricket realized for the first time that their players were bankable commodities.

In 1979 India had played in twenty-six Test matches in the course of just one year. According to Bose, part of the reason for this intense cricketing activity was the fear among the various national cricketing boards that if they didn't keep the players busy they would join Packer's band of merry men (Bose 2002).

In 1975, the first World Cup was contested with all competing nations playing one-day matches. The West Indies, then an unbeatable side, won. At the next World Cup four years later in 1979, the West Indies won again. However in 1983, India emerged as the surprise winner of the third World Cup when it comprehensively beat the all-powerful West Indies in England. It was India's first international title and the country went mad with joy. The re-

turning team had an audience with Mrs. Gandhi, the Indian prime minister, on its victorious return, and overnight the players became national heroes. Coincidentally, in the early 1980s, Mrs. Gandhi embarked on an ambitious expansion of terrestrial networks inside the country. Consequently millions witnessed the first Indian victory in cricket on their television screens.

Jointly with Pakistan, India hosted the following World Cup in 1987. It was the first World Cup to be held outside England. In all, twenty-seven matches were played to capacity crowds at twenty-one venues scattered across the subcontinent. South Asia was awash with cricket. Shifting the World Cup venue was a major breakthrough: England was until that moment the epicenter of international cricket and with the confidence of this knowledge came its authority over the rest of the cricketing world. Shifting the World Cup's venue marked the beginning of the dissembling of England's authority over the game.

Cricket in Contemporary India

Today, India ranks high among the handful of countries that play cricket. It has its fair share of victories and losses, and world-class performances by its cricketing stars. However, as a team, it is constantly criticized for lacking consistency and team spirit. All too often players display bouts of brilliance before succumbing to dismal performances. Apart from the variable performances of the team, the game of cricket in India today is colored by three attributes that lie outside the actual mechanics of the game but nevertheless end up informing the sport at home and abroad. These attributes are sporting nationalism, commercialism, and match-fixing.

Cricket and Nationalism

Cricket has become the arena for an expression of sporting nationalism among some of its supporters, a nationalism that borders on xenophobia. During the British *raj*, cricket was the arena wherein scores could be settled with the colonizers. A victory over the English by the Parsis at the Bombay Gymkhana was the reversal of their humiliating defeat in Persia by the invading Arabs and subsequent exile to India in the eighth century. Similarly when the Hindus won over the British team of the Bombay Gymkhana, the victory was a soothing balm for their humiliating status as a colonized people. It also gave birth to the realization that if the Indians could beat the British at their own game in the sporting field then they could surely wrest independence from them in the political field.

The noise and energy of the Quadrangular (and later the Pentangular) matches were expressions of heightened excitement because allegiances to parochial and religious identities in the intercommunal matches meant that victories or defeats were not just a matter of sporting prowess but of communal and religious prestige. Since independence, the Ranji and Duleep Trophies, with their interprovincial, interzonal matches played by heterogeneous, secular teams, blocked the outlet for hyperemotional nationalism. It was only with the emergence of India as a major cricketing nation after its victories in 1971 that the old excitement returned. This sporting nationalism is particularly evident whenever India plays Pakistan.

Part of this emotional excess lies in the fact that India has no other sport at which it excels. True, there have been a few tennis players such as Leander Paes and Mahesh Bhupathy who have won major victories at Grand Slam matches in tennis, but theirs has been as a doubles act, a neglected side of the tournaments. Paes was also the third Indian to win a junior championship but he never won a major singles title thereafter. Indians now scrutinize the progress of the young tennis star Sania Mirza, who has only just started making her mark in international tennis. Karthikeyan Narain too has just started making a mark in Formula One racing, and the Indian golfer Arjun Atwal has not yet broken through the barrier to become one of the world's top few players.

Between 1926 and 1960 India had been Olympic champions in field hockey. When, in 1960, the Europeans changed the venues to Astroturf surfaces, which favored their power play, the Indian skills of elegant dribbling and passing the ball were diminished. The terrorist acts unleashed on the ordinary people in the Punjab by Sikh separatists in the early 1980s were also major blows to the recovery of Indian hockey, particularly since Punjab is a major hockey-playing center.

In brief, India's performance in sports other than cricket has been especially abysmal as proved by its performance at successive Olympics. At the 2004 Olympics held in Athens, India won just one silver medal while four years earlier at the 2000 Olympics held in Sydney, Indian athletes came home clutching a solitary bronze medal to show its billion-strong population. (In sharp contrast, China, a similarly developing nation with an equally sizable population, is one of the biggest winners at the Olympics.)

With the vacuum created by India's inability to win in any sports other than occasionally in cricket, it is cricket that carries the burden of Indian aspirations. Cricketers are thus asked to redeem the failures of the nation and the brutality of poverty. And the greatest of these burdens falls on the shoulders of a star performer, someone like Sachin Tendulkar, who, as Guha has pointed out, must pacify a billion Indians (Guha 2002).

To make his point Guha quotes the Indian critic, C. P. Surendran, who eloquently points to the Indian hunger for heroes:

> Every time Tendulkar walks to the crease, a whole nation marches with him to the battle arena. A pauper people pleading for relief, remission from the lifelong anxiety of being Indian, by joining in spirit with their visored saviour . . . Tendulkar lifts his gleaming bat, points it like a sword towards the TV cameras after his customary hundred, and a million hands go up in blessing; and in begging, pleading silently for redemption from the oppressive reality of their existence; seeking a moment's liberation from their India-bondage through the exhilarating grace of one accidental bat. One billion hard-pressed Indians. Just one hero . . . (Surendran 1998; also quoted in Guha 2002: 352)

But this intense nationalism in cricket has led to aggressive behavior in the stadiums. Players are sometimes pelted with stones and bottles, which on more than one occasion has led to the dismissal of all spectators from the stadium before the game is allowed to continue. On other occasions spectators have trashed and burned down stadiums. Politicians such as Bal Thackeray, a cricket enthusiast and leader

Indian batsman Sachin Tendulkar raises his bat to acknowledge the crowd during the fifth and final day's play of the second Test match between India and South Africa in Calcutta on 2 December 2004. Off-spinner Harbhajan Singh took seven wickets as India crushed South Africa by eight wickets to clinch the two-Test series 1–0. (Jayanta Shaw/Reuters/Corbis)

of the extreme Hindu nationalist party, the Shiv Sena, who until recently used to run the city of Mumbai like his private fiefdom, have used their hateful ideologies to whip up emotions, have threatened violence during matches with Pakistan, and have even torn up pitches to ambush the matches (*Indian Express* 1999).

Commercialization of Cricket

Another aspect of modern day cricket in India is the rapid commercialization of the sport. India's fortuitous win of the World Cup in 1983 neatly coincided with the expansion of television in the early 1980s and resulted in several tens of millions of spectators watching India's victory on screen. When the subsequent World Cup matches were jointly hosted by India and Pakistan in 1987, advertisers scrambled to promote their products. However the true effects of commercialization were not felt until 1996 when India and Pakistan, this time with Sri Lanka, once again hosted the World Cup. Satellite television had been making rapid inroads into Indian cultural life since 1991 and this time the matches were watched by hundreds of millions, all supporting India's bid for the title, which it, unfortunately, did not even come close to winning.

With the economic liberalization that began in 1991 and hundreds of millions of television viewers watching because of satellite television, more and more of the population had discovered the joys of consumerism. The spread of television has not been confined to the major cities but has entered smaller towns deeper and deeper into the hinterlands, and advertisers have been looking for heroes to endorse their products. The 1996 World Cup was said to have garnered nearly 400 million viewers.

The advertising companies were quick to take advantage of the advertising bonanza that hosting the World Cup offered. Pepsi and Coca-Cola, once banned during the prime ministership of Indira Gandhi, fought a bitter battle to become official sponsors of the match; makers of consumer electronics and fast foods could not get enough air time, so great was the scramble to advertise on television. The advertising frenzy astounded Indian and international observers. In 2002, Indian television networks spent INR 9 billion (US$200 million) to buy the telecast rights to international cricket matches (Malik 2002) and the figure had grown by 350 percent for the 2003 World Cup.

Cricket stars are used for their personal endorsements and so great is their commercial worth that it was feared that India might boycott the 2003 World Cup because Indian cricketers stood to lose several million dollars as a result of ICC's seven-year US$550 million exclusive agreement with Global Cricketing Corporation (associated with Rupert Murdoch's News Corporation) in 2000. Much as they would have liked to, the ICC was in no position to challenge India, whose participation brought in 60 percent of the revenues and half of the world's viewers. While the English and Australian cricketing boards were wealthy enough to withstand the financial strain of a reduced income, the smaller countries such as Sri Lanka, Pakistan, and Kenya would have found it very difficult to continue. This is because broadcasters in India usually buy advertisements in all the tournament matches and if India were not to participate, their advertising revenues would also not be forthcoming to these countries.

Thanks to the advertising bonanza, the Board of Control for Cricket in India (BCCI) is the wealthiest cricket board in the world. Its revenues have risen from INR 20 million (US$500,000) in the 1990s to the current INR 14 billion (US$320 million) in 2004. Much of this turnaround has come from the former secretary, then president, and current patron, businessman Jagmohan Dalmiya. Dalmiya was also president of the ICC, the first Asian to hold the position, where he turned around the fortunes of the ICC from $25,000 when he took over in 1997 to $15 million when he left three years later, with an additional $500-million television contract by establishing the ICC's ownership of the World Cup event and selling the television rights for it (Bamzai 2004).

Despite Dalmiya's obvious Midas touch, there have been rumors of impropriety in the BCCI's accounts. The BCCI is a private body and its accounts are not open to the public for scrutiny. Also, the composition of the company is such that it does not come under any direct government supervision. Besides, none of the board members or delegates to the BCCI are cricketers. Instead the board is packed with powerful local and national politicians to whom the organization provides convenient access to huge funds as well as a national platform on which to perform (Ugra 2004a).

Match Fixing

In 2000, Hansie Cronje, captain of the South African cricket team and a born-again Christian, burst into tears and confessed to having taken money from an Indian bookmaker named Sanjiv Chawla in exchange for deliberately losing matches. On another television channel Kapil Dev, captain of the Indian team also burst into tears and denied having ever taken any money from bookmakers in exchange for throwing matches. Thus was announced, sensationally on global television, the unholy nexus of illegal betting, gangsters, and cricketers—a nexus that has sullied the reputation of India and that of the sport.

Betting on cricket matches has been an age-old activity. One reason for cricket's popularity in the eighteenth and nineteenth centuries in England was that it provided a fertile medium for betting. By the middle of the nineteenth century, public school men had taken the game in hand, and for more than 100 years gambling on cricket was "small beer" (*Economist* 2000b). Bets were placed on the very first match held in India between a team of old Etonians and members of the East India Company in 1804 (Guha 2002). Spread bets on a team's or an individual player's score increased the volume of gambling. In fact, one-day cricket seems to have been designed for betting, and as its popularity spread, gambling became easier. Since betting in India, other than on the racetrack, is illegal, many bookmakers have very close contact with the Indian underworld. In 2003, it was estimated that the World Cup had generated illegal betting business worth INR 300 billion (US$7 billion) (Najmi and Jathar 2003).

At the final match of the 1983 World Cup at Lord's in London, when India, much to the astonishment of the world, overpowered the West Indies team and won, a lot of money changed hands. While the victory renewed interest in the sport and energized the Indian public, for bookmakers it was a black day. There were rumors circulating that Sharad Shetty, the Dubai-based betting kingpin and associate of Indian mafia don Dawood Ibrahim Kaskar, had refused to pay up on his losses of INR 70 million (US$1.5 million) incurred by India's surprise win. Shetty was later shot to death in 2003 by a gang member of Dawood's archenemy, Chhota Rajan. Many have argued that the bookmakers decided to start fixing matches thereafter to avoid the reccurrence of a similar catastrophe.

What the match-fixing revealed was the ease with which bookmakers and members of the Indian underworld could make contact with the international cricketing elite and develop close enough relationships to offer them money to throw matches. One reason that international cricketers allowed themselves to be contacted could be that they receive less of the money generated in the sport than stars of other sports do in their countries. It is reckoned that although most of the income generated in cricket comes from international matches, cricket stars receive just 10 percent of the pot while, in other sports, stars receive around 50 percent. This made bribing players quite a cheap transaction, costing bookmakers just a few thousand dollars (*Economist* 2001a).

It was the confession of Delhi-based jeweler Mukesh Kumar Gupta, one of the alleged bookmakers, to the Indian Central Bureau of Investigation (CBI) that revealed the modus operandi. First, contact was made with a middle-ranking player who was offered financial inducements to make introductions to more important players. These players, in turn, introduced the bookmaker to Pakistani, English, Sri Lankan, West Indian, Australian, and New Zealander cricketers, who were handsomely rewarded in exchange for some simple information about the weather conditions and the state of the pitch. Later bigger demands, such as an agreement to "underperform" or to throw matches, were made for even larger sums of money. According to Gupta some players complied, others did not.

Crucial to the discovery of the alleged corruption of the cricketers was the involvement of the Indian mafia. In fact, it was during a case unrelated to cricket that a Delhi-based detective tapping the phones of two members of the Indian underworld heard the name of Hansie Cronje repeatedly being mentioned in the conversations of those under surveillance. The detective decided to investigate and taped the conversations between Cronje and the Indian bookmaker, Sanjiv Chawla. Once the content of the conversations was leaked to the press, Cronje confessed the extent of his involvement with Indian bookmakers. Cronje died in an air crash in June 2002; Chawla is in hiding in the UK, and other bookmakers named in the match fixing activities are out on bail. The Delhi police have not yet closed the case file and the tapes have been sealed and placed with the Delhi High Court.

However just when it was assumed that the revelations about match-fixing activities were finally over, more rumors surfaced in 2004 when New Zealand captain Stephen Fleming claimed in his biography that an Indian bookmaker named Aushim Khetrapal had offered him and England player Chris Lewis £300,000 (US$550,000) to fix a Test match between the two countries in 1999 (Boock 2004). Khetrapal has denied the charges. Another name mentioned is that of film financier Jagdish Sodha whose connections with a Kenyan cricket captain have caused the latter to be suspended for allegedly taking money from Sodha. In December 2004, the matter was under investigation by the Anti-Corruption and Security Unit of the ICC.

In yet another episode surrounding corruption in Indian cricket, it was revealed in 2004 that Abhijit Kale, a young aspiring player, had tried to bribe the selectors of the BCCI to get on to the national team (*The Sunday Express* 2004). However Kale's alleged misconduct is, as Majumdar points out, nothing new in Indian cricket. Lala Amarnath was once charged with accepting a purse of INR 5,000 from cricket enthusiasts in Calcutta for including a Bengali player in the Indian side (Majumdar 2004b).

Why Do Indians Love Cricket?

Despite the nefarious activities of the bookmakers and cricketers, cricket still invokes a passionate following among Indians. The passion for cricket has prompted the social commentator Ashis Nandy to inaugurate his investigation of why Indians love cricket so much by declaring: "Cricket is an Indian game accidentally discovered by the English" (Nandy 2000: 1). For decades academics have agonized over the reasons for the Indian passion for cricket. "Why is cricket a national passion?" asks Arjun Appadurai. "Why is it not just indigenized but the very symbol of sporting practice that seems to embody India? Why is it watched with rapt attention in stadia from Sharjah (in the Gulf) to Madras and in every other media context as well? Why are the stars of cricket worshipped, perhaps even more than their counterparts in the cinema?" (Appadurai 1998: 110).

Many academics have tried to explain this Indian fascination. Some have contended that it appeals to the Indian temperament. Cricket, according to Ramachandra Guha, indulges Indian taste for chatter and disputation, gossip and debate (Guha 2002). Ashis Nandy has argued that there are mythic structures beneath the surface of the sport that make it profoundly Indian in spite of its Western historical origins (Nandy 2000). Arjun Appadurai offers a link between cricket, gender, nation, fantasy, and bodily excitement or the "erotics of nationhood." He also points to the corporate patronage of cricket whereby many Indian companies took over the task earlier performed by the Indian princes (Appadurai 1998).

There is no doubt that what made cricket so popular in India was nationalism. Cricket had become a reflection, a focus, and an instrument of Indian nationalism. Cricket instilled confidence in the independence movement: if Englishmen treated them as equals on the cricket field, why not off the field? When C. K. Nayudu, a fine, wristy Indian batsman, scored 153 for the Hindus against the MCC in 1926 it had a wider significance: "Every sixer hit by 'C. K.' against the visitors' slow bowlers was as good as a nail in the coffin of the British Empire" (quoted in Guha 2002: 205).

Perhaps the roots of this passion lie in the novelty the sport offered. For the large numbers of urban middle class Indians who embraced the game, it was a case of encountering a new and exciting sport, one that was far more interesting than the Indian options that existed at the time (*gilli danda*, *kabaddi*, and so forth). Second, the game offered social mobility in that mecca of wheeling and dealing that was commercial Bombay. It provided lucrative business contacts with the officials of the *raj* and an opportunity for social advancement. For the Indian maharajas who were patrons of the sport, it offered a route for contact with the British overlord in India and Imperial Britain in London, when they traveled to England as captains of their teams.

Perhaps the roots of the passion lie in the game itself. Cricket is an extremely slow, stately game "invented by the English to give themselves some concept of eternity" as proclaimed by a wit (*Economist* 2001b: 90). The sport required far less exertion than football, rugby, field hockey, and others and, as is apparent from India's performances at international sporting events, physical fitness and unnecessary exertion are not particularly Indian traits. The English philosopher Roger Scruton has pointed out that even the very dress code of pure white flannels "too clean and too pure to suggest physical exertion," although the accompanying "long moments of silence and stillness, stifled murmurs of emotion . . . and subdued applause" have been discarded by the noisy Indian spectators (quoted in Guha 2002: 333).

"To watch cricket," writes Guha, "is to have a long, long break, interrupted by micro-seconds of action." Consequently the structure of the game resonates with the Indian ethos (Guha 2002: 338).

> For cricket is both slow and slow moving, with the action spread out and interrupted instead of fast-paced and concentrated. A ball is bowled, then the bowler walks slowly back to the top of his run. At the end of six balls "Over" is called. The fielders take their time to change positions. A wicket falls, and then the departing batsman contemplatively walks back, and his replacement as leisurely walks in. After an hour's cricket there comes a four-minute drinks break. After two hours, play stops for lunch. This is a forty-minute interval. A twenty-minute break for tea comes at the end of the next session of play. At 5 PM stumps are finally drawn for the day. The players retire to their hotels, to stay there until play resumes the next morning . . . The interrupted nature of play encourages the spectator to participate actively, through barracking and conversation with players on the boundary edge. In between balls and overs, and more so during the longer breaks,

he can talk about the past and future of the game with his fellows. (Guha 2002: 338)

However sociologists and historians of the sport have not touched on one aspect of cricket. Cricket, like field hockey and tennis and unlike football, rugby, and ice hockey, requires very little physical contact among the players. This must have also been most appealing to the middle class Hindus, particularly the Brahmins, who embraced the game in the late nineteenth century, because it allowed them to enjoy a game without "polluting" the purity of their caste. This was particularly true if the lower castes could be persuaded, as was done with Palwankar Baloo by the Poona Brahmins, to take their water and meals outside the perimeter of the gymkhana, thus avoiding intercaste dining, a taboo for the upper castes.

When one adds to these peculiarities of the game the fact that cricket is the only game in which India can compete with the best in the world; the fortuitous arrival of television in India and the nation's first ever World Cup victory; the patronage offered to the sport, first by the maharajas and then the business houses, banks, railways, and other public and private bodies; and the indigenization and vernacularization of the game early in its developmental stages, then the popularity of the game appears natural enough.

Conclusion

Today, cricket is a very lucrative sport in India. It is the most important vehicle for advertising, and cricketing stars are besieged with offers for personal endorsements. This has made the cricketing bodies and the players extremely rich. However there is a serious mismatch between the commercialization of the game and the actual standards of the game as it is played on the cricket fields. While India is one among the top cricket-playing countries, it is not the topmost cricketing nation. That honor, which used to belong to England and the West Indies, currently rests with Australia. India has several star batsmen and bowlers but the team's performance tends to be unpredictable and maverick.

Indian cricket's financial muscle is driven by a buoyant economy and the popularity of the sport, but India has had far too few wins in the important matches to justify the huge advertising revenues. Mihir Bose has warned that the Indian public could easily be turned off the sport that is fast degenerating into all hype and little substance. It is therefore very possible that the television viewers and the advertising media could turn to international football as a more interesting form of entertainment (Bose 2002). Indeed, there are reports that public interest in football, already popular in Kolkata and Goa, is growing.

The next decade is critical for Indian cricket. Currently the sport is full of stars but no winning team, full of money from cricket but no cricketing victory. The moot question that remains is: Will the riches of the BCCI be used to encourage young players and nurture new talent?

A to Z Index

Syed Mushtaq Ali (1914–), a great opening batsman, together with Vijay Merchant was a fast run-getter. He was on the maharaja of Holkar's cricket team and also played for the Muslim Gymkhana in Bombay during the Quadrangulars and Pentangulars. Later he played first class cricket from 1933–1934 until 1951–1952. His son and grandson are both fine cricketers.

Syed Wazir Ali (1903–1950) was a former Indian Test cricketer who toured England in 1932 and 1936 and played against England in India in 1933. A fine batsman with a keen eye, he played for the maharaja of Patiala's team.

Nanik Amarnath Bharadwaj or **"Lala" Amarnath** (1911–2000) was a fiery tempered and independent-minded player for the Hindu Gymkhana, the maharaja of Patiala, and India who was sent back for insubordination from the 1936 tour of England under the captaincy of the maharajkumar of Vizianagaram. His Test debut began in Bombay against England in 1933–1934. He captained India in its 1948 tour of Australia.

Arjun Atwal (1973–) is a promising Indian golfer who turned professional in 1995 and ranks fifty-fifth in the golfing money list. He has yet to win a major tournament title.

Palwankar Baloo (1926–2001), the first member of the untouchable caste, became one of the Test players for India. He was a genius spin bowler who managed to break through the caste barriers and prejudice but not enough to be made captain of the Hindu Gymkhana team.

Donald Bradman (1909–2001) was the greatest cricketer of all time. His appetite for runs was legendary, and the Australian

Bradman's epic career was summed up by the *New York Times* thus: "He simply keeps hitting and running until some sensible person in the stands suggests a spot of tea" (*Economist* 2001b).

Dhyan Chand (1906–1979) started playing field hockey in the army and was included on the Indian hockey team for the 1928 Amsterdam Olympics, where he scored eleven of the side's twenty-eight goals. He was responsible for almost single-handedly helping India win three gold medals during the two subsequent Olympics in Los Angeles (1932) and Berlin (1936).

Jagmohan Dalmiya (1940–) was first treasurer, then secretary, then president, and now is in a newly created position of patron of the Board of Control for Cricket in India. Dalmiya is an inveterate dealmaker and cricket administrator who has turned the sport into a money-making machine not just for the BCCI but also the ICC.

Sunil Gavaskar (1949–) is considered one of the greatest batmen in the history of the sport. "Sunny," as he is known, was a national hero. He made a spectacular debut in the Test series against the West Indies that India won for the first time in 1971. He broke several world records including Donald Bradman's sixty-nine Test centuries (100 runs). He also was the first batsman to have reached a total of 10,000 Test runs. He is now an international broadcaster and commentator on cricket.

Vijay Samuel Hazare (1815–2004) was one of India's finest batmen. He captained the Indian national team after independence and, together with Vijay Merchant, he formed an unbeatable team. Known as a man of few words and not a particularly stylish batsman, he was a darling of the Bombay crowds when he played in the Pentangulars for "The Rest" team. Although not famous as a bowler he nevertheless breached the legendary batsman Don Bradman's defenses not once but twice, a rare feat at a time when Bradman dominated cricket.

Kapil Dev Nikhanj (1959–), an excellent pace bowler and a fine batsman, was one of India's best all rounders. He captained India to the 1983 World Cup victory. Later he was implicated in the match-fixing scandal but was cleared of all charges. His flamboyant lifestyle included marrying a Hindi film starlet. He currently runs his own health and fitness center.

Vijaysingh Madhavji Merchant (1911–1987) was a star batsman who scored a record number of runs in the course of his career. Merchant played for the Hindu Gymkhana during the 1930s and for India in the 1930s and 1940s. He also played for Bombay in the Ranji Trophy matches. He became a writer, administrator, and broadcaster for cricket after he retired from active play at the age of forty.

Sania Mirza (1986–) is a promising professional tennis player who won the Wimbledon Championships Girls' Doubles title in 2003 with Alisa Kleybanova of Russia. She got a wild card entry to the 2005 Australian Open and created history by becoming the first Indian woman to enter the third round of a Grand Slam tournament. In 2005, she became the first Indian woman to win a WTA singles title by beating Alyona Bondarenko of Ukraine in the Hyderabad Open Finals in India.

Karthikeyan Narain (1977–) is the first Indian to create a name for himself in Formula One racing. In 2001 he became the first Indian to test a Formula One car with Jaguar at Silverstone.

C. K. Nayudu (1895–1967) was a stylish and flamboyant batsman who specialized in humbling bowlers by hitting sixes and fours, thus making him a thrilling player to watch. Nayudu played for the maharaja of Holkar's team when not playing for Indian teams that toured England and the Hindu Gymkhana during the Quadrangulars in Bombay. He also served as a colonel in the maharaja's army.

A **one-day** match is a match played over just one day with the teams going in to bat just once instead of twice as in a Test match. Each team is bowled a limited number of overs (usually fifty) and whichever team scores the highest number of runs within the fifty overs is declared the winner.

Over: Six balls consecutively bowled by a bowler to the batsman facing him at the crease constitute an over. At the end of an over, the bowler is changed and another bowler bowls another six balls from the other end of the wicket to the batsman who is facing him at the crease. When no runs are scored during an over, it is known as a maiden over.

K. S. Ranjitsinhji or **Ranji** (1872–1933), the Jam Saheb of Nawanagar, was an Indian prince and a cricketing legend who never played for India, preferring to see himself as an English cricketer. The national Ranji Trophy is named after him. His nephew

K. S. Duleepsinhji was also a good batsman who unfortunately died young.

Sachin Tendulkar (1973–), who started playing international cricket at the age of sixteen, is one of the all-time greats of cricket and is recognized by Bradman as a modern-day incarnation of himself. Not only is Tendulkar a cricketing genius but he is also one of the few men in Indian cricket to be completely untainted by the match-fixing scandals. So feared are his awesome batting skills that it is said by cricket commentators that bookmakers do not fix the odds—or a game—until Tendulkar is out.

A **Test** match is a match that is played over five days with each team playing two innings—that is, going in to bat twice in the course of the match. The scores of a Test match are important because they are counted toward the series' wins or losses.

Bibliography and References

Amarnath, Rajender. *Lala Amarnath: The Making of a Legend.* New Delhi: Rupa, 2004.

Appadurai, Arjun. *Modernity at Large.* Minneapolis: University of Minnesota Press, 1998.

Bahal, Annirudh, and Krishna Prasad. *Not Quite Cricket: The Explosive Story of How Bookmakers Influence the Game Today.* New Delhi: Penguin India, 2000.

Bamzai, Kaveree. "Under the Hammer." *India Today,* 6 September 2004.

Barve, Vijay. "A Mania Called Cricket." *The Illustrated Weekly of India,* 11 April 1971.

Berry, Scylde. *Cricket Wallah: With England in India, 1981–2.* London: Hodder and Stoughton, 1982.

Bharatan, Raju. *Indian Cricket—The Vital Phase.* New Delhi: Vikas, 1977.

Bhatia, Neeru. "Who Will Blink First?" *The Week*, 12 January 2003.

Bhogle, Harsh. *Azhar: The Authorized Biography of Mohammad Azharuddin.* New Delhi: Penguin India, 1996.

Boock, Richard. *Stephen Fleming: Balance of Power.* Auckland: Hodder Moa Beckett, 2004.

Bose, Mihir. *A History of Indian Cricket.* London: Andre Deutsch, 2002.

———. *A Maidan View: The Magic of Indian Cricket.* London: George Allen and Unwin, 1986.

Cashman, Richard. *Patrons, Players, and the Crowd: The Phenomenon of Indian Cricket.* New Delhi: Orient Longman, 1980.

Chambers, Anne. *Ranji, Maharajah of Connemara.* New Delhi: Roli, 2004.

Dadabhoy, Bhaktiar. *A Book of Cricket Days.* New Delhi: Rupa, 2004.

De Mello, Anthony. *Portrait of Indian Sport.* London: P. R. Macmillan, 1959.

Deodhar, D. B. *The March of Indian Cricket.* Calcutta: Illustrated News, 1948.

Dev, Kapil. *Straight from the Heart: An Autobiography.* New Delhi: Macmillan India, 2003.

Docker, E. L. *History of Indian Cricket.* Delhi: Macmillan, 1976.

Economist. "Owzat?" 7 July 2001a.

———. "Donald Bradman." 3 March 2001b.

———. "Ringing the Changes." 6 May 2000a.

———. "Heads, You Lose." 6 May 2000b.

Gavaskar, Sunil. *One Day Wonders.* New Delhi: Rupa, 1986.

———. *Runs 'N Ruins.* New Delhi: Rupa, 1984.

———. *Idols.* New Delhi: Rupa, 1983.

———. *Sunny Days.* New Delhi: Rupa, 1976.

Gibson, Alan. *The Cricket Captains of India.* London: Cassell, 1979.

Guha, Ramachandra. *A Corner of a Foreign Field: The Indian History of a British Sport.* London: Picador, 2002.

———, ed. *The Picador Book of Cricket.* London: Picador, 2001.

———. *Wickets in the East: An Anecdotal History.* New Delhi: Oxford University Press, 1992.

———. *Spin and Other Turns: Indian Cricket's Coming of Age.* New Delhi: Penguin India, 1994.

Harris, Lord. *A Few Short Runs.* London: John Murray, 1921.

Hazare, Vijay. *A Long Innings.* Calcutta: Rupa, 1981.

Indian Express. "Sena Men Spoil Kotla Pitch on Thackeray's Fiat." 7 January 1999.

Keskar, B. V. "Will Cricket 'Quit India' with the British?" *Blitz*, 13 July 1946.

Krishnan, Murali. "Man of Mystery." *India Today*, 20 December 2004.

———. "The Scandal Returns." *India Today*, 22 November 2004.

Majumdar, Boria. *Twenty-Two Yards of Freedom: A Social History of Indian Cricket.* New Delhi: Viking/BCCI, 2004a.

———. *Once Upon a Furore: Lost Pages of Indian Cricket.* New Delhi: Yoda Press, 2004b.

Malik, Ashok. "Cricket Money Wars." *India Today*, 30 September 2002.

Marqusee, Mike. *War Minus the Shooting: A Journey Through South Asia During Cricket's World Cup.* London: Heinemann, 1996.

Mehta, Sir Chunilal V. "Beginnings of Hindu Cricket." In *Diamond Jubilee Souvenir of Parmanand Jivandas Hindu Gymkhana, 1894–1954.* Bombay: PJ Hindu Gymkhana, 1954.

Merchant, Vijay. "The Quadrangulars." *Sportsweek Cricket Quarterly.* April–June 1974.

Najmi, Quaied, and Dnyanesh Jathar. "You Bet!" *The Week*, 2 March 2003.

Nandy, Ashis. *The Tao of Cricket: On Games of Destiny and the Destiny of Games.* New Delhi: Oxford University Press, 2000.

Nayudu, Chandra. *C. K. Nayudu: A Daughter Remembers.* Calcutta: Rupa, 1995.

Patel, Framji. *Stray Thoughts on Indian Cricket.* Bombay: The Times of India Press, 1905.

Patel, Manekji Kavasji. *History of Parsee Cricket.* Bombay: J. N. Petit Parsi Orphanage Captain Printing Press, 1892.

Prospect. "In Fact." May 2004.

Puri, Narottam. *Portrait of Indian Captains.* New Delhi: Rupa, 1978.

Raiji, Vasant. *India's Hambledon Men.* Bombay: Tyeby Press, 1986.

Raiji, Vasant, and Dossa Anandji. *CCI and the Brabourne Stadium 1937–1987.* Bombay: Cricket Club of India, 1987.

Rajaram, G. *Match-Fixing: The Enemy Within.* New Delhi: Har-Anand, 2001.

Ramaswami, N. S. *Indian Cricket.* New Delhi: Abhinav, 1976.

———. *From Porbandar to Wadekar.* New Delhi: Abhinav Publications, 1975.

Ranjitsinhji, K. S. *The Jubilee Book of Cricket.* Edinburgh: William Blackwood, 1897.

Rodrigues, Mario. *Batting for the Empire: A Political Biography of Ranjitsinhji.* New Delhi: Penguin, 2003.

Roy, S. K., ed. *Bombay Pentangular.* Calcutta: Illustrated News, 1945.

Sruton, Roger. *England: An Elegy.* London: Chatto and Windus, 2000.

Sunday Express. "Yehi Hai Right Choice?" 6 June 2004.

Surendran, C. P. "Would You Like to Be Reborn an Indian?" *The Sunday Times of India,* 26 April 1998.

Ugra, Sharda. "Jagmohan Dalmiya: Cricket's Master Player." *India Today,* 27 September 2004a.

———. "Cricket: Going Out of Control." *India Today,* 18 October 2004b.

———. "BCCI Election: 'Playing Politics.'" *India Today,* 11 October 2004c.

10

Consumer Culture

In 1991 Rajiv Gandhi was assassinated in Chennai (formerly Madras) by Tamil separatists while canvassing for the elections. A sympathy vote swept the late Mr. Gandhi's Congress Party into power later that year. However, soon after taking over the reins of government, the new prime minister, P. V. Narasimha Rao, found that foreign exchange reserves had dwindled to US$1.2 billion or just three weeks' worth of imports. India's gold reserves had to be flown to London to help secure a loan from the International Monetary Fund. The country was facing bankruptcy.

As the new finance minister, Dr. Manmohan Singh surprised the world by restoring order to the government finances through cutbacks in wasteful spending and freeing private businesses from bureaucratic restrictions and import controls. Salvaging the economy required the most radical reform ever of the *license raj*, described as "a creaking edifice of central planning held together by miles of red tape" (*Economist* 2004b: 67). The rupee was devalued, import controls were dismantled and customs duties slashed, industrial licensing was liberalized, and the capital markets opened up.

The crisis was overcome, and India's real GDP grew by an average of 5.8 percent a year between 1991 and 2003, up from 5.4 percent in the 1980s and 3.5 percent for decades before that. Foreign exchange reserves grew from the paltry US$1.2 billion to US$18 billion by 1996 and to over US$100 billion by 2003. Under every government since then the pace of reform may have faltered to accommodate various political factions and lobby groups, but the direction of the reform has not changed (Jamieson 2004).

The economic resurgence of India brought a growth in the manufacturing and service industries, and with it a growth in employment in these sectors. Civil servants and public sector workers who number more than 20 million also received substantial salary increments thanks to the recommendations of the Fifth Pay Commission made in 1997. The growth of jobs and increased salaries, combined with lower taxes and import duties, fueled a spending boom, and after decades of austerity, middle class Indians began to revel in the pleasures of consumerism.

Falling prices, due to increased industrial production (and even overcapacity) and falling customs and excise duties, also drove the spending spree. After decades of living with just two brands of cars, refrigerators, and other consumer goods, there was suddenly a profusion of new products, and intense competition between producers to attract customers. Also, with too much money following too few potential borrowers there was easy retail credit; low interest rates were discouraging savings and encouraging spending. (In spite of more and more consumers buying on credit, Indians still remain under leveraged. Buying on credit constitutes barely 4 percent of the GDP, compared with over 20 percent in Thailand, 40 percent in Malaysia, and 60 percent in South Korea.)

The sharp increase in service sector jobs such as IT-enabled services, insurance and finance, retail, and restaurants meant that falling prices coincided with a revival in the job market. Thanks to a combination of all these factors people were able to afford goods that they had never bought before—cars, two-wheelers, refrigerators, microwave ovens, televisions, and so on.

Signs of Modern Consumer Culture

The most visible signs of this new consumer culture are the new shopping malls that have sprung up in all the major towns and cities across India. Unknown in India until the late 1990s, the appearance of the shopping mall was both sudden and surprising. More than 22 malls were built between 2000 and 2003, and another 240 have been built since then.

At first the real estate developers chose the busy shopping districts of the big cities—Bangalore, Chennai, Delhi, Hyderabad, Pune, and Mumbai—in a bid to attract the urban upper middle classes. Crossroads, the first shopping mall in Mumbai, opened in the crowded downtown area in August 1999, and local traffic came to a complete standstill as families rushed to witness the historic event.

The unprecedented success of Crossroads led to more malls being built in other parts of the city. In Mumbai, a teeming metropolis made up of five long, narrow islands sustaining a population of around 16 million, land is extremely scarce for new development. Many of these new shopping malls were built on the premises of abandoned textile mills. Mumbai was once the center of thriving textile mills that were gradually killed off by a combination of sustained union strike actions by workers and steady asset stripping by the owners.

These large highly valued properties lay abandoned for decades because of the government's Urban Land Ceiling (Regulation) Act that had been introduced to safeguard the jobs of the mill workers and prevent the mill owners from profiting from the sale of the land (Raval 2000). The idea was to stop the owners from allowing the mills to run down and then realizing the property values, which were in many cases greater than the income from the mills. However with the transformation of these properties into shopping malls, these dead assets were soon turned into money-spinners. Thus Phoenix Mills, once the hub of Mumbai's thriving textile industry, has been turned into a glittering mall.

In the first phase of mall development large industrial houses such as Tatas (*Westside*), Rahejas (*Globus* and *Shopper's Stop*), Kasliwals (*Landmarc Citi*), and Goenkas (*Musicworld*, *Foodworld*, and

Three new malls opened fifteen miles outside of New Delhi in neighboring Gurgaon, Haryana, in 2002 and are a big hit with the growing middle class. Locals often spend the day window shopping and eating. India's economy was expected to grow 6–7 percent in 2003. (Robert Nickelsberg/Getty Images)

Health and Glow) all joined in the shopping mall boom initiated by Crossroads, and shopping malls were soon built in all the other major towns and cities of India—Bangalore, Delhi, Chennai, Kolkata, Kochi, and so forth.

In the second phase of development that has taken place over the last few years, new malls have been built in the suburbs of major cities and towns, as well as in smaller towns such as Jaipur, Ludhiana, Nagpur, and Indore. For example, Gurgaon, once a small town a few hours' drive from New Delhi, already has fifteen malls. In Mumbai, the new developments have all been in the suburbs of Goregaon, Jogeshwari, Malad, Andheri, Oshiwara, and Kandivli, or away from the islands and on the mainland to the north and east of the city. These suburban developments are extremely important because they cater to more than six million inhabitants. Scores more malls are planned over the next few years in the hope of penetrating deeper and deeper into the hinterland to gain access to the growing middle-class communities located in smaller towns all over the country.

What the Shopping Malls Offer

What these malls offer is something Indians have never enjoyed before—a total shopping and entertainment experience in cool, air-conditioned comfort with a variety of well-made products. For decades Indian manufacturers had operated in a protected market thanks to the ban on imports, producing substandard substitutes for a waiting list of consumers. It was also a time of all kinds of scarcity and food rationing. (Food rationing is still in place but this is to ensure that the poor get the essential foodstuffs at government-controlled prices.) A few decades ago it was the consumers who chased the providers; today it is the producers who pursue consumers with easy credit and a variety of goods.

With greater spending power and exposure to international trends, what has emerged over the last fifteen years is a spending culture where the middle classes, estimated at between 200 and 300 million people, are being encouraged to embrace conspicuous consumption in glitzy malls that offer ready-to-wear clothes, food, leisure activities, and entertainment.

Previously, most Indians shopped for clothes in small, specialty shops for saris and so on, or simply purchased material and had them made by tailors operating out of dusty shops or garages. The new malls such as Westside, Pantaloons, and Shopper's Stop offer ready-made clothes ranging from mass-produced items to exclusive designer clothing. In addition to retail, these newly constructed malls offer entertainment centers that include bowling alleys, pool parlors, fast food restaurants (pizza, burgers, and ice cream), and coffee bars.

The emergence of the shopping malls has transformed urban family life. Hitherto, middle-class families had few places to spend a Sunday together, the choices usually being restricted to eating out in restaurants, going to the movies, staying home and watching television, or visiting relatives. Today the malls have provided a revolutionary way for families to spend Sundays and their leisure time together. Mall developers have put together a series of enjoyable activities, standardized the concept, and sold it as a destination in the hope of capturing four or five hours of the consumers' time. Shopping malls have become one-stop destinations with retail, recreation, entertainment, and eating opportunities that may include theaters, art galleries, cinemas, cyber terminals, and pubs. These malls also offer parking facilities for 300–800 cars. The latest in the development of malls is the growth of specialty malls that focus on wedding trousseaux, gold, and jewelry.

The pleasures of bowling, for example, are an entirely new experience for Indians. In the late 1990s, several bowling centers opened in the major towns and cities, offering the recreational activity as an alternative to pubs and restaurants. The Bowling Co. in Mumbai, the country's largest bowling alley at twenty lanes, which also offers pool, sports bars, video arcades, jazz cafés, and a childcare center, is said to attract 2,200 visitors daily. The Leisuredrome in Chennai, which has forty snooker and pool tables, attracts 4,000 people a day (Ramani and Vetticad 1999). It has future plans for cyber cafés, food courts, miniature golf, and even more bowling alleys.

In the early years of the mall culture, despite crowds of visitors to these new temples of consumption, few showed an inclination to purchase any goods; most people preferred to just wander around and ogle the merchandise on display. The young, who in any case could not afford most of the products, tended to use the malls as a meeting place for friends. In fact, so great were the crowds and so few the actual purchases that some malls began to restrict entry to those with credit cards and mobile

Children play video games at an arcade in a mall in Gurgaon, Haryana, outside New Delhi. (Robert Nickelsberg/Getty Images)

phones, these being deemed signs of bona fide purchasers. However, over the years, more and more consumers are being lured into parting with their money.

The corollary of the frenetic construction of shopping malls has been a boom in the construction industry, and now specialty malls dedicated to construction-related materials as well as flooring, furniture, lighting, acoustics, and hi-tech electronic goods have begun to be built across India.

The new consumerism has also begun to challenge Indian tradition. The young, freed from the qualms felt by their parents, who were brought up austerely with Nehruvian socialism and ancient Hindu ideals of renunciation, positively relish conspicuous consumption. "Rolex," says Mr. Seth (of Equus Red Cell, an advertising agency in Delhi) with his profession's knack for pithy hyperbole, "has replaced religion" (*Economist* 2004a: 39).

Second, and potentially of vast significance for a country as stratified as India, the young and affluent across the country have begun to define themselves not by caste, creed, and language, but by a shared stake in the consumer culture, whose spread has been helped along by television programs and advertising, which now reach over half of all Indian homes. As a result, spending patterns are changing. In the cities, for example, young consumers now change their cars every two years whereas for the previous generation a car was for life.

Economic liberalization and the concurrent boom in information technology–related services have created a generation of wealthy Indians who are distinct from the traditional business families. These newly rich and educated Indians have developed a taste for international luxury brands in cars, watches, shoes, and jewelry. Although they represent just one percent of the entire population, they nevertheless number around ten million consumers, a substantial market. This new breed of consumers of luxury goods enjoys spending, seeing it as a pleasure not a fear. Thanks to their demand, sales have been brisk for Fendi and Louis Vuitton bags and accessories, Cartier watches, Bulgari jewelry, Canali and Hugo Boss suits; and cars from Porsche, Bentley, Rolls Royce, and Ferrari (Bhupta 2004). In fact, most international brands have now opened stores in the big cities.

In addition to spending on clothes and luxury brands, more and more Indians have begun to frequent cafés, pubs, and restaurants.

Café Culture

In 1957, some disgruntled employees of the state-run Coffee Board decided to part ways with the parent company and set up their own Indian Coffee Workers' Cooperative Society. The idea was to set up coffee bars and offer the public affordable coffee. For four decades their 160 outlets across the country were the only dedicated coffee bars that Indians were aware of. The simple interiors and the somnambulant pace of the waiters made it a haven for writers, journalists, artists, poets, and politicians—so much so that the late prime minister Mrs. Indira Gandhi saw the coffee bars as havens of dissent and even had one coffee bar in New Delhi closed down (Bajeli-Datt 2004).

This old world of coffee houses was rudely exposed to the rigors of competition when in 1997 the Indian government removed coffee from its list of restricted commodities. A new breed of indigenous coffee bars along the lines of the Starbucks chain emerged. While the Indian Coffee House catered to the older generations who generally spent the entire day perusing newspapers while nursing a single cup of coffee, the new coffee bars such as Barista, Café Coffee Day, Amarettos, or Qwiky's began to cater to the young and trendy by offering live music, books, and even message boards where patrons could staple their random thoughts, while they sipped exotic concoctions such as frappuccinos, macchiatos, and lattes. What these coffee bars, where a cup of coffee costs the price of a meal, offer above all is a stylish place for youngsters to "chill out" and more importantly to gaze and be gazed at by their contemporaries. It is estimated that the four coffee chains cater to more than 40,000 customers a day.

Starbucks, which already procures some of its Arabica coffee beans from India, has announced plans to enter the Indian market, but the company may find that the market has already been cornered by the indigenous versions. Barista, the leader of the pack, for instance, already runs 152 cafes and 142 express counters in 42 cities and aims to open 80 more cafes in eight cities. It also intends to open coffee bars overseas. Café Coffee Day, which first opened in Bangalore in 1996, is now looking to expand overseas in Dubai, Mauritius, Cyprus, and Singapore (Bajeli-Datt 2004).

Pubs

Accompanying the emergence of the coffee bar are the new liquor bars known in India by the British name of pubs. For decades after India achieved independence, the Indian government was opposed to the consumption of alcohol. The reasons for this were manifold. The most important was that Mahatma Gandhi, the father of the nation who spearheaded the independence movement, was totally opposed to alcohol. This was largely because he saw it as a direct road to ruin for millions of poor workers in the cities and the villages. Gandhian principles apart, socially there has always been distaste, both Muslim as well as Hindu (particularly Brahminical), for imbibition of alcohol.

The sale of alcohol was thus severely restricted by the government, and enthusiasts were required to obtain a permit, which was usually issued on "health" grounds. The rich could often be found huddled in luxury hotels drinking whiskey masquerading as tea, often being poured out of a teapot into teacups. At home, most were careful to draw their curtains before settling down to a peg of local or imported (and usually contraband) whiskey. However, most of the poor, whom these strictures were supposed to protect, drank moonshine, and death or blindness through contaminated alcohol was commonplace.

Prohibition was (and still remains) a matter for state governments. As each state enacted its own legislation regarding the sale and public consumption of alcohol, some states were dry (with prohibitions in place) and others were wet. Some states preferred a compromise with dry days and wet days, and some states regularly changed from being dry to wet and vice versa with each change in the regional government. Each state also has its own laws about the construction of liquor stores, licensing hours, and so on. In some states, licensed liquor shops are closed on the first and seventh day of each month to prevent men from frittering away their wages. In fact, for decades legislators in some southern states were wary of lifting the ban on alcohol sales for fear of provoking the wrath of women, who were vehemently opposed to it. Licensing laws also vary according to the different states but most bars tend to close early—by 11 PM and usually no liquor is served after that hour.

With the passing of the censorious decades and the emergence of a consumer culture, the prohibition of alcohol has been replaced by an active encouragement to imbibe the once-shunned spirits. The reason for the change is that state governments earn very large sums in excise duties from the sale of liquor. The Delhi State Industrial Development Corporation, for example, has the task of running liquor stores in the Delhi region. To this end, it intends to open high-end stores with trained staff and top-of-the-line brands with teller machines in case customers run out of cash. The aim is also to get more women to visit the stores.

The loosening of restriction on alcohol in most states has led to a burst of investment in bars in the major towns and cities. At first, many of these bars tried to go for volume and were open to all and sundry. Now many have increasingly turned their attention to specific segments of society. Bangalore, the hub of India's information-technology industry, is also considered by general consensus to be the capital of the nation's pub culture. The explosion of IT businesses and their offshoots has helped produce a new breed of young professionals with plenty of disposable income. Thus, Bangalore, once a city of parks, gardens, and lakes, and of silk saris and handicrafts,

Shangri-La whiskey in a liquor store. Rangpo, Sikkim. (Macduff Everton/Corbis)

is now the national capital for lounge bars and pubs where the IT sector workers go to unwind, to listen to music, and to drink.

The bars range from upmarket watering holes such as the *F Bar* owned by FTV, the fashion cable television channel, where in the absence of an actual fashion show drinkers can sip under a large screen displaying the closest Indian television comes to soft porn. Some pubs (*Razzberry Rhinoceros* and *Madness*) operate mainly in the afternoons, so that the youngsters can be home by dusk and their parents are none the wiser. Although the young do not have the same spending power as the older clients and often sit clutching a pitcher for the entire afternoon, they give the bar owners profit by virtue of volume because they comprise the largest bar-frequenting segment of the population. Loud music and jammed dance floors constitute their at-

tractions. Many of these bars are located near the colleges to be convenient for frequent visits. The popularity of these bars is such that they are often the venue for celebrations (birthdays, success in examinations, end-of-year parties, and such).

Interestingly, while such pubs are extremely popular with the young, discotheques are not. The absence of a western-style club culture and draconian curfews for noise pollution in cities like Mumbai and Delhi partly explain the lack of enthusiasm for discotheques. Another reason is the Indian preference for singing along with Indian film songs and remixes rather than listening or dancing to trance music (Doshi 2004).

However, the most lucrative pubs are the exclusive bars for the professionals such as *Jazz by the Bay*, the *Cyclone*, Marine Plaza's *Jefferies*, and others that cater to media and marketing executives, film personalities, and professionals such as chartered accountants, lawyers, bankers, and doctors. To keep the place free of the younger groups, some of these clubs have steep membership fees. Some bars, like *Provogue*, have special women's evenings (*Women en Vogue*) to encourage women drinkers. However not all bars are quiet retreats for the professional classes. Some pubs offer live music, have dance floors, and encourage bar-top dancing. Others have special days when celebrities serve at the bar. A few years ago, a fatal shooting that left a model/celebrity bartender dead created panic and scandal at a bar near Delhi. The incident had all the ingredients of a thrilling potboiler—celebrities, alcohol, and a drunk and disgruntled provincial politician's son.

In some cities, such as Chandigarh, the scrapping of building by-laws gave impetus to the growth of a pub culture. Extending hours of operation for pubs, discotheques, and cyber cafés has also added a zing to its nightlife. Despite the changing social scene and ethos surrounding alcohol and bars, some habits die hard. According to the owner of *Aerizona*, a discotheque in Chandigarh, a senior policewoman used to post constables outside the discos and take down the names and addresses of the young frequenters in order to inform their parents.

At the lower end of the social spectrum are the dance bars where women dress in *ghagra-choli* (Indian-style skirts) and dance to Hindi film songs while men sit around nursing their beers. From time to time, the men pick up a few rupees and toss them at the women in gestures of appreciation. The clientele tends to be mixed—from police officers to realtors

and merchants to software professionals, and the amounts of money showered over the women each night runs into tens of thousands rupees each night. The experience of these dance bars has been described in detail by Suketu Mehta in his recently published homage to Mumbai, *Maximum City: Bombay Lost and Found.*

Always on the lookout for novel ideas to promote business, some entrepreneurs have begun attaching bars to their specialty shops. *Scorpion Moon* is a bar attached to *Chand Begum ke Jewels*, an exclusive jewelry store. The bar has long happy hours. According to the owner, jewelry and drinks "gel together because people enjoy getting treated to a drink or two while shopping" (Thomas 2004b: 48). So when men get tired of the long hours women spend agonizing over jewelry, they can step next door for a drink.

Such has been the success of the new pubs and bars that hotels are increasingly worried about losing out to these newcomers. Food and beverage account for nearly 40 percent of a hotel chain's total revenue and they cannot afford to let the new competitors wean away a chunk of their customers. So the hotels too have begun to offer themed pubs (sports bars, jazz bars, and the like) along with specialty cuisine restaurants. This is something of a minor revolution, as many coffee bars in hotels had remained unchanged since the 1970s.

Restaurants

The economic regeneration of India has also led to an increased interest in eating out. Traditional Indians are deeply suspicious of dining in restaurants. Different customs governing the multiplicity of religions that are practiced in India, fiendishly complicated varieties of vegetarianism, social intricacies concerning caste, both of the diners and the cooks, and traditional prohibitions surrounding dining with members of certain castes, in addition to economic constraints such as the lack of disposable incomes had inhibited interest for fine dining in restaurants.

Until recently, varieties of Indian cuisines were enough for most diners—Punjabi snacks, Gujerati *thali*s, south Indian *dosa*s and *idli*s, Bengali sweets, and the ubiquitous Moghlai cuisine. The only foreign food was Chinese, which was adapted to an Indian palate by the small Chinese communities living in Mumbai and Kolkata. Western cuisine, whether French, Italian, or another type, was either uninspiring or considered too bland to be popular.

The younger generations, raised in the cosmopolitan environment of the cities and towns, have embraced international cuisines with enthusiasm. The cuisines offered in the new restaurants are neither traditionally Indian nor entirely western. Instead what is emerging is fusion cuisine—a cuisine that combines western cooking with a dash of Indian spices, or Indian cooking with a dash of western ingredients. *Indigo*, for instance, set in an elegant Victorian building in downtown Mumbai exemplifies the genre with a blend of Mediterranean and Indian cuisines. Other examples of increased interest in Mediterranean cuisine are *Moshe's*, *Café Basilico*, and *Caliente*. With more and more Indians traveling overseas, hot and spicy Thai food has also found a niche in the Indian dining experience.

Celebrities too have started opening restaurants: Sachin Tendulkar, India's star cricketer, has opened two restaurants in Mumbai (*Sachin's* and *Tendulkar's*), as have Hindi films stars Amisha Patel (*Fire-place*), Sunil Shetty (*Mischief Bar* and *Suzie Wong*). Malayalam film star Mohanlal has even ventured as far afield as Dubai (*Tastebuds*) (Rathi 2002).

Traditional Indian food has also been smartened up for the discerning middle classes. Gone are the curry-stained tablecloths and fading menu cards, and signs over washbasins asking customers not to comb their hair in the restaurant. In their place, gleaming new restaurants offer clean, comfortable dining. The traditional Udipi restaurants, named after the district in Karnataka whence the entrepreneurs who set up their cheap and cheerful eateries originated, have for decades offered fast vegetarian lunches accompanied by strong, hot, South Indian coffee. While these continue to be the popular eating places for city dwellers across India, a more contemporary incarnation called *Dosa Diner*, a McDonald's-like fast food chain offers similar traditional Udipi dishes but in more modern surroundings.

In addition to the restaurants are the fast food vendors to be found in all the malls—the pizza chains, hamburger outlets (although in India they serve chicken, lamb, or fish burgers, but no beef or pork out of respect for Hindus who don't eat beef and Muslims who don't eat pork), and ice cream parlors. It is reported that in Delhi at least two new fast food parlors open each day. McDonald's increased its number of outlets in India from 49 to 200 by 2004 and located many of its new outlets in shopping malls.

High Fashion

Haute couture is a nascent industry still in its infancy and valued at around US$35 million, just a fraction of the clothing industry's US$12 billion ready-to-wear Indian ap-

Lakmé is a cosmetics manufacturer who organized a week-long fashion show, highlighting designers, hair stylists, and models. The show's objective was to facilitate a dialogue between designers and trade buyers. Lakmé Fashion Week saw fifty-three designers showcase their collections. The collection modeled is by designer Malini Ramani. New Delhi, 2002. (Baldev/Corbis)

parel market. For decades skilled Indian workers and small companies have been a reservoir of resources for the main fashion houses in the United States and Europe, but few Indian couturiers have managed to make a name for themselves on the catwalks of Milan, Paris, London, or New York. Many have survived on "brown dollars"—clients from the Indian diaspora shopping for weddings and other important occasions when Indians overseas feel the need for traditional yet modern Indian clothing and a fashion statement that would reflect their dual cultural realities.

Now, India has a sizable class of nouveaux riches seeking couture. Their financial muscle has led to millions of additional square feet of retail space for designers to display prêt-à-porter lines in the new shopping malls. The early designers of the 1980s, such Satya Paul and Ritu Kumar, had already carved out niche markets for themselves with the upper class Indian consumers, while Abu Jani and Sandeep Khosla revived age-old Indian techniques in embroidery and mirror-work for those who could afford it. The new crop of contemporary designers feature Tarun Tahiliani, Rohit Bal, Sabyasachi Mukherjee, Suneet Varma, Aki Narula, Raghavendra Rathore, Rajesh Pratap Singh, Wendell Rodricks, Malini Ramani, and Monish Jaisingh, among others, all of whom are still struggling to create a viable industry.

Designers in India face many problems. First, Indian women still prefer to wear

Indian clothes—saris and *salwar* (or *chu-didar*) *kameez* for reasons of tradition. Also western attire does not always flatter the wider-hipped Indian female form. Dresses, skirts, and suits are infrequent although the younger generations, weaned on FTV and MTV channels, have embraced western clothing with greater passion than before. But the young prefer to purchase their clothes from *Fashion Street* and other such makeshift pavement stalls that offer knock-offs at affordable prices for students.

The dilemma the Indian designers face is this: Should their designs ignore local preferences and aim for a global market, or should they cater to the Indian market and be marginalized in the global market for being too Indo-centric? The magic solution for clothes that are Indian in sensibility but with global wearability has not yet been discovered, and the secret to a western cut with an Indian inspiration has not yet been fully unearthed. What Indian designers wish to emulate is the Japanese example, where designers such as Issey Miyake have managed to create successfully their own brands in the global markets by blending Japanese sensitivity with international styles.

However, although the western market may be elusive, many Indian designers have recently entered into agreements with big Indian retail firms. Thanks to the economic growth and boom in consumption, a few have found a nice, lucrative sideline in designing uniforms—for the staff in new private airlines, hotel chains, mobile phone companies, and cinema multiplexes. Designer Hemant Sagar has even designed uniforms for a school in Rajasthan (*The Week* 2004). The Indian film industry also offers designers a great opportunity to be-come a recognized brand, and many vie for an opportunity to dress the goddesses of the silver screen, and achieve the fame that Givenchy did when he dressed Audrey Hepburn in *Breakfast at Tiffany's*. All of these are opportunities that fashion design will explore over the coming years.

Advisers to the industry say that what the designers really need is a credible business profile, which is achievable if they identify their markets, consider corporate tie-ins, and build brands. To transform this cottage industry into a corporate one, it is deemed that designers must institutionalize creativity, think like business managers or acquire one, have an efficient supply-chain management system, and ensure stringent quality control for large-scale manufacturing.

To help the Indian fashion industry corporatize, the Fashion Design Council of India (FDCI) organizes fashion shows and workshops to help designers learn how to overcome problems such as bottlenecks in supplies, manufacturing, and sales, as well as to help them learn to arrange corporate financing. The FDCI has been organizing an annual Indian Fashion Week (IFW) since 1999, offering a chance for young graduates of the fashion design schools across the country to display their talent. In 2004 the IFW, sponsored by the Indian cosmetics brand Lakmé, showcased nearly 60 Indian designers and was attended by nearly 300 (mostly Indian) buyers. There are no precise figures, however, as to the actual amount of business transacted as a result of the shows.

Despite the many false starts (such as holding shows in the months of July and August when most of the potential overseas buyers are away on holiday or by inviting too many celebrities so that genuine buyers found themselves without any seats), the IFW nevertheless offers designers an opportunity to showcase their talents. Acres of publicity in newspapers are achieved thanks to "shocking" publicity photographs: one model dressed in an Indian tricolor miniskirt nearly led to the arrest of designer Malini Ramani for "insulting" the national flag; another indulged in lesbian kisses on stage (in Aki Narula's show in 2003); yet another sported T-shirts depicting gay men in passionate embrace (Manish Arora in 2003). Designers at postshow parties routinely confess to a desire to "push the boundaries" of fashion in their interviews.

All of this has attracted the Indian consumer's attention to a whole new form of entertainment. In fact, so widespread is the perception of haute couture as entertainment, that even the government has not yet accorded it the status of an industry. Before the IFW in 2004, the FDCI spent months trying to convince the government that couture was a genuine industry and did not deserve to be slapped with an entertainment tax as levied on films and other forms of entertainment. Some even see it as a form of pornographic entertainment. Mrs. Sushama Swaraj, the former Indian minister for Information and Broadcasting, threatened to ban FTV, the international cable channel owned by MCN that presents French fashion extravaganzas to an estimated 90 million Indian viewers, for being "pornographic" and "contrary to Indian sensibilities." But, as one journalist remarked, a country that gave the world *Kama Sutra* (the ancient manual of lovemaking) and the erotic statues of Khajuraho was not going to be destroyed by "Naomi Campbell's bare breasts" (Gardner 2003).

E-Commerce

Not all consumption takes place in the shopping malls, and over the last few years there has been a marked increase in e-commerce. The increase in Internet access through the growth of cyber cafés and private Internet connections, and a growing base of credit card holders has led to an increase in online shopping.

Travel-related transactions account for nearly a quarter of total online transactions, followed by books and a variety of impulse purchases such as jewelry, flowers, and gifts. Home appliances, television sets, and music systems are increasingly being purchased from websites such as *Fabmall.com* and *Baazee.com*. Similarly, *Sify* has seen the value of its transactions rise dramatically thanks to alternative payment options such as cash-on-delivery that help to address security concerns. Recently, nearly half of all online shoppers in India were said to have opted for cash-on-delivery.

However, the Internet facilities are also increasingly being availed in payment of bills, applying for home loans, credit cards, or other on-line financial services. *Apnaloan.com* undertakes home loan transactions and processes credit card applications. Remittances sent by Indians working overseas are also transacted on the Internet (Goyal 2003b).

The services industry has also joined the e-revolution. Virtually all bills (telephone, electricity, water, and so forth) and loan installments can be paid online. Banks have become the interface between their customers and service providers. There has also been a growth in online banking because it offers convenience to the customers and lower operational costs to the bank.

Online bookings for railway tickets operated by Indian Railway Catering and Tourism Corporation Ltd. (IRCTC) have been particularly popular. In fact, such was the initial surge in traffic for online train tickets that in 2002 a perplexed Visa (the credit card company) dispatched a high-powered team to investigate the matter.

Customers still need education on the advantages of online shopping. Many are unaware that if they repudiate a transaction charged on their credit card, the payment liability is not on them but on the seller. Second, logistical issues have not yet been overcome. Cash on delivery, a popular payment option, is still not offered by reliable courier companies. Managing state and central taxes has also been a logistical nightmare for online retailers. The government is currently instituting a uniform value-added tax (VAT) to replace the disparate sales taxes.

Mobile phone commerce (m-commerce) is still in its infancy. However, with millions of cellular users in the country and telecommunications firms aggressively pushing for m-commerce, m-commerce may prove popular with buyers (Goyal 2003b).

New Age Spirituality

The economic growth that fueled a taste for consumerism has also given rise to a thirst for spirituality among young Indians. Although materially most middle class Indians have never had it so good, there is increasingly a feeling of alienation and dissatisfaction. As society changes, and the old, traditional social structures are dismantled or transformed, more and more young Indians are also complaining of a sense of insecurity. These feelings of alienation, dissatisfaction, and insecurity have, in some cases, been translated into a genuine quest for inner peace and tranquility.

As a country, India has always been extremely religious. Although Hinduism is the dominant religion (accounting for around 82 percent of the population), most world religions have a following in the country. There are Muslims (11 percent), Sikhs (2 percent), Christians (3 percent), as well as Buddhists, Jews, Jains, Zoroastrians, and others (2 percent combined). Indians overwhelmingly declare themselves to believe in God. A *Marg/India Today* poll conducted in 2002 showed 94 percent of Indians describing themselves as religious. Of these, a third saw themselves as very religious and 56 percent as somewhat religious (Jain 1998). While most Indians still frequent temples, mosques, or churches, and embark on pilgrimages to the various holy shrines, the new, urban, and young middle classes are increasingly attracted to modes of devotion that are more contemporary.

Renunciation, self-restraint, and even abstention from sensual pleasures are important concepts in religions that have originated in India, namely Hinduism, Buddhism, and Jainism. Therefore the economic resurgence and the ability of most urban, middle classes to purchase and enjoy goods and services that they could only dream about before, remains at odds with the underlying austerity that is seen as the Hindu ideal. And it is precisely to reconcile the two contradictory trends—the growing desire to enjoy the new material pleasures that economic growth has brought to Indians and the increasing sense of alienation, dissatisfaction, and insecurity that this material prosperity has created—that some young people have begun to seek spiritual answers.

The new spirituality offers both psychic and physical comfort. It does not require ancient austerities, such as sitting alone on hard rocks on mountaintops, to understand the meaning of life. Nor does it ask the aspirants to choose between spiritual fulfillment and worldly possessions. Instead it asks a spiritual seeker to seek the divine within himself or herself. As one seeker put it: "[The search for God] does not forbid me from going to pubs or discos" (John 2003: 44). And, many of the New Age spiritual solutions emanate from the authority of a *guru* or a spiritual master.

New Age Gurus

Respect for spirituality has been a timeless characteristic of Indian life, and gurus, mystics, and other spiritually enlightened beings from all faiths have always found veneration and devotion among vast swathes of the population. Furthermore, unlike in the West, organized religion and individual quests in mysticism have coexisted harmoniously throughout the centuries.

The arbiters of the new spirituality have embraced modernity, and a plethora of new, urbane, and sophisticated gurus have sprung up across the country—gurus who blend ancient wisdom and modern techniques to concoct a very contemporary spirituality. Some have combined the contemplative or meditative traditions with a variety of esoteric, imported arts. Others talk about relationships and career stress rather than the *Upanishads* and the *Vedas*. And, unlike the traditional gurus, the new generation of teachers are not deified or remote saints but are seen as accessible and aware buddies-cum-psychiatrists who help people navigate the minefield of modern life.

While the older and more traditional gurus and mystics such as Satya Sai Baba and Maa Amritanandamayi still have a large following, the younger generation is more attracted to younger gurus like Bharat Thakur, described by one magazine as the "James Dean of spirituality" (Chopra and Raval 2003: 46). Unlike the older gurus who often wear white or saffron (the Hindu color of religion) to indicate their monastic vows, the new gurus dress in jeans and casual shirts, carry cell phones, and fluently address seminars at IT-related conferences on the stresses and strains of modern life. If some like Bharat Thakur make tantric traditions available to the general populace, others such as Jaya Row employ a modern idiom to explain the intellectual path of *Vedanta*. Not all gurus are necessarily young, but what they do offer is a new form of spirituality and one that is relaxed in its manner of delivery. Although the wisdom they impart is ancient and profound, they present it in a style that is more in tune with the younger generations.

Today there are more and more *satsangs* (group meetings to chant and pray) that take place not in temples or places of worship but in people's homes or hired premises. Also, they are not "oldie" *satsangs* for the "tired, retired and disillusioned" but crammed with young, successful professionals (Vasudev 2003: 54).

In the 1970s, Maharashi Mahesh Yogi introduced meditation to the West, and, thanks to his association with the Beatles, the growth of Transcendental Meditation and *hatha yoga* (physical yoga) throughout the world paved the way for many of the practices that are offered to seekers in India today. There was a time when most ashrams (spiritual refuges) in India (like that of ISKCON and Osho) were mainly peopled by westerners. Today there are more and more Indians who seek spiritual solutions to psychic problems frequenting these places.

Many of the teachers and spiritual guides provide simple, manageable solutions and repackage eternal truths in contemporary formats. Some base their techniques on breathing and lean towards *hatha yoga* and *pranic* healing, Buddhist chants, and *vipassana* (a Buddhist form of mindful action) rather than charitable offerings and unquestioning devotion to the traditional gods. For example, in the new age guru Sri Sri Ravi Shankar's Art of Living program, *pranayama* (or breath control) is a key feature. In addition to courses on meditation and contemplation, *Vyakti Vikas Kendra* (the Art of Living), the ashram (residential center) of Sri Sri Ravi Shankar, offers traditional Indian medicinal (*ayurvedic* and *panchkarma)* treatments.

Thus the contemporary spirituality market offers many choices for New Age therapies. These combine a variety of traditions and provide a smorgasbord of remedies. The mix and match of religions includes Zen and tarot cards, *feng shui* and tranquility candles, scented pillows, *vipassana*, *reiki*, color and crystal therapies, aura and *chakra* healing. Today, conversations about holistic therapies and Karma Quotients (KQs) are commonplace among the Indian chatterati.

The new gurus are also media-friendly and willing to use the power of the mass media to provide help to those seeking spiritual salvation. There are websites to various gurus, spiritual guides, and gods. There are television channels, such as *Aastha* and *Sanskar*, dedicated to spiritual discourse and at least one Christian channel with American and Indian evangelists.

Channels such as Sony and STAR have also added slots for spirituality to their mainstream programs. In addition, the music industry has also been alert to the business opportunities that religion and spirituality offer. Religious/spiritual music constitutes nearly ten percent of the market, and the figure could be even higher if the losses from piracy are factored in. In fact, such is the insatiable demand for religious music that such recordings are frequently out of stock in the stores.

It is estimated that the middle classes spend between 10 and 25 percent of their income on spiritual pursuits. Nationwide, the spiritual market is placed at over INR 250 billion (US$5 billion) with 30 percent annual growth (Chopra and Raval 2003), and this includes the amounts spent on gurus, yoga, and meditation, as well as books, CDs, and television channels.

For those less inclined to spirituality and religion, there is a bewildering array of new spas and luxury hotels that have been quick to offer all kinds of massages, fitness clubs, and beauty parlors at their in-house spas. The growing trend is now towards spas in resorts tucked away from business activity centers. Most spas offer traditional oil massages, yoga, fusion food, Thai massage, and other international treatments. The Golden Palms Spa and Resort, owned by Bollywood film star Sanjay Khan, markets itself as a "life enhancement center." It has a gym and a beauty parlor and offers therapeutic massages, *ayurvedic* massages, Turkish baths, and Swedish massages.

As one aficionado of alternative treatments and new spirituality declared: "The new age spirituality isn't about pursuing nirvana in the next life but attaining mind-body-spirit harmony in this one. Renunciation is for the feeble. The struggle is to find peace in the cacophony of the common-place. The aim is to combine consumerism with happiness" (Chopra and Raval 2003: 48).

Issues

There are two major issues that stand out in the consumer culture that India has so eagerly embraced. The first has to do with the lack of basic amenities amid the grow-ing consumerism, and the second relates to the uneven distribution of wealth between the urban middle classes and the rural poor.

Lack of Amenities

According to the census report of 2001, there are 192 million households in India (each household comprising on average 5.5 persons) but only 179 million residential houses. This leaves thirteen million house-holds with no place to live. Of those who do have a dwelling, only fifty-two percent live in *pukka* houses, while the rest live in houses with no permanent walls or roof. For a third of urban Indian families, the dwelling does not include a kitchen, a bath-room, and a toilet—and in many cases there is no power or water supply (Saran 2003).

Relative to their incomes, Indians enjoy fewer basic amenities such as drinking wa-ter, power, and cooking fuel, than they do consumer products. Only 56 percent of households have both water and electricity supplied to the home; only 65 percent of urban households have water supplied to the home, and the average water supply in the cities is often only available for four hours a day. In the countryside, only 29 percent of rural households have access to water at home.

As for electricity and power, only 88 per-cent of urban households have electricity while in the rural areas the figure drops to 44 percent. Not a single Indian state elec-tricity board (SEB) provides power to all its citizens, and even the best performing states, such as Punjab, Himachal Pradesh, and Goa, provide only 90 percent of elec-tricity needed by households (Saran 2003).

In other aspects of everyday life, only 64 percent of Indians live in houses with kitch-ens. Of those households with kitchens, 76 percent live in urban areas and the rest in rural areas. Most Indian families use fire-wood (52.2 percent), crop residue (10 per-cent), or cow dung cake (9.8 percent) as cooking fuels. Low propane gas, as used in the developed countries, is available to only 17.5 percent of Indians (48 percent in urban areas and only 6 percent in rural areas) while kerosene is used by 6.5 percent of households (Saran 2003). As for telecom-munication, 23 percent of urban families have a telephone connection while only four percent of rural families have the same. Mercifully, the cell phone has pro-vided what the government-run telephone companies have not been able to do.

Just after the economic liberalization in the 1990s, many companies, both Indian and foreign, were disappointed at the Indi-ans' meager appetite for consumer goods. People in India just didn't seem to be buy-ing as many cars, televisions, and refrigera-tors as had been anticipated, even though income levels had risen faster in that decade than ever before. But, as revealed by the census report mentioned earlier, it is not the purchasing power of the people that keeps consumption low but the insuf-ficiency of water and power supplies and the inefficiency of the government pro-viders of the same. And, when incomes grow, as they have done since 1991, people prefer to improve their basic amenities rather than buy consumer products. According to Siddhartha Roy, chief economist at Hindustan Lever Ltd., it is only those who have houses with cement floors, proper bathrooms, kitchens, electricity, water, and gas connections who will be in the forefront of the demand for consumer products (Saran 2003). Some economists feel that companies should produce television sets that run on kerosene if the states are not capable of providing electricity for all.

However, despite the lack of basic infrastructure, many homes without kitchens or toilets possess cars, two-wheelers (scooters and motorcycles), and television sets. In fact, the 2001 census revealed even more startling results: in most states, more households have television sets than toilets, and there are more places of worship (2.4 million) in India than schools, colleges, and hospitals combined.

Uneven Distribution of Wealth

The biggest benefits of market reforms enacted in 1999 have gone to the better-educated, cell phone–toting middle classes rather than the poor peasants, and hundreds of millions of Indians have not seen any of the benefits of the country's economic success. Almost a quarter of India's total economic output is still accounted for by agriculture, and farming accounts for two-thirds of India's employment. Thus, 700 million people live in the countryside far away from call centers and "without even a whiff of cappuccino" (*Economist* 2004a).

An estimated 300 million Indians live on less than a dollar a day and 160 million have no access to clean water. Forty-seven

A five-year-old Indian girl, Rina Kumari, washes herself in the Mahananda river in Siliguri, northeast India, 2005. India's liberalization drive since 1991 has been felt more in cities than on the land, and disparities between urban rich and rural poor have grown. Some 260 million of India's billion-plus people live on less than US$1 a day. According to estimates, several hundred thousand children work as laborers and beg on the streets. (Desmond Boylan/Reuters/Corbis)

percent of children under the age of five are underweight. The average GDP is at US$470, and less than 10 percent of that of America in purchasing-power parity comparisons (Jamieson 2004). Furthermore economic forecasts indicate that by 2008 India's IT and other service exports will account for a third of the country's inflow of foreign exchange, but the same industries would directly employ only 2 million people *in total*. These numbers would constitute only a fraction of the 2 million or so English-speakers who graduate from university *each year*.

However there can be no doubt that India's rural population is better off today than it was in 1991, when Dr. Singh launched his economic program. Famine is almost unknown; education and literacy are slowly spreading; and health care is improving. But hundreds of millions are still landless or homeless, and improvements in education, health care, rural power, water supplies, and transportation have been pitifully slow. Even if globalization and capitalism have made the poor better off, they have increased inequality between the two groups, and it is this inequality that has to be corrected if India hopes to democratically continue the economic boom.

Conclusion

The economic liberalization embarked upon by the Indian government in 1991 unleashed the pent-up dynamism of the Indian middle classes. What followed was an economic boom—not just in the big towns and cities, but also in the smaller towns in the Indian hinterland. The growth in the industrial and services sectors of the economy led to a steady increase in the numbers of the middle classes, who, it is estimated, now number between two and three hundred million. Those who could afford to do so began to enjoy the pleasures of consumerism epitomized by the shopping malls that have mushroomed across the country. After decades of austerity, these middle classes were offered the opportunity to enjoy better household appliances, better clothing, even designer wear,

fine dining, bars, cafés, and other forms of entertainment and pleasurable pastimes.

However the gains of the economic liberalization were not seen to benefit the rural poor, and because India, unlike China, is a democracy, the rural poor expressed their rage at being left out of the pleasures of consumerism by booting out the Bharatiya Janata Party (BJP) in the national elections held in 2004. Many progressive and economic liberalizing governments, such as those in the states of Karnataka and Andhra Pradesh, were also the victims of this backlash.

In place of the BJP, the Congress Party, which had campaigned on a pro-poor platform, and other left-leaning parties, including the Communist parties, made substantial electoral gains. On forming the new government in 2004, the Congress Party promised to generate 7–8 percent growth, alleviate poverty, help farmers, empower women, and raise spending on health care and education. It chose Manmohan Singh, who as finance minister had initiated the economic reforms in 1991, as prime minister. He promised to focus on employment and development issues such as infrastructure, water supplies, and rural welfare.

In order to sustain the economic boom and the consumerist lifestyles, India needs to improve its infrastructure with better roads, new airports and seaports, reliable electricity and power, and a better-educated and healthier work force. It remains to be seen whether the government can manage the competing demands of a market-driven economy linked to a social-spending and welfare program that will win its support from the rural poor, while embracing globalization and keeping the reforms rolling, which privilege the urban middle classes. It remains a precarious combination that has so far eluded many well-intentioned developing countries.

A to Z Index

Anandamayi Ma (1896–1981) was a deeply spiritual woman who moved through various ecstatic states. Her teachings emphasized the need for detachment from the world and religious devotion. She touched thousands of devotees throughout the world by giving them the experience of oneness with God. Her devotees have attributed many miracles to her.

Ayurveda: A holistic system of ancient Indian medicine based on understanding the need to balance the three toxins or *tri-doshas* (*vaat* wind, *pitha* bile, and *kapha* phlegm) that influence our mental and physical health. The Sanskrit word comes from *ayu* (life) and *veda* (science) and encompasses the workings of the mind, body, senses, and the soul.

Rohit Bal entered the fashion industry armed with a first class honors degree in history from New Delhi's prestigious St. Stephen's College. His brother's garment export company offered him his first opportunity for experimentation. Today his client list includes film stars and media personalities. He claims his inspiration comes from fantasy and folklore.

Ritu Beri, a graduate of Delhi University, trained at the National Institute of Fashion Technology in Delhi in the 1980s. She launched her first collection, *Lavanya*, in 1990 and it was a sell-out. Liberty's on Lon-

don's Regent Street is one of the venues where her creations have been displayed.

Hatha yoga: A specific set of physical exercises or postures (*asanas*) that prepares and conditions the body for the spiritual path by quieting it for meditation. The breath is an important component of these exercises. Most of the *yogic asana*, devised thousands of years ago, help to keep the spine flexible and the body supple. The true aim of *hatha yoga* is to strengthen the body and mind for spiritual enlightenment via meditation.

Ritu Kumar, the grande dame of Indian fashion, was one of the earliest designers to bring couture to the public and open a fashion boutique in the 1970s. Most of Kumar's work focuses on reviving craftsmanship in the dying arts of block prints, specialized *zardosi* embroidery, and tie-dye and blending them with modern cuts. The late Diana, Princess of Wales, and Jemima Khan wore her creations. She is very sought after by members of the Indian diaspora seeking bridal trousseaux.

Sabyasachi Mukherjee is an award-winning graduate of the National Institute for Fashion Technology in Kolkata whose very first collection won rave reviews. He is a name to be reckoned with in the Indian fashion scene and he claims that he draws his inspiration from deserts, gypsies, prostitutes, and antique textiles.

Panchkarma, or the five actions, is a traditional cleansing and rejuvenation program for the mind and body. It clears the body of harmful toxins, based on ayurvedic principles and includes oil massages and a special balancing diet.

Raghavendra Rathore, who belongs to a feudal family from Jodhpur, studied fashion at the Parsons School of Design in New York, and later was an apprentice to Donna Karan and then Oscar de la Renta. His creations, sold under the label of *IndePret* give traditional Indian workmanship a modern twist.

Wendell Rodrigues, a fashion designer, a fashion writer, and a patron of the arts, shocked his fellow Goans and Catholics when he married his French lover in 2003. Rodrigues served his apprenticeship in Portugal, has exhibited work in China, and is deeply interested in costume preservation and conservation.

Satsang: The word literally means "the company of truth" and is used to describe a gathering of devotees for the purposes of chanting, meditating, and listening to scriptural teachings or readings.

Satya Sai Baba (1926–) is a guru who has taken the name of the nineteenth century saint Sai Baba (1856–1918) and is known to perform miracles for his several million disciples. His religious headquarters are at Puttaparthi in Andhra Pradesh and there are 30,000 centers around the world. The organization performs charitable works and has established educational foundations.

Sri Sri Ravi Shankar (1956–), born in southern India, is a Vedic scholar who studied with several renowned spiritual masters before becoming a spiritual teacher or guru. He established the Art of Living Foundation in 1982 to promote self-development and health education and he teaches the *Sudarshan Kriya* technique,

which is said to have great medical benefits. His various charitable foundations have initiated projects for the benefit of women and children.

Tarun Tahiliani is one of the most expensive Indian haute couture designers, who specializes in extremely elaborate designs, where delicate Lucknow embroidery is interspaced with Swarovski crystals and semiprecious stones. A graduate of the Wharton School of Business, Tahiliani switched from selling offshore oil to fashion design for the rich and famous in South Asia and the Gulf States. He is credited with designing Jemima Khan's trousseau when she married cricketing star Imran Khan. His new ready-to-wear flagship store is *Ensemble* in Mumbai.

A spiritual master, **Bharat Thakur** is the founder of "Artistic Yoga," which adapts ancient yogic techniques to suit contemporary lifestyles. At his sixty fitness studios, he teaches a combination of yoga and low-impact cardiovascular exercises for promoting weight loss and a stress-free life.

Upanishads: Ancient scriptures that exceed 100 texts of immense variety and style, the *Upanishads* constitute the inspired teachings, visions, and mystical experiences of the ancient sages of India. The word literally means "sitting near steadfastly" and all the texts offer the same teaching in their own ways that the individual soul and God are one.

Vaastu: A 5,000-year-old Indian science dedicated to creating harmony in the home environment also known as the "art of direction." Like *feng shui*, its three basic principles concern the free flow of *prana* (energy) throughout the home; the correct balance of the five elements (earth, fire, air, ether, and water); and the exposure to light, because all three, it believes, influence the health, wealth, and happiness of the family inhabiting the home.

Vedanta: Literally "end of the Vedas," it denotes one of the six orthodox schools of Indian philosophy exemplified by the *Upanishads* and other texts that consider the nature of the self. *Vedanta* is identified with *Advaita* or the philosophy of nondualism.

Vedas: There are four Vedas—*Rig Veda*, *Yajur Veda*, *Sama Veda*, and *Atharva Veda*—and they constitute the most ancient sacred scriptures of the world. They are considered to have been divinely revealed and contain eternal wisdom.

Vipassana: An ancient mediation technique propounded by Gautama Buddha. Its focus is constant and focused self-awareness (awareness of the breath, of sensations, of one's thoughts) with the aim of purifying the mind. The leading proponent of *vipassana* in India today is S. N. Goenka, who has established a Vipassana International Academy in Igatpuri, Maharashtra.

Bibliography and References

Alhuwali, Isher Judge. "The Indian Economy: Looking Ahead." In *Contemporary India.* Pai Panandikar and Ashis Nandy (eds.). New Delhi: Tata McGraw-Hill Publishing Company Limited, 1999.

Assomull, Sujata. "Popular Designs." *Business India*, 1–14 March 2004.

Bajeli-Datt, Kavita. "Hot Hangouts." *The Week*, 25 July 2004.

Bamzai, Kaveree. "Gross Gloss." *India Today*, 9 June 2003.

Bhupta, Malini. "Deluxe India." *India Today*, 22 November 2004.

Business India. "Brush for a Brand." 17 February–2 March 2003.

Chandrasekhar, C. P. "A Bubble Waiting to Burst." *Frontline*, 12 March 2004.

Chopra, Anupama, and Sheela Raval. "New Age Gurus: Guru Chic." *India Today*, 14 July 2003.

Dangor, Kim. "Fashion: Pret Partying." *India Today*, 15 November 2004.

Doshi, Anjali. "It's No Time to Disco." *India Today*, 8 November 2004.

The Economic Times. "Pret Anyone? Fashion Begins at Home." 26 July 2003.

The Economist. "Wealth in Asia: Consuming Passions." 3 January 2004a.

———. "India's Economic Reforms: Can India Work?" 12 June 2004b.

Ezekiel, Hannan. "Process of Liberalisation: No Room for Complacency." *The Times of India*, 6 July 1994.

Gahlaut, Kanika. "Fashion: Big Fat Weddings." *India Today*, 6 December 2004a.

———, with Anil Padmanabhan. "Fashion: Whose Line Is It Anyway?" *India Today*, 18 October 2004b.

———. "Cutting Edge." *India Today*, 10 May 2004c.

———. "Lifestyle/Suburbia: New World of Guppies." *India Today*, 3 November 2003a.

———. "Romp on the Ramp." *India Today*, 4 August 2003b.

———. "Global Designs." *India Today*, 23 June 2003c.

Gardner, David. "Fashion, Sex and Security in India." *The Financial Times*, 10/11 March 2003.

Goyal, Malini. "Consumer Spending: Urge to Splurge." *India Today*, 9 June 2003a.

———. "E-Commerce/Surge in Shopping: Towards Net Profit." *India Today*, 3 November 2003b.

Jain, Madhu. "My God Hasn't Died Young." *India Today*, 5 October 1998.

Jamieson, Bill. "Business Focus: India." *The Business*, 23/24 May 2004.

John, Sangeeta. "Trends: Mind over Matter." *The Week*, 11 May 2003.

Mehta, Suketu. *Maximum City: Bombay Lost and Found*. New York: Knopf, 2004.

Menon, Parvathi. "Closing Factories, Losing Jobs." *Frontline*, 12 March 2004.

Pai Panandikar, V. A., and Ashis Nandy (eds.). *Contemporary India*. New Delhi: Tata McGraw-Hill Publishing Company Limited, 1999.

Ramani, Priya, and Anna M. M. Vetticad. "Invitation to Party." *India Today*, 4 October 1999.

Rathi, Nidhi Taparia. "Lifestyle/Celebrity Restaurants: Star Attractions." *India Today*, 28 October 2002.

———. "Pret Enterprise." *India Today*, 20 January 2003.

Raval, Sheela. "Selling Point." *India Today*, 21 February 2000.

Roy, Saumya. "Fashion: Pardon Your Slip Is Showing." *Outlook*, 4 October 2004.

Sachdeva, Sujata Dutta. "Here's What India's Mega-Rich Stop to Shop." *The Times of India*, 29 June 2003.

Sainath, P. "The Feel Good Factory." *Frontline*, 12 March 2004.

Saran, Rohit. "Census India Household Survey: How We Live." *India Today*, 28 July 2003.

Saran, Sathya. "Designers We Took Notice Of: Meet the Hot Steppers." *Femina*, 1 June 2004.

Singh, Piya. "Bigger Things in Store for Retail." *The Times of India*, 11 August 2003.

Soman, Mangesh. "Rural India Fails to Keep Pace with City Slickers." *The Economic Times*, 21 April 2003.

Thomas, Sunil K. "Boom or Bust?" *The Week*, 5 December 2004a.

———. "Shop and Swig." *The Week*, 8 August 2004b.

———. "Rejuvenation: Spaced Out!" *The Week*, 27 June 2004c.

———. "Designs on the Masses." *The Week*, 9 May 2004d.

Varma, Pavan K. *Being Indian: Inside the Real India*. New Delhi: Penguin Books India, 2004.

Vasudev, Shefalee. "Satsangs: A Date with God." *India Today*, 26 May 2003.

The Week. "Show Stealers." 7 March 2004.

Conclusion

The inexorable growth of the popular culture industry since the 1990s has been driven by the economic growth of the country, itself spurred by the liberalizing measures of the successive governments since 1991. Increased wealth, as more and more people are absorbed into the middle classes (currently estimated at between 200 and 300 million people), has led to increasingly consumerist lifestyles. More Indians travel, eat out, buy designer clothes, and spend money on entertainment and literature. More people own television and radio sets, white goods (such as refrigerators and microwave ovens), consumer electronics, and cars or motorcycles and scooters—and even more aspire to own them.

The circulation figures of newspapers and magazines in English and regional languages show a year-by-year increase, as more and more people earn enough disposable income to purchase a daily newspaper. Television, which comprises 60 percent of all revenues in the entertainment industry, and is accessible to over 75 percent of the urban population and around 30 percent of the rural population, has been the driving force behind the growth of the music and sports (mainly cricket) industries. Advertising on television and in newspapers and magazines relentlessly promotes Indian-made consumer goods and spurred consumerism. But, according to sociologist Kirk Johnson, it has also made the poor more demanding of their rights and helped to blur religious and caste divisions in rural society.

Within the entertainment industry, radical changes are taking place. The film industry, finally recognized as a bona fide "industry" and hence eligible for bank loans and tax breaks, is gradually reforming the manner in which it does business. The unorganized nature of the industry is slowly being transformed to embrace "corporatization" and greater financial transparency. The fragmentation of the industry among individual producers, financiers, distributors, exhibitors, and music company executives, leaving no single entity in overall control, has adversely affected both the quality of films and the profitability of the industry. Industry experts hope that the corporatization of the industry will ensure proper preproduction procedures (completed scripts, tight production schedules, proper contracts for all workers and artists); transparent financing through banks and other lending houses; insurance and comple-

A woman stands next to a mannequin in a
shopping center. Bangalore, 2001.
(David H. Wells/Corbis)

tion guarantees; integrated distribution
plans; and coordinated promotion and
marketing strategies—all of which have
been absent so far.

The growth of multiplex cinemas, encouraged by the state governments
through limited-period tax breaks, has already affected the kind of films being produced. Instead of the all-inclusive romances and melodramas that straddled the
desires of its urban and its rural viewers,
cinema is now increasingly bifurcating into
smart, youth-oriented, city-centric films for
urban viewers and lavish melodramas for
the poorer rural audiences. In the process,
the hegemonic, monolithic, formulaic film
churned out by the film factories is under
siege, and the future should include greater
generic variety. As a result of the efforts by

certain state governments to protect regional cinemas and the decision of film co-
operatives to experiment with low budget
productions, the regional cinemas may find
new and exciting forms of cinematic expression, and more significantly, ones that
can find a cinema to screen their productions.

Another new, influential audience is the
20 million Indians who represent the Indian diaspora but still maintain close links
to their country of origin. A substantial
proportion of these people have been extremely successful financially and constitute an important source of revenue for the
entertainment industry. As a result, Indian
film producers and distributors are paying
greater attention to their desire for entertainment and will continue to do so in the
future.

The growth in television continues unabated, with more and more channels in
all languages offered to the Indian viewers. The global satellite revolution, which
began in India with STAR TV broadcasts
from Hong Kong in 1991, did not swamp
Indian viewers with American products, as
might have been expected. Instead, it gave
birth to hundreds of regional Indian channels, with regional-language soap operas,
news programs, music, and other entertainment. Since 75 percent of urban families have access to terrestrial and 50 percent to satellite television (for rural
households the figures are approximately
30 percent and 10 percent, respectively),
industry analysts are confident of uninter-
rupted growth in the coming years, particularly in the rural sector. Already manufacturers have targeted rural viewers and
begun marketing televisions and sham-
poos—in small one-rupee (three-cent)
packs—in earnest. Television revenues de-

Women at a Western-style water park in Bangalore, 1999. (David H. Wells/Corbis)

pend largely on advertisers, because satellite television is almost exclusively delivered by cable, whose operators pocket most of the subscription revenues. As subscription revenues from the introduction of accessible systems increase, more special interest and niche channels are expected to emerge.

Radio, which is almost entirely in the hands of the government and has near blanket coverage of the whole of India, recently privatized some FM channels. Most of these channels cater to the urban middle classes, and tend to offer the same kind of programs. In the future, as more FM channels are privatized and differences between the government and private entrepreneurs are ironed out, more channels featuring specialist music (Western classical, Indian classical, folk songs) and young,

talented performers are expected to proliferate.

The privatized FM channels, which until now have been playing mostly film music, have adversely affected the music industry and caused a drop in sales. In fact, although the cassette revolution brought forth an unprecedented variety of music, the industry has been plagued by losses caused by widespread piracy and high acquisition costs for film music, accompanied by disastrous box office failures in the film industry. With less investment in the volatile film industry, it might embark on experiments with new genres of nonfilm music and encourage new talent as a cost-effective way of recouping its losses.

The growth of the middle classes is also increasing interest in theater and literature. Indian literature in English is also

Kerala women carrying tealeaf harvest on their heads near Kanjirappally, 1999. (Robert van der Hilst/ Corbis)

supported by the dynamism of the Indian diaspora. Its writers write mainly about India and command million-dollar contracts both in India and abroad—a fact that bears testimony to their global success.

In 2004, the Indian electorate dismissed the coalition BJP government that supported economic reform. Soon afterward, political pundits began to analyze the results. Most pointed to the growing disparity between urban and rural Indians. Two distinct Indias seem to be emerging: the India of the urban areas is affluent, meritocratic, and globalized; the other India lives

in the villages, which are still tied to feudal practices and caste hierarchies. Agriculture, which is very dependent on the erratic monsoons, today accounts for 25 percent of India's gross domestic product (GDP), down from 57 percent in 1951. Yet 70 percent of the population still lives in rural areas and has seen little of the economic wealth that the reforms have generated. Although 69 million people have been lifted out of poverty between 1977 and 2000, 260 million remain trapped below the poverty line. According to the World Bank, 35 percent of India lives on less than US$1 a day. While India has some of the highest numbers of qualified professionals in the world, female literacy stands at just 54 percent. Furthermore, India ranks very low in the world's human development index.

Even the development achieved through economic reform has been very uneven. While states like Maharashtra and Gujerat have achieved very high growth rates, others (Bihar, for example, which is the size of Germany), have living standards on par with Burundi in Africa. Only six of India's twenty-nine states attract direct foreign investment. As agriculture's contribution continues to decline, its place has not been taken by industry, leaving administrators worried about the absence of low- and middle-skilled jobs needed to absorb the displaced rural population and the looming prospect of massive unemployment. The services industry contributes 50 percent of the GDP. Yet the information technology industry and "call centers," which have been growing at rates of 30 and 40 percent each year, will employ, it is estimated, just 4 million people by 2008. The mistake that the BJP political leaders seem to have made was to conflate the achievements of affluent urban India with those of the rural poor, and the election results were seen as a mighty rebuff of the urban elite by the rural poor. The new Congress coalition government elected in 2004, ruling with the help of left-wing parties, hopes to set right this massive imbalance.

The uneven development has raised important questions about the future of India, particularly about the implications of the cultural practices driven by the emerging consumerist middle class. India has been described as a lumbering elephant, big and slow off the mark, particularly when compared with its neighbor and population billionaire, China. Many Indian intellectuals have begun to ponder what it means to be Indian, as can be witnessed by the plethora of books being published on the subject. Others, seeing the gigantic

Indian employees at a call center provide service support to international customers, in the southern city of Bangalore, 2004. The hiring frenzy at call centers in India is the flip side of daily tales pouring out of the United States and Britain, where thousands of software and back-office jobs are being cut as companies take advantage of cheap communications offshore to drive down costs. India is the undisputed leader of emerging markets to which developed economies are outsourcing high-technology jobs. The US$3.6 billion industry in India is forecast to rocket to US$13.8 billion by 2007 with the number of jobs quadrupling to 1 million. (Sherwin Crasto/Reuters/Corbis)

strides made by China, wonder if democracy is truly compatible with the poor, ethnically divided, and hierarchical society that is India. Whatever the answer, the general mood is still one brimming with hope, and the optimism of the entertainment industry promises a prosperous future for India and itself.

Glossary

Abhinaya   Enactment on stage or screen.

Ahimsa   Nonviolence; principle espoused by Mahatma Gandhi.

Akashvani   The Hindi-language name for All India Radio.

Ayurveda   Traditional Indian medicine.

Babuisms   Quaintly Indian manipulations of the English language usually associated with the Indian civil service.

Bhajan   Hindu devotional songs.

Bhakti   Intense devotion to a deity or the divine.

Bhangra   Popular peasant dance form from the Punjab.

Bharat Natyam   A form of classical Indian dance.

Bhava   Emotions expressed by an actor on stage.

Bhavai   Traditional popular theater of Gujerat.

Blade money   The extortionist interest rates charged by the moneylenders.

Bodyline   D. R. Jardine's controversial form of bowling in cricket that aimed at the batsman rather than the wickets and thus endangered the batsman.

Bollywood   Hindi film industry based in Bombay (now Mumbai).

Brahmin   Elite priestly caste among Hindus.

Cablewallahs   Cable operators who deliver satellite television programs to the home.

Chakra   Subtle nerve centers in the physical body.

Company Natak   Professional regional theater companies that formed after the Parsi theaters.

Dharma   Hindu concept of duty and righteousness that govern all our actions; the same word is used for religion, because religion consists of doing one's righteous duty.

DMK   Dravida Munnetra Kazagham, regional political party in Tamil Nadu.

Doordarshan   Government-owned terrestrial television network in India.

Dosas and *idlis*   South Indian pancakes and dumplings.

Fatwa   Death sentence, as passed on Salman Rushdie by Iran's Ayatollah Khomeni for blaspheming Islam.

Ghazal   Urdu poetry inspired by Persian and Arabic poetry.

Gherao   To physically surround a person or a thing; a form of physical intimidation and protest.

Guru   Spiritual guide; teacher.

Gymkhana   A sports club, established by the colonial British in India.

Harijan   "People of God," Gandhi's term for the "untouchable" caste, the lowest in the caste hierarchy.

Hawala   Illegal transfer of money that leaves no paper trail, generally transacted by telephone.

Hazaar   Literally, "a thousand"; colloquially, "a lot," "plenty," "very."

Hinglish   A mixture of Hindi and English; a contemporary, streetwise style of speaking.

Import substitution   Economic strategy to restrict the importation of foreign goods and manufacture them in India instead.

Indipop   Indian pop music in Hindi or English by Indian artists.

IPTA   Indian People's Theatre Association, Communist Party–affiliated theater groups.

Jatra   Traditional popular theater of Bengal.

Kabaddi   Traditional Indian form of sport, also known as *hu-tu-tu*.

Keertan   Religious sermon delivered in song.

Lavani   Erotic song from the *tamasha*, traditional popular theater of Maharashtra.

License *raj*   The Indian government's penchant for licenses.

Lok Sabha and **Rajya Sabha**   The lower and upper houses of the Indian parliament.

Maharaja   Hindu king.

Mahurat   Auspicious moment for a religious ceremony.

Maidan   Open playing field.

Mangalacharana   Opening prayer in song that precedes any performance.

Masala   Spices to enhance the taste of food; "spiced up" action.

Memsahib   A British (or any important) lady.

Mudra   Hand gesture used in the enactment of a play.

Mukhra   Catch phrase in a piece of music.

Multi-starrer   A film with several leading stars.

Narrowcasting   Local programming that targets specific linguistic and cultural groups.

Natya   Drama.

Natyashastra   A scholarly treatise on the performing arts attributed to Bharata, dated circa second century AD.

Nautanki   Traditional popular theater of Uttar Pradesh.

Nawab   Muslim prince.

Nautch **girls**   Dancing girls.

Navaratri   Hindu celebration during nine nights that celebrate the ten avatars (incarnations) of the god Vishnu.

Navya **movement**   The emerging modernist Kannada literature movement.

Nizam   Muslim king.

NRI   Nonresident Indian or an Indian expatriate.

Nrtya   Dance.

Odessa Collective   Malayalam film director John Abraham's film movement, named after a famous scene in Eisenstein's Russian film *Battleship Potemkin*.

Play-back   A song recording that is played back during a film shooting so that actors can lip-synch the words and give the impression of singing.

Prasar Bharati   An autonomous body that oversees Indian radio and television.

Purana   Mythological and historical story; part of the Hindu scriptures.

Raj   Rule, such as British *raj* or British rule; license *raj* or rule by licenses.

Rajah   Hindu prince.

Rasa   Essence of an emotion or feeling, as explained by the *Natyashastra*, Bharata's treatise on the performing arts.

Rashtriya Swayamsevak Sangh (RSS)   An extremist Hindu nationalist political organization, responsible for the assassination of Mahatma Gandhi.

Saas-bahu   Mother-in-law and daughter-in-law; the theme of kitchen politics that dominates television soap operas in India.

Sahitya Akademi   Government-funded body for the promotion of Indian literature.

Salwar- **(or** *chudidar-***)** *kameez*   North Indian form of dress comprising loose (*salwar*) or skin-tight (*chudidar*) trousers, and a shirt.

Sangeet natak   Operatic form of Marathi theater.

Sangeet Natak Akademi   Government-funded body for the promotion of Indian music and theater.

Satsang   An assembly of the devoted; literally, "keeping the company of truth."

Shakti   Physical strength or spiritual/divine energy.

Swadeshi   Indigenous; the boycott of imported British goods undertaken during the struggle for Indian independence.

Tamasha   Traditional popular theater of Maharashtra.

Tantric   Dealing with the religious and magical part of Sanskrit texts.

Upanishad Literally, "sitting near steadfastly"; inspired teachings of the ancient sages; the scriptures exceed a hundred texts and constitute the final and highest knowledge of the Vedas.

Untouchable Lowest caste in the hierarchy; also known as *Harijan* and *dalit*.

Vaishnavism The cult of Vishnu, as against Shaivism, the cult of Shiva.

Vedas Four ancient, authoritative Hindu texts; regarded as divinely revealed.

Yakshgana Traditional popular theater of Karnataka.

Zamindar Feudal landowner.

Zamindari Feudal land-owning system.

Index

About the Author

Asha Kasbekar trained at the National School of Drama in New Delhi, India, and studied drama at the Sorbonne in Paris, France. She was film and drama critic for the *Indian Express* in Bombay and later worked for the British Board of Film Classification in London. She has taught cinema at the School of Oriental and African Studies at the University of London and was a jury member at the Göteborg Film Festival in Sweden in 2003.